I0010631

Enterprise LMS with Adobe Learning Manager

Design and develop world-class learning experiences for your employees, partners, and customers

Damien Bruyndonckx

BIRMINGHAM—MUMBAI

Enterprise LMS with Adobe Learning Manager

Copyright © 2023 Packt Publishing

All rights reserved. No part of this book may be reproduced, stored in a retrieval system, or transmitted in any form or by any means, without the prior written permission of the publisher, except in the case of brief quotations embedded in critical articles or reviews.

Every effort has been made in the preparation of this book to ensure the accuracy of the information presented. However, the information contained in this book is sold without warranty, either express or implied. Neither the author, nor Packt Publishing or its dealers and distributors, will be held liable for any damages caused or alleged to have been caused directly or indirectly by this book.

Packt Publishing has endeavored to provide trademark information about all of the companies and products mentioned in this book by the appropriate use of capitals. However, Packt Publishing cannot guarantee the accuracy of this information.

Group Product Manager: Pavan Ramchandani and Rohit Rajkumar
Publishing Product Manager: Himani Dewan
Senior Editor: Aamir Ahmed
Technical Editor: Saurabh Kadave and Simran Ali
Copy Editor: Safis Editing
Project Coordinator: Sonam Pandey
Proofreader: Safis Editing
Indexer: Manju Arasan
Production Designer: Prashant Ghare
DevRel Marketing Coordinator: Namita Velgekar

First published: June 2023

Production reference: 2300623

Published by Packt Publishing Ltd.
Livery Place
35 Livery Street
Birmingham
B3 2PB, UK.

ISBN 978-1-80461-887-5

www.packtpub.com

As I progressed in the writing of this book, I kept thinking about these few special teachers who have had a profound impact on the person I am today. This book is dedicated to the teachers and instructors who dedicate their lives to changing the lives of others through education. It is not so much the subjects they teach that are important but the life lessons that their everyday behavior and attitude convey. My eternal thanks go to Jacques Baret, my 5th-grade teacher, and Guy Deveux, my 11th- and 12th-grade math teacher, for teaching me the love of a job well done.

– Damien Bruyndonckx

Foreword

I remember when I finished college where I was studying Biology in 1997, there was this wonderful thing called the Internet that was booming with information and seemed like an exciting place to visit and to explore! I immediately knew I wanted to be a part of the web, which meant instead of working with biological systems, it was time to learn computer systems and software technology. IT Networking seemed like a great place to start and the experience of getting those CD-ROMs to learn was truly exhilarating. Running a CD-ROM and learning about the OSI model was eLearning for me at the time.

A few years later, I was lucky enough to get hired by a technical training and consulting company. Classroom training was a core business, and the same type of CD-ROMs would reinforce the learning. A few years after that, my wife introduced me to some people who were in the Macromedia community, which meant shifting from IT/technical topics to Content authoring of training topics using a cool tool called RoboDemo, now Adobe Captivate. IT also meant learning via the browser and not the CD. *Rapid Content Creation* was the thing in 2003 and onward. Not too long after that, the LMS ecosystem started to reveal itself to me through simple tools such as Adobe Connect Training Module all the way up to more Enterprise, complex LMS products. There was A LOT to this eLearning work all of a sudden.

Fast forwarding to the summer of 2015, Adobe Systems announced an LMS product that, after a lot of rumors that the authoring tool company was getting in the LMS space, made a huge splash with Adobe Captivate Prime, now renamed to **Adobe Learning Manager**. Adobe spent three years on the product in pretty much secret and being a part of the beta testing team was very special for me. Along the way I was lucky enough to meet *Damien Bruyndonckx* at an Adobe conference and quickly knew, with his experience in the eLearning space, that I was going to be able to help my own customers more effectively and with more precision. This turned out to be the case and still is today. Damien delivers!

In this book, you're going to learn about Adobe Learning Manager from the standpoint of what a real-deal practitioner of eLearning needs to know to do. There are trainers of eLearning, where they do class after class but sometimes don't really practice what they preach to their students. Damien brings so many skills and experiences to this workbook, which in turn adds value to you as a reader, a student, and so on. This book not only builds on his excellent core work, but you're also going to be able to tap into so many tricks and tips because of Damien's experience as this is a guide from a very experienced professional, passing along real-world knowledge.

Dig-in and Happy LEARNING!

Sean Mullen

Adobe Certified Instructor

Co-Founder, Engage Systems LLC

Contributors

About the author

Damien Bruyndonckx is the founder and CEO of One2Learn, a Belgian company specializing in content development, instructional video, virtual classrooms, and training on the leading eLearning content creation tools. Active in the eLearning industry for over 15 years, Damien has worked with many different customers and LMS implementations. He is a long-time Adobe partner and serves as an instructor for the official Adobe Captivate certification program. Damien is the author of over 30 video training courses for LinkedIn Learning and is the co-author of the *Mastering Adobe Captivate* series by Packt Publishing.

I want to thank the exceptional team that has helped me make this book a reality. Special shout out to my dear friend Yannick Legarff for accepting my invitation to serve as a technical reviewer, and to the awesome team at Packt Publishing. A final word to my sweet Celine, who is always there for me whenever I take on such a crazy project.

About the reviewer

Yannick Le Garrf is a telecommunications engineer and an ISO 27001 and ISO 9001 certified auditor. He started his career as a software development engineer at Hewlett Packard Labs and EADS. He has been working for more than 20 years on digital technologies that are transforming the way organizations communicate and work. He is currently in charge of business development in Europe for MeetingOne, Adobe's international partner for Digital Learning solutions.

Yannick is passionate about the emergence of new ways of learning and how this transforms organizations and society.

Table of Contents

3

Uploading Learning Content and Managing the Content Library   47

4

Creating Skills and Courses   87

Part 2 – Managing Learners and Tracking Learning Data

5

Managing Users   127

6

Enrolling Learners in Courses   169

7

Reviewing the Learner Experience   201

8

Exploring the Instructor Role   229

Part 4 – Administering the Platform

14

15

16

Exploring the Integration Admin Role   447

Preface

Adobe Learning Manager is the award-winning enterprise LMS from Adobe. Just like any other LMS, Adobe Learning Manager allows you to host and deliver any type of learning content to your learners. It also offers state-of-the-art tools for tracking student progress, storing quiz results, generating sophisticated learning reports, and more. But Adobe Learning Manager goes far beyond these standard LMS features. It provides a true learning experience not only for your employees but also for your partners and even your customers. After all, franchisee training is part of your organization's brand image, and a well-trained customer is more likely to be a satisfied and recurring customer. This is why Adobe Learning Manager goes far beyond the traditional boundaries of an enterprise LMS to become a true **Learning Experience Platform** (**LXP**), not only for your organization's employees but also for your suppliers, partners, franchisees, and customers.

This book is designed to help you get started with Adobe Learning Manager quickly and easily. Each feature is described using practical use cases that everyone can relate to, regardless of the size or type of your organization, and the industry in which it operates. You will start your journey by exploring the typical features of any LMS: content upload, course creation, user management, reporting, and so on. Next, you'll learn how to enhance the learner experience by leveraging the built-in gamification, social learning, and AI-powered recommendation features. These will allow you to deliver a truly unique and personalized experience to each learner accessing your account. Finally, you'll learn how to administer the platform and integrate Adobe Learning Manager into your existing IT environment and customer journey using the built-in connectors and/or the Learning Manager API.

Who this book is for

This book is for learning and development professionals, HR managers, corporate instructors, LMS admins, and team leaders looking to set up and manage training and development programs for employees, partners, and customers using Adobe Learning Manager.

What this book covers

Chapter 1, *Introduction to Adobe Learning Manager*, introduces you to the Adobe Learning Manager platform, the Adobe Experience Cloud, and the Adobe Digital Learning ecosystem. It also walks you through activating the trial account you will need to complete the exercises in this book.

Chapter 2, *Customizing the Look and Feel of Adobe Learning Manager*, guides you through basic configuration tasks, including adjusting the look and feel of your account to your organization's branding guidelines.

Chapter 3, Uploading Learning Content and Managing the Content Library, puts you in the role of an author to upload different types of learning content to the content library of your Adobe Learning Manager account.

Chapter 4, Creating Skills and Courses, discusses the concept of skills and walks you through the creation of a custom skill within your account. You will then create a course using the content uploaded to the content library in the previous chapter.

Chapter 5, Managing Users, describes different ways to define various types of users in your **Adobe Learning Manager** (ALM) account. It also describes how to assign users to roles and how to create custom roles.

Chapter 6, Enrolling Learners in Courses, takes you through the creation of course instances, learning paths, and certifications, before showing you how to enroll learners in these learning objects.

Chapter 7, Reviewing the Learner Experience, puts you in the skin of a learner to walk you through the default learner experience provided by Adobe Learning Manager. You will learn about the fluidic player as well as the different ways learners can take courses in Adobe Learning Manager.

Chapter 8, Exploring the Instructor Role, explores the tools and features used by instructors to manage live (face-to-face or virtual) classroom sessions, review learner submissions, and more.

Chapter 9, Configuring and Using Feedback, discusses Kirkpatrick's Four Levels of Learning Evaluation model, which is the theoretical framework behind ALM's feedback features. Then, it walks you through the practical implementation of L1, L2, and L3 feedback in your ALM account.

Chapter 10, Reporting in Adobe Learning Manager, focuses on the advanced reporting features of Adobe Learning Manager and on exporting all kinds of data for further analysis in an external system.

Chapter 11, Badges and Gamification, takes you through the process of configuring and using badges and other gamification features available in Adobe Learning Manager.

Chapter 12, Enabling and Managing Social Learning, describes the social learning engine embedded in Adobe Learning Manager. It shows you how to manage Social Learning from the administrator's perspective and how to use it from the learner's perspective.

Chapter 13, AI-Powered Recommendations for Learners, discusses the use of Adobe Sensei (Adobe's own AI technology) to generate personalized course recommendations for learners. You will also discover the tools administrators use to influence the way the AI works within their ALM accounts.

Chapter 14, Working with Catalogs and Peer Accounts, teaches you how to use catalogs to control who can access which courses. You will also learn how to share your course catalogs with other ALM accounts using the Peer Account feature.

Chapter 15, Working with Messages and Announcements, describes the Adobe Learning Manager announcement and messaging system. You will learn how to create masthead and notification announcements, as well as how to choose and customize the email messages sent by your ALM account.

Chapter 16, Exploring the Integration Admin Role, focuses on how Adobe Learning Manager can be integrated into the existing IT infrastructure of your organization. It walks you through the list of available connectors and helps you make your first steps toward using the Adobe Learning Manager API for custom development and headless deployment.

To get the most out of this book

The book assumes a working knowledge of your operating systems and of the common tools used by most Learning and Development professionals. With Adobe Learning Manager being a cloud-based service, a modern web browser is all you need to follow along with the exercises included in this book.

You can use the free 30-day trial of Adobe Learning Manager to perform the exercises, and *Chapter 1* walks you through the process of activating your trial account. Activating your free trial requires that you have an Adobe ID. If you do not already have an Adobe ID, you can create one for free at `https://account.adobe.com/`.

Finally, you will need to create an email address for each of the users you will create in your trial account. You can use any free email service, such as Gmail, Hotmail, or Yahoo Mail. Detailed information about this process will be provided in the corresponding chapter.

Download the supporting files

You can download the supporting files for this book from here: `https://packt.link/pVa1m`.

We also have other code bundles from our rich catalog of books and videos available at `https://github.com/PacktPublishing/`. Check them out!

Download the color images

We also provide a PDF file that has color images of the screenshots and diagrams used in this book. You can download it here: `https://packt.link/RB7FV`.

Conventions used

There are a number of text conventions used throughout this book.

`Code in text`: Indicates code words in text, database table names, folder names, filenames, file extensions, pathnames, dummy URLs, user input, and Twitter handles. Here is an example: "Type `Cybersecurity Fighter` in the **Badge Name** field."

Bold. Indicates a new term, an important word, or words that you see onscreen. For instance, words in menus or dialog boxes appear in **bold**. Here is an example: "From the administrator home page, click the **Badges** link located in the **Configure** section of the left sidebar."

> **Tips or important notes**
> Appear like this.

Get in touch

Feedback from our readers is always welcome.

General feedback: If you have questions about any aspect of this book, email us at customercare@packtpub.com and mention the book title in the subject of your message.

Errata: Although we have taken every care to ensure the accuracy of our content, mistakes do happen. If you have found a mistake in this book, we would be grateful if you would report this to us. Please visit www.packtpub.com/support/errata and fill in the form.

Piracy: If you come across any illegal copies of our works in any form on the internet, we would be grateful if you would provide us with the location address or website name. Please contact us at copyright@packt.com with a link to the material.

If you are interested in becoming an author: If there is a topic that you have expertise in and you are interested in either writing or contributing to a book, please visit authors.packtpub.com.

Share Your Thoughts

Once you've read *Enterprise LMS with Adobe Learning Manager*, we'd love to hear your thoughts! Scan the QR code below to go straight to the Amazon review page for this book and share your feedback.

https://packt.link/r/1-804-61887-X

Your review is important to us and the tech community and will help us make sure we're delivering excellent quality content.

Download a free PDF copy of this book

Thanks for purchasing this book!

Do you like to read on the go but are unable to carry your print books everywhere? Is your eBook purchase not compatible with the device of your choice?

Don't worry, now with every Packt book you get a DRM-free PDF version of that book at no cost.

Read anywhere, any place, on any device. Search, copy, and paste code from your favorite technical books directly into your application.

The perks don't stop there, you can get exclusive access to discounts, newsletters, and great free content in your inbox daily

Follow these simple steps to get the benefits:

1. Scan the QR code or visit the link below

https://packt.link/free-ebook/978-1-80461-887-5

2. Submit your proof of purchase

3. That's it! We'll send your free PDF and other benefits to your email directly

Part 1 –
Publishing Learning Content

In this part, you will activate your Adobe Learning Manager trial account and perform basic configuration tasks. Then, you will upload various types of learning content to the platform and arrange this content into courses.

This section comprises the following chapters:

- *Chapter 1, Introduction to Adobe Learning Manager*
- *Chapter 2, Customizing the Look and Feel of Adobe Learning Manager*
- *Chapter 3, Uploading Learning Content and Managing the Content Library*
- *Chapter 4, Creating Skills and Courses*

1

Introduction to Adobe Learning Manager

Welcome to *Enterprise LMS with Adobe Learning Manager*. Formerly known as Adobe Captivate Prime, **Adobe Learning Manager (ALM)** is a next-generation **Learning Management System (LMS)** from Adobe. Adobe Captivate Prime was first released in 2015, so it is a relative newcomer in the LMS landscape. Despite its youth, it has already built a solid reputation as one of the best corporate LMSs on the market, as outlined by the numerous awards it has received throughout its young career. In July 2022, Adobe Captivate Prime became Adobe Learning Manager.

Just like any other LMS, you can use Learning Manager to host custom eLearning content, organize that content into courses, maintain a list of users and instructors, enroll learners in courses, track their progress, and more. But **Adobe Learning Manager** (ALM) is much more than that! It has unique features such as a powerful gamification engine, social learning capabilities, as well as an AI-powered recommendation engine that produces personalized training recommendations. This makes ALM a pioneer of the next generation of enterprise LMSs. Some of its features are so disruptive that the industry no longer refers to Adobe Learning Manager as an LMS, but instead uses the acronym **LXP**, which stands for **Learning eXperience Platform**. You can further expand the power of Adobe Learning Manager by leveraging numerous integrations between ALM and other enterprise-grade systems, such as directory services, marketing automation tools, **Content Management Systems (CMSs)**, **Enterprise Resource Planning (ERP)** platforms, eCommerce solutions, and more. This allows organizations to go far beyond the traditional learning management system to design truly comprehensive learning experiences that are part of the customer journey.

You'll explore these features and functionalities throughout this book. You'll begin by exploring the basic LMS aspect of Adobe Learning Manager by uploading custom learning content to the system. Then, you'll organize that content into courses, create different types of users, and assign learners to courses. Next, you'll enhance the learner experience by enabling advanced features such as **gamification** and **social learning**. You will also add a touch of artificial intelligence to provide personalized recommendations to your learners. Finally, you will integrate ALM with the IT systems used in the organization. All this will help you build a complete learning experience not only for your employees but also for your partners, franchisees, customers, and others.

This makes for a lot of exciting features to discover and use cases to discuss, so let's start with the basics. In this first chapter, you will :

- Learn more about what Adobe Learning Manager is.
- Understand how Learning Manager fits into the ecosystem of integrated applications from Adobe.
- Activate your Learning Manager trial account.
- Take a quick tour of Adobe Learning Manager to learn about the interface and available roles.

By the end of this chapter, you will have had a high-level overview of Adobe Learning Manager and will be ready for a detailed exploration of the platform.

What is Adobe Learning Manager?

At its most basic level, Adobe Learning Manager is a **Learning Management System** (LMS). An LMS is a web-based application primarily used for hosting, delivering, administrating, tracking, and reporting learning activities. The concept of LMS dates back to the mid-1990s and first appeared in the higher education sector. Since then, LMSs have evolved to include features such as collaborative learning, social learning, gamification, mobile learning, and more. They have contributed to the advent of new instructional design strategies (such as the flipped classroom) and have moved beyond the tight confines of the education sector to venture into corporate training. Nowadays, LMSs can be found in a very large variety of organizations. From primary schools to large business corporations, the LMS has become a central component of the learning and development strategy of a growing number of organizations.

The main duties of a traditional LMS fall into the following basic categories:

- Training management and delivery.
- User and role management.
- Online assessments and tracking learning progress.
- Automation of various tasks (such as issuing badges and certificates).
- Reporting and analytics.

Adobe Learning Manager being an LMS, it is able to fulfill all these missions. But ALM has a lot more to offer! So, in the next few sections, we'll explore some of the features that set ALM apart from most other LMSs.

Adobe Learning Manager is an enterprise LMS

ALM has been developed from scratch by Adobe. It has not been purchased or acquired. It has been designed, right from the start, as an enterprise LMS. So, even though you can use ALM in a school or university, it is in the corporate environment – more precisely, in large organizations with lots of course material and learners – that the unique features of ALM make the most sense.

Some of the features that establish Learning Manager as an enterprise LMS include the following:

- A dedicated manager view to help managers enroll team members into courses and track their learning progress.

- The ability to integrate off-the-shelf learning content from other ALM accounts or third-party providers.

- Extensive reporting capabilities.

- Integration with other Adobe enterprise-grade services or with the existing ecosystem of tools used in your company (such as directory services, virtual classroom tools, CRM, CMS, ERP, eCommerce, and more).

- The ability for learners to self-enroll in courses they deem relevant and an integrated AI-powered recommendation engine to help learners make their way through massive course catalogs.

- Etc.

Adobe Learning Manager is a cloud-based LMS

There are hundreds of learning management systems out there! Some of them are proprietary software, while others are freely available open source systems developed by communities of users. ALM falls into the former category. It is a closed source proprietary software developed by Adobe.

Some learning management systems can be self-hosted. This means that you can download the system and install it on your own servers. On the other end, ALM is cloud-based. This means that Learning Manager is entirely deployed on Adobe servers and that all of the hosting and IT-related burdens are managed for you by Adobe. This cloud-based approach is in line with the growing trend that's been observed in recent years, as more and more organizations decide to move a growing portion of their tools and services to the cloud.

> **A word on the infrastructure**
> Adobe Learning Manager is deployed on Amazon Web Services with other cloud partners, such as Akamaï and Brightcove, the latter of which offers industry-leading video content delivery. This allows ALM to scale up to very large deployments, sometimes involving hundreds of thousands of regular users.

This model is known as the **Software-as-a-Service** model, also known by its acronym **SaaS**.

Updating Adobe Learning Manager

One of the main advantages of the SaaS model is how the system is updated. Since ALM is entirely hosted and managed by Adobe, all updates are directly deployed by Adobe on the server and are immediately available to all ALM customers.

Adobe constantly updates Learning Manager. As a customer, there is nothing to do on your side to benefit from the latest update.

> **Note**
>
> You can find information about the latest updates at s.
>
> The release notes of all past updates can be found at `https://helpx.adobe.com/learning-manager/release-note/release-notes.html`.

Adobe Learning Manager is a learner-centric LMS

ALM offers a Netflix-like experience: a very large number of courses are available for learners to choose from, just as if you were browsing Netflix's extensive catalog for your favorite movies or series!

This is in sharp contrast to most LMSs used in the education sector, which are designed to help *teachers* implement their instructional strategies. While it is entirely possible for organizations to implement their training strategy using ALM, the overall experience relies on the *learner* being in the driver's seat. This mindset is one of the key elements that makes ALM a **Learning eXperience Platform** (**LXP**) rather than yet another good ol' LMS.

You should now have a better high-level understanding of what ALM is and what differentiates it from other LMS platforms. In the next section, you will explore how ALM fits in with the other tools from Adobe. You'll discover that there is a lot of extra power to leverage when Learning Manager works hand-in-hand with other Adobe products.

Adobe Learning Manager and Adobe Experience Cloud

Products such as Photoshop, Illustrator, InDesign, Premier Pro, and Acrobat have brought the Adobe brand to fame. But do you know about **Adobe Experience Cloud** (**AEC**)?

Adobe Experience Cloud (**AEC**) (formerly known as Adobe Marketing Cloud) is a collection of integrated applications and services for online marketing, web analytics, content management, eCommerce, and more. AEC is used by a wide and growing range of large organizations. It is not as widely known to the general public as the Creative Cloud, but it is one of the world leaders in its own field.

Since July 2022 and the rebranding of Adobe Captivate Prime into Adobe Learning Manager, ALM is an integral part of Adobe Experience cloud. Overall, Adobe Experience cloud comprises more than a dozen services, including :

- **Adobe Analytics**, a web analytics platform.

- **Marketo Engage**, a marketing automation tool.

- **Adobe Commerce**, an eCommerce solution (formerly known as Magento Commerce).

- **Adobe Experience Manager**, a **Content Management System** (**CMS**) and **Digital Asset Management** (**DAM**) solution.

- **Adobe Campaign**, a mass mailing and campaign automation tool

You can use each of these services separately, but it's when they are integrated with each other that the true power of Adobe Experience Cloud emerges. In the next few sections, we will explore some of the most common integrations that exist between Learning Manager and the other components of the Adobe Experience Cloud.

> **More information on AEC**
>
> More information about Adobe Experience Cloud and its components can be found on the official AEC page on the Adobe website at `https://business.adobe.com/`.

ALM and Adobe Experience Manager

Adobe Experience Manager (**AEM**) is a Content Management System (CMS) coupled with a powerful **Digital Asset Management** (**DAM**) platform that allows you to deliver custom content to your target audience. One of the key components of AEM is called *Sites*.

Sites is the CMS component of AEM. It enables organizations to create various types of websites such as the main website of the organization in different languages, product sites, microsites for events or special promotions, and more.

AEM is a tool for marketers, not developers, so building these websites is made easy by using templates and page components that can be dragged and dropped by the page creator. No coding is involved!

Adobe Learning Manager has a built-in connector for two-way communications between Adobe Learning Manager and Adobe Experience Manager.

- From ALM to AEM, the connector allows you to publish learning content hosted in Adobe Learning Manager directly within your Experience Manager site. This allows you to create your own responsive website for Learning Manager with minimal coding effort.

- From AEM to ALM, the connector gives you access to training data (such as Learner progress, quiz results, and more) from the learners taking their courses on the Adobe Experience Manager Site.

This makes it easy to include a learning component into the broader online experience you provide to your employees, users, learners, and customers.

> **More information on AEM**
>
> More information on Adobe Experience Manager can be found on the official Adobe Experience ManagerAEM page at `https://business.adobe.com/products/experience-manager/adobe-experience-manager.html`.

ALM and Marketo Engage

Marketo Engage is the marketing automation tool of Adobe Experience Cloud. It allows organizations to market their products on multiple channels more effectively, including email, social media, websites, and more.

To do that, Marketo Engage collects data about your users, their behaviors on your applications, their intent, how they responded to previous marketing efforts, and more. Thanks to that data and a clever layer of **artificial intelligence (AI)**, your marketing team can segment customers and deliver personalized marketing campaigns that increase lead conversion and business revenues.

With the Marketo Engage connector for Adobe Learning Manager, you can feed the data from your learning platform (such as user addition, course enrollment, course completion, etc.) into your marketing automation system, which allows you to drive marketing campaigns based on learning data coming from your LMS. For example, you can create a marketing campaign that targets the following:

- Users that have completed a certain course,
- Learners that have shown interest in a specific subject matter,
- Users that have acquired a specific badge or completed a certification path.

The possibilities are endless...

The data flow between Marketo Engage and Learning Manager also goes the other way. For example, you can recommend a course to customers that bought a certain product, you can cross-sell learning material to customers that have subscribed to your services or to users that have shared a page on your social media channels, and more.

With such integration, your learning material becomes an integral part of the customer journey. This is where Learning Manager overcomes the traditional LMS to become the cornerstone of your *Learning eXperience Platform* (LXP).

> **More information on Marketo Engage**
>
> You can browse the official Marketo Engage page on the Adobe website for more information: `https://business.adobe.com/products/marketo/adobe-marketo.html`.

ALM and Adobe Commerce

Although Learning Manager does not have an embedded shopping cart, it is easy to integrate with Adobe Commerce using the embedded Adobe Commerce connector. With this connector, you can sell the learning content hosted by Adobe Learning Manager. For example, you can use your website to sell live classrooms, on-demand learning courses, certification exams, video tutorials, and more that are hosted, delivered, and managed by your Adobe Learning Manager account.

> **More information**
>
> More information on Adobe Commerce can be found at `https://business.adobe.com/products/magento/magento-commerce.html`.

Conclusion

In addition to using Adobe Learning Manager standalone as a simple (yet powerful) LMS, you can also integrate it with the other services provided by the Adobe Experience cloud.

One important aspect to keep in mind is that you can integrate Learning Manager with *any* CMS, *any* marketing automation tool, and *any* eCommerce solution, not only with those developed by Adobe. However, if you decide to use Adobe products, you have access to specific connectors that make these integrations a breeze.

Throughout this section, one of the main keywords has been *experience*. As learners and consumers, we are all looking for *experiences* when we browse the internet, use mobile applications, or walk into a store. Nowadays, *experiences* are what we expect brands and companies to deliver. We want these *experiences* to be consistent across devices and channels, and, above all, we want them to be personalized and relevant.

That is exactly the spirit in which the Adobe Experience Cloud has been developed.

Adobe Learning Manager in the Adobe Digital Learning Solutions ecosystem

In addition to being part of the Adobe Experience Cloud, Learning Manager is one of three eLearning-related products developed by Adobe. The other two are Adobe Captivate and Adobe Connect.

Of course, Adobe has developed tight integrations between these three products, so customers using all three of them have some added benefits. That being said, Adobe has taken great care of developing these applications around well-established industry standards such as HTML5, SCORM, and xAPI. This means that Adobe Digital Learning Solutions seamlessly integrates with *any* third-party authoring tool, application, or service, not only with other Adobe-branded solutions.

In this section, you will explore the Adobe Digital Learning tools and services in more detail to better understand how they fit into one another.

> **More information**
>
> More information on Adobe Digital Learning Solutions can be found at `https://www.adobe.com/elearning.html`.

Adobe Captivate

Adobe Captivate is an award-winning eLearning authoring tool. You can use Adobe Captivate to *create* various types of interactive eLearning content, such as compliance training, interactive videos, highly engaging quizzes, virtual reality training, software simulations, and more.

Content created with Adobe Captivate must be deployed on an LMS to be delivered to students. This LMS can be Adobe Learning Manager, but it can also be any other third-party LMS. This is an important consideration. Since Captivate and Learning Manager are both Adobe products, some users believe that content hosted in Learning Manager must be generated by Captivate and that content generated by Captivate can only be uploaded to Learning Manager. **Both these statements are entirely false**:

- The content generated by Adobe Captivate can be uploaded to *any* AICC-, SCORM-, or xAPI-compliant LMS.

- The content hosted on Adobe Learning manager can be generated by *any* authoring tool, providing that the authoring tool can generate an AICC-, SCORM-, or XAPI-compliant package (which they should all be able to do!).

The only benefit you get when you create the learning content with Adobe Captivate is that you have a direct publishing mechanism from Adobe Captivate to Learning Manager, as well as some additional data available in the course reports. Otherwise, the two are completely separate systems.

> **Note**
>
> AICC, SCORM, and xAPI are three standards that are used in the eLearning industry to enable communication between the learning content and the LMS it is hosted on.

To summarize this section, just remember that Adobe Captivate is used to *create* learning content, while Adobe Learning Manager is used to *host*, *deliver*, and *track* learning content.

> **More information**
>
> More information about Adobe Captivate can be found at `https://www.adobe.com/products/captivate.html`.

Adobe Connect

Adobe Connect is an award-winning virtual classroom delivery solution. The learning activities that are delivered by Adobe Connect are said to be *synchronous*, versus the *asynchronous* content generated by Adobe Captivate:

- A *synchronous* learning activity is an activity where all the learners are connected at the same time. A typical synchronous learning activity is a virtual class, but a webinar or a live stream can also be considered a synchronous activity.

- An *asynchronous* learning activity is an on-demand course module that is published on an LMS. Each learner is free to visit the content at their convenience. Typical asynchronous learning activities include instructional videos, online quizzes, PDF files, or PowerPoint presentations that are hosted on an LMS.

An online course can include both synchronous and asynchronous activities. For example, you can ask students to review a series of instructional videos posted online before attending an instructor-led live or virtual class. Mixing techniques in such a way is often called *blended learning*. The overall learning experience that you offer your learners is a blend of asynchronous and synchronous activities. In *Chapter 4, Creating Skills and Courses*, you will learn how to assemble various types of learning activities into courses. For now, all you need to remember is that Adobe Learning Manager supports both synchronous and asynchronous activities.

When it comes to adding synchronous virtual activities to a course, a large array of virtual classroom solutions can be used, with some of the most popular being Zoom, Microsoft Teams, and Google Hangouts. Adobe Connect is just one of the available solutions.

Learning Manager supports *any* virtual class solution, but if you're using Adobe Connect, you have some additional benefits. For example, ALM can automatically retrieve information (such as the room name, the room URL, scheduled meetings, the list of authorized trainers, and more) from your Connect account, making it easy to add an Adobe Connect-powered virtual class to your ALM courses.

> **More information**
>
> For more information on Adobe Connect, you can browse the official Adobe Connect home page at `https://www.adobe.com/products/adobeconnect.html`.

Conclusion

With Adobe Captivate, Adobe Connect, and Adobe Learning Manager, Adobe has a very powerful ecosystem of services and applications that allow you to conduct virtually any kind of online learning activity:

- You can create a wide range of *asynchronous* learning content with Adobe Captivate.
- You can conduct very effective *synchronous* virtual class activities with Adobe Connect.
- Finally, you can *assemble* these building blocks into courses and *deliver* the content to the right learner using Adobe Learning Manager.

Even though this ecosystem is very powerful and well-integrated, Adobe does *not* force you to use all three of these products together.

Adobe Learning Manager seamlessly integrates with *any* asynchronous eLearning authoring tool, providing the chosen tool can generate AICC-, SCORM-, or xAPI-compliant packages (which is something they should all do). Learning Manager also supports *any* synchronous virtual classroom solution, not just Adobe Connect. So, you are free to mix and match any solutions from any vendor when building online courses with Adobe Learning Manager.

That being said, if you decide to stick with Adobe solutions, you will be able to leverage some nice integrations that streamline your workflows and make your life easier.

By now, you should have a good high-level overview of what Adobe Learning Manager is and how it fits into the Adobe ecosystem. If you're like me, I bet that makes you eager to learn about the platform hands-on! Well, that's exactly what you're going to do, starting with the next section.

Getting Access to Adobe Learning Manager

Remember that Adobe Learning Manager is being distributed under the SaaS model, so getting access to ALM is a simple matter of filling out a form to sign up for the service. In the next few sections, you will activate your new ALM trial account and start exploring some basic account settings.

Activating Your Trial Account

ALM is a pay-for service, but Adobe offers a free 30-day trial so that you can test the system hands-on before committing to a pay-for account. It should also give you enough time to go through the information provided in this book.

In this section, you will go through the steps needed to activate your ALM trial account:

1. Open your web browser and go to the following page: `https://business.adobe.com/products/learning-manager/adobe-learning-manager.html`.

2. Click the **Free 30-day trial** button that appears on the page. You may have to wait a few seconds before the button is available.

3. Log in with your Adobe ID. If you don't have an Adobe ID yet, click the **Create an account** link and follow the steps provided. An Adobe ID is necessary to activate your Learning Manager trial account.

4. Once you are logged in, fill in the form that appears on the screen.

While filling in the form, pay close attention to the **Organization name** field. The default URL of your ALM account will be generated based on this particular field.

5. Accept the Adobe Learning Manager terms of use.

6. The system will automatically log you into your new Adobe Learning Manager account as an administrator.

Welcome to Adobe Learning Manager! You are now the proud administrator of a brand-new ALM trial account. Your computer screen should look similar to the following screenshot:

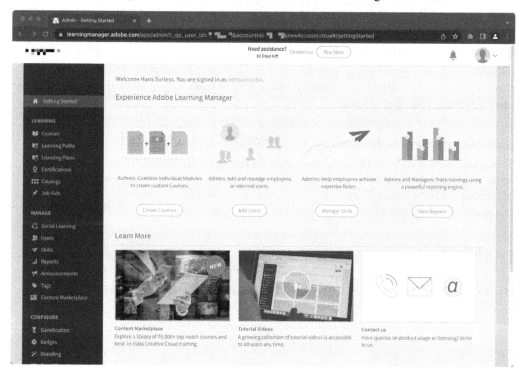

Figure 1.1 – Your first look at the Learning Manager admin interface

> **Important**
>
> If you are using the Firefox or Opera browser, you will see a warning message across the top of the screen, telling you that your browser is not recommended for accessing Learning Manager. At the time of this writing, only Google Chrome, Apple Safari, and Microsoft Edge are recommended by Adobe to access the *admin* portion of Learning Manager. The *learner* experience is also supported by Firefox 57 and higher. More information on the system requirements can be found at `https://helpx.adobe.com/be_en/learning-manager/system-requirements.html`.

Discovering Your ALM Account URL

The last step is to take note of the URL of your new ALM account. This is the address you will use to access the service. It is also the URL you will share with other users (learners, authors, instructors, and others) who need to access your LMS.

Taking a look at the address bar of your web browser, you should see something like `https://learningmanager.adobe.com/app/admin?....`

To discover your account address, the only thing you need to do is log out of your account:

1. Click the user icon located in the upper-right corner of the interface.
2. At the end of the menu, click the **Sign Out** link.

Once you've signed out, take another look at the address bar of your browser. The URL of your ALM account corresponds to the following pattern: `https://learningmanager.adobe.com/<YOUR ACCOUNT NAME>`. Note that your account name is derived from the organization name you filled in when activating your trial account.

> **Customizing your ALM domain**
>
> It is possible to customize the address of your Learning Manager account, but this comes at an additional cost and involves manual intervention from the ALM support team. More information can be found at `https://helpx.adobe.com/learning-manager/custom-domain.html`.

You now have access to a working ALM trial account.

Converting your trial account into a permanent paid account

At the end of your 30-day trial, simply purchase a few licenses to automatically convert your trial into a permanent paid account. At this point, you will need to choose one of the two available licensing models:

- The **Registered User Pricing** model allows you to purchase a fixed number of seats within your ALM account. You can then assign these licenses to individual learners. This model is good for organizations that want to give their employees access to the LMS.

- The **Monthly Active User Pricing** model is great when you have a floating audience, which means when the number of learners varies from month to month. For example, organizations involved in customer education or partner training may not know how many seats they will need along the way, such as when you have an audience that needs only one or two tracked courses a year (say, for compliance reasons). This allows the ALM customer to adjust the number of licenses to the number of users on a monthly basis. Under this licensing model, you are only charged for the number of *active* users, but this requires that you have a minimum of 1,000 monthly active users.

> **Note**
>
> More information can be found at the following URL: `https://business.adobe.com/products/learning-manager/pricing.html`. You can also contact the Adobe Learning Manager sales team at `learningmanagersales@adobe.com`.

Getting to know Adobe Learning Manager

By default, you should be logged in as an administrator. This is indicated at the top of the screen, as shown in the following screenshot:

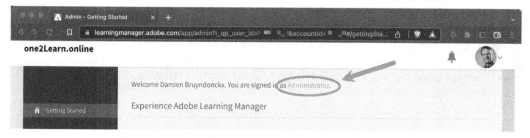

Figure 1.2 – By default, you are signed in as an administrator

The Adobe Learning interface is divided into three main areas:

- The header, across the top of the screen, shows the name of your ALM account on the left and an icon for your user profile on the right. Also, notice the bell-shaped notification icon.

- The dark sidebar on the left-hand side of the interface contains links to the various areas of the system.

- Finally, the main content area displays the most common activities of an ALM administrator. From there, you can create courses, add users, manage skills, and view reports. These activities are the most common administrative tasks. They can also be accessed through the dark sidebar on the left.

Now, let's review the main settings of your new ALM account.

Modifying your user profile

Before going any further, you must take your first steps into customizing your Learning Manager user profile:

1. Click the user profile icon located in the upper-right corner of the screen.

2. In the drop-down menu, select **Profile Settings**.

This opens a dialog box containing your main profile settings. From here, you can customize your user profile. You can also choose your time zone, which is particularly useful when you're scheduling or attending live training events.

But the most important features of this dialog box are the two language choices that it allows you to make:

- **Interface Language** defines the language of the ALM application itself.

- **Content Language** lets you define the default language of the *content* that will be delivered to you. This can be different from the interface language.

In *Chapter 3, Uploading Learning Content and Managing the Content Library*, you will learn how to deploy several language versions of the same course module. The language version of a course depends on the **Content Language** choice the user has made in the **Profile Settings** dialog box.

Let's take the following screenshot as an example:

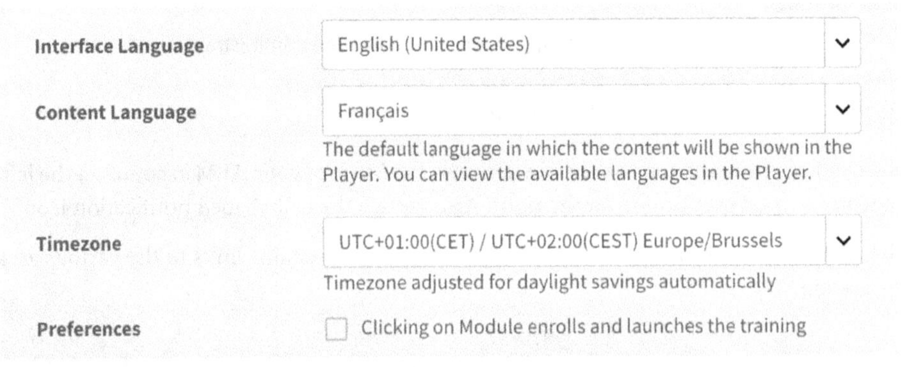

Interface Language	English (United States) ⌄
Content Language	Français ⌄
	The default language in which the content will be shown in the Player. You can view the available languages in the Player.
Timezone	UTC+01:00(CET) / UTC+02:00(CEST) Europe/Brussels ⌄
	Timezone adjusted for daylight savings automatically
Preferences	☐ Clicking on Module enrolls and launches the training

Figure 1.3 – Interface Language and Content Language in the Profile Settings dialog

In the preceding screenshot, **Interface Language** has been set to **English (United States)**. This means that, *for that user*, the Learning Manager application is displayed in American English.

Content Language has been set to **French** (*Français* is the French word for… French). This means that, when this particular user takes a course, the course content will be displayed in French by default (providing, of course, that a French version of the course module is available). If a French version of the course is not available, Learning Manager falls back to the default language of the account.

Another important feature of the **Profile Settings** dialog is the **Download My Learning Transcript (XLS)** link at the bottom of the box. This feature allows each user to download an Excel worksheet containing their personal learning data.

Changing the default language of your account

In the previous section, you learned that Learning Manager distinguishes the interface language (the language of the application) from the content language (the default language of the course modules delivered to the user). You also learned that if the chosen language version of a course does not exist, Learning Manager falls back to the default language of the account. So, in this section, you'll learn how to choose the default language of your ALM account using the following steps:

1. Make sure you are logged in as an administrator, that the **Profile Settings** dialog box is closed, and that you are on the administrator home page.

2. Scroll down to the bottom of the page and click the **Settings** link located at the very bottom of the left column, as illustrated in the following screenshot:

Figure 1.4 – Click the Settings link near the bottom of the left column

This takes you to the **Basic Info** page. Notice that the content in the left column has changed. Also, notice the **Back** link at the very top of the left column, which takes you back to the previous screen.

3. Click the **Change** link located in the upper-right corner of the **Basic Info** area.

4. To change the default language, open the **Locale** drop-down and choose the appropriate default language.

5. Click the **Save** button located in the bottom-right corner of the **Basic Info** form to save your changes and return to the previous screen.

Take some time to read the **Language Change Confirmation** message. This message should be displayed both in the old and new language. It clearly states that each user can override the default platform language using their **Profile Settings**.

6. Click the **OK** button to discard the **Language Change Confirmation** message.

After ALM automatically reloads, the new language should be applied to the system. Note that if you have changed **Interface Language** in your **Profile Settings**, the language that's used is the one of your profile, not the default language of the platform that you just changed.

7. Click the **Change** button in the upper-right corner of the **Basic Info** area again.

Take some time to review the other **Basic Info** properties that can be changed on this page. The **Timezone** property you choose here is the default time zone of the system. Remember that this is yet another setting that each user can override via their **Profile Settings**:

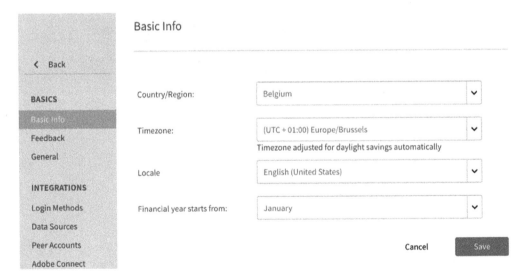

Figure 1.5 – Review the Basic Info properties that can be changed on this page

For the remainder of this book, it is assumed that **English (United States)** is the default locale of your account. It is also assumed that your admin profile uses **English (United States)** as both **Interface Language** and **Content Language**.

8. If necessary, revert to **English (United States)** for the default locale of the platform, as well as for the default languages of your user profile.

9. Make sure you return to the administrator home page before moving on to the next section.

With that, you have examined the options that are available in your user profile, as well as the basic information of your Learning Manager account.

Understanding the main roles

You are currently logged in as an administrator. The main tasks of an ALM administrator are those visible in the top section of the administrator home page:

- Creating courses
- Adding users
- Managing skills
- Viewing reports

In addition to these basic administrative tasks, the administrator is also responsible for maintaining the platform as a whole. Take a look at the links available in the left column to get a better idea of the tasks that fall under the responsibility of an account administrator.

Note that creating course content, managing student activities, grading students, and more are *not* part of the tasks available to administrators. These tasks are assigned to other types of users in the system.

Let's take a quick look at the other roles available by default in Adobe Learning Manager:

1. Click the user profile icon located in the upper-right corner of the interface.

In the menu that opens, take note of the four roles available by default in Adobe Learning Manager. You are currently logged in as an administrator, as shown in the following screenshot:

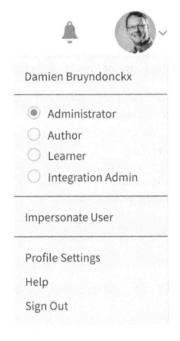

Figure 1.6 – The four default roles that are available in Learning Manager

Now, let's explore the other three roles one by one.

2. Click **Author** in the opened menu. When Learning Manager reloads, you are logged in as an author, as indicated in the welcome message at the top of the main area.

The upper portion of the main content area displays the two basic tasks devoted to an ALM author: **Creating Content** and **Creating Courses**.

Notice that the links available in the left column are not the same as those that were available when you were logged in as an administrator. Take some time to inspect the available links to get a better idea of the tasks assigned to an ALM author.

Now, let's explore the **Learner** role.

3. Click the user icon located in the upper-right corner of the screen.

4. In the menu that opens, choose the **Learner** role.

When Learning Manager reloads, you discover the default learner experience provided by Adobe Learning Manager. This is a very important area of ALM as this is where most users spend most of their time.

Take good note of the areas available on the learner home page. In *Chapter 2, Customizing the Look and Feel of Adobe Learning Manager*, you will learn how to customize this home page.

Also, notice the course recommendations available at the bottom of the learner home page. These are powered by Adobe's own AI technology called **Adobe Sensei**. You will explore the AI-powered features of ALM in more detail in *Chapter 13, AI-Powered Recommendations for Learners*.

Now, let's explore the last default role of Adobe Learning Manager.

5.   Click the user icon located in the upper-right corner of the screen one more time.

6.   In the menu that opens, choose the **Integration Admin** role.

In Learning Manager, the Integration Admin is responsible for connecting your account to the other IT systems used in the organization. The Integration Admin is usually a member of the IT department or a developer. Take some time to review the available connectors. Notice the **Adobe Commerce**, **Adobe Connect**, and **Marketo Engage** connectors, which we've already talked about. Also, notice the **Azure ADFS** connector, which allows you to connect ALM to your corporate Active Directory for user authentication.

7.   From the left column, click the **Applications** link.

This is where you can associate your account with **Adobe Experience Manager – Sites**.

You will explore the **Integration Admin** role in more detail in *Chapter 16, Exploring the Integration Admin Role*. But for now, let's return to your default role of platform administrator.

8.   Click the user icon in the upper-right corner of the screen one last time.

9.   In the menu that opens, choose the **Administrator** role.

When the system reloads, you are back to the default Administrator home page.

In this section, we have briefly reviewed the four default roles available in Adobe Learning Manager.

Summary

Now that we have reached the end of this chapter, you should have a much better understanding of Adobe Learning Manager. ALM is a cloud-based LMS developed by Adobe. It has all the features of a modern LMS platform and you can use it as such. However, Learning Manager has a lot more to offer!

First of all, ALM is one of the many components of the **Adobe Experience Cloud** (**AEC**), a suite of tools used by organizations to create and deliver personalized experiences for every single customer. As such, Learning Manager integrates nicely with the other components of the Experience Cloud, such as Marketo Engage (Marketing automation), Adobe Commerce, and Adobe Experience Manager (CMS and DAM).

Learning Manager is also one of the three products developed by Adobe Digital Learning Solutions. The other two are Adobe Captivate, an award-winning eLearning authoring tool, and Adobe Connect, the virtual class solution from Adobe. Even though Adobe provides easy integrations between these three products, there is absolutely no obligation to use them all together. ALM can host content developed by any authoring tool, including, but not limited to, Adobe Captivate. You are also able to use Learning Manager to schedule and manage synchronous virtual classrooms using any video conferencing system, including, but not limited to, Adobe Connect.

Adobe Learning Manager is designed as an enterprise LMS. As such, it includes unique features specifically for medium and large organizations, such as a dedicated Manager role, extensive reporting capabilities, the ability to share content among various ALM accounts, the ability to include external third-party content in your learning catalog, and more.

In this chapter, you took your first steps into discovering the ALM platform hands-on. You activated your free 30-day trial and explored the basic settings of your personal user profile, as well as the basic information of your account. Finally, you had your first glimpse of the four roles available in the system: Administrator, Author, Learner, and Integration Admin.

In the next chapter, you will continue with the initial setup of your Learning Manager account by reviewing the options available to customize the look and feel of both the user and admin experiences.

2

Customizing the Look and Feel of Adobe Learning Manager

Now that you have a working Learning Manager account, your will concentrate on the initial configuration of the system. One of the first things you'll probably want to customize is the look and feel of your new LMS.

In this chapter, you will explore the main branding and customization features offered by Adobe Learning Manager. You will learn how to change your account's name and URL, upload your logo, and change the color scheme of your account so that it matches your corporate identity. Then, you will explore the options for customizing the learner home page.

Most of these customizations can be done directly on the platform using the admin role, but some more advanced customizations require the intervention of the Adobe Learning Manager support team. At the end of the chapter, we will also discuss another option for customizing the look and feel of your account: using ALM as a **headless LMS**, a feature ALM (formerly Captivate Prime LMS) has pioneered.

By the end of this chapter, the experience provided by your Learning Manager account will match the experience provided by the other digital tools of your organization. To achieve that goal, this chapter covers the following topics:

- Modifying the name and subdomain of your ALM account
- Branding your account by uploading your logo and modifying the color scheme
- Customizing the learner home page
- Using Learning Manager as a headless LMS

This makes for an exciting new chapter in which you will dive deeper into the main options of your Learning Manager account.

Technical requirements

To perform the tasks described in this chapter hands-on, you need to meet the following technical requirements:

- You must have administrator access to a working ALM account (trial accounts are OK).
- You need to have access to your organization's logo and color guide. If you do not have access to these assets, a sample logo and a sample branding guide are available in the `branding` folder of the download associated with this book.

Modifying the name and subdomain of your ALM account

When you activated your ALM account in the previous chapter, a URL was generated automatically based on the organization name you supplied in the account activation form. You will now discover how you can modify the name and/or the URL of your account:

1. Log in to your ALM account as an administrator.
2. Once logged in, scroll down the administrator home page and click the **Branding** link located in the **Configure** section at the bottom of the left column.

This opens the **Branding** section of the administrator application. It should be similar to the following screenshot:

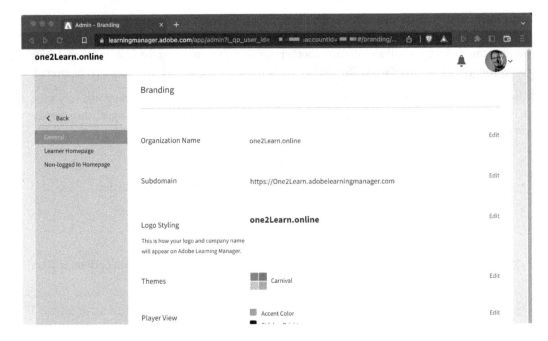

Figure 2.1 – The Branding section of the Learning Manager administrator

At the top of the page, notice the **Organization Name** field. This should match the organization name you supplied when activating your trial account in the previous chapter. It is also the name that appears in the top left corner of the screen, above the left column.

3. To modify the name of your account, click the **Edit** link associated with the **Organization Name** option.

4. Type in the new name and click the **Save** button.

You can also modify the URL of your account using a similar procedure. Note that, using this technique, the URL of your ALM account will always match the following pattern: `https://<yourAccountName>.adobelearningmanager.com`.

This is the reason why this option is called **Subdomain**. The **domain** is `adobelearningmanager.com`, and that portion of the URL cannot be changed. The element that comes between `https://` and `adobelearningmanager.com` is your **subdomain**. That is the only part of the URL that can be changed using this option.

Subdomains on the internet

The concept of **subdomains** is not unique to ALM. It is something widely used across the internet. Take, for example, a company whose main website is `www.company.com`. This company may operate other websites such as `mail.company.com`, `intranet.company.com`, and `shop.company.com`. In this case, `company.com` is the domain, while `mail`, `intranet`, and `shop` are considered subdomains of the `company.com` domain.

---

5. To customize the subdomain of your ALM account, click the **Edit** link associated with the **Subdomain** option.

6. Enter the new subdomain and click the **Save** button to validate it.

Note that only letters (uppercase or lowercase), numbers, and hyphens are allowed for the subdomain. Special characters and spaces are prohibited. Also, note that the subdomain must be unique. Subdomains are allocated on a first-come, first-served basis. If your subdomain of choice has already been taken by another ALM customer, you will see the following error message appear onscreen:

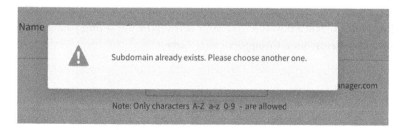

Figure 2.2 – The error message that's displayed when the chosen subdomain already exists

If your subdomain is accepted by the system, you can start sharing your new account URL with the other users of your LMS (administrators, authors, learners, and others). From now on, this is the URL every user will use to access your ALM account.

Using a custom domain

For a growing number of organizations, the requirement to have `.adobelearningmanager.com` in the URL of their LMS is considered an unacceptable limitation that hinders their ability to truly own and manage their brand.

That's why Adobe Learning Manager supports using a custom domain to access your account. Thanks to this feature, you can set up your account under any of the following URL patterns:

- `mycompany.com`
- `lms.mycompany.com`
- `alm.mycompany.com`
- `mycompany.com/learning`

As a prerequisite, you must own or register the domain that you want to use. You must also have access to the SSL certificates and the associated private keys of the custom domain to enable secure communication using the HTTPS protocol.

At the time of writing, the process of setting up a custom domain for your ALM account cannot be completed by an administrator. It involves manual operations by the Adobe support team, as well as your IT department.

> **Configuring a custom domain**
>
> For more information on configuring a custom domain for your account, refer to the following article on the official ALM support site: `https://helpx.adobe.com/learning-manager/custom-domain.html`.

In this section, you learned how to customize the URL of your ALM account. This is an important first step toward taking ownership of your new LMS, but it is not the only form of customization possible. In the next section, you will learn how to *brand* your account by uploading your company logo and by modifying the color scheme used throughout your account.

Branding your Adobe Learning Manager Account

Other important aspects of an organization's corporate image are the logo and the color theme. In this section, you will learn how to upload your logo and modify the color scheme of your ALM account:

1. Make sure you are logged in as an administrator and that you are on the administrator home page.

2. Click the **Branding** link located in the **Configure** section at the bottom of the left column.

This takes you to the **Branding** page of the administrator. From here, you can upload your logo and modify the color theme of your ALM account. Let's review these two options in detail.

Uploading your logo

First, you will upload your company logo using the following procedure:

> **Note**
>
> If you do not have access to a suitable logo image, you can use the sample logo provided in the companion files of this book. Look for the `branding/sampleLogo.png` or `branding/sampleLogo_negative.png` file.

1. Make sure you are on the **Branding** page of the ALM administrator.

2. Click the **Edit** link associated with the **Logo Styling** option.

3. Drag and drop your logo image or click the upload area to select the logo image you want to use. For the best results, it is recommended that you use an image file in `.jpg` or `.png` format.

4. Choose your favorite **Header Style** from the three available options (**Only Logo Image** (default), **Logo Image + CompanyName**, or **Only Company Name**).

5. Click the **Save** button located in the bottom-right corner of the **Logo Styling** section to validate this.

Your logo should now be visible in the upper-left corner of the ALM interface (unless you chose the **Only Company Name** header style), as depicted in the following screenshot:

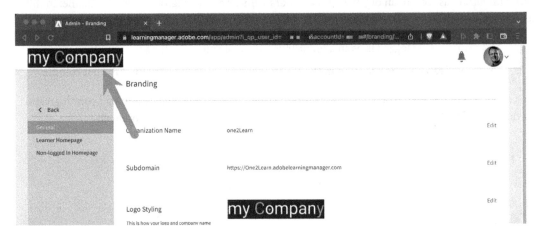

Figure 2.3 – Your logo is displayed in the top-left corner of Adobe Learning Manager

Customizing the color theme

With your logo displayed in the upper-left corner of the header, your account already conveys a very different identity than it did a few minutes ago. But there's still work to be done before it looks like your organization's other online platforms. In this section, you will modify the color scheme of your ALM account so that it matches the visual identity of your organization.

To help you out, Adobe Learning Manager comes with six professionally designed color themes. You will first choose the color theme that takes you closest to the final result you want to achieve. Then, you will further customize the chosen theme to perfectly align it with your corporate colors:

1. Make sure you are logged in as an administrator and that you are on the administrator home page.
2. Click the **Branding** link located in the **Configure** section at the bottom of the left column. This takes you to the **Branding** page of the administrator role.
3. Click the **Edit** link associated with the **Themes** option.

When scrolling down the page, you see the six themes included with Learning Manager. By default, the **Default** theme is applied to any new account.

4. Select any other available theme. You can preview the selected theme in the theme preview section located just above the theme chooser.

Note the left and right arrows located on either side of the theme preview section. These allow you to preview different areas of Learning Manager to control how they are affected by the chosen theme. In the following screenshot, the **Pebbles** theme has been applied, and the theme preview area displays the third available preview image:

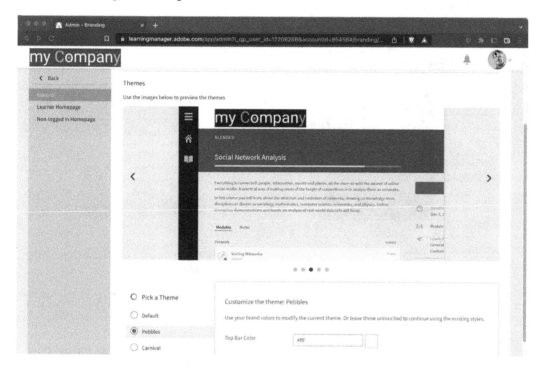

Figure 2.4 – Previewing the Pebbles theme

Continue browsing and previewing the available themes until you find one that you like. The next step is to further customize the chosen theme so that it perfectly aligns with your organization's color guide.

> **Accessing the color guide**
>
> If you do not have access to your organization's color guide, or if your organization does not have a color guide, you can use the sample one provided in the companion files. Look for the `branding/colorGuide.pdf` file.

Adobe Learning Manager lets you customize four different aspects of each theme: **Top Bar Color**, **Accent Color**, **Primary Color**, and **Sidebar Brightness**.

5. To identify which area of the interface is controlled by each of these options, click the **Show Hints** link at the bottom of the theme options area.

This activates hints on the theme preview, as shown in the following screenshot:

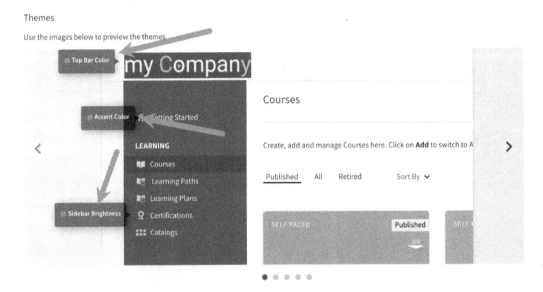

Figure 2.5 – Hints toggled on in the theme preview

Now that you have a better idea of what aspect of the **user interface** (**UI**) each option controls, let's start customizing the top bar color.

6. In the options for the chosen theme, click the **Top Bar Color** field. By default, the top bar color is *#FFFFFF* in every theme. (*#FFFFFF* is the hex code for *white*.)

7. Type in the desired color code or choose the color in the color picker. Click the **Select** button when you're done.

Top Bar Color is the background color of the header area that spans across the top of the interface. Your change is immediately reflected on the theme preview. If you don't like the new color, just repeat the aforementioned actions with another color code until you find a color that you like.

Now, let's modify the **Accent Color** property. The accent color is the color of the icons displayed in the left sidebar.

8. In the options for the chosen theme, open the **Accent Color** dropdown.

9. Choose any color in the list. Your choice is immediately reflected in the theme preview area. If you want to use a custom **Accent Color**, you must first choose **Custom** at the end of the **Accent Color** dropdown; then, you must enter the color code of your custom color or choose it with the color picker.

10. The next option available is **Primary Color**. Just like for **Accent Color**, you can choose another color in the drop-down list. If you want a custom color, you first need to choose **Custom** at the end of the drop-down list; then, you must enter the exact color code you want to use as the primary color.

Unlike the other theme customizations, changing **Primary Color** will not reflect in the theme preview area. **Primary Color** controls some UI elements of the *immersive* user experience. For now, take good notes of the chosen **Primary Color**. You will refer to it in the next section when learning about the *Classic* and *Immersive* user experiences.

The last customization option available for themes is **Sidebar Brightness**. This controls how dark or how light the background of the left sidebar is.

11. Move the **Sidebar Brightness** slider to the left and right while watching the left sidebar in the theme preview area.

Notice that the font color automatically toggles between white and black, depending on the chosen **Sidebar Brightness**.

12. Keep adjusting the **Sidebar Brightness** slider until the left sidebar looks the way you want in the theme preview.

13. Finally, click the **Save** button in the bottom-right corner of the screen to save your changes. After ALM reloads, your new customized theme is applied.

14. Return to the administrator home page before moving on to the next section.

This is how far the built-in options of ALM take you when it comes to customizing the general look and feel of your account. If this feels somewhat limited, you can take your customization to the next level by using ALM as a **headless LMS**, which will be discussed in more detail at the end of this chapter. Keep in mind that you can also use the Adobe Experience Manager (AEM) connector to display the learning content hosted on your ALM account on an AEM site. In such a case, the look and feel of the AEM site define the visual aspect of your learning content.

Customizing the Fluidic Player

The **Fluidic Player** is the component used to display the learning content when a learner takes a course. As such, it is a key component of the Learner Experience. You will learn more about the Fluidic Player in *Chapter 7, Reviewing the Learner Experience*. In this section, we will quickly review the options available for customizing the look and feel of the Fluidic Player:

1. Make sure you are logged in as an administrator and that you are on the administrator home page.

2. Click the **Branding** link located in the **Configure** section at the bottom of the left column, then click the **Edit** link associated with the **Player View** option.

Clicking this link opens the **Player View** section of the **Branding** page. It starts with a preview of the Fluidic Player, followed by a series of options, as shown in the following screenshot:

Player View

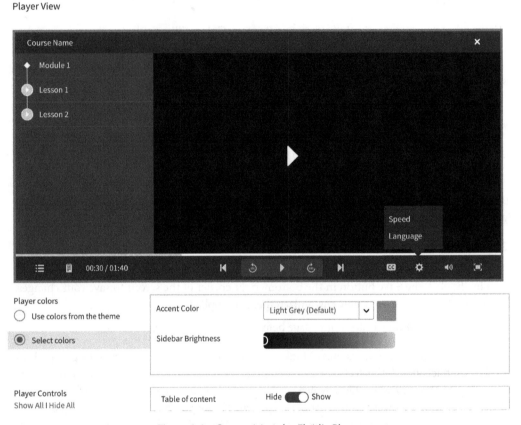

Figure 2.6 – Customizing the Fluidic Player

The options available for customizing the Fluidic Player are straightforward. First, you can apply the theme colors you customized in the previous section to the Fluidic Player.

3. Just below the Fluidic Player preview, select the **Use colors from the Theme** option. If needed, you can further customize the **Accent Color** and **Sidebar Brightness** properties of the Fluidic Player using the same techniques as those used in the previous section when customizing the theme.

4. Further down the page, you can use the switches to enable or disable many of the features available in the Fluidic Player. Feel free to experiment with these switches to get a first idea of what is available in the Fluidic Player. Make sure you turn all switches back to the **Show** position before continuing.

5. When done, click the **Save** button located in the lower-right corner of the **Player View** section of the **Branding** page.

In this section, you had your first glimpse at the Fluidic Player in Adobe Learning Manager and reviewed the options available for customizing it.

Other visual customizations

Adobe Learning Manager allows you to customize other graphical aspects of the platform, such as custom progress icons, custom mouse pointer images, and cusom fonts. Unfortunately, at the time of writing, these additional customizations cannot be completed within the admin interface.

If you need to make these changes, you need to contact the Adobe Learning Manager support team.

> **Contacting the Learning Manager support team**
>
> The email address of the Learning Manager support team is `learningmanagersupport@adobe.com`.

Now that you've completed this section, your ALM account already looks very different from what it looked like at the beginning of this chapter. So far, you stayed in the administrator environment, but in the next section, you will take a look at customizing the learner experience.

Customizing the Learner Experience

Only a small fraction of your users will ever need access to the administrative area of your ALM account. The vast majority of your account users will be *learners* who will use the Learner Experience to browse the course catalog, enroll in courses, take courses, and more. That's why getting the Learner Experience right is a critical aspect of setting up your ALM account. In this section, you'll take your first steps toward taking control of the learner experience.

Understanding the Classic and Immersive experiences

For years, Captivate Prime (remember, *Adobe Learning Manager* used to be called *Captivate Prime*) has provided a certain user experience for learners. This user experience has played a key role in making ALM/Captivate Prime an award-winning LMS. But times change. Whether for listening to music, watching movies or series, shopping online, or accessing public services, the number of platforms has exploded in recent years and users are now much more accustomed to consuming digital experiences than ever before. Their expectations have changed.

Today's digital citizen wants highly personalized experiences that can be consumed seamlessly on any device. Of course, the digital learning industry does not escape this fundamental trend.

As a learner-centric LMS, Adobe Learning Manager takes the Learner Experience very seriously. That's why, in the December 2020 update, the ALM/Captivate Prime team introduced a brand new Learner Experience. This new experience is called the *Immersive* experience, while the original experience is called the *Classic* experience.

The default experience used by any new ALM account is the *Immersive* experience. But, if you have used ALM/Captivate Prime for a longer time, the older *Classic* experience is maintained until you explicitly make the switch to the new *Immersive* experience.

You will now review both of these experiences and have a high-level overview of the options available for each of them.

Discovering the Classic learner experience

We will begin with the *Classic* experience. Remember that this is the older experience provided by the original version of Captivate Prime. If you have just activated your ALM trial account, the default learner experience is the new *Immersive* experience, so to review the *Classic* experience, you must first activate it.

Getting ready

The best way to experiment with the options discussed in this section is to log in to your ALM account twice:

- Once as an administrator
- Once as a learner

To be able to log in twice to the same platform, you can use two different browsers. You need to log in as an administrator using one browser and as a learner using the second browser. If you don't have access to multiple browsers, you can also open a *private* window (sometimes called an *Incognito* window) and log in to your account once in each private window of the same browser.

Remember that to log in as a learner, you first need to log in as an administrator, then switch to the learner role using the user icon located in the upper-right corner of the interface.

Activating the Classic experience

To activate the *Classic* experience, use the browser window where you are logged in as an administrator and perform the following steps:

1. Make sure you are on the administrator home page of your ALM account.

2. Click the **Branding** link located in the **Configure** section at the end of the left sidebar.

3. Scroll down the **Branding** page until you see the **Homepage Experience** option.

For new accounts, the default **Homepage Experience** is the **Immersive** experience, as shown in the following screenshot:

Figure 2.7 – The default Homepage Experience for new accounts is the Immersive experience

If you use an older account, **Homepage Experience** may already be set to **Classic**. In such a case, you can skip the remaining steps in this section.

4. Click the **Edit** link associated with the **Homepage Experience** option.

5. Change **Homepage Experience** from **Immersive** to **Classic**. Note that this immediately reduces the options available further down the page.

6. Click the **Save** button located in the bottom-right corner of the page.

Learning Manager should display a quick message acknowledging that the new options have been successfully saved. You can now switch to the browser window where you are logged in as a learner.

7. Refresh the browser window where you are logged in as a learner.

After the window refreshes, the older *Classic* experience is displayed. It should be similar to what's shown in the following screenshot:

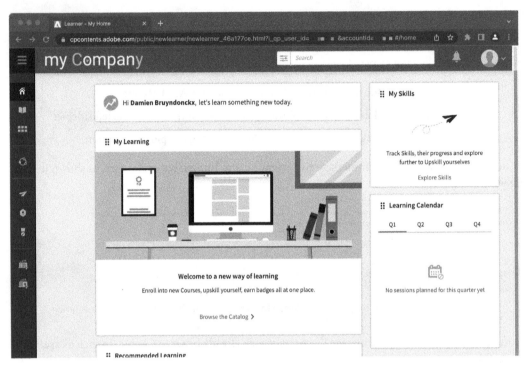

Figure 2.8 – The older Classic experience

Now that the **Classic** experience has been activated, let's take a closer look at it.

Browsing the Classic experience as a learner

In this section, you will simply take a look at the Classic learner experience using the browser window in which you are logged in as a learner. While browsing the Classic experience, keep in mind that your new ALM trial account is currently empty: no custom training material has been uploaded, no user has been defined, and no activity has taken place on your account yet.

Just like the admin experience, the learner home page is divided into three main parts – the header across the top of the page, a sidebar on the left, and the main content area in the middle:

1.   Before going any further, take some time to reduce the width of your browser window.

You should notice that the Classic experience does not properly resize when the width of the browser window changes. The Classic experience is *not* responsive. This means that it is designed for the wider screens of desktop/laptop computers, but not for the narrow screens of tablets and smartphones.

Using the ALM mobile app

To access the training content hosted on your ALM account from a mobile device, you can use the ALM app available for iOS and Android. You will learn more about this mobile app in *Chapter 7, Reviewing the Learner Experience*.

2. Make sure you maximize your browser window before continuing.

3. Click the icon with the three horizontal bars in the upper-left corner of the screen (such an icon is often referred to as a *Hamburger menu*).

This action expands the left sidebar so that you can see the labels associated with each icon. Make sure you are on the **Home** page before moving on.

4. Scroll the learner's home page from top to bottom. Pay close attention to the various sections available.

Each section is a widget that is designed to display specific information. Let's discuss the main widgets in more detail:

Welcome and announcements: This is the first visible widget at the very top of the page. You will use it to display various types of announcements created by the platform administrator. You will learn more about messaging and announcements in *Chapter 15, Working with Messages and Announcements*.

My Learning: This widget displays statistics and provides quick access to all pending activities of the logged-in learner. Since you are currently using a new empty trial account, the **My Learning** widget should be empty.

Recommended Learning: This widget displays the courses that the system recommends to the learner. This widget is powered by Adobe's artificial intelligence called **Adobe Sensei**. You will learn more about this AI-powered feature of ALM in *Chapter 13, AI-Powered Recommendations for Learners*.

Learning Calendar: This widget proposes a chronological view of all upcoming learning events, such as submission deadlines and live or virtual classes in which the user is registered.

5. When ready, click the **Browse the Catalog** link at the bottom of the **My Learning** widget. You can also use the **Catalog** icon in the left sidebar (it is the third icon from the top).

This action takes you to the default learning **catalog**. Notice that a handful of courses are already available in the catalog. These are the default courses available in any new ALM account. You can use them to test various aspects of the platform without spending time creating and uploading content. Even though you can delete these default sample courses, make sure you keep them active for the remainder of this book.

Click any course card to view that course's content. You can also hover over the bottom area of a course card and click the **View Course** link. This action takes you to that course's home page.

6. Click the **Enroll** button located in the top-right area of the page to enroll in this course.

This action will open the **Fluidic Player**, which is the component where the course content is delivered.

7. Click the close icon located in the top-right corner of the Fluidic Player. This takes you back to the course home page.

8. From there, click the **Home** icon at the top of the left sidebar. You can also click the account name or the logo in the top-left corner of the screen.

This action takes you back to the learner home page. Notice that the content of the **My Learning** widget has changed. Since you enrolled in a course, the widget shows some statistics about your progression in that course, as well as a direct link to continue the course where you left off. Also, notice the **My Skills** widget in the top-right corner of the screen, which should display the skills currently in progress.

This little experiment tells us a lot about how these widgets work. The content they display depends on your actions as a learner. This makes the learner home page different for each learner.

Now that you have a better idea of the learner home page in the *Classic* experience, switch back to the admin area of your account to examine how an administrator can customize the *Classic* experience.

Customizing the Classic experience as an administrator

In this section, you will examine the options available to an administrator to customize the *Classic* learner experience:

1. Return to the browser window in which you are logged in as an administrator. Make sure you are on the administrator home page.

2. Click the **Branding** link located in the **Configure** section at the bottom of the left sidebar.

3. Once on the **Branding** page, click the **Learner Homepage** link in the left sidebar.

This takes you to the **Learner Homepage Settings** page. On this page, you can customize both the older *Classic* and the newer *Immersive* layouts. In this section, you will inspect the options available to customize the *Classic* layout, so your first task is to make sure that you are seeing the options for the correct layout.

4. At the top of the **Learner Homepage Settings** page, make sure the **Immersive** switch is disabled, as shown in the following screenshot:

Figure 2.9 – Make sure the Immersive switch is disabled

The rest of the page is divided into two columns. In the right column, you see a preview of the learner home page. This should be very similar to the home page you visited while logged in as a learner.

In the left column, you should see a list of all the widgets available on the learner home page. Notice that you can enable or disable any widget, except for the **Welcome and Sticky Announcements** widget, which cannot be disabled.

5. Disable a few widgets per your liking. Notice that the preview on the right automatically updates as you enable and disable widgets.

You can also use the preview on the right to rearrange the enabled widgets.

6. Move the widgets around in the preview area using simple drag-and-drop actions.

7. Once the learner home page looks the way you want, click the **Save** button located in the upper-right corner of the **Learner Homepage Settings** page.

8. When done, return to the browser window in which you are logged in as a learner to review the changes you just made.

9. Refresh the page and confirm that it conforms to the new settings you have defined in the administrator area.

Tip

If you want to quickly return to the default settings of the *Classic* experience, switch back to being an administrator and click the **Reset to Default** link located next to the **Save** button in the upper-right corner of the **Learner Homepage Settings** page.

In this section, you discovered the *Classic* learner experience and the options available to customize it. In the next section, you will take a closer look at the *Immersive* experience.

Discovering the Immersive learner experience

Now that you have a better idea of what the *Classic* learner experience looks like, you will spend time discovering the new *Immersive* experience and the options available to administrators for customizing it.

Before doing so, let's reflect on the current situation. At the moment, the old *Classic* experience has been activated. The new *Immersive* experience is available, but it is not activated. If you're using an old ALM/Captivate Prime account (one that was activated before December 2020), the current situation may be similar to what you're experiencing on your account.

In this section, you will pretend to be an older ALM/Prime customer that wants to switch from the old *Classic* experience to the new *Immersive* experience. In this case, you want to make sure that the new *Immersive* experience meets your requirements before going live and making it available to your learners. So, you will leave the *Classic* experience enabled while discovering and setting up the *Immersive* experience behind the scenes. It is only when the new experience will be ready for production that you will make the switch for your learners.

Getting ready

To work through the examples in this section, you have to find a way to experiment with the new *Immersive* experience as an administrator, while leaving the older *Classic* experience enabled for your learners until you are ready to make the switch. Fortunately, there is a way to achieve this in ALM using the following procedure:

1. Make sure you are logged in as an administrator.
2. Open a new tab or a new browser window.
3. In the new tab, browse to the following URL: `https://learningmanager.adobe.com/app/learner?learnerLayout=IMMERSIVE`.
4. Enter your email ID and/or your password if prompted to do so.

Thanks to this trick, you can experience the new *Immersive* learner experience while regular learners using your ALM account still use the older *Classic* experience.

Browsing the Immersive experience

Now that you have access to the new *Immersive* experience, let's take a closer look at it.

First, notice that the header (across the top of the screen) and the left sidebar are the same as in the *Classic* experience. The most obvious differences are in the main content area. That being said, there is another very important (yet a little less obvious) change that's introduced by the *Immersive* experience:

1. Reduce the width of your browser window.

While doing so, notice that the *Immersive* experience perfectly fits any screen width. Unlike the *Classic* experience, the *Immersive* experience is *responsive*. This means that it automatically adjusts to any screen width, making it possible to enjoy the new experience on virtually any device.

2. Maximize your browser window before continuing.

The *Immersive* experience offers a Netflix-like interface, similar to the experience offered by many of the platforms we have become accustomed to. The area at the top is called the *Masthead*. Just like the old **Welcome and Announcements** widget, administrators can use it to display announcements and messages to learners:

Figure 2.10 – The Masthead is the large area at the top of the Immersive experience

In *Chapter 15, Working with Messages and Announcements*, you will learn how to create such announcements and how to target them at various types of learners.

Just under the Masthead, in the **My Learning List** area, you should find the course you enrolled in while in the *Classic* experience in the previous section.

3. Scroll down the *Immersive* experience to the very bottom of the page, taking the necessary time to identify each section.

You should recognize the old widgets from the *Classic* experience in the different sections of the *Immersive* experience, but with a fresh, modernized (and responsive) look.

Toward the bottom of the page, you should also notice some new sections that have no equivalent in the old *Classic* experience. These sections are used to display various types of personal recommendations. The content of these sections is unique to each learner and automatically generated by the AI-powered recommendation engine of Adobe Learning Manager:

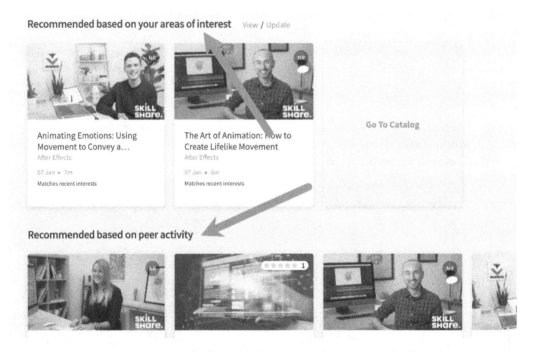

Figure 2.11 – A powerful AI-powered recommendation engine displaying
various types of recommendations that are unique to every learner

Customizing the Immersive experience as an administrator

Now that you have a better idea of what the *Immersive* experience looks like, let's go back to the ALM administrator and review the options available to customize the *Immersive* experience:

1. Return to the administrator home page of your account.
2. Click the **Branding** link located in the **Configure** section at the end of the left sidebar.
3. Once on the **Branding** page, click the **Learner Homepage** link in the left sidebar to open the **Learner Homepage Settings** page.
4. At the top of the **Learner Homepage Settings** page, toggle the **Immersive** switch on.

This action displays the options for the *Immersive* experience. A preview of the *Immersive* experience is displayed on the right-hand side of the page. This preview should be similar to the learner home page you reviewed in the previous section. The available options are displayed in the left column.

5.   Take some time to inspect the available options. Most of them should be self-explanatory.

Note that some sections of the home page (**Recommended by <your account name >** and **Browse by Catalog**) are not enabled by default. This is because these sections need some additional input from the administrator before they can display the relevant content. You will review these options in more detail in *Chapter 13, AI-Powered Recommendations for Learners*.

6.   Similar to what you did when customizing the *Classic* experience, you can use the preview on the right to rearrange the sections of the *Immersive* home page using simple drag-and-drop actions. Note that some sections (such as the **Masthead** area, the **My Learning** section, and the **Footer** area) cannot be rearranged in such a way.

7.   When done, click the **Save** button located in the upper-right corner of the screen.

8.   Return to the browser tab/window in which the *Immersive* experience is displayed (use the following link if that tab/window is no longer open: `https://learningmanager.adobe.com/app/learner?learnerLayout=IMMERSIVE`).

9.   Refresh the page and confirm that it conforms to the new settings you established in the administrative area.

You now have a better idea of what the *Immersive* experience is and the options available to an administrator to customize it.

Switching to the Immersive layout

At this point, you have successfully configured the new *Immersive* experience the way you want. Now, it's time to go live and introduce this new experience to your learners.

In this section, you will first revert to the default settings of the *Immersive* experience (this is necessary for all future examples presented in this book). Then, you will officially switch your Learning Manager account to the new *Immersive* experience:

1.   Return to the administrator home page of your account.

2.   Click the **Branding** link located in the **Configure** section at the end of the left sidebar.

3.   Once on the **Branding** page, click the **Learner Homepage** link in the left sidebar to open the **Learner Homepage Settings** page.

4.   At the top of the **Learner Homepage Settings** page, make sure the **Immersive** switch is toggled on.

5.   Click the **Reset to Default** link located next to the **Save** button in the upper-right corner of the screen.

You are now ready to save the configuration of the *Immersive* experience and make it available to your learners.

6. Click the **Save** button located in the upper-right corner of the page.

7. When done, click the **General** link at the top of the left sidebar to return to the main **Branding** page.

8. Once on the **Branding** page, scroll down until you see the **Homepage Experience** option. Confirm that it is currently set to **Classic**.

9. Click the **Edit** link associated with the **Homepage Experience** option.

10. Switch **Homepage Experience** to **Immersive** (this action modifies the options available further down the page. You will review these options in *Chapter 13, AI-Powered Recommendations for Learners*).

11. Click the **Save** button located in the bottom-right corner of the page.

This last action is what makes the switch to the *Immersive* experience effective for all learners using your ALM account.

> **Important note**
>
> For the remaining examples in this book, we assume that the default *Immersive* experience is enabled in your account.

Customizing the Non-Logged In Homepage

As discussed in *Chapter 1, Introduction to Adobe Learning Manager*, customers using both **Adobe Learning Manager** (**ALM**) and **Adobe Experience Manager** (**AEM**) can configure a special connector to display ALM training content on their AEM sites. In doing so, the system must be able to grant some access to the training content to site visitors, whether or not they are logged into ALM. This is the purpose of the **Non-logged In Homepage** section available in the left column.

Enabling the **Non-logged In Homepage** section requires configuring the **Training Data Access** connector. This special connector is available out of the box for customers who have purchased ALM and AEM together. If you do not have an AEM account alongside your ALM account, you can purchase the Training Data Access connector for an additional fee and activate the **Non-logged In Homepage** option anyway.

Since this feature requires an additional purchase, it will not be discussed any further in this book, but more information can be found on the official ALM help site at `https://helpx.adobe.com/learning-manager/administrators/feature-summary/non-logged-in-experience-learners.html`.

Going headless with Adobe Learning Manager

If you want to take customization to the next level and offer your learners an eLearning experience that is completely your own, Learning Manager offers the unique ability to go **headless**. This can be very useful in the following situations:

- You do not want to be limited to the native customization options available in Adobe Learning Manager.

- There are learning assets/Catalogs/Programs you'd like to be featured in a more prevalent, custom fashion.

- You want to add a learning dimension to an existing highly customized digital experience.

- You want to combine content coming from various sources (a **Content Management System** (**CMS**), **Learning Management System** (**LMS**), marketing automation, big data, and so on) into a single online experience.

First, let's try to understand what *headless* means in the context of a web application such as a CMS or an LMS.

Typically, a CMS or an LMS has two distinct parts:

- **A publicly available area**, also known as the **frontend**. In the case of an LMS, this area is the experience provided to the learner taking the courses hosted on the platform.

- **An administrative area**, also known as the **backend**. This area is available to administrators only. It is mainly used to edit the content available to the general public. Note that Adobe Learning Manager, has further divided the administrative area into the *Administrator*, *Author*, and *Integration Admin* roles.

In classic CMS or LMS platforms, these two spaces are tightly coupled. This means they are hosted under the same domain and are managed by the same platform. For example, your public-facing website might be accessible through `www.company.com`, and the administrative area of your website might be hosted at `www.company.com/admin`. By comparing these two URLs, you can see that the public area and the administrative area are both deployed on the same site under one unique domain name.

Going headless means that the frontend (the public-facing part) and the backend (the administrative area) are *decoupled*. In other words, they can be two completely different systems using different technologies, being hosted on two distinct IT infrastructures, and using two completely different domain names.

When you choose to go *headless*, you only use the administrative areas of Adobe Learning Manager, but you do not use the built-in learner experience. When taking courses, learners use a custom website that leverages the Adobe Learning Manager API to access course content and data to be displayed.

At the time of writing, Learning Manager is one of the very few LMSes on the market to offer such a capability. To make it possible, ALM offers the following two features:

- You can embed the Fluidic Player into your website using a technique that is similar to how a YouTube video is embedded on a web page.

- Learning Manager offers a comprehensive **Application Programming Interface** (**API**). The developer of your website can use this API to remotely query Learning Manager for content, and display that content within your custom website. Your website can also use the ALM API to post data (such as users' progress in courses, quizzes, survey results, submitted assignments, and more) to the Learning Manager backend.

If this sounds rather technical to you, don't worry! Implementing a headless LMS is the job of a developer. As an ALM user or administrator, you should not worry about the nitty-gritty details of implementing a headless LMS.

The main takeaway of this section is that the course content and all learning interactions offered by your Learning Manager account can be delivered to the learner through your custom website.

Summary

In this chapter, you made your Adobe Learning Manager account your own by customizing the name of your account and the URL at which it is accessible. You also customized the look and feel of your account by uploading your logo and making the platform use the colors of your corporate identity. These are critical steps in making Adobe Learning Manager part of the overall digital experience your organization aims to provide to its employees, partners, suppliers, and customers.

You also discovered that Adobe Learning Manager can be used as a headless LMS. This allows you to decouple the learning experience from the ALM backend, which makes virtually any customization possible.

You are now one step closer to providing a highly engaging experience to your learners. That being said, there is still work to be done before you can welcome your first learners into your new LMS. Indeed, your account is still empty. It lacks both the custom course content that you shall provide to your learners and the learners themselves!

You will solve one of these two issues in the next two chapters, in which you will learn how to upload custom learning modules to the platform and how to assemble these modules into courses.

Uploading Learning Content and Managing the Content Library

In the previous chapter, you took ownership of your Learning Manager account by changing its visual appearance so it matches your brand identity. That was an important first step, but your LMS is still lacking two of its most critical ingredients: content and learners.

In this chapter, you will introduce the first of these two missing ingredients: the content. First, we will discuss where the content hosted on your Learning Manager account comes from. This can be either off-the-shelf content from third-party libraries or custom content that you upload to the platform yourself.

Then, you'll switch to the **Author** role and upload different types of learning content (such as videos, interactive quizzes, Word documents, presentations, etc.) to the **Content Library** of your ALM account. You will also learn how to upload **Job Aids** and discuss the difference between regular modules and Job Aids.

Finally, you will explore how to manage your Content Library in the long run. This includes uploading new versions of existing content, adding multiple language versions of a module, and retiring outdated content.

By the end of this chapter, you'll have a thorough understanding of the Content Library and its key role in managing content in your Adobe Learning Manager account.

To reach this goal, the following topics will be covered in this chapter:

- Getting content into Adobe Learning Manager

- Creating custom course modules

- Managing the Content Library

- Creating Job Aids

It's finally time to upload some content to the cloud so learners can access it through your Adobe Learning Manager account.

Technical requirements

To perform the tasks described in this chapter, you'll need to meet the following technical requirements:

- You must have Administrator and Author access to a working Learning Manager account (it can be a free trial account).

- You need to have access to various types of learning content (videos, documents, presentations, and SCORM packages) that you can upload to your Content Library. If you do not have access to such content, sample files are provided in the `courseContent` folder of the download associated with this book.

- Optionally, you need access to the latest version of Adobe Captivate if you want to experiment with the direct upload workflow from Adobe Captivate (the free 30-day trial version of Adobe Captivate is OK).

Getting content into Adobe Learning Manager

Unlike many other LMSs (especially those LMSs targeted at the education market), Learning Manager does not have any built-in, browser-based, content authoring capabilities. This means that all the content hosted on your ALM account has to be brought in from outside the system.

Basically, the content available to your learners can come from two types of sources:

- You can integrate third-party, off-the-shelf content libraries into Learning Manager

- You can upload your own custom learning content to the platform

Let's take a closer, high-level look at these two options.

Integrating third-party, off-the-shelf content

There are many learning content providers out there and it is not uncommon for organizations to subscribe to external learning content libraries to give them personnel access to a wide range of learning resources.

Some of the most famous providers are LinkedIn Learning (previously known as Lynda.com), Udemy, OpenClassrooms, and Pluralsight. These suppliers provide tens of thousands of courses in many languages covering a wide range of topics. More and more workers have access to this type of extended learning material through their employers. In fact, access to this type of content is increasingly considered part of the standard employment package provided by employers.

But organizations do not offer access to such content just for the sake of it! They want a return on investment, which means they need data out of this training effort. For example, they want to know which employees are actively engaged in learning new skills so that those employees can be rewarded with a pay raise, or by being promoted to a higher position. Organizations also want to make sure each employee has spent some time upskilling themselves so that everyone stays up to date in their respective roles, that the required certifications and compliance training have been effectively and successfully taken by each employee, and so on.

This is where a platform such as Adobe Learning Manager comes into play. By integrating this external content into the LMS, Learning Manager can track every interaction with the course material and generate meaningful reports from that data. Learning Manager is also able to use its AI-powered recommendation engine to harness these massive repositories of training content and provide personalized recommendations that match current industry standards as well as each learner's personal requirements and interests.

To make this integration possible, Adobe Learning Manager provides a handful of connectors out of the box. Lots of these providers also offer APIs, which your development team can use to make the content available as course catalogs in your Learning Manager account.

Uploading your own custom content

In addition to the external content discussed in the previous section, most organizations also need to train their workforce on specific topics relevant to their specific business, regulations, workflows, and tools. Another use case is when an organization wants to train external users such as providers, contractors, or even customers. That's why Adobe Learning Manager also offers the ability to upload your own custom course material.

Remember that Learning Manager does *not* include any built-in authoring tools, so this custom content must be produced outside of ALM.

Conclusion

Learners using your Learning Manager account have access to both the external content provided by third-party providers and the custom content produced by your own internal instructional designers. Both types of content are tracked by the system, and both types of content are used by the AI-powered recommendation engine to generate custom recommendations for each learner. This allows Adobe Learning Manager to fit into an increasingly wide range of organizations and use cases.

Integrating external content is made possible through a handful of connectors available out of the box, as well as through APIs that your IT and dev teams can leverage to integrate that content into your Learning Manager account. Custom content must be made outside of ALM because there are no built-in authoring tools in the platform.

In the next section, you will log in as an author and start uploading custom modules to the Content Library of your ALM account.

Creating custom course modules

In this section, you will discover the Author role by uploading custom training content to your Content Library.

Logging in as an Author

Uploading custom content is a task devoted to the Author role. You will now switch to the Author role in order to upload training content. Let's get started:

1. Log in to your ALM account. By default, you should be logged in as an Administrator.
2. Click the user icon in the upper-right corner of the screen and switch to the **Author** role.

When Learning Manager reloads, you should be logged in as an Author. You immediately notice that the home page of an Author differs from the home page of an Administrator, as shown in the following screenshot:

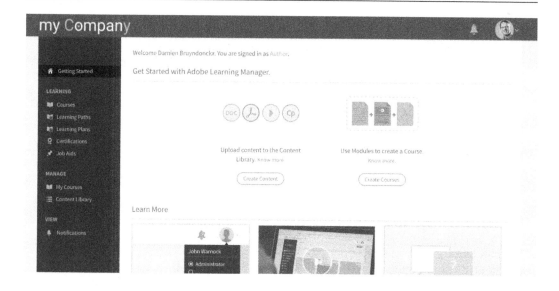

Figure 3.1 – A first look at the Author home page

The tasks devoted to an Author and the tools needed to perform these tasks are accessible through the links of the left sidebar. Two of these tasks are considered to be the main tasks of an ALM author. Links to these two tasks are available at the top of the main content area. These two tasks are as follows:

- **Upload content to the Content Library**

- **Use Modules to create a Course**

Looking at the links on the left sidebar, you'll discover words such as **Modules**, **Courses**, **Learning Programs**, **Learning Plans**, **Job Aids**, and more. Before going any further, let's take some time to understand the meaning of these words in Adobe Learning Manager.

Modules, courses, and learning programs

When you upload a file to the Content Library, you create what Learning Manager calls a **Module**. The *module* is the smallest content unit available in Learning Manager. In other words, each video tutorial, Word document, PDF file, PowerPoint presentation, and SCORM package that you upload to the platform is considered a module.

Note that the modules you upload to Learning Manager are all *asynchronous* learning activities. As discussed in *Chapter 1, Introduction to Adobe Learning Manager*, an asynchronous learning activity is an on-demand piece of learning content that each learner is free to review at their own pace and convenience.

These modules can be arranged into **Courses**. From this perspective, a course is just a series of modules bundled together. While this definition of a course is enough to get you started, in the next chapter, *Chapter 4, Creating Skills and Courses*, you will discover that a course is a little bit more than that as it can also contain *synchronous* activities not included in the Content Library.

Going up one more step, courses can further be arranged into **Learning Programs**. A learning program is a bundle of courses that complement each other.

Throughout the course of this book, you'll discover even more ways to arrange the instructional content available in your ALM account. But for now, you have enough insight to move on to the next section where you will take your first steps into the Content Library.

A first look at the Content Library

The **Content Library** is where all your custom asynchronous modules reside in your ALM account. Every uploaded module ends up in the Content Library, regardless of which author uploaded a particular file. In other words, Author A can see the content uploaded by Author B and vice versa. It is possible to segment the Content Library into folders, which can be made public or private. This feature will be discussed in the *Using Content Folders* section, later in this chapter.

To have access to the Content Library, it is necessary to be logged in as an Author:

1. Make sure you are logged in as an Author and that you are on the Author home page.

2. Click the **Content Library** link located in the **Manage** section of the left sidebar.

This action takes you to the **Content Library** Notice that, by default, a selection of modules is already available in the Content Library of your trial account, as shown in the following screenshot:

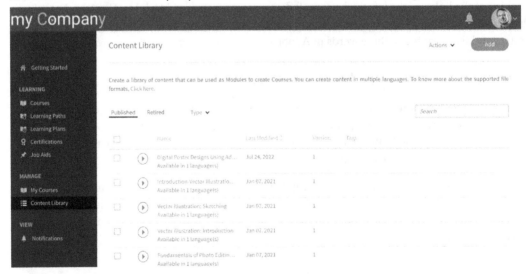

Figure 3.2 – When using a trial account, sample modules are already available in the Content Library

You can use these sample modules to test the features of Adobe Learning Manager without going through the burden of creating and uploading your own content.

3. To add more modules to the Content Library, click the **Add** button located in the upper-right corner of the screen. This takes you to the **Add New Content** form.

4. Take some time to inspect the **Add New Content** form. When you're ready, click the logo in the top-left corner of the screen to return to the Author home page.

5. Once on the Author home page, click the **Create Content** button located in the upper section of the main content area.

This last action takes you back to the **Add New Content** form. Remember that the links available in the top section of the main content area of the home page are shortcuts to the most common tasks devoted to an Author.

6. Click the **Back** button located at the top of the left sidebar. This action takes you back to the **Content Library** page.

The learning content hosted in your LMS can be made up of a wide range of file types including MP4 videos, Word documents, PowerPoint presentations, PDF files, interactive quizzes, and SCORM packages. Before moving on to uploading content, let's take some time to review the types of files supported by Adobe Learning Manager.

7. A quick definition of the Content Library can be found at the very top of the **Content Library** page. Read through this definition; then, click the **Click here** link, as shown in the following screenshot:

Figure 3.3 – The Click here link at the end of the Content Library definition

This takes you to the **Content Library** page of the official Adobe Learning Manager user guide where you will find the list of supported content types.

> **Note**
>
> It is wise to bookmark this page of the ALM user guide so that you'll have the list of supported content types at your fingertips. https://helpx.adobe.com/learning-manager/authors/feature-summary/content-library.html.

8. Take some time to review the list of content types supported by Adobe Learning Manager.

Note that ALM differentiates between *interactive content* and *static content*:

- **Static Content** is content for which the learner is essentially passive. Typical static content consists of MP4 video tutorials, audio podcasts, and text documents.

- **Interactive Content**, on the other hand, is content that makes the learner active. Typical interactive learning content includes quizzes, surveys, interactive videos, and scenario-based training. This interactive content is created by dedicated eLearning authoring tools such as Adobe Captivate, Articulate Storyline, iSpring, and others, and it is uploaded to Learning Manager as either SCORM-, AICC-, or xAPI-compliant packages.

You should now have a better idea of what the Content Library is and the different types of files that can be uploaded to Adobe Learning Manager. In the next two sections, you will upload new modules to the Content Library and review the available options.

Uploading static content

It's time to upload your first custom modules to the Content Library. You will start by uploading some static content, which consists of a Word document, a PDF file, a PowerPoint presentation, and an MP4 video.

> **Getting access to content**
>
> To complete the exercises in this section, you can use any file at your disposal. You can also use the sample files provided in the `CourseContent` folder of the download associated with this book. Note that most of these sample files contain only placeholder text.

Let's start by uploading a Word document to the Content Library:

1. From the Author home page, click the **Create Content** button located in the topmost section of the main content area.

Remember that this action takes you to the **Add New Content** form. Note that there are only two pieces of information that are required: the **Name** and **Add Content File** fields.

2. Type in the name of the new module in the **Name** field.

3. Drag and drop a Word document into the **Add Content File** field. (You can use both the `.doc` and the `.docx` file formats.)

> **Tip**
>
> If you do not have a suitable Word document available, you can use the `courseContent/ Theory of file extensions - Part 1.docx` file of the download associated with this book.

4. As a best practice, take some time to enter a meaningful description in the **Description** field (max 400 characters) and a duration (in minutes) in the **Duration** field.

   Note that the **Duration** field is used for informational purposes only, so that learners know what to expect, but it has no impact on how Learning Manager delivers the content.

The last remaining field is the **Tags** field at the bottom of the form. Tags will be discussed in the *Working with tags* section later in this chapter.

The **Add New Content** form should now look as follows:

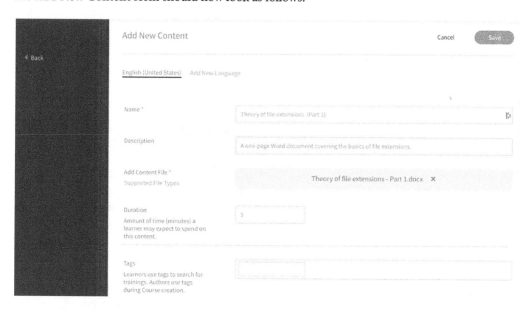

Figure 3.4 – The Add New Content form

You are now ready to save your new module to the Content Library.

5. Click the **Save** button, located in the upper-right corner of the screen.

This takes you back to the Content Library, where you should see your new module at the top of the list. Note that Learning Manager needs to process the new content before it is made available. Processing time varies depending on various factors, such as file type, size, and complexity.

6. Click the new module when Learning Manager has finished processing it.

This last action reopens the form you used to upload the module a few minutes ago with a new section available at the bottom of the page, as shown in the following screenshot:

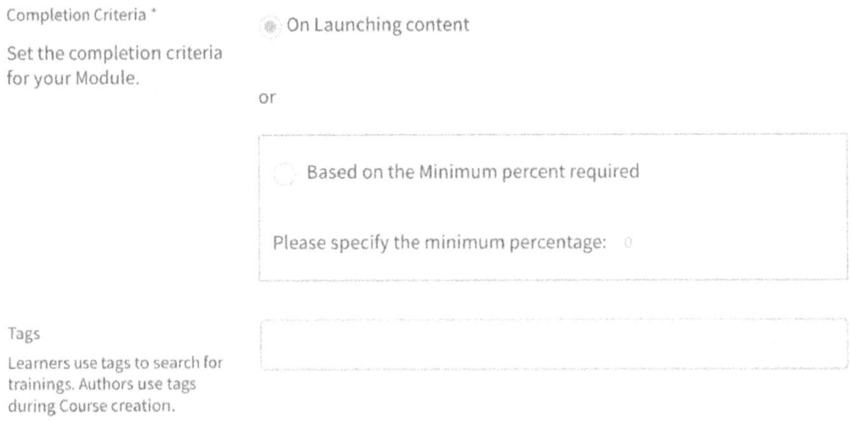

Completion Criteria *

Set the completion criteria for your Module.

○ On Launching content

or

○ Based on the Minimum percent required

Please specify the minimum percentage: 0

Tags

Learners use tags to search for trainings. Authors use tags during Course creation.

Figure 3.5 – New options are available when Learning Manager has finished processing the content

This new section contains additional options that depend on the content type being uploaded. That's why these options can only be made available after Learning Manager has finished processing the content.

In the case of static content, these additional options allow you to define the completion criteria. The completion criteria instruct ALM about when the content is considered complete. This is very important because Learning Manager can be configured to give access to the next module of a course only when the previous module has been completed. Learning Manager also uses the **Completion Criteria** property of each module in a course to determine whether a badge can be awarded, whether a skill has been achieved, whether a certification has been obtained, and so on:

- If you leave **Completion Criteria** at its default value of **On Launching content**, it means that the module is considered *complete* as soon as the learner opens the Word document.

- If you want to make sure the learner spends time reading the document, you can change **Completion Criteria** to **Based on the Minimum percent required** and specify a minimum percentage. For example, if you set a minimum percentage of 50%, that means this module is considered complete when the learner has reviewed at least 50% of the document.

Setting a completion criterion

As instructors, it can be tempting to always set the completion criteria at 100% to ensure that the whole content is reviewed by each learner. However, in practice, this is not always a good idea. In the case of a Word document, for example, the learner may read the entire document without actually scrolling to the very end (especially if the document is very short). In such a case, the module will not be marked as completed by Learning Manager, even if the learner has reviewed 100% of the information contained in the file. To work around this problem, some authors set the completion criteria at around 90%, although in my opinion, the completion criteria for a static text-centric document can remain at the default value of **On Launching content**.

7. If you need to modify **Completion Criteria**, be sure to click the **Edit** button located in the upper-right corner of the screen to activate the form. In this example though, click the **Cancel** button to close the form without making any changes.

Before going any further, take some time to upload a few additional files using the very same process:

8. Create a new module by uploading a PDF file. If you do not have access to a suitable PDF file, you can use the `courseContent/Theory of file extensions - Part 2.pdf` file provided in the download that comes with this book.

9. Create one more module by uploading a PowerPoint presentation. If you do not have access to a suitable PowerPoint presentation, you can use the `courseContent/WelcomeToTheCourse.pptx` file provided in the download that comes with this book. (You can use both the `.ppt` and the `.pptx` file formats.)

10. After Learning Manager has finished processing the PowerPoint presentation, change the **Completion Criteria** property of your PowerPoint-based module to a minimum percentage of **100%**.

In the case of a PowerPoint file, a completion criterion of 100% makes a lot more sense since it is very easy for Learning Manager to track the slides that have been reviewed by the learner.

11. Create yet another module by uploading an MP4 video file. If you do not have access to a suitable video file, you can use the `courseContent/phishing-address.mp4` file provided in the downloads associated with this book.

Uploading closed captions for video files

When editing your video-based module after Learning Manager has finished processing it, you'll discover an additional field that is available for video-based content only. It allows you to upload a closed captioning file in **WebVTT** format. A WebVTT file is a text file used to display timed text on top of a video viewed over the internet. It is an industry standard that most video editing tools can produce. Such files use the `.vtt` file extension.

At the end of this section, you should have four additional custom course modules based on four different file types uploaded to your Content Library, as shown in the following screenshot:

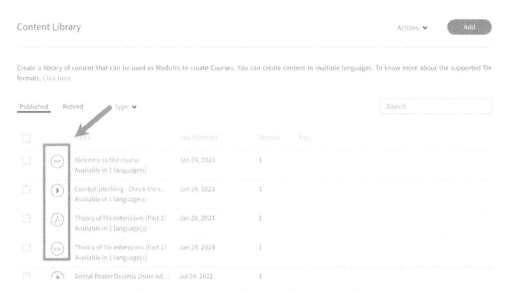

Figure 3.6 – Four new custom modules are visible in your Content Library

Notice that the content type of each module is identified by an icon, as outlined by the rectangle in the preceding screenshot.

In this section, you reviewed how to upload static content to your Learning Manager account. In the next section, you will continue your exploration of the Content Library by uploading *interactive* course modules.

Uploading interactive content

As instructors, we know that the more active the learner, the more effective the learning. Therefore, it is essential to keep the learner actively engaged in the learning process. Online learning offers a wealth of new opportunities to create interactive learning content using dedicated tools and widely supported industry standards.

Typical *interactive* learning content includes the following:

- Quizzes and surveys
- Scenario-based training
- Serious games
- Interactive software demonstrations and simulations
- Interactive videos

Some of the most popular authoring tools used to produce such interactive content include Adobe Captivate, Articulate Storyline, iSpring, and TechSmith Camtasia. All of these authoring tools have one thing in common: they can generate either an AICC-, a SCORM-, or an xAPI-compliant package.

Before going any further, let's take some time to understand what AICC, SCORM, and xAPI are.

Understanding AICC, SCORM, and xAPI

When using interactive content, you want to collect data about the behavior of your learners as they interact with the content. For example, you want to retrieve the results of a quiz, the chosen scenario, the results of a survey, the points collected during a game, or the completion status of a given module. To provide this capability, the interactive content must be able to communicate with the LMS on which it is hosted.

AICC, SCORM, and xAPI are the three standards used in the eLearning industry to enable this communication. They describe how the content and the LMS should communicate and provide resources to achieve this communication.

Adobe Learning Manager is compliant with all three of these standards. This means that you can upload content created by *any* authoring tool that is compliant with *either* the AICC, the SCORM, or the xAPI standard to Learning Manager.

Now, let's spend some time defining these three standards.

AICC stands for **Aviation Industry Computer-Based Training Committee**. The AICC committee was formed in 1988 by the main aircraft manufacturers, and in 1993, it came up with what is regarded as the first interoperability specification for LMS platforms. On December 11, 2014, the AICC committee announced that AICC would be dissolved and that the AICC standard would no longer be maintained. Learning Manager still supports AICC for backward compatibility with older authoring tools, but new content should not be made AICC-compliant anymore.

> **More information**
>
> More information on AICC can be found on Wikipedia at `https://en.wikipedia.org/wiki/Aviation_Industry_Computer-Based_Training_Committee`.

SCORM stands for **Sharable Content Object Reference Model**. SCORM is maintained by the **Advanced Distributed Learning** (ADL) project of the US Department of Defense. The first version of the SCORM standard was released in January 2000. Nowadays, two versions of SCORM are still widely used across the industry:

- **SCORM 1.2**, which was released in October 2001
- **SCORM 2004**, whose first edition was released in January 2004

Adobe Learning Maanger supports both SCORM 1.2 and all the editions of SCORM 2004. At the time of writing, and despite being relatively old, SCORM is still the most popular standard used in the eLearning industry.

> **More information**
>
> More information on the SCORM of the standard can be found at `https://scorm.com/`.

Experience API (xAPI) is the newest standard. It is meant to replace the aging SCORM specification. Preliminary work on xAPI started in October 2010, and a preliminary draft was released in September 2011 under the name *Tin Can API*. The first official version was released in April 2013, when the project name was changed from *Tin Can* to *xAPI*.

xAPI was built under the assumption that people always learn, but not necessarily within the tight boundaries of their corporate LMS. This led to one of the most interesting and disruptive aspects of xAPI: the fact that xAPI no longer reports learning interactions to an LMS but to a **Learning Record Store (LRS)** instead.

An LRS is a database that records and stores learning experiences. Interestingly, an LRS can exist inside or outside an LMS. This allows game manufacturers, mobile app developers, content providers, and others to implement an LRS within their ecosystem and record the countless learning experiences of their users, regardless of these experiences happening inside or outside an LMS.

Another interesting aspect of xAPI is the fact that multiple LRSes can communicate to exchange data.

At the time of writing, xAPI is gaining a lot of traction, mainly in the United States. In the rest of the world, and especially in Europe, xAPI is having a harder time breaking through as it raises concerns about privacy, a topic Europeans are very picky about. That being said, there is no doubt that xAPI will be the new standard for the eLearning industry in the not-too-distant future.

Adobe Learning Manager includes an LRS and fully supports xAPI, which makes it a future-proof LMS solution.

> **More information**
>
> More information on xAPI can be found at `https://xapi.com/`.

Now that you have a general understanding of what AICC, SCORM, and xAPI are and know that Adobe Learning Manager supports all three of these standards, it's time to put this new knowledge into practice by uploading interactive modules to your Content Library.

Creating interactive modules

Regardless of the standard used, all these interactive modules are packaged in `.zip` files. An AICC-, SCORM-, or xAPI-compliant LMS is supposed to be able to take in that ZIP package, unzip it, and find its way around. In other words, deploying these interactive modules on an LMS should be as easy as uploading a `.zip` file and watching the LMS do all the heavy lifting for you!

Let's experiment with uploading a SCORM-compliant `.zip` package to Adobe Learning Manager hands-on:

1. Make sure you are logged in as an Author and that you are on the Author home page.

2. Click the **Create Content** button located in the upper section of the main content area. This action takes you to the **Add New Content** page.

3. Type the name of your new module in the **Name** field. Remember that this information is required.

4. Drag and drop the `.zip` file of the SCORM package you want to upload to the **Add Content File** field. You can use any SCORM-compliant package you have access to. If you do not have access to any suitable package, you can use the `courseContent/identifyFhishing_scorm2004.zip` file provided in the download associated with this book.

> **Note**
>
> The SCORM package provided in the download was created with Adobe Captivate, but it could have been created with any SCORM-compliant authoring tool for it to work within Adobe Learning Manager.

5. As a best practice, take some time to fill in the optional **Description** and **Duration** fields.

6. Once you have finished filling out the form, click the **Save** button in the upper-right corner of the page.

Clicking the **Save** button takes you back to the Content Library. Learning Manager is now processing your new course module. So far, the process of uploading an interactive SCORM-compliant module to the Content Library is the same as the process of creating a static module.

7. When Learning Manager has finished processing your new module, click it in the Content Library to reopen the form.

As for static content, additional options are now available at the bottom of the form, but this time, the options are different, as shown in the following screenshot:

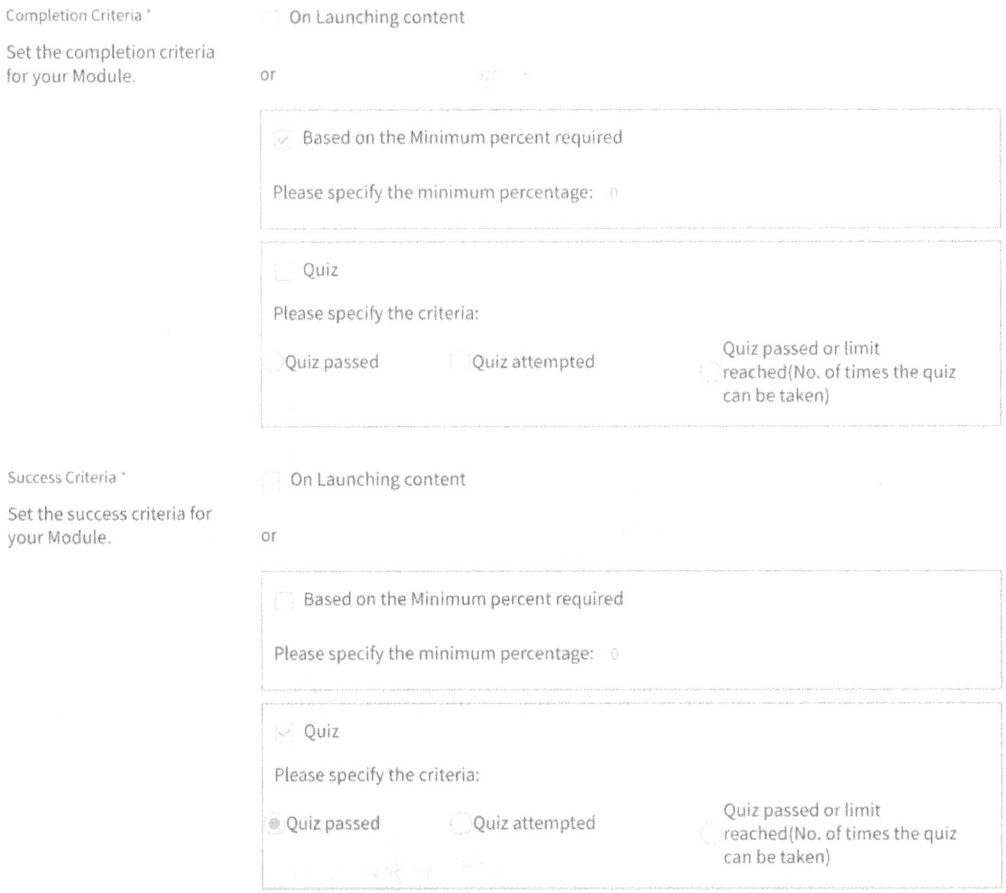

Completion Criteria *

Set the completion criteria
for your Module.

On Launching content

or

Based on the Minimum percent required

Please specify the minimum percentage: 0

Quiz

Please specify the criteria:

Quiz passed   Quiz attempted   Quiz passed or limit
                                              reached(No. of times the quiz
                                              can be taken)

Success Criteria *

Set the success criteria for
your Module.

On Launching content

or

Based on the Minimum percent required

Please specify the minimum percentage: 0

Quiz

Please specify the criteria:

Quiz passed   Quiz attempted   Quiz passed or limit
                                              reached(No. of times the quiz
                                              can be taken)

Figure 3.7 – Additional options available for a SCORM 2004 package

Remember that you are uploading an *interactive* module. This means that the learner viewing this module will be asked to perform actions within the module. These actions can be as simple as clicking buttons, but they can also be drag-and-drop interactions, click-and-reveal interactions, games, quizzes, and more. The author of the module can also grade these interactions, awarding (or removing) points to (or from) the learners as they progress in the module. Also, remember that the SCORM (or AICC or xAPI) standard allows for communication between your training module and the LMS. This communication capability is used to report interactions and scores to the LMS.

This interactivity layer makes it possible to differentiate the *completion criteria* from the *success criteria*. The completion criteria determine when this course module can be considered *complete* for a particular learner, whereas the success criteria determine whether the learner has *passed* or *failed* this particular course module.

These criteria are set by the module author within the authoring tool when creating the SCORM package. Learning Manager only reads this data from the uploaded .zip file. You can, however, modify these criteria within Adobe Learning Manager.

8. Click the **Edit** button located in the upper-right corner of the page.

9. Modify the completion criteria and/or the success criteria as needed.

10. Click the **Save** button in the upper-right corner of the page to confirm the changes and return to the Content Library.

You should now have one more module available in your Content Library. Note that, in this section, you uploaded a SCORM 2004-compliant package, but the process is the same when uploading a SCORM 1.2 package, an AICC package, or an xAPI-compliant package.

In the next section, you will review the process of uploading an interactive module directly from Adobe Captivate.

Uploading interactive content from Adobe Captivate

Learning Manager supports interactive content created by *any* authoring tool, provided that the authoring tool is capable of generating either an AICC-, a SCORM-, or an xAPI-compliant package.

That being said, if you are using Adobe Captivate as your authoring tool of choice, you do have access to one extra feature, which allows you to upload your content directly from Adobe Captivate to Adobe Learning Manager.

> **Note**
>
> The steps of this exercise refer to Adobe Captivate 2019. So, you must have Adobe Captivate 2019 (or higher) installed on your computer to perform this exercise. If you use a newer version of Adobe Captivate, the steps outlined here will, most likely, differ slightly, but the general idea remains the same. Adobe Captivate is available for both macOS and Windows. A free 30-day trial can be downloaded at https://www.adobe.com/products/captivate/download-trial/try.html. The trial version has the same capabilities as the permanent version, with one exception: the content produced by the trial version expires at the same time as the trial. If you do not have access to Adobe Captivate, simply read the following steps to get a general understanding of the process.

Let's review the process of uploading content from Adobe Captivate to Adobe Learning Manager hands-on using the following steps:

1. Open Adobe Captivate 2019 (or higher).

2. Use the **File – Open** menu item to open the courseContent/extensions_Quiz.cptx file, which is available in the download associated with this book.

Let's review the content of this file and some of its settings before uploading it to Learning Manager.

3. Adobe Captivate 2019 looks a bit like PowerPoint. On the left side, in the **Filmstrip** panel, notice that this project is made up of five slides. Slide 1 is an introductory slide, slides 2, 3, and 4 are three quiz question slides, and finally, slide 5 is the quiz result slide.

4. Use the **Quiz – Quiz Preference** menu item to open the **Quiz Preferences** dialog box.

Even if you haven't seen Captivate before, take some time to examine the **Quiz Preferences** dialog box. At the top of the box, notice that *reporting* is enabled for this particular project (see **1** in the following screenshot). Also, notice that this project uses the *SCORM 2004* standard (see **2** in the following screenshot). Finally, the other options that are available in the **Quiz Preferences** dialog (see **3** in the following screenshot) roughly match the **Completion Criteria** and the **Success Criteria** options available in Adobe Learning Manager:

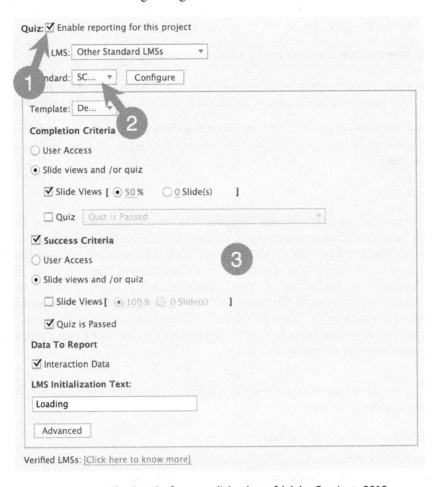

Figure 3.8 – The Quiz Preferences dialog box of Adobe Captivate 2019

Now, you will close the **Quiz Preferences** dialog and upload this course module to the Content Library of your Learning Manager account.

5. Click the **Cancel** button in the lower-right corner of the **Quiz Preferences** dialog to close the box without saving any of the changes you may have made.

6. Click the **Publish** icon located in the main toolbar of Adobe Captivate. Choose **Publish to Adobe Learning Manager** from the menu that opens.

7. Review the information contained in the **Publish to Adobe Learning Manager** dialog. Then, click the **Publish** button in the lower-right corner of the box.

8. When Captivate has finished publishing the content, click the **Continue to Publish** button.

9. Enter the email address associated with your Learning Manager account and click the **Submit** button. If multiple ALM accounts are associated with your email address, choose the account you want to upload this module to.

10. Enter your password and click the **Continue** button.

After logging into your Learning Manager account, a form very similar to the **Add Content** form of Adobe Learning Manager appears on the screen. Note that the **Completion Criteria** and **Success Criteria** options are already available and that they have been set to the same values as those that were supplied in the **Quiz Preferences** dialog of Adobe Captivate.

11. Enter the name of your new module in the **Content Name** field. Note that this is the only required information in this form.

12. As a best practice, take some time to enter a description in the **Short Description** field.

13. When ready, click the **Publish** button located in the upper-right corner of the form.

After clicking the **Publish** button, your course module is uploaded directly from Adobe Captivate 2019 to the Content Library of your Learning Manager account. When the upload is finished, an **Upload Complete** message appears on the screen.

14. Click the **Visit Adobe Learning Manager** button located at the end of the **Upload Complete** message.

This action takes you directly to the Content Library of your ALM account, where your new interactive module is already available, as shown in the following screenshot:

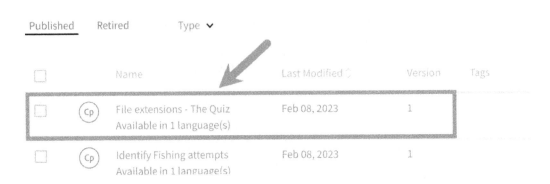

Figure 3.9 – The interactive module uploaded from Captivate being processed in the Content Library

> **Note**
> If you do not have access to Adobe Captivate 2019 but still want to upload this interactive module to your Content Library, you can upload the `courseContent/extensions_quiz.zip` file from the download associated with this book using the steps outlined in the *Uploading interactive content* section, earlier in this chapter.

In this section, you learned how to upload an interactive course module to your Content Library directly from the Adobe Captivate authoring tool. There are some additional benefits to using Adobe Captivate together with Adobe Learning Manager:

- The Adobe Captivate Table of Content integrates nicely with the **Fluidic Player** of your ALM account (the Fluidic Player is the component that delivers the course. It will be discussed in more detail in *Chapter 7, Reviewing the Learner Experience*).

- Adobe Learning Manager honors Captivate's controls for showing/hiding the Table of Contents and the Playbar.

- Closed Captions created in Adobe Captivate integrate with the closed Caption controls of Learning Manager.

- The ability to configure the completion and success criteria within Learning Manager without republishing the content from Adobe Captivate.

Besides these additional benefits, remember that Adobe Learning Manager can host content created by *any* tool and that the content generated by Adobe Captivate can be uploaded to *any* LMS.

After reading the previous few sections, you should have a couple of additional custom course modules available in your Content Library. In the next section, you will review the features of the Content Library that allow you to manage these modules in the long run.

Managing the Content Library

Now that you have some content in your Content Library, it is time to review the features that allow you to manage the course modules available in your Learning Manager account.

Searching for content

All content uploaded to your Learning Manager account goes into the Content Library. As various authors keep uploading content, the Content Library quickly becomes a huge list of course modules that proves difficult to manage.

Hopefully, the Content Library provides a handful of very effective features that allow you to search for and filter content. Let's review them now:

1. Make sure you are logged in as an Author and are on the Author home page.

2. Click the **Content Library** link in the **Manage** section of the left sidebar to access the Content Library.

This gives you access to the long list of course modules available in the Content Library. By default, the content is sorted by date, with the newest content at the top of the list. You can change that order by clicking the arrows next to the **Last Modified** column header, as shown in the following screenshot:

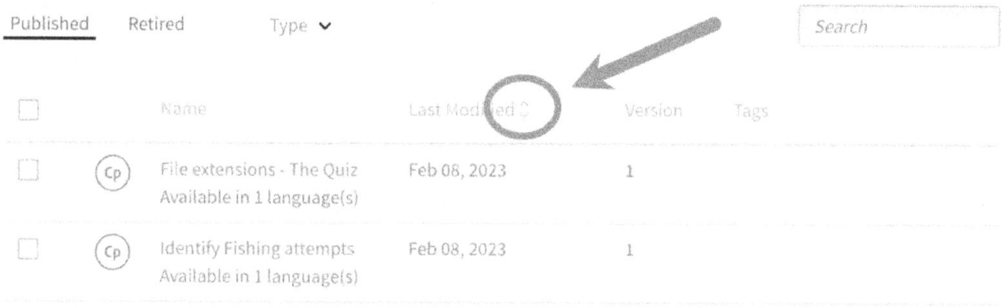

Figure 3.10 – You can change the sort order of the course modules in the Content Library

Another feature is the **Search** field, visible on the right side of the screen, which allows you to search by name and by tags.

Now, let's perform a quick experiment with the **Search** field.

3. Type a keyword in the **Search** field. See how Learning Manager lists the available modules and tags in the drop-down list.

4. Click one of the modules displayed in the search dropdown. If no module is available, simply type another keyword in the **Search** field until you have a positive result.

After this operation, the Content Library shows a filtered list of modules, which makes it much easier to spot the one you're looking for.

5. Click the **Clear** link that appears above the list to clear the filter.

The next feature is the **Type** dropdown, which allows you to filter the list by *used* and *unused* modules. Unused modules are those modules not currently included in any course. This should be the case for all the modules you uploaded in the previous section of this chapter. Let's check this out hands-on:

6. Open the **Type** dropdown and click the **Unused** option.

7. Confirm that the list of unused modules includes all the modules you uploaded in the previous section.

8. Next, open the **Unused** dropdown and choose the **All** option to return to the complete list of available modules.

These are the main options for sorting and filtering the modules available in the Content Library. In the next section, you will learn how you can further divide your Content Library into folders.

Using Content Folders

In the previous section, you discovered that the Content Library is a long list containing every module available in your account. There are some advantages to this default behavior:

- As an author, you can take advantage of the modules that have been uploaded by other authors to create and update courses.

- Any author can add a language version to any module. This feature is very useful in organizations where different teams are responsible for creating different language versions of the same content. You don't have to be the author of the original content to upload a translation. This makes it much easier to manage the different language versions of a module.

- Every author can also update, retire, and delete *any* course module. This makes it easy to delete content created by a contractor or an employee who no longer works for the organization or has moved to a different position.

If it feels strange for you to consider this default behavior as an advantage, remember that Adobe Learning Manager is designed as an enterprise LMS. Therefore, it is assumed that the content available in the Content Library belongs to the organization, not to any particular content author or instructor. This is very different from the mindset that prevails in most schools and universities.

That being said, there are instances where this default behavior is somewhat limited, even in the corporate world:

- As a company, you may contract with many agencies providing course content. You may not want Agency A to have access to the list of course modules provided by Agency B.

- You may have confidential course content that should only be accessed by a specific team of users with proper accreditation.

- As authors add content to Learning Manager, the content library can become very busy, resulting in a long scroll down the content library home page. Of course, the search feature is available, but for some users, searching and editing a module may be easier and more familiar with a good ol' folder system.

- Maybe you simply want to organize your Content Library in a way that seems appropriate to you.

For all these reasons, plus those not listed here, it is possible to create Content Folders to segment the Content Library and ensure that only authorized personnel have access to the content.

Creating Content Folders

Folders must be created beforehand by an administrator. Therefore, you will now return to the administrator role and create a couple of Content Folders. Then, you will return to the author role and put content in these folders:

1. Make sure you are logged in as an Administrator and that you are on the Administrator home page.

2. Click the **Settings** link located in the **Configure** section at the end of the left sidebar. This takes you to the **Basic Info** page.

3. Click the **Content Folder** link in the **Advanced** section of the left sidebar.

This takes you to the **Content Folder** page. By default, there are no *Content Folders* available in a new Learning Manager account, but that doesn't mean there is no important information on this page. Take some time to read the statement at the top of the page. It gives you a lot of very useful information about what *Content Folders* are and how they work:

Figure 3.11 – The statement at the top of the Content Folder page contains lots of useful information

First, note that administrators need to create *Custom Roles* to define who can access what folder. Creating Custom Roles will be covered in *Chapter 5, Managing Users*. Until then, all folders are visible to all users (which partially defeats the purpose of creating folders in the first place, but bear with me – more answers will be provided in *Chapter 5, Managing Users!*).

Another interesting aspect is that deleting a folder does *not* delete the content of that folder. This is because folders are just logical containers stored in the ALM database. They are used to segment the Content Library and/or add an extra layer of security, but they are not *actual* folders like the ones you create on your computer to organize your files.

4. Click the **Add** button in the upper-right corner of the page to create a new Content Folder.

5. Enter the name of the new folder in the **Name** field. As a best practice, also supply a quick description in the **Description** field.

6. Click the **Save** button to create your first Content Folder.

7. Repeat the preceding process to create a couple more Content Folders.

You should now have a few Content Folders available, as shown in the following screenshot:

Content Folder   Actions ∨   Add

Add, edit and delete folders here. Content Folders allow authors to organize content in specific folders. Administrators can set the visibility of folders using Custom Roles. Deleting a folder does not delete the content within it. Learn more.

	Name	Description
☐	eLearning Pro	This is the content uploaded by the eLearningPro LTP agency.
☐	French content team	Content uploaded by the French content team
☐	R & D - CONFIDENTIAL	Content visible only to members of the L&D department.
☐	US content team	English content uploaded by the US content team.

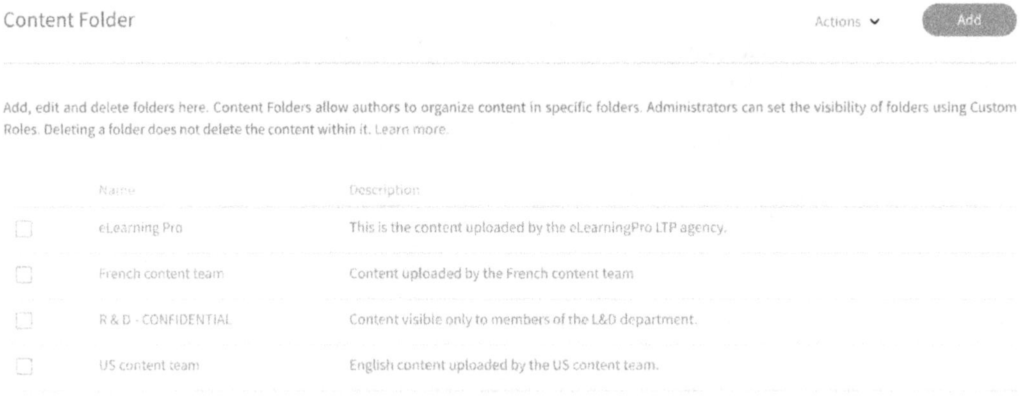

Figure 3.12 – The list of Content Folders available in your ALM account

Now that you have a few Content Folders available, let's go back to the Author role to put those folders to work.

Adding Content Modules to folders

Creating Content Folders is a task devoted to a Learning Manager Administrator, but putting modules into folders is part of the Author role:

1. Switch back to the Author role and click the **Content Library** link located in the **Manage** section of the left sidebar.

2. Click the **Add** button, as if you wanted to add a new module to the Content Library.

As shown in the following screenshot, a new field is available in the **Add New Content** form:

Add Content File *
Supported File Types

Drag & drop a file or click here to select.

Add to Folder *

Search

Add to 'Public' folder to make it
available to all authors

Duration

Amount of time (minutes) a
learner may expect to spend on
this content.

Figure 3.13 – The Add to Folder field is available after you define Content Folders in your account

Now, let's take a closer look at this field to find out how to add modules to a content folder.

3. Click the **Search** area associated with the **Add to Folder** field.

This reveals the list of all the available Content Folders. You should recognize the folders created in the previous section. If you do not want to add this module to a particular folder, choose the **Public** folder, which is the default folder visible to all users of your ALM account.

Now you will add existing modules to these Content Folders. To do this, you must return to the main page of the Content Library.

4. Click the **Cancel** button in the upper-right corner of the form to return to the **Content Library** page.

Back on the main page of the Content Library, you can see the **Folders** column in the list of available modules. At the moment, all the modules are in the **Public** folder. Just above the list of modules, you also see two additional filters: **Folders** and **All Authors**.

You will now move one of your custom modules into one of the folders you created earlier:

5. Use the checkboxes column to select one of the available modules.

6. With one module selected, click the **Actions** button located next to the **Add** button in the upper-right corner of the page.

As shown in the following screenshot, an **Organise Content** menu item containing additional sub-options is displayed in the **Actions** menu. Unfortunately, these options are not available, even though a module has been selected:

Figure 3.14 – Organise Content options are not available in the Actions menu by default

To enable the **Organise Content** options of the **Actions** menu, it is necessary to use the **Folders** filter located above the list of modules.

7.   Open the **Folders** filter and select the **Public** folder from the drop-down list.

This action filters the list of modules so that only the modules in the **Public** folder are displayed. Since all modules are currently in the **Public** folder, nothing changes on the screen.

8.   If needed, you can also add a **Type** filter to show only the unused content, or the **All Authors** filter to show only the modules that *you* have uploaded.

9.   Use the checkboxes to select all the modules you uploaded earlier in this chapter.

10.   Return to the **Actions** button in the upper-right corner of the screen. Since the **Folder** filter is active, the **Organise Content** option is now available.

11.   Select **Organise Content – Move Contents to Folder** to open the **Move Content** dialog box.

12.   Use the **Search** field to search for the name of the destination folder. Once found, click the folder name in the drop-down list. Note that you can choose multiple destination folders if needed.

13.   When ready, click the **Confirm** button in the lower-right corner of the **Move Content** dialog. A quick message should confirm that the move operation has been successful.

14.   When done, click the **Clear** link to remove all the active filters and return to the complete list of modules available in the Content Library.

As shown in the following screenshot, some modules have been moved to another content folder:

		Name	Folders	Last Modified	Version	Tags
☐	(Cp)	File extensions - The Quiz Available in 1 language(s)	US content team	Feb 08, 2023	1	
☐	(Cp)	Identify Fishing attempts Available in 1 language(s)	US content team	Feb 08, 2023	1	
☐	(PPT)	Welcome to the course Available in 1 language(s)	US content team	Jan 28, 2023	1	
☐	(▶)	Combat phishing - Check the s… Available in 1 language(s)	US content team	Jan 28, 2023	1	
☐	(⅄)	Theory of file extensions (Part 2) Available in 1 language(s)	US content team	Jan 28, 2023	1	
☐	(DOC)	Theory of file extensions (Part 1) Available in 1 language(s)	US content team	Jan 28, 2023	1	
☐	(▶)	Digital Poster Designs Using Ad… Available in 1 language(s)	Public	Jul 24, 2022	1	
☐	(▶)	Using Movement to Convey a F…	Public	Jan 07, 2021	1	

Figure 3.15 – Some modules are now in the US content team folder

This is how you can move new and existing modules into folders. If you return to the **Organise Content** item of the **Actions** button in the upper-right corner of the screen, you see that two more operations are available:

- **Copy Content to Folder** is a somewhat misleading label. Remember that Content Folders are just logical containers. The module is stored only *once* on the system and then linked to one or more of these folders. Copying content to a folder simply means that you *link* a module to at least one more folder, but there is no *actual* copying of the content involved. In other words, you do not consume any more disk space after this "copy" operation.

- **Unlink Folder** is used to remove the link between a content module and one or more folders. Note that the content *must* exist in at least one folder, so you cannot use the **Unlink Folder** operation on the modules that are linked to only one folder.

Moving existing modules into folders can be very helpful for organizing content as your Learning Manager authors and usage grows over time!

In this section, you learned how to create Content Folders as an administrator and how to use them as an author. In *Chapter 5, Managing Users*, you will learn how to restrict access to these folders by defining Custom Roles.

But for now, let's continue your journey of discovering the features of the Content Library. In the next section, you will learn how to upload new versions of your existing course modules.

Uploading new versions of your content

There are numerous instances where one or more modules need to be updated:

- Someone finds a bug (such as a typo or a content issue) in a module.

- Your organization updates its brand identity, which requires updating old course modules.

- A new policy or a legal change needs to be implemented in a compliance course or certification.

- A third-party vendor has made enhancements or improvements to popular content and has made the update available to you.

Adobe Learning Manager has a built-in versioning system that makes uploading new versions of your modules a breeze. Let's take a look at it:

> **Tip**
>
> If you want to follow along but do not have access to any suitable files, you can use the `courseContent/Theory of file extensions - Part 1 - Version 2.docx` file from the download associated with this book. If you use that file, you will update the course module associated with the Word document you created earlier in this chapter.

1. Make sure you are logged in as an Author and that you are on the Author home page.
2. Click the **Content Library** link located in the **Manage** section of the left sidebar to open your **Content Library**.
3. Once on the **Content Library** page, click the module that you want to update.
4. Click the **Edit** button in the upper-right corner of the page.

To update a module, you need to remove the current file that is associated with your module and replace it with a new version of that file.

5. Click the *delete* icon associated with the file currently loaded in the **Add Content File** field to remove the current file from the module, as shown in the following screenshot:

Figure 3.16 – Remove the file currently associated with the module you want to update

The next operation is to upload the new file:

6. Drag and drop the new version of the file into the **Add Content File** field.

7. When ready, click the **Save** button located in the upper-right corner of the screen.

This action takes you back to the Content Library. When ALM has finished processing your updated module, version 2 of your course module is made available in the Content Library, as shown in the following screenshot:

Figure 3.17 – Version 2 of your course module is made available in the Content Library

Making the updated content available to learners

In this example, you updated a module that is not yet part of any course. Therefore, the update has no impact on the courses or learners currently active in your account.

But what happens when the updated course module is already part of one or more courses and learners have already enrolled in these courses? To find out how Learning Manager handles such a situation, it is necessary to go back to the Administrator role:

1. Click the user icon located in the upper-right corner of the screen to switch back to the **Administrator** role.

2. When on the Administrator home page, click the **Settings** link located at the end of the left column. This action takes you to the **Basic Info** page.

3. From there, click the **General** link located in the **Basics** section of the left sidebar. This takes you to the **General** settings of your account.

4. Scroll down the page until you find the **Module Version Update** option.

5. Click the **Edit** link associated with the **Module Version Update** option of the **General** settings.

As shown in the following screenshot, the update applies to all learners by default, which means that both existing learners and new enrollments receive the updated content.

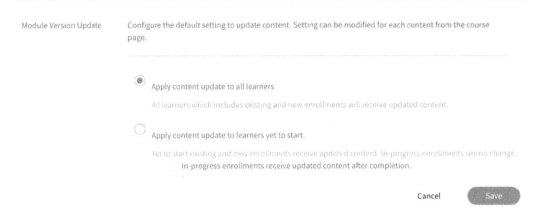

Figure 3.18 – The Module Version Update option of the General account settings

You can also choose to deliver the updated content only to future learners. Future learners are those who will enroll in the updated course after the date of the update, and those who enrolled before the update but have not yet started the course at the time of the update.

The **In-progress enrollments receive updated content after completion** checkbox allows you to further refine this behavior. When selected, currently enrolled learners still receive the old version of the content when they take the course (in fact, they receive the most recent version available at the time of their enrollment). If they decide to revisit the course after completing it, then they are provided with the updated content.

Regarding the completion and success criteria for learners who have already reviewed the old version of the content, the basic principle is that *learners retain everything they have already accomplished*. In other words, the completion and success statuses of learners who viewed the old version of the content are maintained, even if these criteria have been changed by the update.

Note that when updating a module that is already part of one or more courses, a small icon appears in the Content Library next to the updated module. You must click this icon to update the courses that use this content. Until you click this icon, the old version of the module is maintained. This action is illustrated in the following screenshot:

Figure 3.19 – Click this icon to update the module in all courses that use this content

Thanks to this built-in versioning system, it is very easy to keep track of each version of a module. But this is not the only way to update a module. In the next section, you will add additional language versions to one of the modules of your Content Library.

Adding language versions

Many of the organizations using Adobe Learning Manager have a global presence with teams of workers spread across different regions of the world. For these organizations, it is sometimes necessary to provide the same course content in different languages to ensure equal access to the content for each worker. In some countries, local regulations mandate that content be provided in the official language of the country.

For these reasons (plus all the ones not listed here), Learning Manager supports delivering the same content in various languages. Let's explore this feature hands-on:

> **Tip**
> If you want to follow along but do not have access to any translated content, you can use the `courseContent/Théorie des extensions fichiers (Part1)_FR.docx` file from the download associated with this book (it is the French translation of the Word document used earlier). If you use that file, you will add a French version to the course associated with the Word document you created earlier in this chapter.

1. Make sure you are logged in as an Author and that you are on the main page of **Content Library**.

2. Open the module you want to add a language version to.

3. Click the **Edit** button located in the upper-right corner of the screen.

At the moment, only one language version of this module is available, as shown in the following screenshot:

Figure 3.20 – The default version of a module corresponds to the default language of your account

By default, the first language version of a module corresponds to the default language of your account, which is English (United States) in this example. Changing the default language of your account was covered in the *Changing the default language of your account* section of *Chapter 1, Introduction to Adobe Learning Manager*.

4. Click the **Add New Language** link located in the upper-left area of the form.

5. Select the language(s) you want this module to support. Note that you can select as many languages as needed.

6. Click the **Save** button in the lower-right corner of the **Select Languages** dialog box. This action adds one new tab across the top of the form for each of the chosen languages.

7. Switch to another language tab and fill in the form with the module information in that particular language.

8. Click the **Save** button located in the upper-right corner of the screen to save your changes.

This action takes you back to the Content Library. The multilingual course module is made available after Learning Manager finishes processing the file.

As discussed in the *Modifying your account settings* section of *Chapter 1, Introduction to Adobe Learning Manager*, each user can choose both the *interface language* and their preferred *content language* in their profile settings.

Learning Manager automatically serves the language version of a module that matches the preferred content language the user has chosen in their profile settings (if one is available). If a corresponding content language is not available, Learning Manager automatically falls back to the default language of the account (English (United States), in this example).

In this section, you learned how to upload additional language versions of a module, and how that relates to the default language of the account and to the preferred *content language* that each user can choose in their **Profile Settings** page.

In the next section, you will learn how to retire and delete outdated modules.

Retiring and deleting content

When a module is no longer relevant or undergoes a complete revision (possibly by a contractor other than the one who created the original version), it is necessary to remove this module from the Content Library. Retiring and deleting content may also be helpful as the number of authors, and therefore the amount of content, grows over time.

Learning Manager does not allow you to *remove* the published content directly. You must first *retire* the content and only then can you remove it. Perform the following steps to retire an existing course module:

1. Make sure you are logged in as an Author and that you are on the **Content Library** page.

2. Use the checkboxes to select the course module(s) you want to retire.

3. Click the **Actions** button located in the upper-right corner of the screen and choose the **Retire** action.

This action moves the selected module(s) from the list of *published* modules to the list of *retired* modules.

4. Click the **Retired** tab located above the list of modules, as shown in the following screenshot:

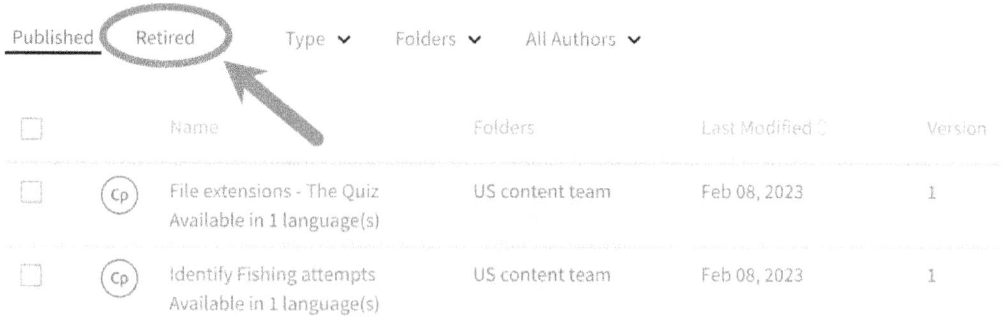

Figure 3.21 – Click the Retired tab located above the list of modules

A retired module is no longer visible to Authors when creating a new course. However, existing courses that currently use the retired module *are not affected* by the retirement.

You will now *actually* delete the module(s) that you have previously retired:

5. While in the list of retired modules, use the checkboxes to select the modules you want to delete.

6. Click the **Actions** button located in the upper-right corner of the screen.

Two actions are available in the **Actions** menu. **Republish** allows you to move the selected module(s) back to the **Published** list. This makes the module(s) available again when creating new courses.

7. Click the **Delete** action to delete the selected retired module.

Take some time to read the message displayed on the screen. This message warns you that the content will be permanently deleted. But, at the same time, the deleted module continues to exist in the courses that currently use it. So, it is not *actually* deleted from the system. A deleted module can no longer be used when creating new courses *and* can no longer be republished. It is only when all the courses using those modules will themselves be deleted that the module will be gone once and for all.

Thanks to this system, you can safely retire and delete modules without bearing the risk of compromising the learning experience of learners currently enrolled in courses using the modules you retire/delete.

Working with tags

As discussed in the *Searching for content* section earlier in this chapter, tags are keywords used to help the internal search engine of Adobe Learning Manager, making it easier to search for objects throughout the system.

Tags can be associated with a wide range of learning objects, including the course modules discussed in this chapter. By default, both administrators and authors can create tags, but you can change this default so that only administrators can create tags. This ensures that the tags available in your account remain consistent (no typos, no duplicates, compliance with naming conventions, etc.).

You will now head back to the administrator area of your ALM account and create a handful of tags. Then, you will return to the Author role and see how tags can be associated with a course module:

1. Click the user icon in the upper-right corner of the screen and switch back to the **Administrator** role.

2. From the Admin home page, click the **Tags** link located in the **Manage** section of the left sidebar. This action opens the **Tag Management** page of the administrator.

3. Click the **Settings** tab available at the top of the page, next to the **All Tags** tab.

4. Next, click the **Edit** link associated with the **Tag Creation Access** option.

As shown in the following screenshot, both Admins and Authors can create tags by default.

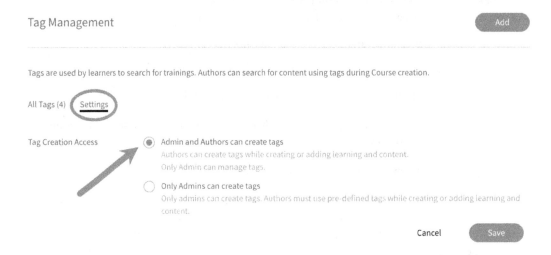

Figure 3.22 – By default, Admins and Authors can create tags

You will now modify this default so that only Administrators are allowed to create new tags.

5. Select the **Only Admins can create tags** option and click the **Save** button.

6. Now, return to the **All Tags** tab of the **Tag Management** page.

7. Click the **Add** button located in the upper-right corner of the screen to open the **Add a Tag** dialog.

8. Enter the name of the tags you want to create. You can create multiple tags at once by separating the tags with a comma, a semi-colon, or a line break.

9. When the screen looks as follows, click the **Create** button in the lower-right corner of the **Add a Tag** dialog to create the new tag(s):

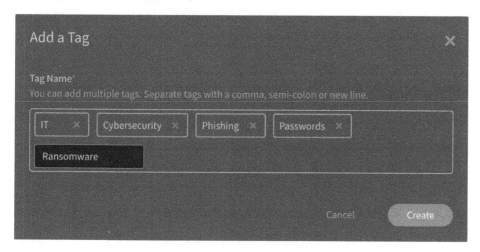

Figure 3.23 – You can create multiple tags at once

Confirm that the newly created tags appear on the **Tag Management** page of the administrator.

10. Take some time to inspect the features available on the **Tag Management** page; most of them are self-explanatory. Pay special attention to the options available in the **Actions** menu.

Now that you have a few tags available in your account, you can return to the Author role and associate these tags with the modules you created earlier in this chapter:

11. Click the user icon in the upper-right corner of the screen to switch back to the **Author** role.

12. When on the Author home page, click the **Content Library** link located in the **Manage** section of the left sidebar.

13. Click any of the modules you created earlier in this chapter.

14. Then, click the **Edit** button located in the upper-right corner of the screen.

15. Scroll down the page until you see the **Tags** field.

16. Enter the name of the tag in the **Tags** field. When the tag you are looking for appears in the list, click it to associate it with the module being edited. Note that you can add multiple tags to the same module.

17. When done, click the **Save** button located in the upper-right corner of the screen.

These tags can now be used as keywords in the **Search** field of Adobe Learning Manager to search for this particular module, making it easier for Authors to find their way around the Content Library of your account.

By now, you should have a good understanding of how the Content Library of Adobe Learning Manager works and of the features available to create, update, retire, and delete your custom modules. You have also seen how administrators can create tags and how those tags can be associated with modules in the Content Library. In the next section, you will review the creation of job aids and discuss the differences between regular modules and job aids.

Creating Job Aids

Job aids are similar to the modules of the Content Library but with a few key differences, as outlined here:

- Learners can access Job Aids without enrolling in a course.
- You may, however, link Job Aids to courses, but access to Job Aids is not dependent on any completion or success criteria.
- Job Aids can only be static content (documents, presentations, videos, and so on) and web links. Interactive content cannot be used as Job Aids.

You can think of Job Aids as cheat sheets or handouts, similar to those you receive at the end of conferences, briefings, or live classes. Learners can refer to job aids for quick reference when performing any activity or task.

The process of creating Job Aids is very similar to the process of creating modules in the Content Library. Let's review it using the following steps:

1. Make sure you are logged in as an Author and that you are on the Author home page.
2. Click the **Job Aids** link located at the end of the **Learning** section in the left sidebar.

This action takes you to the **Job Aids** page. By default, there are no job aids available in your account.

3. To create a new Job Aid, click the **Create** button in the upper-right corner of the **Job Aids** page.
4. Type the name of the new job aid in the **Name** field. Note that this information is required.
5. The only other required information is the **Content** field, where you can choose to supply a file or a link to a web page.

6. Copy/paste the link or drag and drop the file that makes up the content of the new Job Aid.

7. As a best practice, take some time to provide a meaningful description in the **Description** field.

The other fields are all optional, but some of them deserve an additional explanation.

Shared Job Aids are visible to any author when creating a course. **Private** Job Aids are only visible to the author that has uploaded them. Note that this option only modifies the visibility of the Job Aids for authors when creating courses, but it has no effect on learner access to the Job Aid.

Skills and **Levels** will be discussed in *Chapter 4, Creating Skills and Courses*.

8. Add the required information in the **Job Aids** creation form, as shown in the following screenshot:

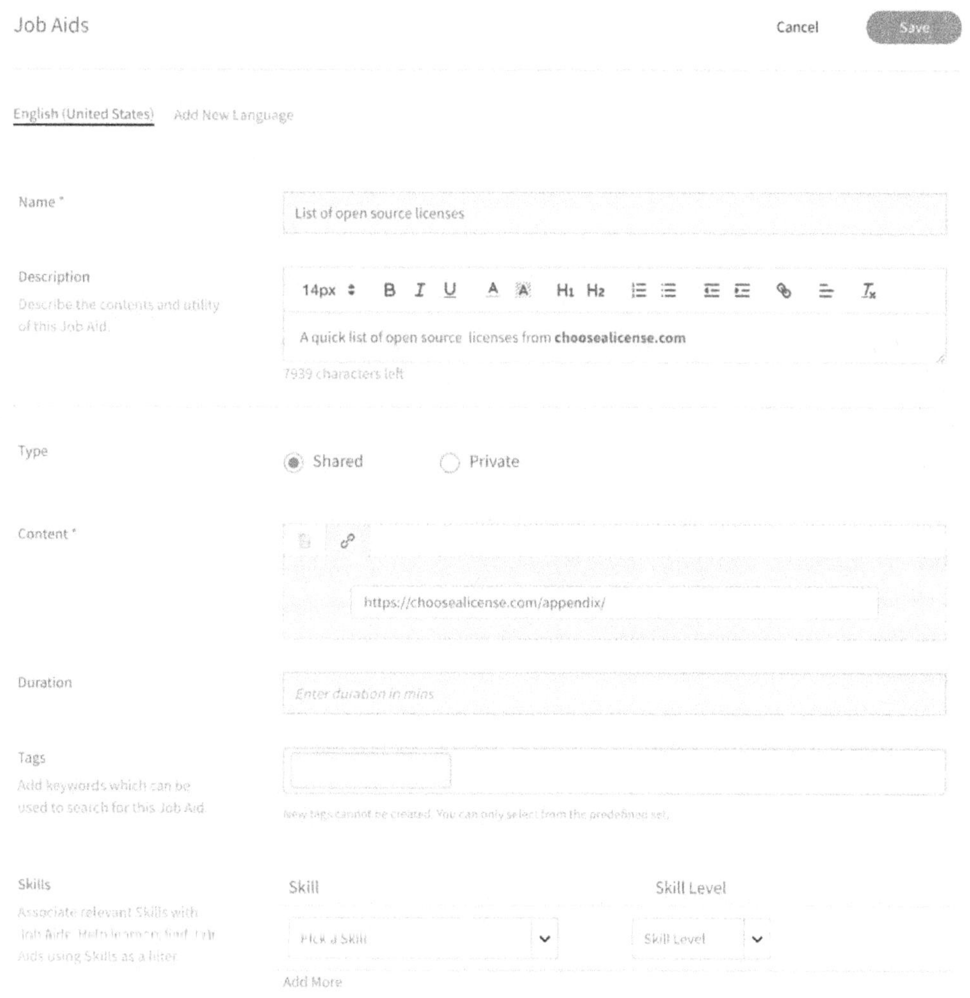

Figure 3.24 – Adding the required information in the Job Aids creation form

9. Click the **Save** button in the upper-right corner of the screen to save the changes and create the new Job Aid.

This action takes you back to the **Job Aids** page, where the new job aid is visible in the list. Similar to the **Content Library** page, the **Job Aids** page contains all the features necessary to manage your Job Aids in the long run.

10. Click the *gear* icon associated with your Job Aid to reveal the available options, as shown in the following screenshot:

Figure 3.25 – Options available to manage job aids

Use the **Edit** option to modify the Job Aid. This includes adding additional languages using a process very similar to the one used to add language versions to modules in the Content Library.

The **Withdraw** option for Job Aids is similar to the **Retire** option for modules. Use it to remove Job Aids from the list without removing them from the courses they are linked to.

Take some time to experiment with those features hands-on before moving on to the next chapter. You will find out that working with Job Aids is very similar to working with modules.

In this section, you learned about Job Aids. You reviewed the options available to create, edit, withdraw, and delete the Job Aids available on the system. You also learned about the elements that make Job Aids different from regular content modules.

Summary

At this point, you have an in-depth understanding of how the Content Library works and have uploaded many different types of modules to your Learning Manager account.

We first addressed the question of the origin of the content available on your account. You discovered that this content can be provided by third-party vendors or uploaded directly to the Content Library. You also discovered the wide range of file types supported by Adobe Learning Manager and the distinction between *static* and *interactive* content.

Speaking of interactive content, you learned about the AICC, SCORM, and xAPI standards, which are used across the eLearning industry to enable communication between the content and the LMS. Remember that interactive learning content is packaged as `.zip` files and that a compliant LMS must be able to unzip these packages, read their content, and deploy the training modules automatically.

Uploading content to the Content Library is only the first step. The content must be able to live in the long run and stay relevant to your learners. That's why Adobe Learning Manager is equipped with a built-in versioning system. You can also provide multiple language versions of the same content.

Finally, you discovered Job Aids and discussed the key differences between Job Aids and regular course modules.

But your learners do not enroll in *modules*, they enroll in *courses*. The modules you have created in this chapter are only the fundamental building blocks of courses that are yet to be created.

Assembling modules into courses and reviewing the options pertaining to course creation is what you will study in the next chapter.

4

Creating Skills and Courses

In the previous chapter, you uploaded custom content modules to the Content Library of your Learning Manager account. But this content is not yet available to learners as these modules are only the fundamental building blocks used to create courses. Building courses is precisely what you will do in this chapter.

Before creating courses, let's think about the reasons why learners take courses in the first place and why organizations spend so much time, effort, and money to make courses available to theiwr personnel. The answer to both questions lies in one word: **skills.**

Learners take courses because it allows them to acquire new skills (*reskilling*) or to update existing skills (*upskilling*). As for organizations, they know that in a competitive environment, skilled employees are one of the cornerstones of success and profitability. Therefore, both for learners and organiwzations, it is essential to align courses to skills. This allows learners to choose the courses they want to take based on their interests and/or job requirements. It also allows organizations to track thwe skills acquired by each employee to ensure that their staff stays on the leading edge and that the skills available in the organization remain relevant in an ever-changing marketplace, not to mention mandatory compliance training in organizations (such as government entities), where acquiring new skills and updating existing skills is considered a function of the position.

In this chapter, you will take your first look at the Skills Manager by creating a new custom skill. Then, you will assemble content modules into courses and review the wide range of options available for creating various types of courses.

By the end of this chapter, you will have published two custom courses so that your Learning Manager account will be ready to welcome its first learners. To achieve this goal, this chapter covers the following topics:

- Creating custom skills with the Skills Manager
- Creating Courses
- Adding different types of modules and content to courses
- Linking courses to skills
- Updating, retiring, and deleting courses

These topics make for another chapter full of great features and exciting discoveries.

Technical requirements

In order to perform the exercises in this chapter, you need to meet the following technical requirements:

- You need Administrator and Author access to a working Learning Manager account (which can be a free trial account)
- You need to have some custom content modules available in your Content Library

If you have completed the exercises in the previous chapters, you are ready to go! If not, you can use any course modules at your disposal to complete the exercises in this chapter. Just keep in mind that the provided instructions are based on the exercises from the previous chapters, so feel free to adapt them to your situation.

Managing skills

Acquiring skills is the expected outcome of any learning activity. It is the primary reason why learners take courses and why organizations decide to invest time and money in training their personnel. For organizations, it is essential to ensure that the skills available in the workforce match the business goals of the organization, current regulations, and the requirements of an ever-changing marketplace.

As the enterprise LMS of choice, Adobe Learning Manager features a comprehensive Skills Manager. The primary purpose of this feature is to provide organizations with a tool to help them align learning with business.

Let's look at an example to understand the main idea behind the skills manager.

With the sudden increase of employees working from home, an organization has observed a significant rise in cyber attacks and other malicious activities that threaten the digital security of the organization. After analysis, it has been determined that this increase is partially due to the lack of employee awareness about cybersecurity, which results in many best practices not being observed. Because a single successful attack (such as a ransomware attack) could potentially be disastrous for the organization, the organization has decided to upskill all employees in cybersecurity. It was also decided that members of the IT department should undergo additional training so that they can make the IT infrastructure more secure and adapted to remote work.

One way to implement this strategy with Adobe Learning Manager is to define a custom *IT Security* skill using the Skills Manager. This new skill shall have the following properties:

- You will define two levels for this skill. Level 1 represents basic IT security awareness and best practice training, while Level 2 represents more advanced technical knowledge on the topic.
- You will assign courses to these two levels of the *IT Security* skill. Employees taking these courses receive credits and when they reach a certain number of credits, they are awarded the Level 1 or Level 2 Cybersecurity skill.
- Finally, you will assign the *IT Security – Level 1* skill to every employee and the *IT Security – Level 2* skill to the members of the IT department.

This approach allows you to define exactly what course material falls into *IT Security – Level 1* and *IT Security – Level 2*. It also allows you to track the progress of each learner in acquiring the skill. This information allows you to document the effectiveness of the learning (did IT security *actually* increase after a given number of employees acquired the IT Security skill?), send reminders to the learners that are yet to acquire the skill, and more.

Creating a custom skill

Now that you have a general understanding of what skills are and what they allow you to do in Adobe Learning Manager, it is time to log in as an administrator and define the new *IT Security* skill by performing the following steps:

1. Log in to your ALM account as an Administrator and make sure you are on the **Administrator** home page.
2. Click the **Skills** button located in the **Manage** section of the left sidebar.

This gives you access to the list of existing skills. Note that, by default, your Adobe Learning Manager account comes with a handful of skills already defined, as shown in the following screenshot:

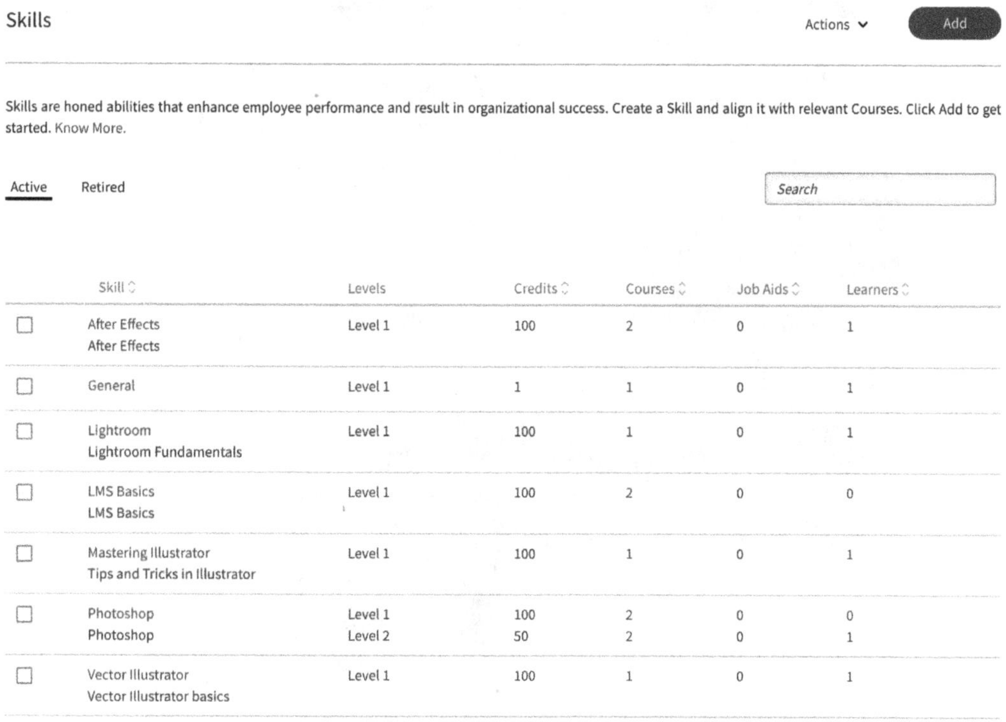

Skills   Actions ∨   Add

Skills are honed abilities that enhance employee performance and result in organizational success. Create a Skill and align it with relevant Courses. Click Add to get started. Know More.

Active   Retired   Search

Skill ◇	Levels	Credits ◇	Courses ◇	Job Aids ◇	Learners ◇
After Effects After Effects	Level 1	100	2	0	1
General	Level 1	1	1	0	1
Lightroom Lightroom Fundamentals	Level 1	100	1	0	1
LMS Basics LMS Basics	Level 1	100	2	0	0
Mastering Illustrator Tips and Tricks in Illustrator	Level 1	100	1	0	1
Photoshop Photoshop	Level 1 Level 2	100 50	2 2	0 0	0 1
Vector Illustrator Vector Illustrator basics	Level 1	100	1	0	1

Figure 4.1 – A handful of skills are available in your ALM trial account

Now, add one more skill to the list by performing the following steps:

3. Click the **Add** button located in the upper-right corner of the screen. This opens the **Add Skill** form.

4. Type the name of the new skill in the **Skill Name** field (IT Security, in this example).

5. As a best practice, type a short description into the **Description** field.

6. Increase the number of credits needed to reach level 1 to 50 credits.

7. Click the + **Add** link located on the right-hand side of the **Levels** heading to add a second level for this skill.

8. Increase the number of credits needed to reach level 2 to 50 credits.

9. Leave all the other fields (**Badge**, **Skill Domain**, and so on) at their default values.

10. When the form looks like the following screenshot, click the **Save** button:

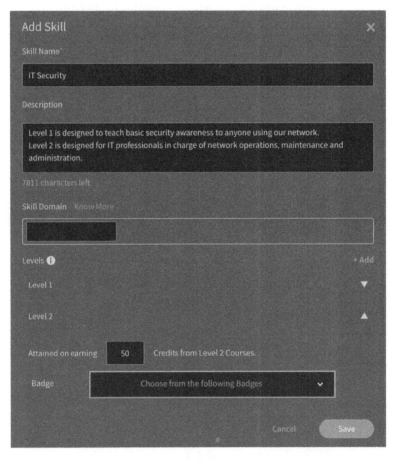

Figure 4.2 – Click the Save button after completing the Add Skill form

After clicking the **Save** button, you should see the new **IT Security** skill in the list.

With the current settings, learners are awarded the *IT Security – Level 1* skill when they accumulate 50 credits by taking courses linked to that particular skill and level. They are awarded the *IT Security – Level 2* skill when they accumulate 50 additional credits by taking courses linked to level 2 of the skill. You will learn how to link courses to skills in the *Linking courses to skills* section, later in this chapter.

> **Badges and skill domains**
>
> When defining the IT Security skill, you noticed the ability to assign a **Badge** to each level. Badges are a great way for learners to display the skills and certifications they have acquired. You will learn more about defining and using badges in *Chapter 11, Badges and Gamification*. It is also possible to link a skill to a **skill domain**. This is used by the AI-powered recommendation and curation engine of Learning Manager. This feature will be discussed in *Chapter 13, AI-Powered Recommendations for Learners*.

Now that you have created a new custom skill, you will use the features of the Skills Manager to manage it in the long run.

Modifying an existing skill

If needed, you can easily modify an existing skill by performing the following steps:

1. Make sure you are logged in as an Administrator and that you are on the **Skills** page.
2. Click the name of the skill you want to modify.
3. Modify the skill as per your requirements (note that it is not possible to remove an existing level) and click the **Save** button in the bottom-right corner of the form when you're done.

If you change the number of credits needed to achieve a skill, be aware that learners retain the skills they've already acquired, even if they no longer have enough credits under the new rule.

> **A general rule**
>
> As a general rule, learners always keep what they have been granted (skills, certification, credits, badges, and so on).

In this section, you learned how to modify an existing skill. Now, let's review how skills can be retired and deleted.

Retiring and Deleting Skills

Skills can be aligned with projects or business goals that come and go. Maintaining skills related to older projects or products, or those that are no longer relevant for whatever reason, can be confusing for learners. These are reasons why you may want to remove skills from your Learning Manager account.

When it comes to removing a skill, you must first *retire* the skill before you can *remove* it. When a skill is retired, it can no longer be associated with any course, job aid, or learner. However, existing associations remain. Only after all items associated with a particular skill have been removed can the retired skill be removed as well. This allows you to smoothly retire and delete skills without affecting the user experience. Perform the following steps to retire and then delete a skill:

1. Make sure you are logged in as an Administrator and that you are on the **Skills** page.
2. Use the checkboxes in the first column to select one or more skills.
3. Open the **Actions** menu located next to the **Add** button in the upper-right corner of the form and choose to **Retire**.

The retired skills are still available in the **Retired** tab of the **Skills** page, as shown in the following screenshot:

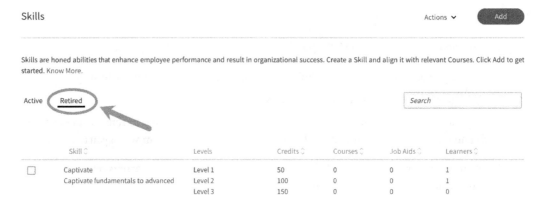

Figure 4.3 – The retired skills are available in the Retired tab of the Skills page

Once on the **Retired** tab, you can decide to either *republish* retired skills or completely *delete* them.

4. From the **Retired** tab of the **Skills** page, use the checkboxes in the first column to select one or more retired skills.
5. Open the **Actions** menu located next to the **Add** button in the upper-right corner of the form and choose either the **Republish** or **Delete** action.

In this section, you learned how to use the skills manager of your account to create, edit, retire, and delete custom skills. As an example, you created a new custom skill named *IT Security* and defined two levels for this particular skill.

Creating skills is an important preliminary step to creating courses, which will be discussed in the next section.

Creating courses

Back in *Chapter 3, Uploading Learning Content and Managing the Content Library*, you uploaded various types of modules to Adobe Learning Manager. In the previous section, you created a custom Skill. Everything is now in place for you to create your first custom course.

Creating a self-paced course

At its most basic level, a course is a simple list of learning activities. In this section, you will create a self-paced course using the modules you uploaded in the previous chapter.

Creating courses is a task devoted to an author, so first, you need to log in as an Author:

1. Log in to your Learning Manager account and click the user icon located in the upper-right corner of the screen to switch to the **Author** role.

2. From the **Author** home page, click the **courses** link located in the **Learning** section of the left sidebar. This takes you to the **Course Catalog** page.

3. Click the **Add** button located in the upper-right corner of the screen.

This action takes you to the course creation form. Note that you can also reach this form by clicking the **Create Courses** link directly available on the **Author** home page.

4. Type the name of your new course in the **Course Name** field (Fundamentals of IT Security, in this example). Note that this is required information.

The next piece of required information is the list of content modules that make up this course.

5. Click the **Add Modules** link located in the **Content** option of the **Modules** section of the form. This action opens the **Select Module Type** dialog box, as shown in the following screenshot:

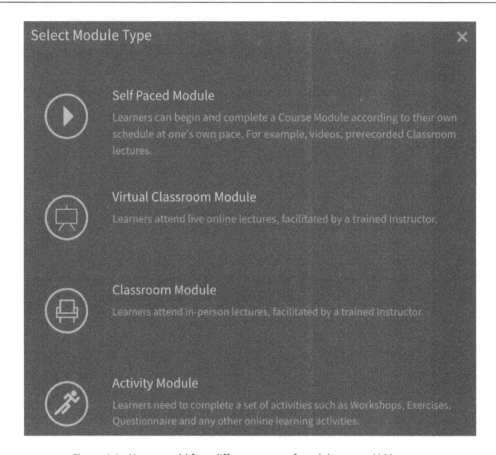

Figure 4.4 – You can add four different types of modules to an ALM course

There are four types of modules you can add to a Learning Manager course. In this first example, you will only add a few self-paced modules. These modules are the *asynchronous* learning activities you uploaded to the Content Library in the previous chapter.

6.   Click the **Self Paced Module** option.

This action opens the **Self Paced Module** dialog, which provides a list of all the modules available in the Content Library of your account. Note that you can use the search field at the top of the box to search for the module you are looking for.

7.   Use the checkboxes in the first column to select the module(s) you want to add to your course. In this example, select all the modules you uploaded to the Content Library in the previous chapter.

8.   When ready, click the **Add** button located in the lower-right corner of the **Self Paced Module** dialog.

This last action takes you back to the main form with the selected modules visible in the **Content Modules** section, as shown in the following screenshot:

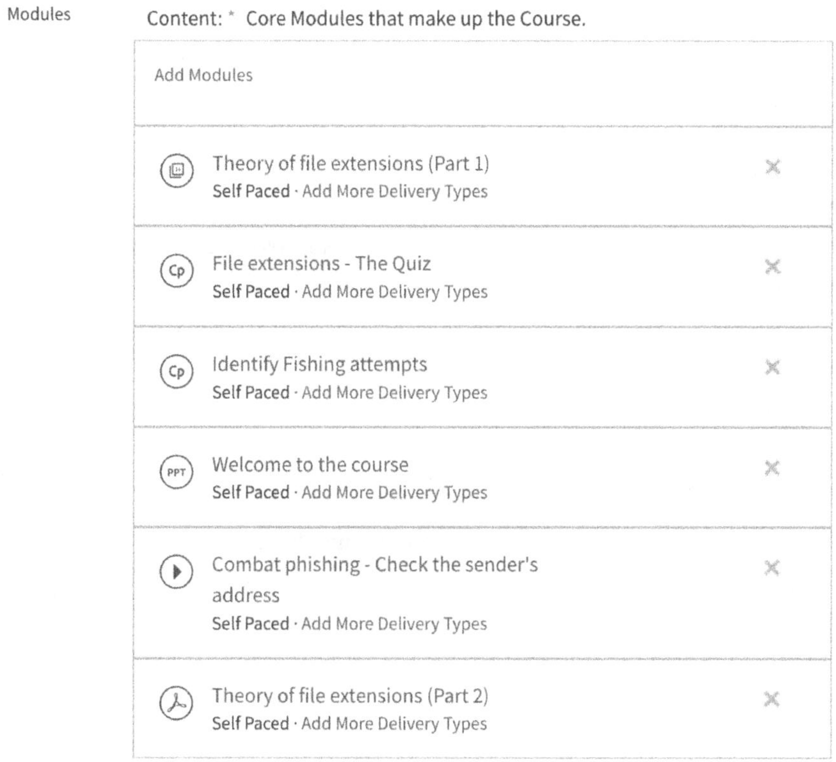

Modules

Content: * Core Modules that make up the Course.

Add Modules

Theory of file extensions (Part 1)
Self Paced · Add More Delivery Types

File extensions - The Quiz
Self Paced · Add More Delivery Types

Identify Fishing attempts
Self Paced · Add More Delivery Types

Welcome to the course
Self Paced · Add More Delivery Types

Combat phishing - Check the sender's address
Self Paced · Add More Delivery Types

Theory of file extensions (Part 2)
Self Paced · Add More Delivery Types

Figure 4.5 – The selected modules are visible in the Content Modules section of the form

If needed, you can reorder the modules by dragging them up and down. After completing the preceding steps, you have provided the two required pieces of information.

9. Click the **Save** button located in the upper-right corner of the page.

This action takes you to the **Settings** page of this particular course, where a few additional pieces of information are required before Learning Manager allows you to publish this course. This is what you will do in the next section of this chapter.

10. For now, click the **Back** button located at the top of the left sidebar to return to the **Course Catalog** page of the Author role.

The **Course Catalog** page lists all the courses in your Learning Manager account. The course you have just created is not yet part of this list. Since you still need to provide some additional information, the new course is currently in a *draft* state.

Linking Courses to Skills

At this point, your new course is in a *Draft* state. Before you can publish it, you must link the course to one or more skill(s) and supply the name of the course author by performing the following steps:

1. Make sure you are logged in as an Author.
2. From the **Author** home page, click the **courses** link located in the **Learning** section of the left sidebar.
3. At the top of the list, click the **Draft** tab to access the list of courses currently in a *draft* state. In this list, you should find the course you created in the previous section.
4. Click the course card of the new course to return to the course creation form.
5. Click the **Settings** link located in the left sidebar.
6. At the top of the page, open the **Pick a Skill** drop-down list.
7. Choose the **IT Security** skill you created earlier in this chapter.
8. Open the **Level** drop-down list and choose level **1**.
9. Finally, type 30 in the **Credits** field.
10. Type the first few letters of your name in the **Author(s)** field. Click your full name when it appears in the list.
11. Click the **Save** button located in the upper-right corner of the page.

The upper section of the **Settings** page should now look as follows:

Figure 4.6 – Your course awards 30 credits for the IT Security – Level 1 skill

With the current settings, your course awards 30 credits toward the *IT Security – Level 1* skill. Keep in mind that a learner must earn 50 credits before achieving this skill. Therefore, this course is not sufficient to achieve this specific skill.

This is a very common pattern in Adobe Learning Manager. Imagine that three different courses are associated with the *IT Security – Level 1* skill:

- The *Fundamentals of IT Security* course (which is the course you are building in this section) awards 30 credits

- The *How to come up with a strong password* course (which hasn't been created yet) will award 20 credits

- Finally, the *How to back up your computer* course (also not yet created) will award 20 credits as well

With the preceding parameters, the *IT Security – Level 1* skill will be awarded to any learner who has taken at least two of these three courses, one of which is the *Fundamentals of IT Security* course. This illustrates how skills can be used to make a course mandatory while providing learners with some options for achieving the skill.

Technically, your course is now ready to be published. That being said, you want to provide the best possible experience for your learners. So, in the next section, you will add some additional data to make your course more attractive and improve its discoverability.

Customizing a course and making it discoverable

Courses are only useful when users can enroll in them. In *Chapter 6, Enrolling Learners in Courses*, you will discover that, although administrators and managers can enroll learners in courses, Learning Manager is built around the idea of a *self-service learning platform*, where a Course Catalog is made available to learners so that they can enroll *themselves* in the courses they are interested in. A course catalog can contain thousands of courses, so you must make your course discoverable to the learners who might be interested in taking it.

As an author, there are a few things that you can do to increase your course discoverability within the platform:

- You can provide a **Brief Description** and a **Detailed Overview** of the course. This increases the chances that a mere interest converts into an actual enrollment. The internal search engine of Learning Manager also uses this content to index your course and relate it to the proper keywords.

- You can link your course to tags. Tags were discussed in the *Working with tags* section of *Chapter 3, Uploading Learning Content and Managing the Content Library*.

- You can inform Learning Manager about the target audience of the course. By doing so, the search engine of Learning Manager gives more prominence to your course when a learner in the target audience searches the catalog. This also requires the creation of users and user groups, which will be discussed in *Chapter 5, Managing Users*.

- Finally, you can make the course visually appealing by providing a **Banner Image** and a **Cover Image**.

In this section, you will add this additional metadata by performing the following steps:

1. From the **Author** home page, click the **Courses** link located in the **Learning** section of the left sidebar.

2. At the top of the list, click the **Draft** tab to access the list of all courses currently in a *draft* state.

3. Click the **Fundamental of IT Security** course to open it.

4. Provide a **Brief Description** and a **Detailed Overview** of the course.

Brief Description appears on the Course Card, which is visible both in the catalog itself and on the search results page when using the built-in search engine. It should be very short (a maximum of 140 characters) and should contain the main keywords related to your course.

Detailed Overview is a longer description of your course (up to 1,500 characters). It appears on the course page once the learner has clicked the course card. In other words, learners who reach the **Detailed Overview** have already expressed an interest in the course. This is why the **Detailed Overview** can be much longer than the **Brief Description**. The **Detailed Overview** should contain information such as the course content, learning outcomes, methodology used, and so on.

> **Sample descriptions**
>
> Examples of **Brief Description** and **Detailed Overview** can be found in the `ITSecurity/ fundamentals_description_EN.pdf` file in the download provided with this book.

Before hitting the **Save** button, you will upload both a **Cover Image** and a **Banner Image** for the course.

> **Sample images**
>
> You can use any image at your disposal to complete the steps in this process. If needed, sample images are provided in the `/ITSecurity` folder of the download associated with this book. If you're using your own images, the recommended size of the cover image is 300 pixels by 300 pixels, and the recommended size of the banner image is 1,600 pixels by 140 pixels, as stated in the official ALM user guide at `https://helpx.adobe.com/be_en/learning- manager/system-requirements.html`.

Let's upload the necessary images.

5. Drag a suitable cover image on the **Cover Image** field at the end of the course **Overview** form.

6. Also, drag a suitable banner image to the **Banner Image** field.

7. Click the **Save** button located in the upper-right corner of the screen.

8. When done, click the **Preview as learner** link located in the **Preview** section of the left sidebar.

This action opens the course page as a learner will see it when the course is published. Notice the banner image, which is visible at the top of the page, the detailed overview, and the list of modules included in the course.

9. Take some time to inspect the other elements present on the course page. When you're ready, click the **Back** button at the top of the left sidebar to return to the **Course Catalog** page.

10. If needed, click the **Draft** tab at the top of the page to access the list of courses currently in a *Draft* state.

You should see the new cover image on the list of **Draft** courses, as shown in the following screenshot:

Figure 4.7 – The cover image is used on the Course Card displayed in the Learning Catalog

Choosing course images

These course images represent yet another opportunity to brand your Learning Manager account. This can be a branded image or a stock image edited for internal branding so that the appearance of your account remains consistent and courses are easily recognizable.

In this section, you made the course more discoverable by adding a **Brief Description** and a **Detailed Overview**. You also customized the look and feel of your course to make it stand out in the Course Catalog, which increases the likelihood that learners will click the course card and enroll.

Your course is almost ready to be published. However, there is one last important aspect to discuss before you can finally make it available to learners: the course completion criteria.

Defining the course completion criteria

In *Chapter 3*, *Uploading Learning Content and Managing the Content Library*, you defined the completion and success criteria for each content module. But courses also have their own completion and success criteria.

This aspect of course creation is very important because completing a course allows the learner to earn skills credits and badges, among other things. As discussed later in this chapter, a course can also serve as a prerequisite for other courses, so completing a course can become a requirement for enrolling in other courses.

Let's take a look at the course completion and success criteria by performing the following steps:

1.   Make sure you are logged in as an Author and return to the **Draft** tab of the **Course Catalog** page.

2.   Click the **Fundamentals of IT Security** course card.

3.   Scroll down the page until you see the modules that make up this course.

Just below the list of modules, you find the **Sequencing of Modules** and **Mandatory Modules** options, as shown in the following screenshot:

Figure 4.8 – Default configuration of the Sequencing of Modules and Mandatory Modules sections

With this default configuration, the learner can view the course modules in any order, but all the modules must be marked as *completed* for the course to be considered *complete*.

4.   Change the **Sequencing of Modules** option to **Ordered**.

5.   Click the **Save** button in the upper-right corner of the page.

With this new configuration, the learner must review the modules in the order you have defined. As an author, remember that you can change the order of the modules with a simple drag-and-drop action.

Before publishing the course, remember that the *completion* criteria are not the same as the *success* criteria. In other words, you can *complete* a course but not *pass* it. In this case, you want to define how Learning Manager handles multiple attempts.

Allowing multiple attempts

Unfortunately, the **Multiple Attempts** option is *not enabled by default*. So, first, you have to switch back to the Administrator role to enable this option for your account. Then, you must return to the Author role to configure it for your course. Let's take a look:

1. Click the user icon located in the upper-right corner of the screen and return to the **Administrator** role.

2. From the **Administrator** home page, click the **Settings** link located at the end of the **Configure** section of the left sidebar.

3. Then, click the **General** link in the left sidebar to open the **General** settings page.

4. Locate the **Multiple Attempts** option and select the **Enable** checkbox. This is the action that enables the advanced *success* and *completion* options for Authors when creating courses.

5. Return to the **Author** role.

6. From the **Author** home page, click the **courses** link in the **Learning** section of the left sidebar.

7. Click the **Draft** tab to access the courses currently in *Draft* state.

8. Click the **Fundamentals of IT Security** course to open it.

9. Notice the new **Allow multiple attempts** option at the top of the **Modules** section of the course **Overview** page, as shown in the following screenshot:

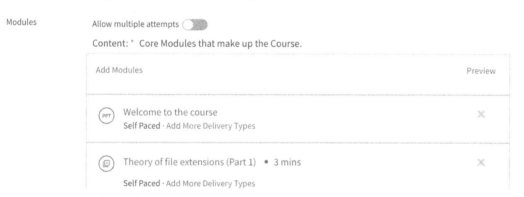

Figure 4.09 – The Allow multiple attempts option appears atop the Modules section

10. Toggle the **Allow multiple attempts** option *on*.

11. Take some time to examine the available options, but do not modify any of them.

12. Click the **Save** button in the upper-right corner of the page.

Turning the **Allow multiple attempts** option on displays a **Retake** button in the learner experience when the learner fails an interactive module.

While examining these options, keep in mind that they only apply to the *interactive* modules of your course. As discussed in *Chapter 3, Uploading Learning Content and Managing the Content Library*, interactive content modules are those that are created using specialized eLearning authoring tools (such as Adobe Captivate, Articulate Storyline, Lectora, iSpring, and others) and uploaded to Learning Manager as AICC-, SCORM-, or xAPI-compliant packages:

- The **Set Attempts at** drop-down list allows you to adjust these options at the *course* level or the *module* level. When choosing **Course level**, you apply the same values to all the interactive modules of your course. If you choose **Module level**, you can adjust these options for each interactive module separately.

- The **Stop new attempt once module is completed & passed** option hides the **Retake** button as soon as the learner has both *completed* and *passed* the interactive course module.

- The **Lock module between attempts** option allows you to block access to a module for a certain amount of time. The learner is unable to start the next attempt until the lock time has elapsed.

- The **Set time limit to complete module** option allows you to specify a time limit for completing the module. If the learner does not complete the module within this time limit, the attempt automatically ends with an *Incomplete* status.

These advanced options allow you to implement a very large array of instructional design strategies. Of course, you don't need to go through all these options every time you create a course. Sometimes, the default options work just fine.

In this section, you learned how to specify the success and completion criteria of a course. Now, your course is finally ready to be published, which is what you will do in the next section.

Publishing a course

At this point, your course is still in *Draft* state. This means that it is currently invisible to learners searching the Course Catalog, so it is not yet open for enrollment. To make it an official component of the Course Catalog and to start accepting enrollments, you must *publish* the course by performing the following steps:

1. From the **Author** home page, click the **Courses** link in the **Learning** section of the left sidebar.
2. Click the **Draft** tab to access the courses currently in *Draft* state.
3. Hover over the lower portion of the course card and click the **Publish Course** link.

That's it! Your course is now officially part of the Course Catalog and is open for enrollment. Publishing a course also makes new options available to Authors. Let's quickly review these new options.

4. Click the **Published** tab to access the list of courses currently being published in the Course Catalog.
5. Click the card of your newly created course. This takes you to the **Overview** page of the course.

While on the **Overview** page, take a look at the left sidebar and notice the availability of a bunch of new options, as shown in the following screenshot:

Figure 4.10 – New options are available in the left sidebar once the course has been published

These options are only available once the course has been published.

The **Email Templates** option will be covered in *Chapter 15, Working with Messages and Announcements*, while the **Instances** option will be covered in *Chapter 6, Enrolling Learners in Courses*.

At this point, you have gone through the process of creating and publishing a self-paced course.

Self-paced means that learners can take the course at their convenience. The course is delivered automatically by Adobe Learning Manager with little to no human intervention.

Most of your custom courses will probably be self-paced courses, like the one you just published. But Adobe Learning Manager can also be used to create instructor-led courses, which is what you'll learn about in the next section of this chapter.

Creating an instructor-led course

The course you created in the previous section only contains a bunch of self-paced *asynchronous* content modules. There's nothing wrong with that! Many excellent online courses are simple collections of self-paced asynchronous learning modules.

That being said, Adobe Learning Manager also supports adding *synchronous* modules to a course. *Synchronous* modules are instructor-led training delivered live, either face-to-face, or using a virtual classroom environment such as Adobe Connect, Zoom, or Microsoft Teams.

This capability allows Adobe Learning Manager to address the following use cases:

- You can create courses that include only *synchronous* learning activities. In *Chapter 8, Exploring the Instructor Role*, you will review the features of Adobe Learning Manager for managing course attendance, waitlists, reminders, and more.

- You can create courses that include a blend of self-paced asynchronous activities and synchronous face-to-face or virtual classes. For example, you can schedule a live class after learners have reviewed several self-paced modules (considered prerequisites to the live class). This **blended learning** approach is very popular with learners and trainers alike because it combines the benefits of both the asynchronous and synchronous learning approaches.

Now, let's create an instructor-led *synchronous* course using the following steps:

1. Make sure you are logged in as an **Author** and that you are on the **Author** home page.

2. From the **Author** home page, click the **Create Courses** link located in the main content area. This action takes you to the course creation form.

3. Type the name of your new course in the **Course Name** field (Advanced IT Security, in this example).

4. As a best practice, take some time to add a **Brief Description**, as well a **Detailed Overview**. For this exercise, you can use the example provided in the ITSecurity/advanced_ Description_EN.pdf file of the download associated with this book.

5. Also, add a **Cover Image** and a **Banner Image** to increase the course's discoverability in the course catalog. In this example, you can use the images available in the ITSecurity folder of the download associated with this book.

So far, creating an instructor-led course follows the same process as creating a self-paced course. In the next section, you will add modules to your course. This is where things will start to differ.

Adding instructor-led activities to a course

Let's add an instructor-led *synchronous* training activity to the course you are currently building.

There are two types of instructor-led classroom modules: the **Virtual Classroom Module**, which takes place online, and the **Classroom Module**, in which learners attend face-to-face lectures.

The main differences between a self-paced *asynchronous* module and a *synchronous* module (face-to-face or virtual) is the fact that a *synchronous* module is time-dependent. The modules you will create in this section will have a **Start Date** and **Time**, as well as an **End Date** and **Time**.

This raises the question of learner enrollment. What happens when a learner enrolls in the course *after* the start/end date of the synchronous course activity? This is the purpose of course **instances**, which will be covered in *Chapter 6, Enrolling Learners in Courses*.

First, let's take a look at how to create a **Virtual Classroom Module**.

Defining a Virtual Class Module

This exercise picks up where the previous section left off. Use the following steps to add a **Virtual Classroom Module** to your course:

1. Click **the Add Modules** link located at the top of the **Content** section. This action reopens the **Select Module Type** dialog.

2. This time, choose the **Virtual Classroom Module** option to add a live instructor-led virtual class to your course.

3. Take a first look at the fields available in this form, but do not complete any of them yet.

Now let's take a look at the **Details** section of the form. This is where you define the practical details of the online class (such as the conference URL and the scheduling details).

The **Conference URL** is used to redirect the user to *any* virtual class or video conferencing solution available (even if the chosen solution is *not* from Adobe). For example, if your organization uses Zoom, simply schedule the class in your Zoom account and copy/paste the Zoom link in the Conference URL field.

The **Conferencing System** dropdown lists the conferencing systems that have been integrated with your ALM account using one of the connectors available in the Integration Admin role. You will explore the Integration Admin role in *Chapter 16, Exploring the Integration Admin Role*. If you have not configured any of these connectors, only the **Other Services** option is available in the list.

The added value of integrations

Since you can configure a **Virtual Classroom Module** by copying and pasting a link created from your web conferencing solution of choice, you may wonder what added value there is in having an integration admin configure connectors beforehand. Using the built-in connectors enables data exchange between your ALM account and your virtual classroom service. In particular, this data exchange enables the automatic retrieval of data such as attendance and engagement data from your virtual classroom solution. This data can then be used by the built-in ALM reports, which will be covered in *Chapter 10, Reporting in Adobe Learning Manager*.

At the end of the form, notice the **Location** and **Seat Limit** fields. Here you can specify the physical location where the class will actually take place. This allows you to address a very common use case, where some learners are physically present with the instructor in the classroom or lecture hall, while the course is also broadcast online for the other learners. If your classroom activity is only virtual, leave the **Location** and **Seat Limit** fields empty.

4. Take some time to inspect the other fields available on this form.

Because defining a virtual class requires that you have access to a video conferencing solution, we will not go any further with defining a **Virtual Classroom Module** in this book, so you will now cancel the current process.

5. Click the **Cancel** button located in the lower-right corner of the **Virtual Classroom** dialog to cancel the creation of the **Virtual Classroom Module**.

In the next section, you will explore adding a **Classroom Module** in your course.

Defining a Classroom Module

In this section, you will explore adding the second type of instructor-led activity: the **Classroom Module**. This section picks up where the previous section left off, so you should be on the **Overview** page of the **Advanced IT Security** course in the Autor role. Use the following steps to do create a **Classroom Module**:

1. Click the **Add Modules** link located at the top of the **Content** section. This action reopens the **Select Module Type** dialog.

2. This time, choose the **Classroom Module** option to add a face-to-face instructor-led class.

3. Fill in the form with the required information, as shown in the following screenshot.

Figure 4.11 – Adding a Classroom Module to your course

Before moving on, notice a few interesting features in the **Classroom Module** dialog.

First, the **Scheduling Assistant** is designed to help you schedule your class by showing you the current schedule for your chosen **Instructor** and **Location**.

> **Using the Scheduling Assistant**
>
> For the **Scheduling Assistant** to work as intended, you must first define **Instructors** and **Locations**. Defining instructors is covered in *Chapter 5, Managing Users*. Defining locations must be done by an administrator beforehand, using the **Settings | Classroom Locations** page of the Admin role.

Also notice the **Timezone** field. If you leave it empty, it defaults to the **timezone** defined for the account in the **Settings | Basic Info** page of the Admin role as discussed in *Chapter 1, Introduction to Adobe Learning Manager*.

4. When ready, click the **Done** button, located in the lower-right corner of the form.

The **Seat Limit** field is important for class registration and waitlist management. In this example, make sure you choose a low seat limit (**5**, in the preceding screenshot).

Also, notice the **Instructor** field. You probably tried to enter your name in the **Instructor** field when creating the activity, but since you are not yet identified as a potential instructor within the system, Adobe Learning Manager won't let you do this. Assigning roles to users will be covered in *Chapter 5, Managing Users*. Until then, you can safely leave this field empty.

The **Do you want to add a quiz score for this Module** checkbox allows you to decide if a grade is awarded to learners attending this class. Assigning grades to the class attendees is one of the responsibilities devoted to the instructor. You will explore the instructor role in *Chapter 8, Exploring the Instructor Role*. Until then, make sure you leave this box and the **Allow Instructor to mark success** boxes deselected.

> **Authors versus instructors**
>
> Coming from the education sector, it took me a while to understand the reason for distinguishing authors from instructors. After all, in most schools and universities, an instructor is the person who both *creates* a course and *teaches* it. But things are different in the corporate world, and Adobe Learning Manager is an enterprise LMS. In large organizations, the L&D department may be responsible for designing courses that are delivered all over the world, in different branches and in different languages, by a multitude of instructors. In such a case, the *author* of the course is the L&D department, while the *instructors* are the people responsible for delivering that training. Of course, the same person can be both author and instructor, but this is much less common than in the education sector.

Adding more delivery types

Now, imagine the following situation. You are organizing a face-to-face training session, but at the same time, you want to record the session and make it available to learners asynchronously. When registering for the course, learners will have the choice of registering either for the face-to-face class or for the recorded version of the training.

Perform the following steps to add another delivery type to the Classroom module you just created:

1. Still on the course creation form, click the **Add More Delivery Types** button associated with the **Classroom** module you created in the previous section. This action is illustrated in the following screenshot:

Figure 4.12 – Adding more delivery types to your classroom module

2. In the **Modules Details** dialog, select the **Self Paced Module** checkbox.
3. Click the **Add Content** link located toward the bottom of the **Module Details** dialog.
4. Select the self-paced module that will be delivered to learners enrolling in the recorded version of the course. Click the **Add** button when you're done.

    For this example, choose any available self-paced module. In a real-world situation, you would have to wait until the recording of the first live class is available before selecting that video recording as the content for the self-paced delivery type.

5. Click the **Done** button.

There are many instances where it is helpful to deliver the same modules using different delivery types, as outlined in the following examples:

*   An instructor is on medical leave for a few months, so his/her face-to-face classes have been temporarily replaced by self-paced modules (for example, recordings of previous classes).
*   Your instructors cannot teach in every language. Therefore, for some languages, you must provide self-paced modules (for example, a recording of the live class with subtitles in different languages) in place of the instructor-led class.

- Varying local regulations may require that certain modules of your course be extended in some parts of the world and not in others. For example, a 3-minute self-paced module in one country may require a 3-hour webinar in another country.

- In a situation where some learners need to take this course urgently, but there are no sessions scheduled in the near future, these learners can enroll in the self-paced recorded version of the course and attend at any time.

- You may simply want to provide the best possible learning experience for all learners, regardless of their learning styles.

You can now proceed with the remaining steps of the course creation process.

6. Click the **Save** button located in the upper-right corner of the screen. This action saves the course and takes you to the course **Overview** page.

7. Use the **Course Skills** section to award **30** points towards the **IT Security Level 2** skill to all learners who successfully complete this course.

8. Add yourself as the **Author** of the course.

9. Click the **Save** button located in the upper-right corner of the page.

10. Finally, click the **Back** button located at the top of the left column to return to the **Course Catalog** page.

Congratulations! You have just created a second custom course in your Adobe Learning Manager account. This second course contains only one *synchronous* module, which can be either a face-to-face **Classroom Module** or a **Virtual Classroom Module**. Since the new course has not yet been published, it is currently in **Draft** mode.

You have now reviewed the options that you will use most often when creating custom courses in your Adobe Learning Manager account. But instructional designers are creative people who imagine all sorts of unique use cases and subtle nuances. To accommodate these requirements and enable instructional designers to implement their training strategies, Adobe Learning Manager offers a wide range of additional options for creating all kinds of training. This is what you will explore in the next section.

Advanced options for courses

Every organization is unique, every industry has its training challenges and compliance requirements, and instructional designers each each have their own vision of what corporate training should be like. As the enterprise LMS of choice, Adobe Learning Manager must be able to accommodate a wide range of situations. This is what you will explore now, starting with the special **Activity Module** in the next section.

Working with the Activity Modules

In addition to **Self-Paced Modules**, **Virtual Classroom Modules**, and **Classroom Modules,** Adobe Learning Manager supports the **Activity Module**. You can use it when learners need to complete some kind of activity, such as an assignment or a workshop, or when viewing an external resource such as a YouTube video.

You will now add an activity module at the end of the **Fundamentals of IT Security** course you created earlier using the following steps:

1. Make sure you are logged in as an **Author** and that you are on the **Author** home page.
2. Click the **Courses** link located in the **Learning** section of the left sidebar to open the **Course Catalog** page.
3. Click the **Fundamentals of IT Security** course card to open the course details.
4. Click the **Edit** link located in the upper-right corner of the page to start editing the course.
5. Scroll down the page until you see the list of modules included in this course.
6. Click the **Add Modules** link in the **Content** section to reopen the **Select Module Type** dialog.
7. Click the **Activity Module** at the bottom of the list.

As shown in the following screenshot, there are four types of activity modules available in the **Type** drop-down list:

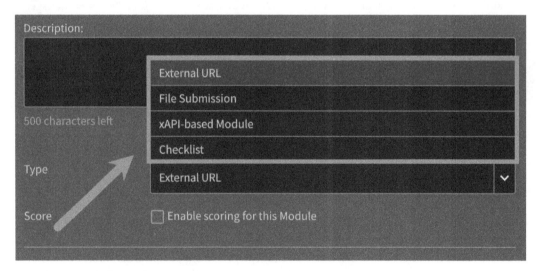

Figure 4.13 – There are four types of Activity Modules available

In the next few sections, you will explore these four types of activities one by one, starting with the **External URL** activity in the next section.

Creating an External URL activity

In today's interconnected world, there is a plethora of educational content available all over the internet. Therefore, it is not always necessary to reinvent the wheel when creating your courses. Sometimes, redirecting learners to these external resources is the most effective solution, both from an instructional perspective and in terms of cost control. The External URL activity can also be learning content that is contracted out to a third-party provider that does not allow files to be uploaded to your LMS.

Starting from where the previous section left off, use the following steps to add an **External URL** activity to the **Fundamentals of IT Security** course:

1. Enter the title of your **Activity Module** in the **Title** field. As a best practice, also supply a short description in the **Description** field.

2. Choose **External URL** in the **Type** field.

3. Copy/paste the URL of the activity in the **URL** field. This is the most important piece of information on the form.

4. Finally, enter the approximate duration (in minutes) of the activity in the **Duration** field.

5. Make sure the **Activity Module** form looks like the following screenshot before clicking the **Add** button:

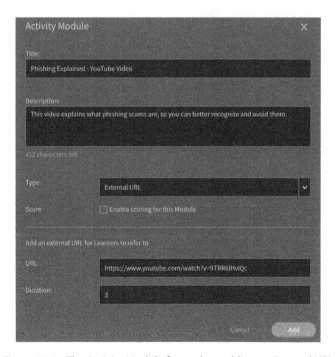

Figure 4.14 – The Activity Module form when adding an External URL

After clicking the **Add** button, the new activity is added as an additional module to the course.

6. Feel free to reorder the modules as required.

7. When you're ready, click the **Republish** button located in the upper-right corner of the screen to save and publish the changes.

Read the **Confirmation Required** message. Since no learners are enrolled in your course yet, you can safely click the **Proceed** button.

> **Advanced YouTube Embedding using the External URL activity**
>
> When the external URL is a YouTube video, you can use the URL available in the Embed option of YouTube so that the video is displayed directly in the Fluidic Player and the learner does not have to leave Learning Manager to visit the external URL. The schema of such a URL is as follows: `https://www.youtube.com/embed/ressourceID`.

Creating a File Submission activity

Having learners submit individual assignments is an effective way to assess their new skills. Adobe Learning Manager makes it easy to set up this type of activity using the **File Submission** activity module. Once the learner has uploaded the assignment, an instructor must review the submitted work to grade it.

You will now add a File Submission activity to the Advanced IT Security course using the following steps:

1. Make sure you are logged in as an **Author** and that you are on the **Author** home page.

2. Click the **Courses** link located in the **Learning** section of the left sidebar to open the **Course Catalog** page.

3. Click the **Draft** tab to see the list of courses currently in a *Draft* state.

4. Click the **Advanced IT Security** course card to open the course details.

5. Scroll down the page until you see the list of modules included in this course.

6. Click the **Add Modules** link in the **Content** section to reopen the **Select Module Type** dialog.

7. Click your **Activity Module** at the bottom of the list.

So far, creating a **File Submission** activity follows the same steps as creating an **External URL** activity.

8. Enter the title of your **Activity Module** in the **Title** field. As a best practice, also supply a short description in the **Description** field.

9. Choose **File Submission** in the **Type** field.

10. As you are yet to define potential instructors in your account, leave the **Submission Instructor(s)** field empty for now.

11. Optionally, enter the estimated duration (in minutes) in the **Duration** field.

12. When you're ready, click the **Add** button located in the lower-right corner of the form.

The new **File Submission** activity is added as a second module in your course. Since you now have two modules in your course, you need to make sure that the **Module Sequencing** and **Mandatory Modules** options are defined correctly.

13. Toggle the **Sequencing of Modules** option to **Ordered**.

14. Make sure that the **Mandatory Modules** option is set to **All**.

15. Click the **Save** button in the upper-right corner of the page to save the changes.

This is how easy it is to add a **File Submission** activity to your Adobe Learning Manager courses. In *Chapter 8, Exploring the Instructor Role*, you will assign an instructor to this activity and review how instructors can access and grade submitted assignments.

Creating a Checklist activity

In occupations where the practical aspect is highly important, it is useful to visit learners directly on the job to assess their new skills after they have completed their training. This is especially useful in production plants, supply chains, first aid training, safety training, and other areas.

The **Checklist** activity is a list of items that a designated instructor must evaluate as they monitor learners on location in their daily work.

You will now add a checklist activity at the end of the **Advanced IT Security** course you created earlier by performing the following steps:

1. Return to the **Overview** page of the **Advanced IT Security** course.

2. Scroll down the page until you see the **Modules** section.

3. Click the **Add Modules** link located at the top of the **Content** section.

4. Click the **Activity Module** option to open the **Activity Module** form.

5. Enter the title of your **Activity Module** in the **Title** field. As a best practice, also supply a short description in the **Description** field.

6. Choose **Checklist** in the **Type** field.

There are two checklist types available: the **Yes/No** checklist and the **1-5** checklist. If you choose **Yes/ No**, the instructor will answer either *Yes* or *No* to each item on the checklist. If you choose **1-5**, the instructor shall rate each item of the checklist on a scale of 1 to 5.

7. Choose **Yes/No** in the **Checklist Type** field.

8. Type 3 in the **Pass Criteria** field. This means that the checklist is considered *passed* when three items or more have a *Yes* as an answer.

9. Click the **Add** link in the **Checklist Questions** field to add a minimum of three questions to your checklist.

This last action is shown in the following screenshot:

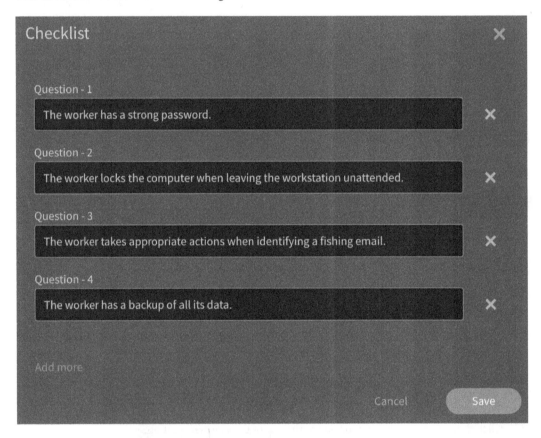

Figure 4.15 – Enter a minimum of three questions in your checklist

As you work out the questions, keep in mind that the instructor should be able to answer each one with a *Yes* or a *No*.

10. When you're done, click the **Save** button to save the questions.

11. Leave the **Instructor** field empty for now. Optionally, you can type a note for the instructor in the **Note to Instructor** field.

12. When you're ready, click the **Add** button in the lower-right corner of the form to make the new activity part of the course content.

13. Finally, click the **Save** button in the upper-right corner of the page to save the changes.

The **Checklist** activity is yet another assessment tool available in Adobe Learning Manager. Use it to complement other assessment activities and to provide the organization with meaningful data measuring learning effectiveness.

Discovering the xAPI activity

xAPI is the new communication standard of the eLearning industry. As discussed in *Chapter 3, Uploading Learning Content and Managing the Content Library*, xAPI was designed under the assumption that learners always learn, but not necessarily within the tight boundaries of your corporate LMS. This type of activity module allows you to grab learning data generated by external systems and make it part of the Learner track record. It allows learners to take course modules outside of Adobe Learning Manager while still being tracked by the system.

In this section, you have reviewed the **Activity Module** by adding three different types of activities to your course. After completing the last few sections, the main content of the course is now in place. But Learning Manager allows you to specify other types of content, such as **Prework**, **Job Aids**, and other additional **Resources**. This is what you will look at in the next section.

Other types of learning material

So far, the modules you have added to the course represent the main content of the course. It is this content that each learner must review to progress through the course, complete it, and earn the credits that the course awards.

But Adobe Learning Manager supports other types of learning material as well. This is what you will review in this section:

1. Return to the **Overview** page of the **Advanced IT Security** course.
2. Scroll down the page until you see the **Modules** section.

You should already have three modules in the **Content** section, as shown in the following screenshot:

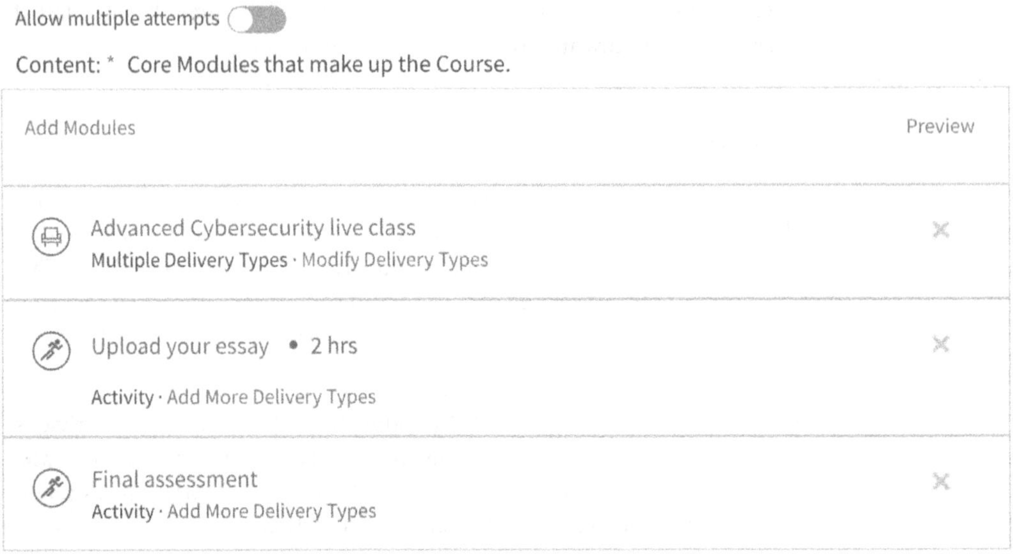

Allow multiple attempts ⬤

Content: * Core Modules that make up the Course.

Add Modules	Preview
🖥 Advanced Cybersecurity live class Multiple Delivery Types · Modify Delivery Types	✕
✎ Upload your essay • 2 hrs Activity · Add More Delivery Types	✕
✎ Final assessment Activity · Add More Delivery Types	✕

Figure 4.16 – The content modules currently in the course

Scrolling down the page, you find two additional sections you can use to add **Prework** modules and **Testout** modules.

Using Prework modules

Prework modules are modules designed to help learners prepare for the course. This type of learning content is often used in the following situations:

- Adding self-paced modules explaining how Learning Manager works from the learner's perspective

- Adding a video to introduce the course author(s) and/or instructor(s)

- Providing an optional live or virtual class to introduce the course

- Providing some material to help learners determine if they meet the course prerequisites or if they have the correct skills or work experience before they take the training

When adding **Prework** modules to a course, keep in mind that learners are *not* required to view these modules to complete the course and earn credits. This is the main difference between regular **Content** modules and **Prework** modules: **Content** modules *are required* to complete the course, while **Prework** modules are *not*.

The process of adding **Prework** modules is the same as the process of adding regular **Content**.

Using Testout modules

Staff training costs time and money, so organizations want to ensure that the right training is being provided to the right audience. In large organizations, it is not uncommon to bulk-enroll large groups of individuals in courses. While this practice makes it easier to administer the LMS, it also increases the chances of enrolling people who are already familiar with the course topic, wasting these people's time and the organization's money. **Testout** modules allow learners to demonstrate their mastery of the subject, thus allowing them to skip the course altogether.

Another use case for **Testout** modules is within the government space, where many courses require yearly attendance, even if the material has not changed. One possible way to help learners (and the LMS owners) is to offer Testouts. This helps save the learner's time, as well as provide data that proves topic mastery.

Adding Testout modules is done in the same way as adding regular Content modules and Prework modules.

Linking Job Aids to courses

As discussed in the *Creating Job Aids* section of *Chapter 3*, *Uploading Learning Content and Managing the Content Library*, Job Aids are training content that learners can access without enrolling in a course. Think of these as cheat sheets or handouts, similar to those you receive at the end of conferences or live classes.

While it is not required to enroll in the course to access Job Aids, you can still associate relevant Job Aids with your course by performing the following steps:

1. Make sure you are logged in as an Author and return to the **Overview** page of the **Advanced IT Security** course.
2. Click the **Settings** link located at the top of the left sidebar.
3. Scroll down the page until you see the **Job Aids** field.
4. Click the **Add Job Aids** link and start typing in the name of the Job Aid you are looking for.
5. Click the name of the Job Aid when it appears in the list.
6. Repeat this process for the other Job Aids you want to link to this course.
7. When you're done, click the **Save** button in the upper-right corner of the page to save the changes.
8. Click the **Preview as learner** link in the **Preview** section of the left sidebar to test your changes.

As shown in the following screenshot, Job Aids are available to learners from the right sidebar of the course:

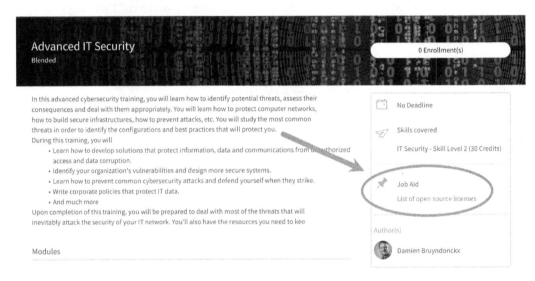

Figure 4.17 – Job Aids are accessible from the right sidebar of the course

In this section, you reviewed the process of linking Job Aids to courses. In the next section, you will add additional resources to your course.

Adding resources to the course

In addition to modules (Content, Prework, and Testout) and Job Aids, Adobe Learning Manager allows you to upload additional resources to your courses. Note that uploading additional resources is not required to publish the course.

Typically, this extra course material is used in the following situations:

- To make the assets needed to complete an assignment available to learners

- To provide sample files for a course

The main difference between these resources and the Job Aids discussed in the previous section is that Job Aids can be accessed without enrolling in a course, whereas resources are linked to a particular course and can only be accessed by the enrolled learners. Also, the same Job Aid can be linked to multiple courses, while a specific resource is linked to a specific course (if you want to use the same resource in multiple courses, it is necessary to reupload the same file multiple times).

Resources can be files that you upload to the system or links to other sites. Perform the following steps to add resources to your course:

1. Make sure you are logged in as an Author and return to the **Overview** page of the **Advanced IT Security** course.

2. Click the **Settings** link located at the top of the left sidebar.

3. The **Resources** field is located toward the very end of this form.

From here, you can upload files and/or enter links to other sites that will be used as **Resources** for this course. Don't forget to click the **Save** button in the upper-right corner of the page to save your changes.

After completing the previous few sections, all the content of your course is now in place. In the next section, you will learn how to specify **prerequisites** for your course.

Defining Course Prerequisites

Every instructor knows that learning is a journey made up of steps that must be taken in the right order. Enrolling someone in an advanced course when that person does not have the basic knowledge is both a waste of time and money. This is the main reason why you want to define prerequisites for your courses.

In Learning Manager, prerequisites are other courses that you suggest the learner take before enrolling in this course. By default, these prerequisites are only suggestions, which means that Learning Manager does *not* force learners to meet these prerequisites before enrolling in a course. However, you can make these prerequisites mandatory, which prevents learners from enrolling if they have not completed the prerequisite course(s).

Perform the following steps to define the prerequisites for your course:

1. Make sure you are logged in as an Author and return to the **Overview** page of the **Advanced IT Security** course.

2. Click the **Settings** link located at the top of the left sidebar.

3. Scroll down the page until you see the **Prerequisites** section.

4. Click the **Add Prerequisites** link and start typing in the name of a course you consider a prerequisite for this course.

5. Click the name of the chosen course when it appears in the list. In this example, add the **Fundamentals of IT security** course as a prerequisite.

   You can add multiple prerequisites by repeating the last two steps as many times as needed. If there are multiple prerequisites, you can easily reorder them with simple drag-and-drop actions.

6. Select the **Enforce Prerequisites** checkbox to make it mandatory.

7. Don't forget to click the **Save** button in the upper-right corner of the page to save your changes.

8. Click the **Preview as learner** link in the **Preview** section of the left sidebar to test the effect of your last change.

As shown in the following screenshot, **Prerequisite Courses** (if any) are displayed above the course content on the course page:

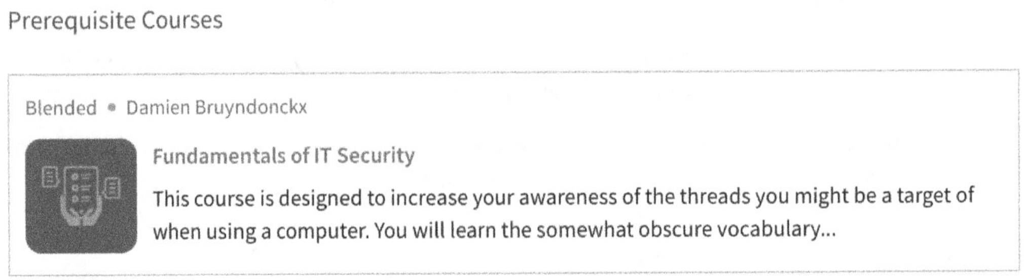

Prerequisite Courses

Blended • Damien Bruyndonckx

Fundamentals of IT Security

This course is designed to increase your awareness of the threads you might be a target of when using a computer. You will learn the somewhat obscure vocabulary...

Figure 4.18 – Prerequisite Courses are visible above the course content

In this section, you learned howw to add prerequisites to your course. In the next section, you will add multiple language versions of a course.

Defining multiple language versions of a course

In *Chapter 1, Introduction to Adobe Learning Manager*, you learned that the LMS is available in multiple languages. In *Chapter 3, Uploading Learning Content and Managing the Content Library*, you learned how to upload multiple language versions of the same module and how Learning Manager chooses which language version to deliver to each learner.

The same basic reasoning applies to courses. The original language of the course is the same as the default language of the platform (*English (United States)*, in this example), but you can specify various information such as **Course Name**, **Short Description**, and **Detailed Overview** in multiple languages. Let's take a look at this:

1. Make sure you are logged in as an Author and return to the **Overview** page of the **Advanced IT Security** course.

2. Click the **Add New Language** link located next to the **English (United States)** tab at the very top of the form:

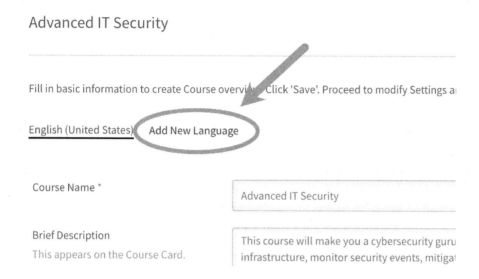

Figure 4.19 – The Add New Language link

3. Select one or more additional languages from the list and click the **Save** button in the lower-right corner of the **Select Languages** box. This adds additional language tabs at the top of the course **Overview** page.

4. Fill in the localized **Course Name**, **Brief Description**, and **Detailed Overview** fields in every language tab.

5. Don't forget to click the **Save** button in the upper-right corner of the **Overview** page when you're done.

With these additional language versions, learners can browse the Course Catalog in their language. Don't forget that learners can also choose their preferred content language via their personal **Profile Settings** (see the *Modifying your account settings* section of *Chapter 1, Introduction to Adobe Learning Manager*). With that in mind, imagine that a learner has chosen French as his/her preferred content language. In such a case, one of these situations can occur:

- If a French version of the course is available, the French **Course Name**, **Short Description**, and **Detailed Overview** information are presented to this learner when browsing the Course Catalog. When taking the course, the French version of the course module is provided to this learner by default. If a French version is not available for a module, plan B is to serve the content in the default language of the platform (*English (United States)*, in this example). In other words, for this learner to have a completely localized experience, you need to translate both the information of the course itself *and* all the modules included in the course.

- If a French version of the course is not available, Learning Manager falls back to providing the language version that corresponds to the default language of the platform (*English (United States)*, in this example), so the learner sees the **Course Name**, **Short Description**, and **Detailed Overview** information in the default language. That being said, if one or more modules included in the course has a French version, that version of the module is presented to the learner.

You are now ready to publish the **Advanced IT Security** course.

6. While on the **Overview** page of the **Advanced IT Security** course, click the **Publish** button located in the upper-right corner of the screen.

7. Read the **Confirmation Required** message asking you to provide a completion deadline for this course. This will be done in *Chapter 6, Enrolling Learners in Courses*. For now, you can safely ignore this warning and click the **OK** button.

8. Return to the **Published** tab of the **Course Catalog** page.

After completing these steps, you see both of your custom courses in the Course Catalog of your Learning Manager account.

Editing a published course

There are several reasons why it is useful to modify a published course – for example, new regulations, policy changes, or a new software version require you to update courses. Editing a published course is very similar to creating a course. Let's take a look:

1. From the **Author** home page, click the **courses** link in the **Learning** section of the left sidebar to access the Course Catalog.

2. Click the course you wish to update. This takes you back to the course **Overview** page, where *all fields are disabled by default.*

3. Click the **Edit** button in the upper-right corner of the page to unlock the form.

4. Make the necessary changes.

5. When you're ready, click the **Republish** button to commit your changes.

By default, republishing a course sends an email to all learners currently enrolled in the course to notify them about the update. In *Chapter 15, Working with Messages and Announcements*, you will learn how to enable/disable and customize these notifications.

Also, be aware that updating courses in such a way does *not* change the completion and success criteria that have already been achieved by currently enrolled learners.

> **Updating content**
>
> As a general rule, remember that, when modifying any type of content available in the system, Learning Manager never takes away what has already been granted to learners.

In the next section, we will briefly discuss retiring and deleting courses.

Retiring and deleting courses

From time to time, it may be necessary to delete a course altogether. This can happen when one of your products reaches its end of life, when you decide to no longer work with a given provider, when a given software solution has been discontinued, or when a new version of a course is created from scratch.

Similar to modules, skills, and other types of content available in Learning Manager, you cannot directly *delete* a course. You must *retire* it first. In a nutshell, a course can have several statuses, as outlined here:

- A *published* course accepts new enrollments.

- When the course is *retired*, it is removed from the Course Catalog and does not accept any new enrollments. Currently, enrolled learners continue to view the course normally. Also, a *retired* course can still be republished, in which case it returns to the Course Catalog and starts accepting new enrollments again.

- When a course is *deleted*, it is completely removed from your Learning Manager account. All the data about the course is lost and learners lose access to it. That's why you need to proceed with great care when deleting a course. Note that a course must be in the *retired* state before it can be deleted.

Perform the following steps to retire and then delete a course:

1. From the **Author** home page, click the **Courses** link in the **Learning** section of the left sidebar to access the **Course Catalog** page.

2. Hover over the bottom section of the course card of the course you want to retire.

3. Click the **Retire Course** link. Take some time to read the message and click the **Yes** button to confirm the retirement of the course.

4. Click the **Retired** tab located above the list of courses on the **Course Catalog** page.

5. Hover over the course card of the course you want to republish/delete.

6. Click either the **Publish Course** or **Delete Course** link.

In this example, make sure you do *not* delete any course. Just click the **Publish Course** link to reestablish the course in the course catalog.

In this section, you learned how to retire, republish, and delete courses. It is not uncommon for a course to remain for several months or even years in the *Retired* state to allow learners to complete it before it is permanently deleted. Some organizations also decide to keep their old courses in the *Retired* state without ever deleting them to keep them in their archives.

Summary

In this chapter, you learned that Adobe Learning Manager features a comprehensive skills manager. Thanks to this feature, organizations can align skills to courses and track the skills available in the organization. As for learners, they can use skills to better select the courses they want to enroll in. A handful of skills are available by default in Adobe Learning Manager, but you can also define your own custom skills and assign them to courses.

You also reviewed the options for creating courses. A course can be a simple list of self-paced asynchronous modules. A course can also contain face-to-face or virtual synchronous instructor-led classes, as well as various types of activity modules such as external URLs, file submissions, and checklists. Prework and Testout modules, as well as Job Aids and other Resources, can also be added to courses. All these options make it possible to implement a wide range of instructional design strategies using Adobe Learning Manager.

At this point, however, your LMS is still missing one final ingredient before learning can finally take place. That last ingredient is the users who will use the LMS to take courses. Managing users is what you will learn about in the next chapter.

Part 2 – Managing Learners and Tracking Learning Data

Now that courses are available in your ALM account, you need students. In this second part, you will provision users to your account, enroll them into courses, manage and track their learning progress, collect their feedback, and generate all sorts of sophisticated reports.

This section comprises the following chapters:

- *Chapter 5, Managing Users*
- *Chapter 6, Enrolling Learners in Courses*
- *Chapter 7, Reviewing the Learner Experience*
- *Chapter 8, Exploring the Instructor Role*
- *Chapter 9, Configuring and Using Feedback*
- *Chapter 10, Reporting in Adobe Learning Manager*

5
Managinswg Users

After reading the previous chapter, there is some learning content hosted on your Adobe Learning Manager account. This content is ready to be delivered to your learners. Except... you don't have any learners yet! In this chapter, you will review the tools and features used to manage users accessing your ALM account.

When it comes to user management, there are two important aspects to keep in mind: **authentication** and **authorization**. *Authentication* answers the question, "Who are you?" while *authorization* answers the question, "What can you do?"w

For authentication, you can define users directly within Adobe Learning Manager, but in most (if not all) large organizations, users are already defined in some kind of corporate directory. As the enterprise LMS of choice, Adobe Learning Manager can retrieve user data from virtually any third-party system, either through a dedicated connector or by automatically importing CSV files via an FTP connection.

You can also decide to integrate Learning Manager with your **single sign-on** (**SSO**) infrastructure, providing that your organization has a **Security Assertion Markup Language** (**SAML**) 2.0-compliant SSO provider. This allows users to authenticate only once and gain access to multiple enterprise applications, including Adobe Learning Manager.

When it comes to authorization, Learning Manager adopts a role-based approach. You have already learned about the main default roles of the system (*Administrator, Author, Integration Admin, and Learner*), but you can also define custom roles to fit the specific needs of your organization.

Finally, Learning Manager distinguishes between internal and external users. Internal users are employees of your organization, while external users are customers, partners, suppliers, contractors, and others who need to access your LMS.

The features described in this chapter are a little more technical than in the previous chapters. In most organizations, user management is a task for the IT department, who use dedicated server-side tools and network management applications. That being said, user management is such an important topic that we recommend it to every reader. Furthermore, the exercises in this chapter are very important for the upcoming chapters in this book.

By the end of this chapter, various types of users coming from different sources will be able to log in to your ALM account. To achieve this goal, this chapter covers the following topics:

- Creating internal and external users
- Working with user groups
- Managing roles
- Configuring data sources and login methods

The wide range of options available allows Adobe Learning Manager to fit into virtually any corporate environment. This also means that there's an exciting new chapter ahead! So, let's get started!

Technical requirements

To perform the exercises in this chapter, you need to meet the following technical requirements:

- You need Administrator access to a working Learning Manager account (which can be a free trial account)
- Sample files are provided when needed, but you can also choose to use your own files
- You need access to a spreadsheet editor (such as Microsoft Excel or Apple Numbers) to edit CSV files

In this chapter, you will create five new users: three Learners, one Instructor, and one Manager. So, in addition to the aforementioned requirements, you need to create five email addresses: one for each of these future users. You can use any email provider, such as Gmail, Yahoo Mail, or Outlook. Four of these email addresses will be used to create four different Adobe IDs.

Take the necessary time to create these five email addresses before moving on to the next section.

Creating internal and external users

Organizations do not use Learning Manager only to train their employees. They can also use it to train their customers, partners, suppliers, contractors, franchisees, and more. This is the reason why Learning Manager recognizes two main types of users – internal users and external users:

- **Internal users** are the employees of the organization
- **External users** are people outside the organization who need access to your Learning Manager account

External users can be assigned the role of author and manager, but cannot be administrators or integration admins. Other than that, the user experience is mostly the same for both internal and external users.

It is possible to provide different learning content to internal and external users using different learning catalogs. This will be covered in *Chapter 14*, *Working with Catalogs and Peer Accounts*.

In the next few sections, you will review various ways of creating internal and external users.

Creating internal users

Let's start by reviewing the mechanisms used to create internal users. To do so, you need to be logged in as an Administrator and perform the following steps:

1. From the **Administrator** home page, click the **Add Users** link located in the top section of the main content area. You can also click the **Users** link located in the **Manage** section of the left sidebar.

This takes you to the **Internal Users** page, as shown in the following screenshot:

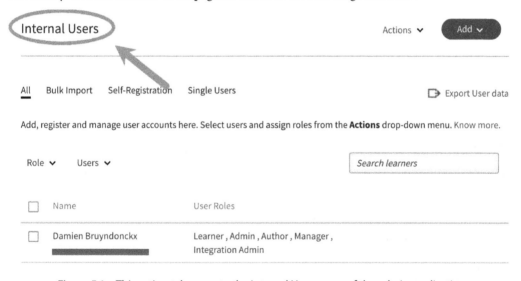

Figure 5.1 – This action takes you to the Internal Users page of the admin application

At this point, if you are using a Learning Manager trial account, the only internal user available should be yourself!

2.   Click the **Add** button located in the upper-right corner of the screen.

As shown in the following screenshot, there are three ways of adding internal users to the system:

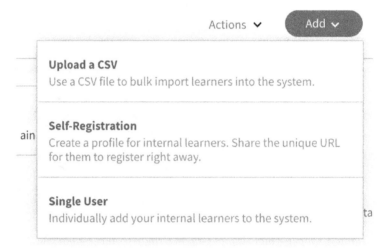

Figure 5.2 – There are three main options for adding internal users to the system

In the next few sections, you will review these three options one by one.

Creating a single user

The first way to create internal users is to use the **Single User** option, which allows you to create one user at a time. You will use this option to create a new learner named *Learner 01*:

1.   From the **Internal Users** page, click the **Add** button located in the upper-right corner of the screen.

2.   Click the **Single User** option to open the **Add User** form.

3.   Type Learner 01 in the **Name** field.

4.   Enter the email address that you created for **Learner 01** in the **E-Mail** field. Note that **Name** and **E-mail** are the only two required fields.

5.   Type Marketing Specialist in the **Profile** field.

6.   Leave the **Manager's Name** field empty for the moment.

7.   When you're ready, click the **Add** button.

Take a moment to read the message that appears on the screen. It tells you that the user has been successfully added and that Learning Manager has sent the user a welcome email with instructions for logging into your ALM account.

8.   Click the **Close** button to close the message and return to the **Internal Users** page.

A new internal user named **Learner 01** has been added to the list. Notice that this new user has been automatically assigned the **Learner** role, as shown in the following screenshot:

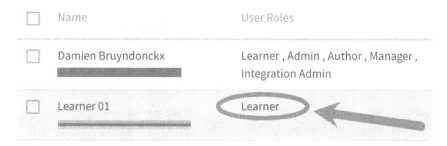

Figure 5.3 – Learner 01 has been automatically assigned the Learner role

When you created the user, *you did not provide any password*, so how can this new user log in to your ALM account? The answer lies in the welcome email the user receives from the system. To better understand how it works, let's examine the default user onboarding experience.

Inspecting the default user onboarding experience

In the previous section, you created a new internal user named *Learner 01* using one of the email addresses you created at the beginning of this chapter.

At this point, *Learner 01* should have received the welcome email from Adobe Learning Manager. You will now log into *Learner 01*'s email account and review this welcome email by performing the following steps:

1.   Log into the email account you created for *Learner 01*.

2.   Confirm that *Learner 01* has received a welcome email from your ALM account.

As shown in the following screenshot, the welcome email explains that users must use their **Adobe ID** to log into your Learning Manager account. If the user does not have an Adobe ID yet, the welcome email provides a link to a page where the new user can create one for free:

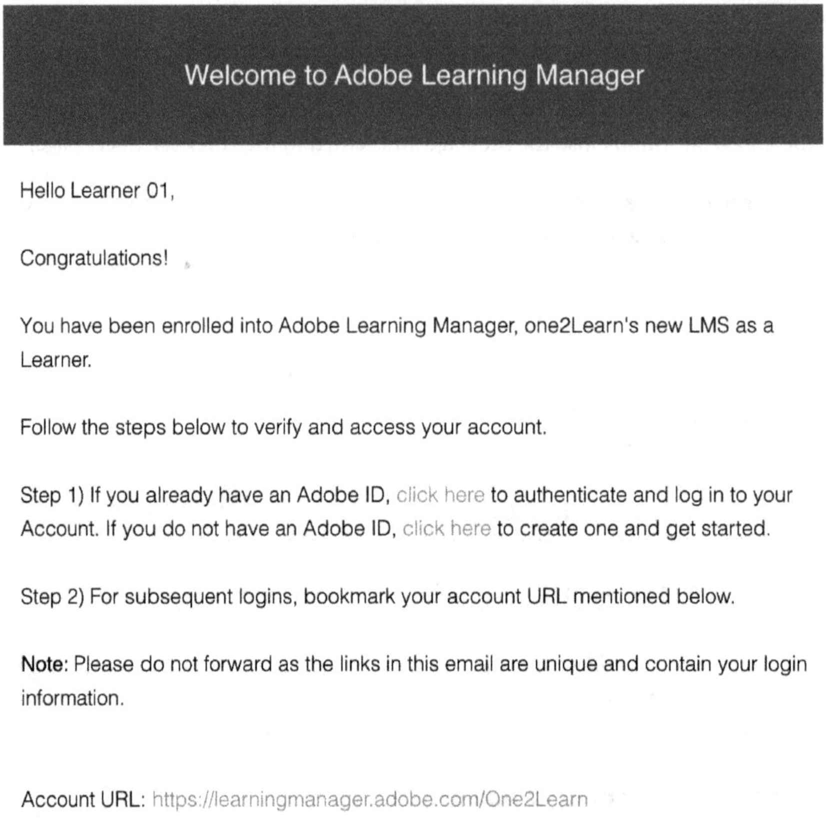

> # Welcome to Adobe Learning Manager
>
> Hello Learner 01,
>
> Congratulations!
>
> You have been enrolled into Adobe Learning Manager, one2Learn's new LMS as a Learner.
>
> Follow the steps below to verify and access your account.
>
> Step 1) If you already have an Adobe ID, click here to authenticate and log in to your Account. If you do not have an Adobe ID, click here to create one and get started.
>
> Step 2) For subsequent logins, bookmark your account URL mentioned below.
>
> **Note:** Please do not forward as the links in this email are unique and contain your login information.
>
> Account URL: https://learningmanager.adobe.com/One2Learn

Figure 5.4 – The welcome email received by Learner 01

By default, the authentication mechanism used by Adobe Learning Manager is the Adobe ID. In the *Configuring Login Methods* section later in this chapter, you will learn how to enable other authentication mechanisms for your ALM account so that users can log in using their corporate credentials rather than an Adobe ID.

> **Customizing the welcome email**
>
> In *Chapter 15, Working with Messages and Announcements*, you'll learn how to customize the messages sent from the platform, including the welcome email discussed here.

Now that you have defined *Learner 01* as a new internal user, you will switch hats and be that user for a short while.

> **Connecting as a new user**
>
> To log into your Learning Manager account as a new user without logging out of your administrator account, use a different browser or a new private window of the same browser.

3. If the email address of the new user is already associated with an Adobe ID, you can directly log into your Learning Manager account using the first link provided in the email. If there is no Adobe ID associated with this email address yet, click the second link and go through the process of creating a free Adobe ID.

When you log into your account as *Learner 01*, you are automatically redirected to the Learner experience. The user icon in the upper-right corner of the screen does not give this user the ability to visit any other roles:

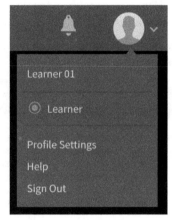

Figure 5.5 – The new user can only visit the Learner experience

In this section, you created a new internal user named *Learner 01*. You discovered that Learning Manager uses **Adobe ID** as the default authentication mechanism, which requires each of your learners to have an Adobe ID to access your account.

The workflow described in this section is useful for adding a limited number of learners to your account. But if you have a large number of users to define, you want to import those users in one go using a CSV file. This is what you will explore in the next section.

Importing users from a CSV file

You will now create two additional users: *Learner 02* and *Instructor 01*. Instead of creating these two users one by one using the **Single User** option described in the previous section, you will create these two users by importing a CSV file containing the necessary information. Of course, in real life, you can use the CSV import process to create more than just two users at a time. So, for this demonstration, let's assume that the CSV file contains several hundred users.

> **CSV**
>
> CSV stands for *Comma-Separated Value*. A CSV file is a text file containing data items separated from each other by a comma. This type of file can be edited by any spreadsheet application, such as Microsoft Excel, Open Office Calc, or Apple Numbers. When reading the file, the spreadsheet software moves to the next column each time it encounters a comma and to the next line each time it encounters a line break. A very wide range of applications support exporting and importing data in CSV format, which makes CSV one of the preferred ways for exchanging information between virtually any system.

Before starting the actual import, let's examine the CSV file provided in the download associated with this book by performing the following steps:

1. Open the `users/internalUsers.csv` file of the download associated with this book using the default spreadsheet application installed on your system.

2. Take some time to inspect the content of the file. You should find four rows and six columns, as shown in the following screenshot:

	A	B	C	D	E	F
1	Employee name	Employee eMail	Employee ID	Department	Job Title	Location
2	<YOUR NAME HERE>	<YOUR EMAIL HERE>	ADMIN	ADMIN	CEO	<YOUR CITY HERE>
3	Learner 02	<ADD EMAIL HERE>	L547896	Marketing	Marketing Specialist	San Jose
4	Instructor 01	<ADD EMAIL HERE>	I596321	Learning & Development	Senior Trainer	New York
5						

Figure 5.6 – The internalUsers.csv file, as seen in Microsoft Excel

3. Type your full name (as it appears in your existing user profile in Learning Manager) in cell A2 and the associated email address in cell B2.

When you import users using a CSV file, a manager is *always* defined for the users you import. If you do not explicitly provide this information in a dedicated column of the CSV file, the system defines one of the existing platform administrators as the **Manager** of the imported users. To make this possible, the chosen administrator must be part of the CSV import and must be defined *before* the other users. This is why you need to add your name in the first line of the CSV file.

4. Type the email address you created for *Learner 02* in cell B3 and the email address you created for *Instructor 01* in cell B4.

5. When you're done, save the CSV file and close the spreadsheet application. The CSV file is now ready to be imported into Adobe Learning Manager.

6. Return to the **Internal Users** page of the admin role.

7. Click the **Add** button located in the upper-right corner of the screen and select the **Upload a CSV** option.

8. Drag and drop the `internalUsers.csv` file into the **Upload a CSV** window.

9. Now, you need to map the columns of the CSV file to the fields of the **Add User** form using the drop-down lists that appear on the screen.

   Map the **Name** field to the **Employee name** column of the CSV file, the **E-mail** field to the **Employee email** column, and the **Profile** field to the **Job Title** column. Leave the **Manager's ID** field empty for now.

   Before moving on, notice that the **Employee ID**, **Department**, and **Location** columns of the `.csv` file are not mapped to any Learning Manager fields. This does not mean that these extra columns have no impact. More on this in the *Working with Active Fields* section, later in this chapter.

Troubleshooting column mapping

If the column mapping does not work as expected, check that the separator used in the CSV file is indeed a comma (,). Depending on the regional settings of your system, the separator may have been replaced by a semicolon (;). To solve this problem, open the CSV file in a text editor (such as Notepad on Windows or TextEdit on Mac) and use the **Find and Replace** feature of the text editor to replace all semicolons (;) with commas (,).

---

10. When you're ready, click the **Save** button in the lower-right corner of the **Upload a CSV** window.

11. A message will inform you that the CSV upload was successful and that the CSV file is currently being processed by the system. Click the **Close** button to return to the **Internal Users** page.

After a short while, two additional users appear in the **Internal Users** list. As shown in the following screenshot, these two users are currently **Unregistered**, which means that they do not yet use a Learning Manager license and therefore do not yet have access to the system:

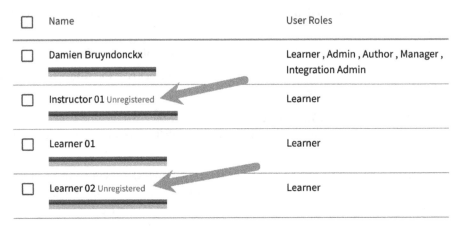

Name	User Roles
Damien Bruyndonckx	Learner , Admin , Author , Manager , Integration Admin
Instructor 01 Unregistered	Learner
Learner 01	Learner
Learner 02 Unregistered	Learner

Figure 5.7 – Instructor 01 and Learner 02 are currently marked as unregistered users

12. Click one of the two **Unregistered** users to open its detailed information.

13. Notice that *you* are defined as the Manager of that user.

Instructor 01 and *Learner 02* are now part of the **Internal Users** list, but they do not have access to the platform yet. You will register these two users in the next section.

> **Save the .csv file**
>
> Make sure you save the .csv file you used in this section. You will need it again in the *Working with Active Fields* section later in this chapter.

Registering imported users

In the previous section, you created *Instructor 01* and *Learner 02* using a CSV import. These users are currently marked as **Unregistered** users.

Unregistered users have not received the welcome email and therefore cannot yet log into the system. Perform the following steps to register these users:

1. Make sure you are logged in as an Administrator and that you are on the **Internal Users** page.

2. Use the checkboxes in the first column to select the two **Unregistered** users. If you have a large number of **Unregistered** users to select, you can use the **Users** filter located above the list of users.

3. Click the **Actions** link located in the upper-right corner of the screen and select the **Register** option.

4. Click **Yes** to confirm. This action registers the users and sends the welcome email.

5. Click the **Close** button to clear the **Users Registered Successfully** message.

You should now take the necessary time to log into the email accounts of *Instructor 01* and *Learner 02* to create their Adobe IDs. This will give them the ability to log in to your Learning Manager account.

Note that, at this time, the *Instructor 01* user is defined as a regular Learner, so when logging in as *Instructor 01*, you are automatically redirected to the Learner experience. You will assign the *Instructor* role to that user in the *Managing roles* section later in this chapter.

> **Your new Manager role**
>
> Since you have been defined as the Manager of *Instructor 01* and *Learner 02*, you should now have access to the **Manager** role, which you can access using the user icon in the upper-right corner of the screen. If you do not see the new **Manager** role in the menu, log out of the system, then log back in. You will explore the manager role in more detail in *Chapter 6, Enrolling Learners in Courses*.

At this point, you should have a total of four registered users in your Learning Manager account: yourself, as the platform administrator, as well as *Learner 01*, *Learner 02*, and *Instructor 01* currently registered as Learners.

In the next section, you will create one more internal user using a self-registration link.

Creating a self-registration link

In the last two sections, you, the account administrator, created new users. In this section, you will allow users to register *themselves* to your ALM account. The idea is to generate a self-registration link and share that link with users who might be interested in joining your Learning Manager account. Users can then click the link and fill out a form to register *themselves* on the platform.

Once properly configured, this feature does not require any further intervention from you. Let's get started:

1. Make sure you are logged in as an administrator and that you are on the **Internal Users** page.

2. Click the **Add** button located in the upper-right corner and choose the **Self-Registration** option. This opens the **Add Self-Registration** profile form.

3. Enter a profile name in the **Profile Name** field.

4. Enter your name in the **Manager's Name** field. It is important to note that the manager must be a user who is already registered on your ALM account. The chosen manager does not need to be an administrator; you can choose any learner as a manager.

Note that the **Profile Name** and **Manager's Name** fields are the only two required fields in this form.

5. As a best practice, also supply a short **Description** for this self-registration profile.

6. You can also supply an optional image using the **Add Image** field. (A sample picture is provided in the download associated with this book. Look for the `branding/o21DevTeam.png` image.)

7. When the **Add Self-Registration Profile** form looks as follows, click the **Save** button located in the lower-right corner of the form:

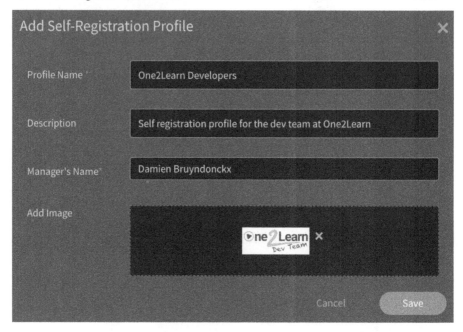

Figure 5.8 – Filing in the Add Self-Registration Profile form

After saving the new self-registration profile, Adobe Learning Manager generates a unique URL that you must share with potential learners. This unique URL is displayed onscreen and is also sent by email confirming the creation of the new self-registration profile.

You can create as many self-registration profiles as needed (keep an eye on the number of user licenses you have purchased!). For example, each department of the organization can have a self-registration profile with a different manager assigned to each profile. This allows you to add users to your account without any action being required from an administrator, all while respecting the hierarchical structure of your organization.

Using a self-registration profile to auto-register as a learner

Now that a self-registration profile is active, you will switch hats again and put yourself in the shoes of a user who wants to register to your ALM account. You will use the self-registration link you configured in the previous section to create *Manager 01*.

Keep in mind that, by default, all internal users must have an Adobe ID. So, one of the steps in the self-registration process is for users to create their own Adobe ID. Let's experiment with this workflow by performing the following steps:

1. Open a new private window in your web browser (or another browser altogether).

2. Paste the auto-registration URL you generated in the previous section in the address bar. This takes you to the Adobe **Sign in** page.

3. Click the **Create an account** link to create a new Adobe ID for *Manager 01*.

4. Fill in the **Create an account** form and click the **Create account** button when you're done.

5. You should be automatically redirected to the Learner experience of your ALM account and logged in as *Manager 01*.

Take a look in the upper-right corner of the screen. You should recognize the image you uploaded while defining the self-registration link in the previous section:

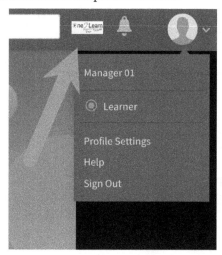

Figure 5.9 – The self-registration image is visible in the top-right corner of the screen

At the end of this section, you have yet another learner registered on your ALM account. In the *Managing roles* section, later in this chapter, you will make this new user a manager, but for now, you will return to the Administrator role to review how the self-registration link can be managed in the long run.

Administering self-registration links

In this section, you will take on your Administrator hat again and review the options available for managing the new self-registration link:

1. Return to the Administrator application on the **Internal Users** page. Confirm that *Manager 01* has been included as a **Learner** in the list of **Internal Users**.

2.   Above the list of users, click the **Self-Registration** tab, as shown in the following screenshot:

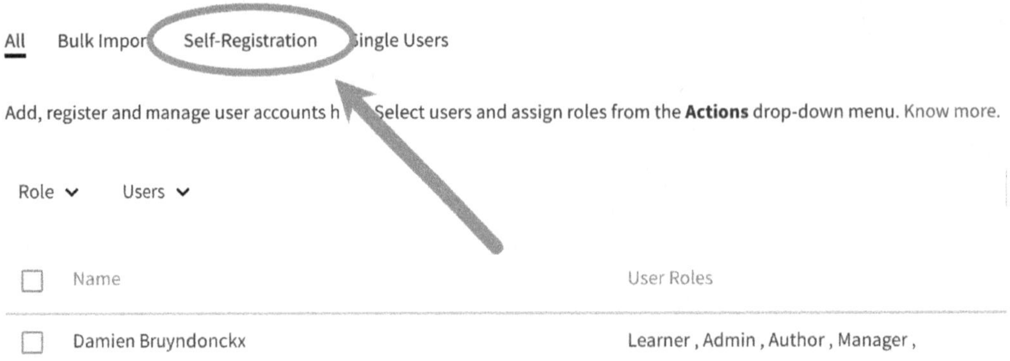

All   Bulk Import   Self-Registration   Single Users

Add, register and manage user accounts h   Select users and assign roles from the **Actions** drop-down menu. Know more.

Role ⌄   Users ⌄

☐   Name   User Roles

☐   Damien Bruyndonckx   Learner , Admin , Author , Manager ,

Figure 5.10 – Clicking the Self-Registration tab above the list of users

This takes you to the list of self-registration profiles, where you can see the number of learners who have used each of these profiles to register for your ALM account.

3.   Hover over the profile you created in the previous section. This reveals a link icon that you can use to copy the self-registration link to the clipboard.

4.   Click the profile name to open the **Edit Self-Registration Profile** form, where you can modify the profile's **Description** and image. Note that you cannot modify the **Profile Name** or **Manager's Name** fields.

5.   Click the **Cancel** button to close the form.

6.   Click the number that appears in the **No. of People** column for your registration profile. This takes you to the list of learners who have used this self-registration profile to register to the platform.

7.   Click the **Internal** link located in the **Users** section of the left sidebar to return to the list of **Internal Users**. Then, click the **Self-Registration** tab to return to the list of self-registration profiles.

8.   Use the checkbox in the first column of the list to select the self-registration profile you created earlier.

9.   Open the **Actions** button located in the upper-right corner of the screen to inspect the available actions.

There are three actions available in this list:

- The **Delete** action deletes the selected self-registration profile(s). Be very careful when using this action as it also deletes all the users that have used these self-registration profiles to register to your ALM account.

- The **Pause** action allows you to temporarily disable the selected registration profile(s). This prevents additional users from registering using that link but does *not* remove or disable users already registered. That's why the **Pause** action is usually preferred to the **Delete** action described previously.

- The **Resume** action restores the possibility to self-register using that link.

These actions give you all the necessary tools to create and manage internal users and self-registration profiles.

In the next section, you will learn how to add external users to your ALM account.

Creating external users

So far, you have created internal users. Internal users are individuals who are part of your organization. A typical internal user is a regular employee. However, there are many use cases where people outside your organization also need access to your account. These include the following:

- You need to provide access to customers who have purchased training from you

- You need to provide training to external partners, suppliers, franchisees, or contractors

- You must provide Instructor access to an external provider that your organization has contracted to deliver instructor-led courses

- Your organization has outsourced the creation of training materials to external eLearning agencies, and you want to provide Author access to the people working in those agencies so that they can upload the content they create directly to your account

Users who are not part of your organization are considered external users. They enjoy the same experience as internal users except that they cannot be made Administrators or Integration Admins.

External users can only be created through an **External Registration Profile**, similar to a self-registration profile used by internal users. Perform the following steps to create an external registration profile:

1. Make sure you are logged in as an Administrator.

2. From the **Administrator** home page, click the **Users** link located in the **Manage** section of the left sidebar.

3. Then, click the **External** link located in the **Users** section of the left sidebar. This takes you to the **External Users** page.

4. Click the **Add** button located in the upper-right corner of the screen to open the **Add External Registration Profile** form.

5. Type a profile name in the **Profile Name** field.

6. Type an email ID in the **Manager Email** field. This is the email ID of a contact person in the external organization. Details about this registration profile, along with instructions on how to use it, will be sent to this email address upon profile creation. This is not to be confused with the **Manager** role within ALM.

> **Tip**
> Enter a working email address you have access to in the **Manager Email** field so that you can review the default email message ALM sends to external managers.

7. Type a number in the **Seats Allotted** field. This represents the maximum number of learners that can register through this registration profile. Keep in mind that Adobe Learning Manager is a paid product that is charged by the seat, so this is very important information for controlling your costs.

8. Select an expiry date in the **Expiry** field. This is a deadline after which it is no longer possible to register users using this profile. However, existing users continue to have access to the platform after the **Expiry** date.

That's it for the required fields, but before hitting the **Save** button and creating the external registration profile, let's review the other fields of the form.

9. As a best practice, enter a short description in the **Description** field. You can also provide an image using the **Add Image** field. (A sample image is provided in the download associated with this book. Look for the `branding/xTernalCo.png` image.)

10. Click the **Advanced Settings** link located in the lower-left corner of the form.

11. Enter a number in the **Login Requirement** field. Registered users that do not log in to your account for the specified number of days are automatically deleted. This ensures that you are not charged for seats that are not *actually* used by learners.

12. You can also specify a comma-separated list of domains in the **Allowed Domains** field. Typically, you would enter the external organization's email domain(s) in this field. This prevents users who do not have an email address in that (these) domain(s) from registering to your account using that link.

13. Finally, you can check the **Email Verification Required** checkbox if you want Learning Manager to validate the external user's email address before officially registering the user.

14. When the **Add External Registration Profile** page looks as follows, click the **Save** button located in the lower-right corner of the form. This opens a message showing the unique URL to that registration profile:

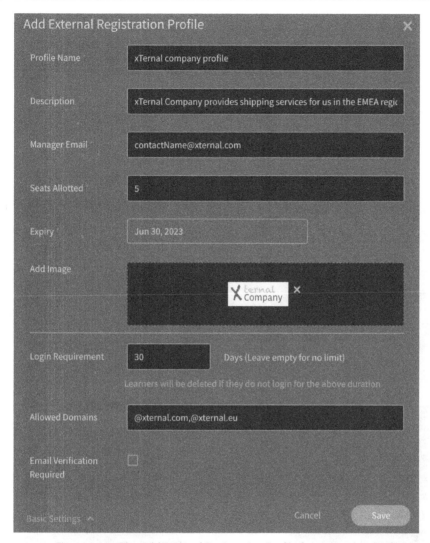

Figure 5.11 – The Add External Registration Profile form completed

Manager versus Manager

The **Manager Email** property you used when creating the external registration profile has nothing to do with the **Manager** role within Adobe Learning Manager. It is the email address of a contact person in the external organization who is responsible for distributing the link to your external registration profile. This contact person does not have access to your ALM account, neither as a learner nor as a Manager, unless of course this person registers using the external registration link, in which case that person is considered an external learner by Adobe Learning Manager.

15. Click the **Close** button to close the message and return to the **External Users** page of the Administrator role, where the new external registration profile is visible in the list.

16. The last step is to make this profile active by toggling the **Status** button *on* in the last column of the list.

The new external registration profile is now up and running. An email containing the unique link to this registration profile is sent to the **Manager Email** address you supplied when defining the registration profile, as illustrated in the following screenshot:

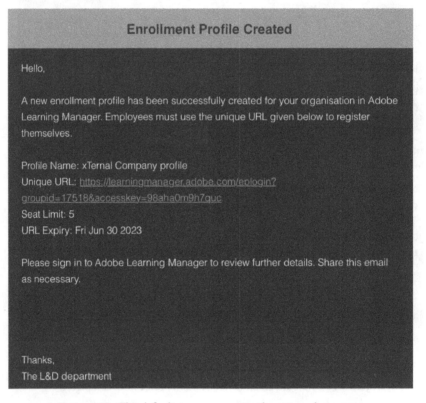

Figure 5.12 – The default message sent to the external manager
when creating an external enrollment profile

In the next section, you will pretend to be an employee of this external organization that needs to access your ALM account. You will use the registration profile you just created to register.

Registering as an external user

Now that you have a working external registration profile, let's switch hats again and become, for a few moments, that external employee who needs access to your Adobe Learning Manager account. You will use this technique to create a user named *Learner 03*. Follow these steps:

1. Open a new private window in your web browser.

2. Navigate to the unique link of the external profile you created in the previous section.

> **Tip**
>
> If you no longer have access to the unique link for the external registration profile, go to the **External Users** page of the administrator role in ALM and hover over the external registration profile to make two icons appear. The *envelope* icon allows you to resend the manager email, while the *chain* icon allows you to copy the link to the external registration profile to the clipboard.

3. Fill in the registration form to create a new user named *Learner 03* using the email address you created for *Learner 03* at the beginning of this chapter.

4. Click the **Register** button when you're done.

This last action creates a new external user in Adobe Learning Manager. It also redirects that user to the Learner experience of your account. Looking at the top-right corner of the screen, you see the logo of the external organization that you uploaded when defining the external registration profile, as shown in the following screenshot:

Figure 5.13 – The new external user being redirected to the learning experience of your Prime account

Notice that, by default, external users do *not* have to create an Adobe ID to access your account. They must also log in to Adobe Learning Manager using a special login page that is emailed to them when they register. These are other important differences between internal and external users. In the *Configuring login methods* section, later in this chapter, you will review the options available to decide on the login methods for both internal and external users.

To conclude this section, let's return to the Admin role of your account to review the options used to administer external users in the long run.

Administering external users

Now that you have a working external user profile and a user has used this profile to register to your account, you will go back to the Admin role and review the options that allow you to administer external users:

1. Return to the Administrator role of your Adobe Learning Manager account.
2. From the **Administrator** home page, click the **Users** link located in the **Manage** section of the left sidebar.
3. Next, click the **External** link in the **Users** section of the left sidebar. This takes you back to the **External Users** page, where the external registration profile you created earlier is visible.

From here, a few key pieces of information about the external user profile are available at a glance. As shown in the following screenshot, you can see the number of **Seats Used**, the **Expiry** date, **Login Requirement**, as well as its **Status**:

	Partner Org Name	Seats Used	Expiry	Login Requirement	Status
☐	xTernal Company profile	1 / 5	Jun 30, 2023	30 days	⬤

Figure 5.14 – Key information about external user profiles is available at a glance

4. Click the external user profile name visible in the first column of the list. This opens the **Edit External Registration Profile** form, which you can use to modify the information about the external registration profile.
5. Click the **Cancel** button to close the form.
6. Click **Seats Used** to access a list of users that have registered using this external registration link.
7. Click the **External** link located in the **Users** section of the left sidebar to return to the **External Users** page.

8. Use the checkbox in the first column of the **External Users** page to select the registration profile you created previously.

9. Click the **Actions** button in the upper-right corner of the screen to review the available actions.

There are two actions available in the list: the **Pause** action and the **Resume** action. Use the **Pause** action to temporarily disable the ability to create new users via this external registration profile. Note that existing users retain their ability to log into your Learning Manager account, even though the external registration profile has been paused. You can use the **Resume** action to restore the ability for external users to register using this external registration profile. This feature is useful for seasonal staff who need to register during a given period.

10. Click the **Status** toggle button to toggle the external registration profile *off*.

When the external registration profile is turned off, three things happen. First, it is no longer possible to create new users via that external registration profile; second, existing users that were created via that external registration profile lose their ability to log into your account; and third, the licenses used by this registration profile are released, which means that they can be reassigned to other users. These are the nuances that make *deactivating* an external registration profile different from *pausing* it. Toggling an external registration profile off is useful in situations such as the end of a partnership, the end of a training agreement, the acquisition or closure of an external partner, and so on.

11. Before moving on to the next section, make sure you reactivate the external registration profile by turning its **Status** back *on*.

With that, you have created all the users you need to continue with the exercises in this book. Before moving on, here is a quick summary of the users you created in the last few sections:

- You should have five users, in addition to your original Administrator profile.
- Four of those users are internal users, while the fifth one is external.
- The internal users are named *Instructor 01*, *Learner 01*, *Learner 02*, and *Manager 01*. The external user is named *Learner 03*.
- At the moment, all these additional users are learners. You have not yet assigned special roles to any of them.
- You have also successfully tested the ability to log in as these users.

Creating these users has given you a comprehensive overview of the various ways you can create users in Adobe Learning Manager. You manually created a user using the **Single User** option, you imported users using the **CSV Import** option, and you created **Self-Registration** links for internal users, as well as an **External Registration Profile** for external users.

You are now ready to move on to the next section, where you will learn how to grab custom pieces of information about the users of your account.

Working with Active Fields

When creating users in the previous sections, you only had to provide basic user information. This is in contrast to most corporate directories, which contain much more information about employees. Data such as the department, employee ID, location, language, and more is very common. This additional data plays a vital role in the day-to-day operations of an organization. Moreover, the way this information is organized, as well as its content, is specific to each organization.

As an enterprise LMS, Adobe Learning Manager understands the importance of this additional metadata to your organization. Therefore, it allows you to capture this data and use it in different areas of the system, such as user management, skills management, learner enrollment, reporting, and more.

In Learning Manager, this is the purpose of **Active Fields**, which you can define and customize according to your specific needs. This is what you will discover in this section using the following steps:

1. Make sure you are logged in as an Administrator.
2. From the **Administrator** home page, click the **Users** link located in the **Manage** section of the left sidebar. This takes you to the **Internal Users** page.
3. Click the **Active Fields** link located in the **Advanced** section of the left sidebar.

This last action takes you to the **Active Fields** page, where you can define additional fields for both internal and external users, as shown in the following screenshot:

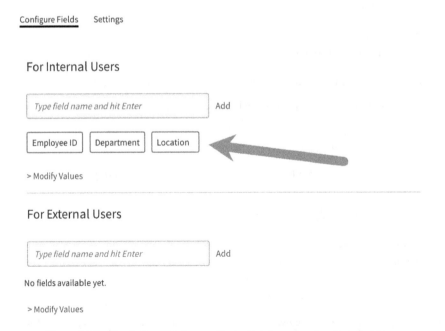

Figure 5.15 – The Active Fields page for both internal and external users

For internal users, notice that three fields (the **Employee ID**, **Department**, and **Location** fields) have already been defined (see the arrow in the preceding screenshot).

Activating and customizing CSV fields

These three extra fields correspond to the three unmapped columns of the CSV file that you imported in the *Importing users from a CSV file* section, earlier in this chapter. By default, these extra fields have no influence on Adobe Learning Manager and no data has been entered into any of these fields. You can change this default behavior by performing the following steps:

1. Click the **Settings** tab, as illustrated in the following screenshot:

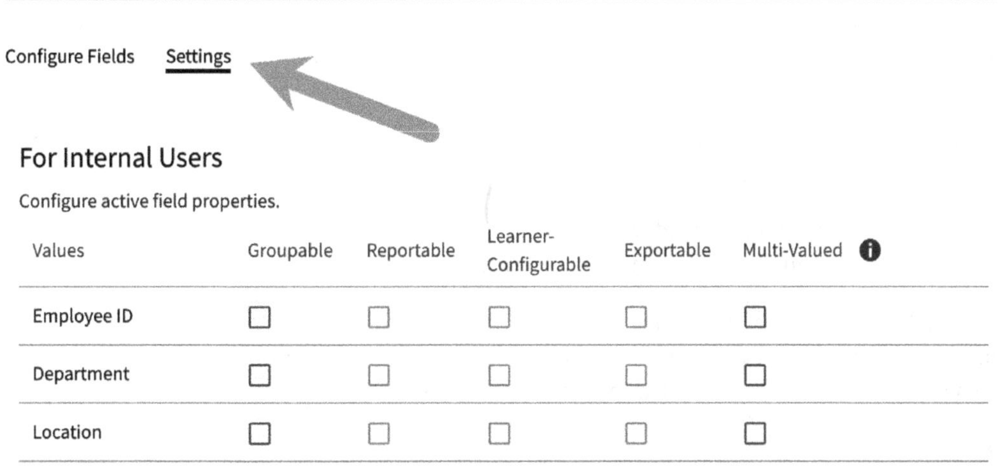

Configure Fields   Settings

For Internal Users

Configure active field properties.

Values	Groupable	Reportable	Learner-Configurable	Exportable	Multi-Valued ⓘ
Employee ID	☐	☐	☐	☐	☐
Department	☐	☐	☐	☐	☐
Location	☐	☐	☐	☐	☐

Figure 5.16 – Click the Settings tab to reach this page

This action takes you to a page with a table containing the three CSV fields and several checkboxes. By default, none of these checkboxes are selected, as shown in the preceding screenshot.

2. Select the **Groupable** checkbox for the **Department** and **Location** fields. This action also selects most of the other checkboxes.

By selecting the **Groupable** checkbox, you instruct Adobe Learning Manager to automatically create additional user groups based on these fields. Since the **Employee ID** field is unique to each employee, there is no point in creating groups based on that field. This is why you left this field unselected. You will learn more about automatic and custom user groups in the *Working with user groups* section later in this chapter.

The **Reportable**, **Learner Configurable**, and **Exportable** checkboxes were automatically selected when you selected the **Groupable** checkbox:

- The **Reportable** checkbox makes the field available in reports created by Adobe Learning Manager. You will learn more about the reporting features of Adobe Learning Manager in *Chapter 10, Reporting in Adobe Learning Manager*.

- The **Learner Configurable** checkbox determines whether learners have access to these fields when they complete their user profile.

- The **Exportable** checkbox determines whether this field is part of the reports you can export from Adobe Learning Manager. This will be discussed along with the other reporting features in *Chapter 10, Reporting in Adobe Learning Manager*.

This is a very powerful feature! It allows you to import any piece of information into Adobe Learning Manager and use it to create user groups and reports. Most of the time, you do not want users to tamper with this data.

3. Deselect the **Learner Configurable** checkbox for all the fields to prevent learners from tampering with this data via their user profile.

4. Click the **Save** button located in the upper-right corner of the page to save the changes. You should receive an email confirming these changes.

These extra fields have now been activated and configured. At this point, it does not change anything about the platform or the user experience provided by your ALM account since no data has been entered into these fields at this time. Data will be entered into these fields during the next `.csv` import.

Let's give it a try by importing the `.csv` file we used in the *Importing Users from a CSV File* section again.

5. Click the **Internal** link located in the **Users** section of the left sidebar.

6. Click the **Add** button located in the upper-right corner of the screen and choose the **Upload a CSV** option.

7. Drag and drop the `users/internalUsers.csv` file you used in the *Importing Users from a CSV File* section earlier in this chapter into the **Upload a CSV** field.

8. Since you have already used this same file for a previous import, Learning Manager should remember the column mapping, but double-checking is always helpful.

9. Click the **Save** button to start the import process and close the **CSV Upload Successful** message.

It should not take long for Learning Manager to process this small `.csv` file. Once the processing is complete (watch for a notification in the *Bell* icon in the upper-right corner of the screen), you will take your first look at the **User Groups** section of the Admin role.

10. Click the **User Groups** link located in the **User Groups** section of the left sidebar.

Once on the **User Groups** page, notice that Adobe Learning Manager has already created several user groups automatically. Because you selected the **Groupable** checkbox for the **Location** and **Department** fields in the .csv file, Learning Manager has automatically created user groups based on these fields:

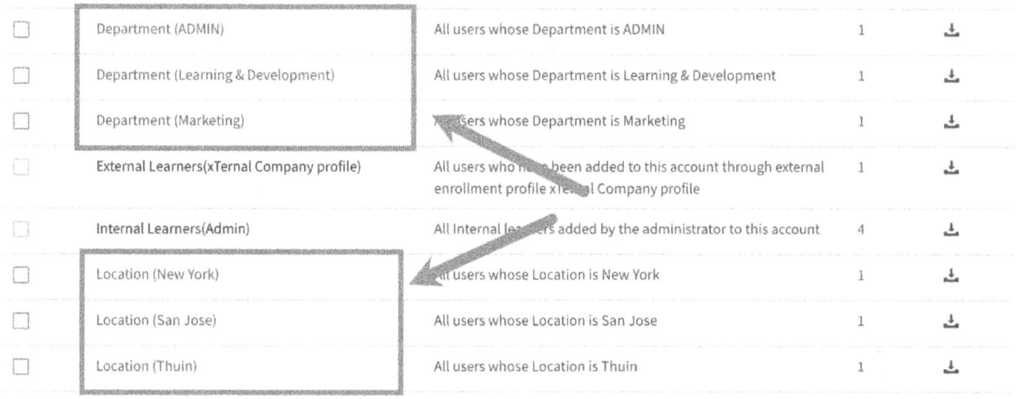

☐	Department (ADMIN)	All users whose Department is ADMIN	1	⤓
☐	Department (Learning & Development)	All users whose Department is Learning & Development	1	⤓
☐	Department (Marketing)	users whose Department is Marketing	1	⤓
☐	External Learners(xTernal Company profile)	All users who have been added to this account through external enrollment profile xTernal Company profile	1	⤓
☐	Internal Learners(Admin)	All Internal learners added by the administrator to this account	4	⤓
☐	Location (New York)	All users whose Location is New York	1	⤓
☐	Location (San Jose)	All users whose Location is San Jose	1	⤓
☐	Location (Thuin)	All users whose Location is Thuin	1	⤓

Figure 5.17 – Learning Manager creates User Groups based on the Groupable fields of the .csv file

You will learn more about **User Groups** in the *Working with User Groups* section later in this chapter.

In this section, you activated, configured, and populated the Active Fields that are present in the CSV file used to import users into your ALM account. In the next section, you will create additional **Active Fields** from scratch.

Creating Custom Active Fields

Adobe Learning Manager also allows you to create additional custom fields from scratch. In this section, you will create the *Hobbies* field to allow users to enter their hobbies in their user profile. After all, this can be an important piece of data for skills management, as the skills you acquire from your hobbies can be valuable in the workplace. Let's get started:

1. Make sure you are logged in as an Administrator and that you are on the **Users** page.

2. Click the **Active Fields** link located in the **Advanced** section of the left sidebar.

3. Make sure you are on the **Configure Fields** tab and not on the **Settings** tab.

4. Type Hobbies in the **Type field name and hit Enter** field for **Internal Users** and hit the *Enter* key or click the **Add** link.

5. Next, click the **Modify Values** link in the **Internal Users** section of the page.

6. Open the **Select Field** dropdown and choose the **Hobbies** fields.

7. Inspect the available options, but do not modify anything at this time. Click the **Done** button when you're ready.

8. Finally, click the **Save** button located in the upper-right corner of the page.

Thanks to these steps, you have created a new custom field from scratch. This one is a free text field where users can type anything they want: they are not restricted to a drop-down list of predefined elements. Let's take a look at it.

9. Click the **Internal** link located in the **Users** section of the left sidebar.

10. Click your name in the list of users to open the details of your user account.

11. Click the pencil icon located in the upper-right corner of your user's details to open the **Edit User** form.

Confirm that the **Hobbies** field is now available at the end of the **Edit User** form. Don't hesitate to enter your hobbies before clicking the **Save** button:

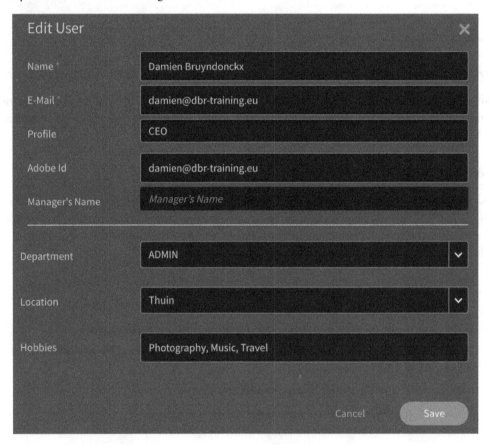

Figure 5.18 – The Hobbies field is now available at the end of the Edit User form

After completing the last few sections, you have added three additional fields to the user form. You will now review how users can enter data in these fields.

Entering data in the additional custom fields

In the previous sections, you created three additional fields: the **Department** and **Location** fields, which came from the CSV file you imported earlier in this chapter, and the **Hobbies** field, which you created from scratch.

You also entered your hobbies in the **Hobbies** fields of your user account manually. As an administrator, you could enter this information for each user, one by one, but that would quickly become tedious. A better approach is to have users enter this data themselves the next time they log in. Well, it turns out this is exactly the default behavior of Adobe Learning Manager! Let's check this out by performing the following steps:

1. Open another browser or a new private window of your web browser.

2. Use this new private window to log into your ALM account as *Learner 01*.

3. Once logged in as *Learner 01*, you are immediately prompted to enter your hobbies in the **Hobbies** field.

4. Enter some data in the **Hobbies** field and click the **Proceed** button.

Note that users can only enter their hobbies; they do not have access to the **Location** and **Department** fields. This is because you deselected the **Learner Configurable** checkbox for these last two fields in the administrator area.

5. Click the user icon in the upper-right corner of the screen to log out as *Learner 01*.

6. Once logged out, browse the URL that was sent by email to *Learner 03* when that user registered to your ALM account.

> **Accessing the custom login page**
>
> If you do not remember the custom login URL or if you no longer have access to this email, go to the **External Users** page of the Admin role and hover over the external registration profile you created earlier. Click the *chain* icon that appears to copy the custom link to the clipboard. Then, return to the private browser window and paste the link in the address bar. When the page loads, click the **Already Registered** link to access the custom login page.

When logging in as *Learner 03*, notice that the **Complete Profile** form does *not* appear. This is because *Learner 03* is an external user and you created custom fields for internal users only.

7. Make sure you log out as *Learner 03* before moving on.

Thanks to this default behavior, each user is prompted to enter data in the new custom fields the next time they log in.

In the last few sections, you examined the **Active Fields** feature of Adobe Learning Manager, which allows you to customize the user form and capture additional data. In subsequent chapters, you'll see how this additional metadata enhances the platform's reporting capabilities. But for now, let's move on to the next section, where you'll learn more about **User Groups**.

Working with user groups

As the list of users grows, it quickly becomes difficult to manage users individually. This is one of the reasons why administrators generally prefer to manage groups of users.

When creating user groups, you want to group users based on common characteristics. This can be the members of a team, users working at a specific location, users speaking a certain language, users that have the same manager, users that have the same role, and so on. Grouping people in this way has several advantages:

- First, it facilitates users and skills management. For example, you can enroll a group of users in a course rather than enrolling each learner individually. You can also assign skills to user groups rather than assigning skills to each user.

- It also simplifies the automation of certain tasks. For example, when a user becomes a manager (that is, when the user becomes a member of the managers' group), that user is automatically enrolled in the management onboarding course.

- Groups are also useful for reporting purposes.

In Adobe Learning Manager, you can have an infinite number of groups, each user can be a member of an infinite number of groups, and a group can be a member of another group. We'll take a closer look at this in the next few sections.

Inspecting autogenerated groups

Adobe Learning Manager understands that creating groups and manually assigning users to groups is a daunting, time-consuming, and error-prone task. The Learning Manager team has also noticed that some groups are very common across many organizations. Therefore, a large number of groups are automatically generated by the system based on various aspects, such as roles, user hierarchy, active fields, and more. Let's review these autogenerated groups by following these steps:

1. Make sure you are logged in as an administrator.

2. From the **Administrator** home page, click the **Users** link located in the **Manage** section of the left sidebar. When on the **Users** page, click the **User Groups** link in the left sidebar.

This takes you to the **User Groups** page. Notice that a large number of groups are already available. These user groups have been automatically generated by Adobe Learning Manager. Taking a look at the list of autogenerated groups, you should see the following:

- Some groups, such as **All Admins, All Authors**, and **All Learners**, are based on the user role within the ALM account.

- The **All External Users** group lists all the external users, regardless of the external registration profile used to register to Learning Manager. In addition to that, other groups are automatically generated for each of the external registration profiles defined on your account.

- Groups such as **<your name>'s Team** are automatically generated based on the user hierarchy defined by the **Manager Email** field of the user profile.

- One group is created for each profile. **Profile** is another field present in the user creation form. Most of the time, it corresponds to the user's job title or department within the organization. This type of autogenerated group is very useful as it represents more or less the way your organization is structured.

- Also, remember that some groups have been automatically generated based on the custom fields defined on the **Active Field** page, as discussed in the *Working with Active Fields* section earlier in this chapter.

You can view the list of users in each group by clicking the number in the **No. of People** column. Take some time to inspect these **Auto-generated** groups and the users they contain.

These groups are automatically *generated* and *maintained* by Adobe Learning Manager. So, when users are added, deleted, or updated, these groups are modified accordingly without any action from you.

These auto-generated groups may be all you need to effectively manage the users of your Learning Manager account, but your organization may also need other, more customized user groups. That's why Learning Manager also allows you to create custom groups. This will be discussed in the next section.

Creating custom groups

In this section, you will create the *Advisory Board* group. This group comprises the CEO, some managers, and some employees. It does not correspond to any department, location, role, or hierarchical relationship in the organization and therefore cannot be automatically generated by Adobe Learning Manager.

Perform the following steps to create a new custom user group:

1. From the **User Groups** page, click the **Add** button located in the upper-right corner of the screen. This brings up the **Add User Group** form.
2. Enter Advisory Board in the **Name** field.
3. As a best practice, take the necessary time to supply a short **Description** for your new group.

Finally, you must supply the list of group members. You can add group members individually using either their username or their email ID. You can also select groups of users to create a hierarchy of nested groups.

In this example, you will add a few individual users to the group using their usernames.

4. Use the **Search** field in the **Include Learners** section of the **Add User Group** dialog to look for users. Include yourself, **Manager 01**, and **Learner 02** in the group.

5. When you're done, click the **Save** button located in the lower-right corner of the **Add User Group** form.

Your new custom user group is now visible in the **User Groups** list, as shown in the following screenshot:

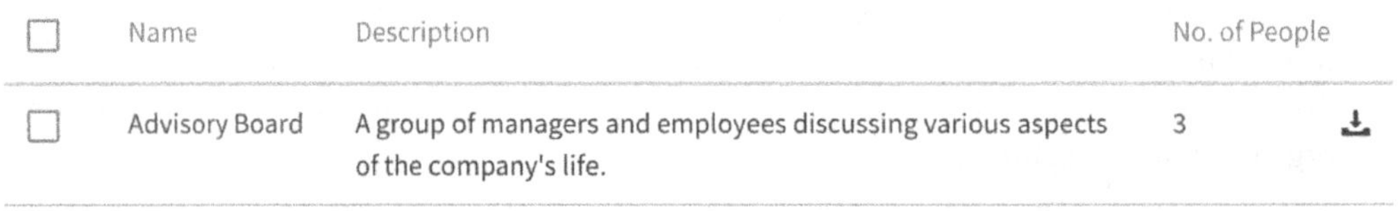

	Name	Description	No. of People	
☐	Advisory Board	A group of managers and employees discussing various aspects of the company's life.	3	⬇

Figure 5.19 – Your new custom user group appears in the User Groups list

To edit the group, click the group name within the list. You can also use the checkbox in the first column to select one or more groups, then the **Actions** button in the upper-right corner of the page to delete the selected group(s). Note that the autogenerated groups cannot be deleted and that deleting a group does *not* delete the users that were a part of the deleted group. Finally, you can filter the list of groups displayed on the screen using the **All**, **Auto-Generated**, and **Custom** tabs, as well as the **Search** field at the top of the page.

In this section, you created a custom group and added users to that group. In the next section, we will discuss how to assign roles to the user of your Learning Manager account.

Managing user roles

Within a platform such as Adobe Learning Manager, *authentication* and *authorization* are the two fundamental aspects of user management. So far in this chapter, we have only focused on authentication. Authentication answers the question *Who are you?*

In this section, you will focus on the *authorization* aspect of user management. Authorization answers the question *What can you do?* Indeed, just because you can authenticate on a platform does not mean that you are allowed to use all its features. For example, learners cannot create courses, authors cannot delete users, and so on. Only the administrator is allowed to access every corner of the platform.

In Learning Manager, authorization is role-based. This means you need to create roles and define what each role can do on the platform. Then, you assign users to these roles.

There are five basic roles already defined in Adobe Learning Manager: **Learner**, **Author**, **Instructor**, **Integration Admin**, and **Administrator**. Let's take a look at them:

- The **Learner** role is the default role assigned to each new user (internal or external). A learner can browse through the Course Catalog, enroll in courses, take courses, and more.

- The **Author** role applies to instructional designers and content creators. They can be internal or external users, and they have access to the Content Library to upload instructional content and create new course modules. They can also assemble these modules into courses and learning programs.

- The **Instructor** role is for teachers that conduct live and virtual class activities. They also review the assignments that have been uploaded by learners through the file submission activity and fill in the checklists defined in the checklist activities.

- The **Integration Admin** role is typically for IT professionals or developers, whose job is to configure the connectors that integrate Adobe Learning Manager with other systems in your organization and to develop applications that use Learning Manager as a backend. Note that external users cannot be made Integration Admins.

- Finally, the **Administrator** role is for those who are in charge of the day-to-day management of your account. They can add and remove users, assign roles to users, create skills, enroll users in courses, and more. They are also in charge of the general setup and maintenance of the platform.

These roles are considered *explicit* roles because they must be explicitly assigned to users by an administrator.

In addition to these five roles, Learning Manager also contains an *implicit* role: **Manager**. This role is considered implicit because it is automatically assigned to a user when their email address is supplied in the **Manager Email** field of another user. Managers can manage the learning of their team members. For example, a manager can enroll team members in courses, approve or reject enrollment requests, generate team reports, track performance, and so on.

You will review the **Manager** role in more detail in *Chapter 6, Enrolling Learners in Courses*, as well as in *Chapter 9, Configuring and Using Feedback*.

For now, you will return to the Admin role of Adobe Learning Manager and start assigning these roles to the users you created in the previous sections.

Assigning explicit roles to users

Now that you have a better understanding of the default roles available in Learning Manager, let's return to the user list and assign roles to users:

1. Make sure you are logged in as an Administrator.

2. From the **Administrator** home page, click the **Users** link located in the **Manage** section of the left sidebar. This takes you to the **Internal Users** page.

3. Use the checkbox in the first column to select the **Instructor 01** user.

4. Click the **Actions** button located in the upper-right corner of the screen and select the **Assign Role** action.

5. Click **Make Instructor** to assign the instructor role to the **Instructor 01** user.

6. Repeat these steps to also assign the **Author** role to the **Instructor 01** user.

As you do so, notice the **Remove Role** option in the list of available actions. Taking a closer look at it, you see that the **Learner** role cannot be removed from a user. In other words, everyone in Learning Manager is a learner!

Before moving on to the next section, let's quickly review the roles that can be assigned to external users.

7. From the **Internal Users** page, click the **External** link located in the **Users** section of the left sidebar.

8. Click the **Seats Used** link associated with the external registration profile you created in the *Creating external users* section, earlier in this chapter.

9. Use the checkbox to select **Learner 03**.

10. Click the **Actions** link located in the upper-right corner of the screen.

11. Hover over the **Assign Role** action and notice that an external user can only be made an **Author** or a **Manager**.

With that, you've learned that an external user cannot become an **Administrator** or an **Integration Admin**. You also learned that, for external users, the **Manager** role is explicit, which is yet another difference between internal and external users. This makes a lot of sense since external users are outside your organization, so you don't have access to information about the role and hierarchy level of external users within their respective organizations.

Once designated as a **Manager**, the external user automatically becomes the manager of all the other *existing and future* external users using the same external registration profile. Also, note that you cannot remove the manager role from an external user.

Assigning the Manager role to an internal user

As discussed at the beginning of this section, there is one additional role available in Adobe Learning Manager: the **Manager** role. The **Manager** role is special in that it is not considered an *explicit* role. To become a manager, you only need to be defined as the manager of another user. Let's check this out by performing the following steps:

1. From the **Administrator** home page, click the **Users** link located in the **Manage** section of the left sidebar to open the **Internal Users** page.

2. Click **Learner 01** in the list of internal users to reveal this user's details.

3. Click the pencil icon associated with **Learner 01** to open the **Edit User** form.

4. Change the value of the **Manager's name** field to define **Manager 01** as the manager of **Learner 01**.

5. Click the **Save** button when you're done.

6. Repeat these steps to make **Manager 01** the manager of **Learner 02** as well.

Once you've done this, you notice that the **Manager** role has automatically been assigned to **Manager 01**, as shown in the following screenshot:

Figure 5.20 – The Manager role is automatically assigned to Manager 01

With **Manager 01** now designated as the manager of **Learner 01** and **Learner 02**, Adobe Learning Manager has automatically created additional User Groups based on this new hierarchy. Let's check this out.

7. Click the **User Groups** link located in the left sidebar.

8. Notice the new **Manager 01's Team** and **Manager 01's Direct Team** groups that have been automatically generated. Also notice that both these groups contain two users.

To better understand the difference between the *Team* and the *Direct Team*, you will now examine the automatically generated groups bearing your name.

9. Still on the **User Groups** page, spot the **<your name>'s Direct Team** group. Once done click the **No. of People** property associated with that group (normally, **2**).

After performing the previous exercises, there should be two users in your direct team: **Instructor 02** and **Manager 01**.

10. Close the **<your name>'s Direct Team** dialog.

11. Now, click the **No. of People** property associated with the **<your name>'s Team** group (normally, **4**).

As shown in the following screenshot, **<your name>'s Team** group also includes **Instructor01** and **Manager 01**. However, since **Manager 01** is a manager in its own right, this user also has its own team. The users in that team are not included in your *direct team*, but they are still part of your *team* at large. The difference between the team and the direct team is the way Learning Manager handles a multi-level hierarchy:

Figure 5.21 – Your team also includes the users of the Manager01 team

Assigning the Manager role

In this section, you used the features of the Admin role to manually define **Manager 01** as the manager of **Learner 01** and **Learner 02**. This technique is good enough for demonstration purposes, but in real life, you will use the `.csv` file import technique to automatically define the user hierarchy that exists in your organization.

Deleting a Manager

Adobe Learning Manager does not allow you to delete a user with the Manager role. To delete a manager, you must first assign a new manager to all users who have the user to be deleted as a manager.

In this section, you reviewed the built-in roles of Adobe Learning Manager. These roles should cover your basic needs, but there are many scenarios where they do not quite fit the bill. That's why Learning Manager allows you to create custom roles, which is what we will cover in the next section.

Creating custom roles

As an enterprise LMS, Adobe Learning Manager allows you to implement a wide range of business requirements. Part of that flexibility relies on the ability to define custom roles. This allows you to address hundreds of custom business requirements, including the following:

- By default, an Administrator is responsible for both the daily operation of your account and for implementing your organization's training strategy. Using custom roles, you can split the Administrator role into a *Platform Admin* role (the main configuration of your account, creating internal and external users, branding your account, and so on) and a *Training Admin* role (enrolling users in courses, managing skills, badges and certifications, generating reports, and more).

- You may want junior authors to only be able to upload new content to the Content Library so that assembling this content into courses remains the prerogative of senior authors. This can be achieved by creating a *Junior Author* custom role.

- You want certain users to be able to run some reports, but without giving them full access to the Admin or Manager role.

Now that you have a better idea of the importance of custom roles, let's review the steps required to create one:

1. Make sure you are logged in as an Administrator.

2. From the **Administrator** home page, click the **Users** link located in the **Manage** section of the left sidebar to access the **Internal Users** page.

3. Then, click the **Custom Roles** link located at the end of the **Advanced** section in the left sidebar to access the **Custom Roles** page.

4. Click the **Create Role** link located in the **Roles** column.

5. Enter a name for the new role (Junior author, in this example) in the **Name of Role** field.

6. Next, you need to specify **Privileges** for the new role. For the *Junior Author* example, you can allow either **Full Control** or access to **Selected Folders** of the Content Library under the **Account Privileges** section.

    Take some time to browse all the privileges that can be included in a **Custom Role** and try to imagine how *your* organization could take advantage of all the possibilities offered by this feature.

    Also, notice the **Scope for Feature Privileges** section, which allows you to restrict the privileges that are allocated to this role to specific catalogs and/or user groups (catalogs will be discussed in *Chapter 14, Working with Catalogs and Peer Accounts*).

7. Finally, use the **Search for users** field in the **Users** section at the very bottom of the form to select the users you wish to assign this custom role to. For this example, assign this custom role to **Learner 01**.

   Note that only internal users can be assigned such custom roles.

8. When you're ready, click the **Save** button located in the upper-right corner of the screen.

From now on, when *Learner 01* logs into your ALM account, that user will see an additional custom role in the **User** menu located in the upper-right corner of the screen, as shown in the following screenshot:

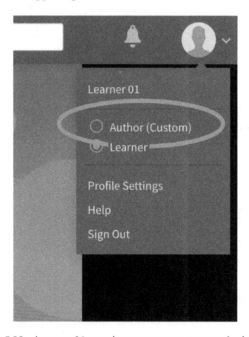

Figure 5.22 – Learner 01 now has access to a custom Author role

The wide range of possible combinations makes custom roles a very powerful feature. There are so many complex scenarios that it is impossible to cover them all in this book.

> **More information on Custom Roles**
>
> For more information on custom roles and privilege management, please refer to the following page, from the official Learning Manager user guide: `https://helpx.adobe.com/learning-manager/administrators/feature-summary/custom-role.html`.

In this section, you created the **Junior Author** custom role and assigned it to the **Learner 01** user. In the next section, we will discuss the login methods and the **Single Sign-On (SSO)** options available in Adobe Learning Manager.

Configuring Login Methods

When creating users, remember that Adobe Learning Manager does not ask for any user password. This is because Learning Manager does not have any authentication mechanism of its own (except for authenticating external users).

When an internal user tries to log into Adobe Learning Manager, the system relies on an external authentication mechanism to authenticate that user. The default authentication mechanism of Adobe Learning Manager is an *Adobe ID*.

Relying on an external authentication service to authenticate users has several advantages:

- As an organization, you can use a single external authentication service to grant a user access to an unlimited number of applications. This technique is called SSO. The idea is to authenticate once against a central authentication service, which, in turn, gives users access to all the services they are allowed to use. This avoids the need for users to authenticate individually to each service. It also saves the organization from maintaining separate authentication directories for each of the applications used in the organization.

- When users change their password, that change is made at the central authentication service. Thus, the new password is immediately available for all applications that the authentication service gives access to. The user does not need to change the password for each service.

- When an employee leaves the organization, deleting the user account at the central authentication service revokes that user's access to all of the organization's applications at once.

- A central authentication service facilitates the daily management of users by the IT team: updating a user in the central authentication service automatically adjusts the access rights of this user to all tools and applications across the organization.

SSO has so many benefits, especially for large organizations, that Learning Manager didn't bother developing its own authentication mechanism. Instead, it is designed to integrate seamlessly with the authentication mechanism available in your organization.

If your organization does not have a centralized authentication mechanism, then Adobe provides its own: the Adobe ID. This is nothing more than a central authentication service that gives you access to all the online services provided by Adobe. The Adobe ID you use to access Learning Manager can also be used to access your Creative Cloud account or other online services, such as Adobe Express, Adobe Colors, the Adobe eLearning community, and others.

Because Learning Manager is designed to use an external SSO provider, it is very easy to configure it to use your organization's SSO provider rather than the Adobe ID. That's what you'll explore in this section. Let's get started:

1. Make sure you are logged in as an Administrator.

2. From the **Administrator** home page, click the **Settings** link located in the **Configure** section at the end of the left sidebar.

3. Then, click the **Login Methods** link located in the **Integrations** section of the left sidebar. This takes you to the **Login Methods** page, where you can define how internal and external users authenticate to Adobe Learning Manager.

As shown in the following screenshot, the default **Login Method** for internal users is **Adobe ID**, while the default login method for external users is **Adobe Learning Manager ID**:

Internal Users

Default Login Method
This will be the default login method
if multiple SSO is not configured

> Adobe ID   ⌄

Internal Users can log into this account using their Adobe Ids.

☐ Enable Multiple Single Sign-On(SSO) for login

External Users

Default Login Method
This will be the default login method
if multiple SSO is not configured

> Adobe Learning Manager ID   ⌄

External users can log on to this account after creating their Adobe Learning Manager username and password.

☐ Enable Multiple Single Sign-On(SSO) for login

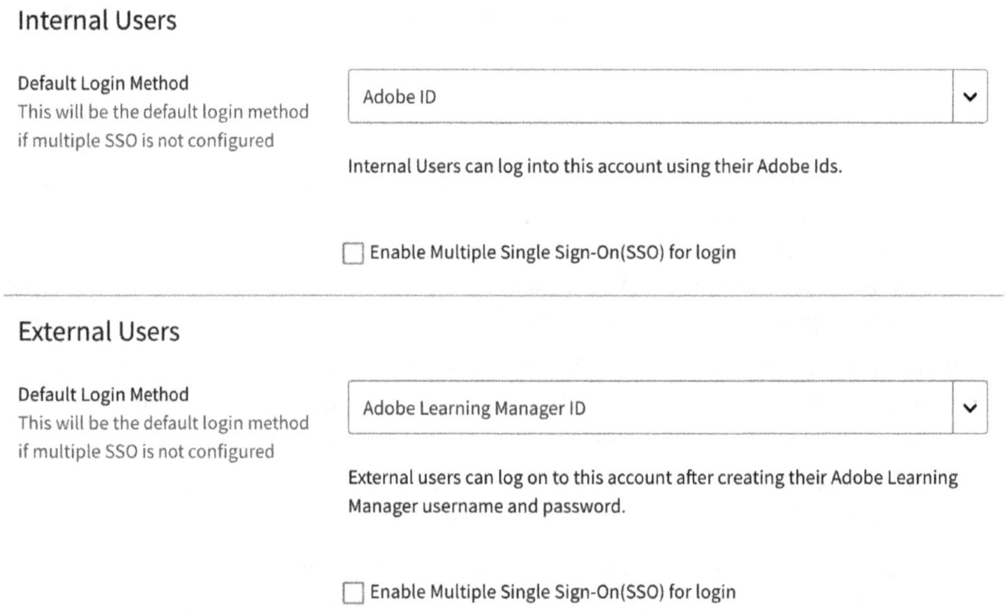

Figure 5.23 – The default login methods for internal and external users

Interestingly, **Adobe Learning Manager ID** is the only authentication mechanism specific to Learning Manager. It is an exception to the all-external authentication strategy used by the platform for internal users.

4. Open the **Login** drop-down list for **Internal Users** to inspect the available options.

5. Select the **Single Sign-On** option.

Remember that the Adobe ID *is* an SSO mechanism, so the **Single Sign-On** option simply allows you to switch from one SSO provider (Adobe ID) to another (your own)!

Now, you need to provide an SSO configuration in the **SSO Setup** field. Unfortunately, no **SSO Setup** is currently available in the drop-down menu.

6. Switch to the **Single Sign-On (SSO) Configuration** tab located at the top of the page.

7. Click the **Add new SSO Configuration** link.

These last two actions are depicted in the following screenshot:

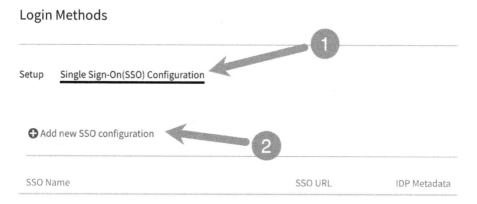

Figure 5.24 – Configuring a new SSO provider

Clicking the **Add New SSO Configuration** link opens the **SSO configuration** dialog, where you need to provide the details of your organization's SSO provider. When done, you must return to the **Setup** tab and choose the defined **SSO Configuration** in the **SSO Setup** drop-down menu.

Detailing these options is beyond the scope of this book and configuring SSO requires performing configuration steps both in Adobe Learning Manager and your organization's SSO provider. Don't hesitate to contact the Learning Manager support team for more instructions on how to integrate ALM with your internal SSO provider.

SAML 2.0

Your SSO provider must be SAML 2.0-compliant to be used with Adobe Learning Manager. The **Security Assertion Markup Language** (**SAML**) 2.0 standard is an XML-based protocol that uses security tokens to exchange information between a central authentication service and the resource the user wants to access. You can find more information on the SAML 2.0 Wikipedia page at `https://en.wikipedia.org/wiki/SAML_2.0`.

Since it is not possible to demonstrate this possibility in this book, you will now cancel the process and return to the default situation.

8. Close the **SSO Configuration** dialog and return to the **Setup** tab of the **Login Methods** page.

9. Open the **Default Login Method** drop-down menu and switch back to **Adobe ID**.

Before moving on, notice the **Enable Multiple Single Sign-On (SSO) for login** checkbox. It allows you to configure multiple SSO providers for your Learning Manager account so that you can use different SSO providers for different groups of users in your organization. You can also use this capability to authenticate multiple types of external users using their respective SSO providers.

> **Multiple SSO providers**
>
> More information on multiple SSO logins can be found in the official Learning Manager User Guide at `https://helpx.adobe.com/learning-manager/administrators/feature-summary/multiple-sso-logins.html`.

In this section, we discussed SSO and you discovered the login methods available in Adobe Learning Manager for authenticating internal and external users.

We've discussed a lot of options in this chapter, and you may have a hard time figuring out how to put it all together. So, we'll do a quick recap in the next section.

Putting it all together

The exercises in this book are designed to help you discover how Learning Manager works and help you explore all its features at your own pace. But these exercises hardly represent the day-to-day operations of a real-life Learning Manager account, where thousands of learners interact with thousands of courses every day. Not to mention the fact that in large organizations, employees come and go and constantly change positions.

When setting up your Learning Manager account, you should not only consider how you will initially *configure* your account but also how you will *maintain* your account over time. Here are a few considerations to help you out:

- The SSO provider only provides the *authentication* mechanism. It only determines who knocks on the door and verifies that this person has access to your Learning Manager account; it does not know about the inner workings of Adobe Learning Manager. For example, your SSO provider doesn't know what roles are available in Learning Manager, so it can't *authorize* users, only *authenticate* them.

- Setting up an SSO provider does not exempt you from uploading user data to Adobe Learning Manager using the CSV file import or any other available mechanism. Users must exist both in Learning Manager and in your SSO provider directory.

- Since employees constantly come and go or change positions within the organization, your internal employee directory is constantly updated. Therefore, don't forget to regularly synchronize your internal directory with the users list of Adobe Learning Manager to reflect new hires, departures, promotions, and more.

In *Chapter 16*, *Exploring the Integration Admin Role*, you will configure various connectors available in Adobe Learning Manager to automate the constant synchronization of your internal employee directory with the user list of Adobe Learning Manager.

> **Best Practices Guide to set up Learning Manager**
>
> To help you figure out the first steps in configuring your Learning Manager account, Adobe has created a Best Practices guide, which is available at `https://helpx.adobe.com/learning-manager/administrators/getting-started.html`.

Summary

Now that you've come to the end of this chapter, learning can finally start on your account as all the needed ingredients are now properly in place:

- In *Chapter 3, Uploading Learning Content and Managing the Content Library*, you created modules by uploading various types of learning activities to your Content Library

- In *Chapter 4, Creating Skills and Courses*, you assembled these learning modules into courses, and you assigned skills to courses

- Finally, in this chapter, you added the users that will bring your Learning Manager account to life

First, you learned that Adobe Learning Manager distinguishes between internal and external users. Typically, internal users are the employees of the organization, while external users are individuals from third-party organizations who need access to your Learning Manager account.

You also reviewed several ways to create new internal and external users. Internal users can be created one at a time using the **Single User** option, in bulk using the **Upload a CSV** option, or through self-registration links, which you cwan define as an administrator. For external users, it is necessary to create external registration profiles to allow these users to register themselves to the platform.

Adobe Lewwarning Manager is designed to authenticate users through an external SSO provider. This can be the SSO provider of your organization or Adobe's own SSO solution, also known as *Adobe ID*. The only exception to this general rule is the possibility for external users to use an Adobe Learning Manager ID to authenticate to the platform.

Finally, you learned that Learning Manager adopts a role-based approach to authorization. Six roles are automatically defined in the system: **Administrator**, **Author**, **Integration Admin**, **Instructor**, **Manager**, and **Learner**. However, you can create custom roles to address a very wide range of complex use cases.

Now that all of these ingredients are in place, it is possible to start enrolling learners in courses. Learning Manager offers many options for this purpose, addressing numerous instructional design strategies and business requirements. This is what you will review in the next chapter.

Enrolling Learners in Courses

A recipe has two main parts: te *ingredients* and a second part called *Instructions*, or *Method*. After reading the previous chapters, the ingredients section of your digital learning recipe is complete. In this chapter, it's finally time to move on to the *Method* section and see how these ingredients will be combined for learning to occur.

The first question you will explore in this chapter is, *What do learners enroll in?* At first glance, the answer to this question seems obvious: learners enroll in courses. But upon closer inspection, Adobe Learning Manager offers many nuances and variations, such as **Course Instances**, **Learning Paths**, **Learning Plans**, and **Certifications**, all of which will be discussed in this chapter.

The second question to consider is, *Who can enroll learners in courses?* Again, there is an obvious answer: as discussed earlier, Learning Manager is designed as a learner-centric LMS, so learners typically enroll *themselves*. Therefore, in this chapter, you will examine the enrollment experience from the learner's perspective. That being said, organizations are subject to regulations that require learners to take compliance training; some professions require constant recertification, not to mention each organization's training and development strategy, which also plays a role in determining who should learn what. I like to say that a successful learning and development strategy is where the desires of learners meet the needs of organizations. This is why administrators and managers also have a role to play when enrolling learners in courses.

In this chapter, you will review several enrollment workflows, such as administrator enrollment and manager approval. Of course, these various enrollment methods can be combined, which offers unmatched flexibility to learners, managers, and organizations alike.

By the end of this chapter, you will have a solid understanding of how learners and learning content come together and how this helps organizations implement their overall learning and development strategy. To achieve this goal, this chapter covers the following topics:

- Reviewing the course options that affect enrollment
- Creating course instances
- Taking advantage of Learning Paths and Certifications

- Learner self-enrollment
- Enrollment by Administrators and Managers
- Automatic enrollment using Learning Plans

There are a lot of exciting new features to discover, so let's jump right in!

Technical requirements

To perform the exercises in this chapter, you need to meet the following technical requirements:

- You need Administrator and Author access to a working Learning Manager account (it can be a trial account)
- In addition to the administrator account mentioned previously, you need access to at least three different learner accounts and one manager account
- Your account must host at least one course with a synchronous (face-to-face or virtual) activity and one course with an activity that has multiple delivery methods enabled

If you have completed the exercises in the previous chapters, you should be ready to begin this chapter immediately. If you have not read the previous chapters, make sure you meet the aforementioned requirements before proceeding. You can also read through the steps without doing the practical exercises.

The steps described in the exercises in this chapter are based on the learning content and user profiles defined in the previous chapters. Feel free to adapt these steps to your situation if you have not read the previous chapters.

Reviewing the course options affecting enrollment

Back in *Chapter 4, Creating Skills and Courses*, you created two custom courses. At that time, you went through almost all the options related to course creation, except for a few properties associated with defining the preferred target audience for the course and how learners enroll in the course. You will now return to the Author role and explore these options by performing the following steps:

1. Make sure you are logged in as an Author to your Learning Manager account.
2. From the **Author** home page, click the **Courses** link located at the top of the **Learning** section in the left sidebar.
3. Click the course card of the **Fundamentals of IT Security** course you created in *Chapter 4, Creating Skills and Courses*.
4. Once the course is open, click the **Settings** link located in the left sidebar.

This takes you to the settings page of your course, where the **Enrollment Type**, **Unenrollment**, and **Who should take this Course?** options are available. These options were not discussed in *Chapter 4, Creating Skills and Courses*.

5. Click the **Edit** link located in the upper-right corner of the screen.

6. Open the **Enrollment Type** drop-down and inspect the available options.

    Self Enrolled is the default value. Using this option, learners can browse the course catalog and enroll *themselves* in the course. This is exactly the type of experience Learning Manager aims to promote, so it's not surprising that this is the default.

    When using the **Manager Nominated** option, only managers can enroll their team members in the course.

    Finally, with the **Manager Approved** option, learners can browse the course catalog to send an enrollment request to their manager for approval.

7. Choose **Self-enrolled** in the **Enrollment Type** dropdown.

> **Changing the enrollment type**
>
> When changing **Enrollment Type**, you cannot change to a more restrictive option. For example, changing from **Self Enrolled** to **Manager Approved** is not possible. When in doubt, choose a restrictive **Enrollment Type** when you create the course, as this allows you to switch to a more permissive option later. As a workaround, you can also duplicate the course, choose a more restrictive **Enrollment Type** for the copy, and retire the original.

8. Leave the **Unenrollment** checkbox *deselected*.

9. Scroll down to the bottom of the page until you see the **Tags** and **Who should take this Course?** options.

As discussed in the *Working with tags* section of *Chapter 3, Uploading Learning Content and Managing the Content Library*, tags are keywords that help the internal search engine index courses to make them more discoverable in the Course Catalog.

For the **Who should take this course?** option, you can define the preferred target audience of the course by supplying one or more profiles. As discussed in *Chapter 5, Managing Users*, **Profile** is one of the fields in the **Add User** form. Most of the time, the profile corresponds to the *job title* of the learner.

10. Type the name of an existing profile in the **Who should take this Course?** field. Click the desired profile when it becomes visible in the list. You can repeat this operation to add multiple profiles if needed.

    For this example, make sure you leave the **Who should take this Course?** field empty.

11. Finally, click the **Republish** button in the upper-right corner of the screen to save your changes.

Thanks to these steps, you should have a better understanding of the course options affecting enrolment. You also learned how to define a preferred target audience for the courses hosted on your account.

Working with course instances

To understand course instances, it is necessary to remember that a Learning Manager course can include both *synchronous* and *asynchronous* modules. As a reminder, *asynchronous* activities are self-paced modules that learners can review at their convenience, while *synchronous* activities require learners and instructors to be present together at the same time, either face to face or online.

But there is another major difference between *synchronous* and *asynchronous* activities: *synchronous* activities are time-bound, while *asynchronous* activities are not.

Let's take a quick example. Imagine it's early April and you're creating a course that includes a virtual classroom activity scheduled for, say, mid-May. If learners register for the course before the end of April, all is well. But if they register later, they may not have enough time to complete the required prework before attending the mid-May class. Even worse: what happens if learners enroll in the course *after* the scheduled class date?

Another example is when your organization wants to offer the same synchronous activity in various countries and/or in different languages. In such a case, you need to schedule several instances of the same (live or virtual) class in different locations, time zones, languages, and possibly with different instructors.

You can also use course instances with courses containing self-paced modules only. This can be very useful for reporting and feedback purposes. Feedback and reporting will be covered in *Chapter 9, Configuring and Using Feedback*, and *Chapter 10, Reporting in Adobe Learning Manager*, respectively.

To address these use cases, you need to define **Course Instances**. In this section, you will create two instances for the **Advanced IT Security** course:

1. Make sure you are logged in as an **Author**.

2. From the **Author** home page, click the **Courses** link located in the **Learning** section of the left sidebar.

3. Click the **Advanced IT Security** course to open it.

4. Scroll down the **Overview** page until you see the **Modules** section.

As depicted in the following screenshot, there are three modules in this particular course:

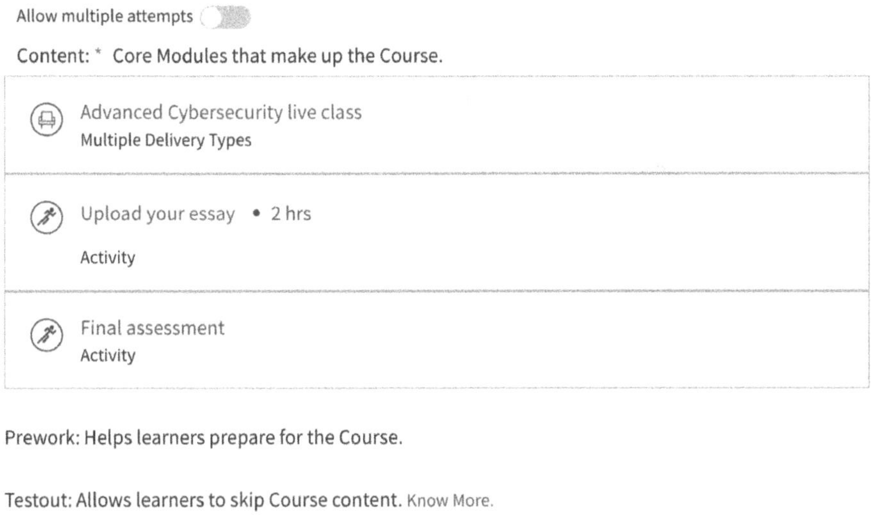

Allow multiple attempts

Content: * Core Modules that make up the Course.

Advanced Cybersecurity live class
Multiple Delivery Types

Upload your essay   • 2 hrs

Activity

Final assessment
Activity

Prework: Helps learners prepare for the Course.

Testout: Allows learners to skip Course content. Know More.

Figure 6.1 – The Advanced IT Security course contains three modules

The first one is a *synchronous* Classroom module. However, back in *Chapter 4, Creating Skills and Courses*, you enabled multiple delivery methods for this module, so it can also be delivered as a self-paced asynchronous learning activity. The second module is a **File Submission** activity, while the third module is a **Checklist** activity.

All these modules require an *instructor*. This instructor is responsible for conducting the live class, reviewing the assignments submitted by the learners, and filling out the checklist. It can be the same instructor for all activities or different instructors for each.

> **Note**
> File submissions and checklist activities were discussed in *Chapter 4, Creating Skills and Courses*.

Creating course instances

Creating **Course Instances** is something both administrators and authors can do. For this example, let's do this as an administrator by performing the following steps:

1. Make sure you are logged in as an **Administrator**.

2. From the **Administrator** home page, click the **Courses** link located in the **Learning** section of the left sidebar.

3. Click the **Advanced IT Security** course card.

4. When the course opens, click the **Instances** link located at the top of the **Manage** section in the left sidebar.

As shown in the following screenshot, a **Default instance** should already be defined. Since there is still some information you need to provide (such as the designated instructor for example), this **Default instance** is currently in the **Retired** state and is not yet accepting enrollments:

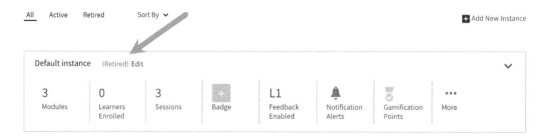

Figure 6.2 – A Default instance should already be defined

You will now create two additional instances for this course: one for the North American region and one for the **Europe Middle East Africa (EMEA)** region.

5. Click the **Add New Instance** link located in the upper-right corner of the **Instances** page.

6. Type the desired session name (North American Spring Session, in this example) in the **Instance Name** field. Note that, at this point, this is the only required information.

7. If needed, you can enter a **Completion Deadline**. Learners must complete the course by the selected date to receive credit for the course.

8. Click the **Show More Options** link to reveal additional options.

    If needed, you can enter an **Enrollment Deadline**. After this date, the course instance will no longer accept enrollment. Learners can still enroll in the course but using other course instances.

    You can also enter an **Unenrollment Deadline**. After this date, enrolled learners can no longer unenroll.

9. Finally, you can enter a **Timezone**. Note that this is required information that defaults to the main **Timezone** you specified for your account, as discussed in the *Modifying your account settings* section of *Chapter 1, Introduction to Adobe Learning Manager*.

10. That's it for the main settings of the new course instance. Make sure your screen looks similar to the following screenshot before clicking the **Save** button:

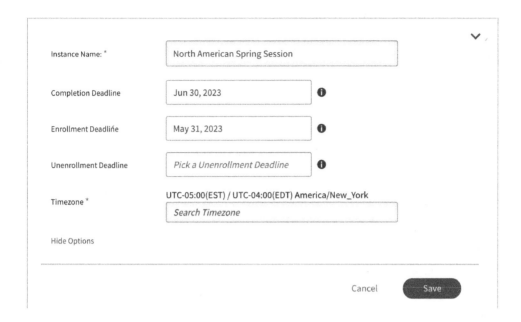

Figure 6.3 – The main settings of the new course instance

The first step in creating a new course instance is complete. You will now finalize the new course instance by providing the necessary details for the different sessions.

11. From the **Instances** page of the **Advanced IT Security** course, locate the course instance you created in the previous section.

12. Click the **Sessions** link in the properties of the course instance to open the list of modules. This operation is illustrated in the following screenshot:

Figure 6.4 – Clicking the Sessions link of the new course instance

This is where you provide instance-specific details for all the activities that require it. In this example, this is where you supply the details of the live class, such as the start and end date, the instructor, the venue, and the seat limit.

13. Click the pencil icon associated with the **Advanced Cybersecurity live class** module.

14. The previous action opens a form where you can define the necessary information for the classroom module in this particular course instance.

    Choose a **Start Date** and an **End Date** that is consistent with the **Completion Deadline** and the **Enrollment Deadline** you defined in the previous section.

    Choose **Instructor 01** as the Instructor for this session. Note that you can define multiple instructors if necessary.

    For the sake of the demonstration, choose a very low **Seat Limit** of 2. This will allow you to review the **Waitlist** options in subsequent chapters.

    Complete the other fields as per your requirements.

15. When you're ready, click the blue checkmark at the bottom-right corner of the form to validate these session details.

You will now assign an instructor to the other two modules of the course.

16. Click the pencil icon associated with the **Upload your essay** activity.

17. Choose **Instructor 01** as the instructor for this activity. This means that **Instructor 01** is responsible for reviewing the assignments uploaded by learners enrolled in this course instance. Click the blue checkmark at the bottom-right corner of the form when you're done.

18. Repeat these steps to assign **Instructor 01** as the instructor for the **Final assessment** activity, which is a *Checklist* activity, as defined in *Chapter 4, Creating Skills and Courses*.

Make sure you provide all the necessary information where appropriate; otherwise, the learners enrolling in this course instance may not be able to complete the course as expected.

19. Repeat the whole process to create a second course instance named EMEA Summer Session.

    Choose any appropriate **Completion Deadline** and **Enrollment Deadline**.

    Choose the **Continental European Time (CET) Timezone**.

    Enter all the required session information for the **Advanced CyberSecurity live class** module.

    For this course instance, choose *yourself* as the instructor for all activities.

When you're done, you should have two additional course instances available for the **Advanced Cybersecurity** course, as shown in the following screenshot:

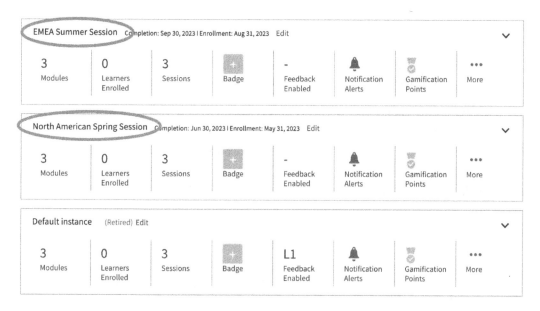

Figure 6.5 – Two additional course instances are available for your custom course

> **Note**
>
> The remaining course instance properties, such as **Badge**, **Feedback**, and **Notifications**, will be discussed in future chapters.

Now that you have a better understanding of what Course Instances are, you understand that learners enroll in *Course Instances* and not in *courses*, per se.

Choosing an alternate delivery method

In *Chapter 4, Creating Skills and Courses*, you chose the **Classroom** and **Self-paced module** delivery types for the first module of the **Advanced IT Security** course. This was done to address the situation where a learner wants to enroll in the course, but no session is scheduled in the near future. In such a case, the learner can watch a video recording of a previous class instead of attending a face-to-face training session.

You will now implement this strategy using the **Default instance** that was automatically created for this course. First, you will rename this instance; then, you will change the delivery type of the first module. Perform the following steps:

1. Make sure you are logged in as an **Administrator** and that you are on the **Instances** page of the **Advanced IT Security** course.

2. Click the **Edit** link associated with your **Default instance**.

3. Change **Instance Name** to `Self-paced` and leave all the other fields empty. Click the **Save** button when you're done.

Thanks to the previous steps, you have renamed the **Default** instance to **Self-paced**. You will now select the appropriate delivery type for the first module of the course.

4. Click the **Modules** link associated with the **Self-paced** instance. This action opens the **List of modules** available in the course.

5. Open the drop-down menu associated with the **Advanced Cybersecurity live class** module and choose the **Self Paced** option.

6. Click the blue checkmark in the bottom-right corner to validate the change.

The last few actions are depicted in the following screenshot:

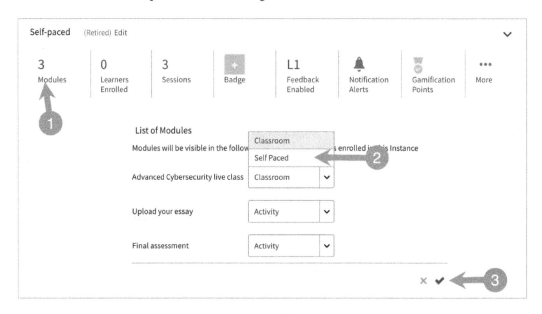

Figure 6.6 – Changing the delivery type for the first module of the course

7. Now, click the **Sessions** link associated with the **Self-paced** instance and define **Instructor 01** as the instructor for the remaining two activities.

> **Deadlines for Self-Paced courses**
>
> By choosing the **Self-paced** delivery type for the first module, it is the entire instance that is essentially self-paced. This allows learners to enroll at any time and take the course at their own pace, so the **Completion Deadline**, **Enrollment Deadline**, **Unenrollment Deadline**, and **Timezone** options make little sense here.

There is one last thing we must do for this course instance to start accepting new enrollments.

8. Click the blue arrow located in the upper-right corner of the **Self-paced** course instance.

9. Choose the **Reopen instance** option in the menu that opens. Thanks to this action, the **Course Instance** is no longer in the **Retired** state and can accept enrollments.

These last two steps are depicted in the following screenshot:

Figure 6.7 – Reopening the retired course instance

With that, you have three instances in the **Advanced IT Security** course. Two of these instances use the *Classroom* delivery type for the first module. One class will be taught in North America, and the other in Europe. The last instance uses the **Self-paced** delivery type for the first module. Learners who enroll in this instance will watch a video recording of a previous live class rather than attending face-to-face training.

> **Choosing the right video file**
>
> The .mp4 file of the class recording was selected from the **Course Library** when we created this course in *Chapter 4, Creating Skills and Courses*.

In the next section, you will review the **Default** course instance associated with the **Fundamentals of IT Security** course that you also created in *Chapter 4*.

Exploring the Default Instance of a Self-paced course

Even if you do not explicitly create course instances, a **Default instance** is automatically created whenever you create a new course. Let's take a quick look at the default course instance of the **Fundamentals of IT Security** course:

1. Make sure you are logged in as an **Administrator** and that you are on the **Courses** page.

2. Click the **Fundamentals of IT Security** course card.

3. When the course opens, click the **Instances** link located in the **Manage** section of the left sidebar.

As shown in the following screenshot, a default instance has been automatically created for this course:

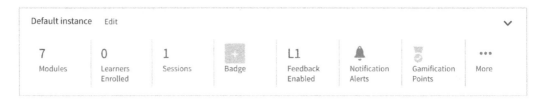

Figure 6.8 – The Default instance of the Fundamentals of IT Security course

Since this course only includes self-paced, asynchronous learning activities that are automatically delivered by Adobe Learning Manager, there is no need to configure multiple sessions or assign instructors to the activities being delivered. In other words, this default instance is all your course needs to get up and running and start accepting enrollments.

In the next section, you will explore how course instances can be retired and reopened.

Retiring course instances

When a course has multiple instances, learners can choose which instance they want to enroll in. Sooner or later, this will reveal one of the biggest mysteries all event organizers inevitably face: some course instances will be in high demand, and others not at all. This is especially problematic if the course contains live class activities with limited seating. Waitlists can quickly fill up, which can lead to a logistical nightmare and unhappy learners.

This is one of the circumstances in which retiring a course instance is very useful. A retired instance no longer appears in the course catalog and does not accept new enrollments. Learners who are already enrolled keep their status and take the course as if nothing had happened to the course instance they are enrolled in!

Perform the following steps to retire a course instance:

1. From the **Courses** page of the **Admin** role, click the **Advanced IT Security** course card.
2. Click the **Instances** link located in the **Manage** section of the left sidebar.
3. Click the down arrow located in the upper-right corner of the course instance you wish to retire.
4. Click the **Retire instance** option in the menu that opens, as illustrated in the following screenshot:

Figure 6.09 – Clicking the Retire instance option in the menu that opens

Now, let's imagine that, in response to increasing learner demand, you decide to move the course to a larger venue and assign an additional instructor. You can now accommodate many more learners than originally planned, so you want to reopen the course instance so that you can start accepting new enrollments again.

5. Locate the retired instance that you wish to reopen. If necessary, you can use the **Retired** tab located above the list of instances.

6. Click the down arrow in the upper-right corner of the course instance you wish to reopen.

7. Click the **Reopen instance** option in the menu.

Note that when the enrollment deadline or the first synchronous activity has passed, Learning Manager *automatically* retires the course instance.

After reading this section, you know enough about instances to go through the remaining exercises of this chapter. The main takeaway is that learners do not enroll in *courses* but in *course instances*. In the next section, you will learn how to bundle courses together using **Learning Paths**.

Working with Learning Paths and Certifications

Until now, you have always assumed that learners enroll in *courses* (actually, course *instances*, as discussed in the previous section). In this section, you will discover that, although this is often the case, it is not always true. There are many examples where it makes sense to group courses and enroll learners in a series of courses rather than a single course. These include the following:

- You offer different levels of courses on the same subject (for example, photography level 1 and photography level 2) and you want to allow learners to enroll in the full curriculum in one go.

- You want to split longer courses into chapters, but Learning Manager does not provide such a chaptering concept. You can work around this limitation by grouping multiple courses and treating each course as a chapter of a larger curriculum.

- Your organization implements internal certifications to allow employees to become trainers, managers, or whatever you can think of. These certifications require learners to take multiple courses. So, you want to group them to make the certification discoverable in the course catalog and to make enrollment easier.

- Many jobs (accounting, HR, project managers, and so on) require ongoing training, and you want to define a series of courses that make up this ongoing certification program.

The preceding examples are just a few of the many situations where such course bundling is relevant. Adobe Learning Manager offers many features to address this type of use case. This is what you will review in this section.

Creating Learning Paths

Let's start with **Learning Paths**. In Adobe Learning Manager, a Learning Path is a simple collection of courses. You can use it to group a set of related courses or create a longer curriculum in which each course is considered a chapter.

To illustrate this feature, you will use some of the courses that are automatically available with your Learning Manager trial account to create a Learning Path dedicated to photo editing using Adobe Lightroom and Adobe Photoshop.

Creating Learning Paths can be done by both Administrators and Authors, so let's create a new Learning Path by performing the following steps:

1. From the **Administrator** home page, click the **Learning Paths** link located in the **Learning** category of the left sidebar.

   This takes you to the **Learning Paths** page of the administrator role.

2. Click the **Add** button located in the upper-right corner of the page.

3. Type Mastering Photo Editing in the **Learning Path Name** field. Note that, at this point, this is the only required field of the form.

4. As a best practice, also provides a **Learning Path Overview** and the **Benefits of this Learning Path** in the corresponding fields.

   Sample text for these two fields is provided in the masteringPhoto/masteringPhoto_desc.pdf file of the download associated with this book.

5. You can also provide a **Cover image** and a **Banner Image** to make this **Learning Path** attractive in the course catalog.

   If needed, sample images are provided in the download associated with this book. Look for the masteringPhoto/masteringPhoto_Banner.png and masteringPhoto/masteringPhoto_Cover.png files.

The other fields are very similar to those you used when creating courses in *Chapter 4, Creating Skills and Courses*.

6. Take some time to inspect the other available options. Then, click the **Save** button in the upper-right corner of the page.

This concludes the first part of creating a new **Learning Path**. When the page reloads, a wealth of additional links are available in the left column, as illustrated in the following screenshot:

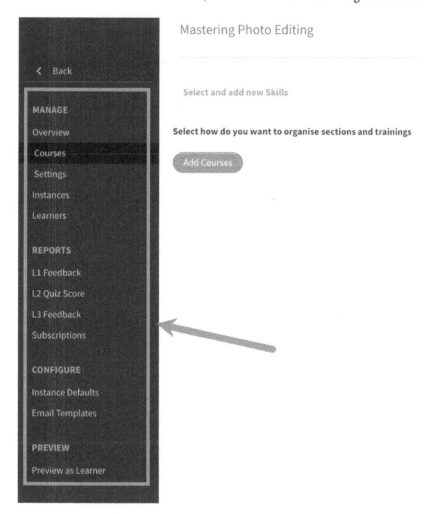

Figure 6.10 – When the page reloads, new links become available in the left sidebar

Most of these links are the same as those available for courses. Speaking of courses, the next step is to select the courses included in this new Learning Path.

Adding courses to a Learning Path

Since a Learning Path is a set of courses, the most important step in creating one is to choose the courses that are part of it. This section picks up where the previous section left off: you are on the **Courses** page of the Learning Path you started to create in the previous section.

Perform the following steps to add courses to this Learning Path:

1. Click the **Add Courses** button.
2. Use the tools in the window that opens to search for the desired courses. In this example, you can use the **Search** field to search for the `PhotoShop` and `Lightroom` keywords.

   When you spot a course you want to add to the Learning Path, select the checkbox in the upper-left corner of the course card.

   Repeat this operation for all the courses that should be added to the Learning Path.

These steps are illustrated in the following screenshots:

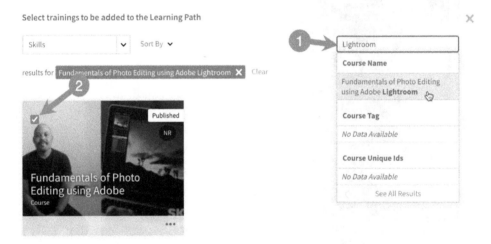

Figure 6.11 – Choosing the courses included in the Learning Path

3. Click the **Save** button once you have selected all the desired courses.
4. If needed, you can reorder the courses using drag-and-drop actions.
   You can also adjust your **Completion Requirements** using the tools available on the right-hand side and choose whether you want to enforce the order in which you set the course. By default, **Completion Requirements** is set to **All** courses and the order is *not* enforced.
5. When you're ready, click the **Publish** button in the upper-right corner of the page.

From now on, this new Learning Path is available in the course catalog and is open for enrollment. In the next section, you will review the options for managing the Learning Paths available in your account, which includes editing, retiring, and deleting Learning Paths.

Managing Learning Paths

Maintaining Learning Paths is very similar to maintaining individual courses. It is a task devoted to both administrators and authors. Let's take a quick look at the available options by performing the following steps:

1. From the **Administrator** or **Author** home page, click the **Learning Paths** link located in the **Learning** section of the left sidebar.

2. Hover your mouse over the lower area of the card of the Learning Path you wish to work with.

Most of the available options are the same as they are for individual courses, as shown in the following screenshot (note that Authors do not see the **Enroll Learners** option):

Figure 6.12 – The options available for Learning Paths

As with courses, note that you cannot delete a Learning Path without first retiring it.

There is, however, one option specific to Learning Paths that requires further investigation. It relates to how Learning Paths Instances and Course Instances work together to create **Flexible Learning Paths**. This is the subject of the next section.

Creating Flexible Learning Paths

As discussed in the *Creating Course Instances* section, earlier in this chapter, learners do not enroll in *Courses* but in *Course Instances*. The same is true with Learning Paths.

In this section, you will examine how Course Instances and Learning Paths Instances work together to give learners a smooth learning experience. The general workflow is as follows:

- Create several Courses and add course instances as needed.
- Create a Learning Path and add courses to it
- Create the needed instances of the Learning Path and map Learning Path Instances to Course Instances.
- Enroll learners in the desired Learning Path instance.

This is just the general workflow. There are some interesting nuances and variations available, which you can review by performing the following steps:

1. When on the **Learning Paths** page of the **Administrator** or **Author** role, open the Learning Path you want to work with.

2. Click the **Instances** link located in the **Manage** section of the left sidebar.

Just like with courses, Adobe Learning Manager has created a **Default instance** for your Learning Path.

In this example, the courses that are part of the Learning Path only contain self-paced modules, so this **Default instance** is all you need to provide the expected learning experience. But this may not always be the case, so let's inspect the available options anyway.

3. Click the **Courses** link of your **Default instance** to open the **List of Courses** included in the Learning Path.

From here, you can decide to go one of two ways:

-   You can choose a specific course instance for each of the courses included in the Learning Path using the drop-down list available next to each course. Using this option, learners enrolling in this instance of the Learning Path are automatically enrolled in the chosen instances of each course.

-   You can also select the **Enable Learners to Choose instances (Flexible Learning Path)** checkbox, which allows learners to choose the instance they wish to enroll in for each of the courses included in the Learning Path.

In this example, these options are not relevant since the Learning Path only contains courses that do not have multiple instances defined.

After reading this section, you should have a pretty good understanding of Learning Paths and the various options available in Learning Manager for creating and maintaining them. It is now time to move on to the next section, where you will learn about **Certifications**.

Creating Certifications

Certifications are similar to the Learning Paths discussed in the previous section, in that they also allow you to enroll learners in a series of courses rather than in a single course. But certifications add a few more things to the mix: several *days to complete* and the possibility of creating *recurring* certifications with automatic learner re-enrollment.

Creating Certifications is very similar to creating Learning Paths. It is a task both administrators and authors can accomplish. Let's examine it hands-on by creating the *Certified IT Security pro* certification:

1. From the **Administrator** or **Author** home page, click the **Certifications** link located in the **Learning** section of the left sidebar.

2. Click the **Add** button located in the upper-right corner of the screen.

3. Type `Certified IT Pro` in the **Certification Name** field.

4. Type `30` in the **Days to complete** field located further down the page. This means that learners who enroll for this certification have 30 days to complete it. If the certification is not completed within this time frame, the learner shall *not* be certified.

    Note that, at this point, the **Certification Name** and **Days to complete** fields are the only two required fields.

5. As a best practice, take the necessary time to type a **Description** and **Certification Overview** in the corresponding fields.

    You can also supply a **Cover Image** and a **Banner Image** to make the certification stand out in the course catalog.

    Sample files are provided in the `/certification` folder of the download associated with this book.

6. Scroll down the page until you see the **Type** field.

Here, you can choose between a **Recurring** or a **Perpetual** certification. A recurring certification expires after a certain **Validity** period, requiring learners to constantly recertify to maintain their status. In contrast, a perpetual certification never expires. For example, you can use a perpetual certification to certify people in a specific version of a software application.

7. For this example, choose a **Perpetual** certification.

8. Further down the page, notice the **Certification Issuer** field.

The default value is **Internal**. This means that the certification is entirely controlled by your organization. In such a case, you use Adobe Learning Manager to deliver the courses, so it is easy for the platform to track the completion status of each course and to automatically award the certification when a learner has successfully completed all the courses.

External certifications are organized by third parties and can be recognized by a wide range of organizations in various industries. Examples include CPR and First Aid training, compliance certifications from government-approved operators, and more. In these situations, the courses are delivered outside of Adobe Learning Manager, so it is impossible to automatically track course completion and certification. To solve this problem, Learning Manager offers the following two choices:

- Managers can approve the certification after a member of their team has achieved the certification

- The learner can self-declare the completion of the certification

Note that **Certification Issuer** cannot be changed after the certification has been published.

9.   In this example, choose **Internal** for **Certification Issuer**.

10. Take a quick look at the other options. They should be self-explanatory for the most part.

11. When you're ready, click the **Save** button located in the upper-right corner of the screen.

This action creates the new certification and places it in *draft* state. When the page reloads, you are redirected to the **Courses** page for the new certification.

12. Click the **Catalog** tab located in the upper-left area of the page.

13. Search for the **Fundamentals of IT Security** course you created in *Chapter 4, Creating Skills and Courses*. When you find it, hover over the lower area of the course card and click the **Add** link.

     Repeat this process with the **Advanced IT Security** course.

14. Return to the **Curriculum** tab located in the upper-left corner of the screen.

15. Confirm that the chosen courses are visible in the **Curriculum** tab. Notice the **Completion Requirements** drop-down list located above the list of courses.

16. When you're ready, click the **Publish** button located in the upper-right corner of the page.

Just like for Courses and Learning Paths, clicking the **Publish** button makes the Certification officially part of your course catalog. From now on, the certification is open for enrollment.

> **Note**
>
> You must provide at least one course before you can publish an *internal* certification. *External* certifications can be published without mentioning any course.

The options for maintaining Certifications are mostly identical to those used for maintaining Learning Paths and Courses and will not be further discussed here.

After reading these few sections, you have seen that courses are *not* the only thing learners can enroll in:

- First of all, you discovered instances and realized that learners enroll in *instances*, not in *courses* per se.

- You also bundled several Courses into a Learning Path. Learners enrolling in such a Learning Path enroll in all Courses that are part of the Learning Path.

- Finally, you created a Certification. Certifications are similar to Learning Paths, but they add a time limit for completion, as well as the ability to create recurring certifications with automatic learner re-enrollment.

Now that your course catalog contains a variety of learning objects for learners to enroll in, it's time to move on to the next section, where you'll *actually* enroll learners in those learning objects.

Self-Enrollment by Learners

In Adobe Learning Manager, self-enrollment is the preferred way to enroll for a course. The new *immersive* learner home page has been designed as a Netflix-like interface where learners can browse the catalog and enroll in courses, similar to browsing Netflix's vast catalog to find the next movie or series they want to watch.

In this section, you will examine this self-service learning approach by logging into the platform as *Learner 03* and experiencing enrollment from the learner's perspective.

Using the Impersonate User feature

To log in as *Learner 03*, you can simply open a new private browser window and log in as *Learner 03* as you did in previous chapters. This is possible because you know the username and password of all active users in your Learning Manager trial account.

Without a doubt, this does not reflect reality. A more realistic situation is when a support staff member has to help learners find their way in the platform. In this case, the support staff do not know the password of each learner and therefore cannot log in as someone else to troubleshoot an issue.

The **Impersonate User** feature of Adobe Learning Manager allows Administrators to switch hats and take on another user's identity for a short while. Let's use it to log in as *Learner 03* using the following steps:

1. Open a new browser or a new private window of the same browser.
2. In that new window, log into your Learning Manager account using your usual Admin credentials.
3. Click the **User** icon located in the upper-right corner of the screen.
4. Choose the **Impersonate User** option, as shown in the following screenshot:

Figure 6.13 – Clicking the Impersonate User option

5. Use the **Search** field to search for **Learner 03**.

6. Click the **Proceed** button when you're ready. Take some time to read the message and click the **Proceed** button again.

When Learning Manager reloads, *you are Learner 03*! Note that you did not have to enter Learner 03's password to access this page. That's the magic of the **Impersonate User** feature and what makes it different from logging in as another user, as in the previous chapters.

When using the **Impersonate User** feature, there are a few things to keep in mind:

- Only administrators (and custom admins with proper permissions) can use the **Impersonate User** feature.

- The maximum duration of an impersonate session is 60 minutes.

- You can only impersonate active users; unregistered users cannot be impersonated.

- During the impersonation session, the system *actually* thinks that you are the impersonated learner. Everything you do has an impact on the impersonated learner's experience and learning record. However, a special impersonation report is available in Learning Manager if needed.

More information on the **Impersonate User** feature is available on the official Learning Manager help site at `https://helpx.adobe.com/be_en/learning-manager/administrators/feature-summary/impersonation-learner-manager.html`.

Now that you can act as *Learner 03*, let's review the default course enrolment experience.

7. Click the **Go To Catalog** link in the **My Learning List** section at the top of the **Learner** home page.

By default, all the active learning objects available for enrollment are visible in the course catalog. This includes the *courses* themselves, but also *learning paths* and *certifications*.

8. Hover over the lower area of the **Fundamentals of IT Security** course you created in *Chapter 4, Creating Skills and Courses*. This reveals a *brief description* and the *skills* associated with this course, as well as the **View Course** link.

   Click the **View Course** link.

9. Take some time to review the information available on the course page. When you're ready, click the **Enroll** button located in the upper-right area of the page.

The course begins as soon as you click the **Enroll** button. You will review the learning experience in more detail in *Chapter 7, Reviewing the Learner Experience*. For now, you will close the course, return to the learner home page, and enroll *Learner 03* in the **Advanced IT Security** course as well.

10. Click the **Close** icon located in the upper-right corner of the screen. This takes you back to the course overview page.

11. Click the **Home** icon at the top of the left sidebar to return to the **Learner** home page.

Once you're back on the home page, confirm that the **Fundamentals of IT Security** course appears in the **My Learning List** section, as shown in the following screenshot:

Figure 6.14 – The Fundamentals of IT Security course on the home page

12. Hover your mouse over the icons visible on the left edge of the screen. Then, click the **Catalog** icon to return to the **Course Catalog**.

13. When you're back in the **Course Catalog** click the **Advanced IT security** course.

14. Because the **Advanced IT Security** course contains multiple instances, you must choose the instance you want to enroll in, as shown in the following screenshot:

Figure 6.15 – Choosing the instance you want to enroll in

15. In this example, choose **North American Spring Session** (see the arrow in the preceding screenshot).

16. Take some time to review the information available on the Course overview page. When you're ready, click the **Enroll** button in the upper-right corner of the page.

Because the first module of this course is not self-paced, clicking the **Enroll** button does not automatically start the course as in the previous example.

17. You can now end the *Impersonate* session by clicking the **Logout** button at the top of the page.

In this section, you reviewed the default learner enrollment experience. Remember that this self-service learning approach is at the heart of the thinking that led to the creation of Adobe Learning Manager in the first place.

But there are other ways to enroll learners in courses. In the next section, you will learn how Managers and Administrators can enroll learners without them asking.

Enrolling Learners in courses

Allowing users to self-enroll in courses is certainly a great idea, which assumes that many learners will *actually* take advantage of it to continuously improve their skills.

Unfortunately, we all know that this concept is sometimes more of a utopia than a reality. Furthermore, there is no guarantee that the courses that learners choose to enroll in will magically match the needs of the organization. That's why administrators and managers can also enroll learners in courses without them asking. This is what you will review in this section.

Enrollment by Administrators

In this section, you will return to the Administrator role and enroll *Learner 01* in the **Advanced IT Security** course. Let's get started:

1. Make sure you are on the **Courses** page of the **Administrator** role.

2. Hover over the bottom section of the **Advanced IT Security** course card.

3. Click the **Enroll Learners** option to open the **Enroll Learners** dialog.

4. Use the **Select Instance** dropdown to select the same course instance you enrolled *Learner 03* in in the previous section.

5. Use the **Search** field of the **Include Learners** section to enroll Learner 01.

You can repeat this operation to enroll additional learners. You can also enroll **User Groups** rather than individual learners. **User Groups** were discussed in the *Using User Groups* section of *Chapter 5, Managing Users*.

Using inclusion and exclusion sets

When using groups of learners, you can create **inclusion sets**. An inclusion set is a list of groups. The learners that get enrolled in the course are those that are a part of *all* the groups listed in an inclusion set. For example, an inclusion set containing the **All Admins** and **All Managers** groups enrolls learners that are *both* admins *and* managers. Similarly, you can use **exclusion sets** to exclude individual learners or groups from the inclusion sets defined in the **Include Learners** section of the dialog.

6. Take some time to inspect the other options available in the **Enroll Learners** dialog.

    When the **Enroll Learners** dialog looks as follows, click the **Proceed** button located in the lower-right corner of the dialog:

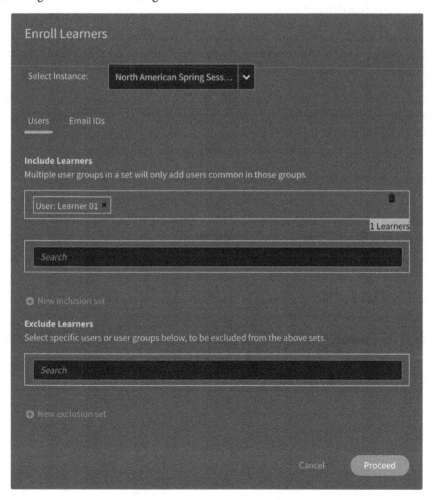

Figure 6.16 – Click the Proceed button when you're done

7. Take some time to read the **Summary** and confirm that it reflects your intentions. If needed, click the **Advanced Options** link to enter an **Additional Comment** that documents this enrollment.

8. When you're ready, click the **Enroll** button.

By completing this section, two learners have been enrolled in the same course instance of the **Advanced IT Security** course:

- *Learner 03* self-enrolled in the course in the previous section

- In this section, you enrolled *Learner 01* using your Admin privileges

In the next section, you will review how Managers can enroll their team members in a course.

Enrollment by Managers

Managers can also enroll learners in courses. The only difference is that Managers can only enroll the members of their team, while administrators can enroll any active learner available in your Learning Manager account.

When you created users back in *Chapter 5, Managing Users*, you defined *Manager 01* as the manager of both *Learner 01* and *Learner 02*. You will now log in as *Manager 01* and go through the process of enrolling *Learner 02* in the same course instance you used in the previous two sections when enrolling *Learner 01* and *Learner 03*. Perform the following steps to make this happen:

1. Open a new browser or another private browser window and use it to log in to your account as *Manager 01*. You can also use the **Impersonate User** feature described previously.

2. By default, *Manager 01* is logged in as a regular learner. Click the **User** icon in the upper-right corner of the screen to switch to the **Manager** role.

3. On the **Manager** home page, click the **Courses** link located in the **Learning** section of the left sidebar.

4. Click the **Advanced IT Security** course. When the course opens, click the **Learners** link available in the **Manage** section of the left sidebar

5. When on the **Learners** page, click the **Enroll** link, as shown in the following screenshot:

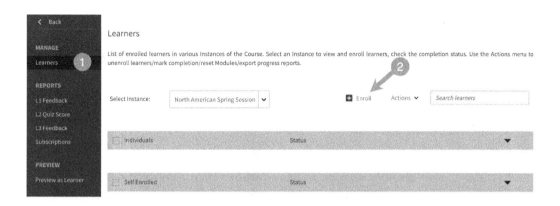

Figure 6.17 – Clicking the Enroll link

6. Use the **Select Instance** dropdown to select the same course instance as in the previous two sections.

7. Use the **Search** field of the **Include Learners** section to select Learner 02.

Note that only learners in the *Manager 01* team appear in the list. This is the only difference between enrolling users as a Manager and enrolling users as an Administrator.

8. Click the **Proceed** button located in the lower-left corner of the **Enroll Learners** dialog. Confirm that the **Summary** reflects your intentions and click the **Enroll** button.

This takes you to the **Learners** page of the selected course. From here, you can see the list of learners enrolled in each course instance.

9. Use the **Select Instance** dropdown to select the instance you enrolled learners in.

10. Expand the **Individuals** and **Self Enrolled** sections to reveal the learners for each category.

As shown in the following screenshot, only **Learner 01** is visible in the **Individuals** section of the chosen instance, even though *Learner 02* and *Learner 03* are also enrolled in the same course instance:

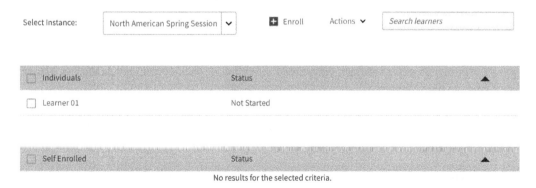

Figure 6.18 – Only Learner 01 appears in the list of enrolled learners

Don't worry! This situation is perfectly normal and can easily be explained by the following points:

- Since you are currently logged in as a Manager, you only see data about your team members. This explains why *Learner 03* does not appear in the list.

- As for *Learner 02*, remember that, when creating the instance, you specified a **Seat Limit** of 2. With the enrollment of *Learner 01* and *Learner 03*, the seat limit has been reached and the course instance is currently full!

Therefore, *Learner 02* has been added to the **waitlist**. Unfortunately, Managers do not have access to the waitlist. This is something only administrators and instructors have access to. You will review this in the *Viewing enrolled learners* section, later in this chapter.

But for now, let's touch on another workflow in which learners need **Manager approval** to enroll in a course.

Enrolling with Manager approval

Back in the *Reviewing the course options that affect enrollment* section, earlier in this chapter, you inspected the **Enrollment Type** option for courses, and you discovered that one of the available options is **Manager Approved**.

Using this option, learners cannot self-enroll in courses. Instead, they send an approval request to their manager, who must approve or reject it. Although the course you are using in these examples does not make use of this workflow, let's take a quick look at how managers can approve or reject such enrollment requests:

1. From the **Manager** home page, click the **Notifications** link located in the **View** section of the left sidebar.

   This takes you to the **Notifications** page. This is where all recent notifications are displayed. This includes pending enrollment requests sent by team members.

2. Click the **Pending Tasks** tab located in the upper-left corner of the **Notifications** page.

A list of all possible notification types appears on the screen. At the moment, *Manager 01* has no pending tasks, but you should see the **Approve Learner** and **Certification Approval** sections:

- The **Approve Learner** section is where managers approve or reject the enrollment requests of their team members.

- The **Certification Approvals** section relates to external Certifications. Since external certifications take place outside of Adobe Learning Manager, formal approval of the certification by a Manager may be required. This was discussed in the *Creating certifications* section, earlier in this chapter.

In the next section, you will discover yet another way Learning Manager allows you to enroll users in courses.

Automatic enrollment using Learning Plans

Learning plans are yet another way of enrolling users in courses. What makes them special is that learner enrollment is fully automatic once a Learning Plan has been defined.

You can use Learning Plans to automatically enroll learners in *Courses*, *Learning Paths*, and *Certifications*. This automatic enrollment is triggered by an event that you choose when you create the Learning Plan. This feature is very useful in many situations, including the following:

- You want to automatically enroll new learners in onboarding courses.

- You want to automatically enroll learners in courses when they join or leave a group. For example, when someone becomes a manager (that is, when someone joins the automatically-generated **All Managers** group), that person is automatically enrolled in a course on *Management Best Practices*. You can use the same technique to automatically enroll learners when they change positions, move to a new department, and more.

- You want to ensure that users are only enrolled in a given course once they have completed a previous course. This is one of the ways to enforce prerequisites.

- You want to automatically enroll learners in courses on a certain date – for example, you need to train people when a new product is released, after an organization acquisition has been made official, or when a new branch opens.

In this section, you will create the **New Learner Onboarding** Learning Plan. For the sake of this demonstration, you can use any of the courses available in your Learning Manager trial account. In reality, you would, of course, create an onboarding course before creating the corresponding Learning Plan.

Perform the following steps to experiment with creating a Learning Plan:

1. Make sure you are logged in as an Administrator.

2. From the **Administrator** home page, click the **Learning Plans** link located in the **Learning** section of the left sidebar.

3. Click the **Add** button in the upper-right corner of the page.

4. Type New Learner Onboarding in the **Learning Plan Name** field.

5. Open the **Occurs When** drop-down menu and inspect the available events.

   Depending on the selected event, additional options appears on the form. Take some time to review these events and their associated options.

6. When you're ready, choose the **New Learner is added** event.

7. Use the search field under **Training** to look for the Courses (or *Learning Paths* or *Certifications*) that you want to associate with this Learning Plan.

8. Click the **Save** button in the upper-right corner of the page when it looks as follows:

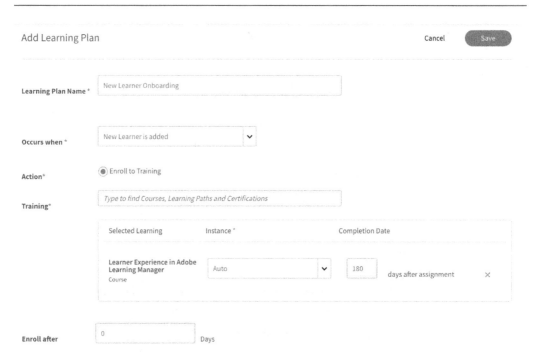

Figure 6.19 – Creating a new Learning Plan

9.   The last step is to enable the new Learning Plan.

Back on the **Learning Plans** page, use the checkbox to select the Learning Plan you just created.

10. Click the **Actions** button in the upper-right corner of the screen and choose the **Enable** option.

From now on, each time a new user is added to the platform, that user is automatically enrolled in the *New Learner Onboarding* Learning Plan and is given 180 days to complete the associated course(s).

This makes for a lot of options for enrolling learners in courses. So, in the next section, you will review the list of enrolled learners using the Admin role of Adobe Learning Manager.

Viewing Enrolled Learners

In the *Enrollment by Managers* section, earlier in this chapter, you discovered how managers can list the learners that are enrolled in a course. But managers only see data about their team members. Also, they do not have access to the waitlist. Only administrators and instructors have a comprehensive overview of all the learners enrolled in a given course.

In this section, you will review the list of enrolled learners from the administrator's perspective. The instructor role will be covered in more detail in *Chapter 8, Exploring the Instructor Role.*

Perform the following steps to review the list of learners that have enrolled in the **Advanced IT Security** course:

1. Make sure you are logged in as an administrator and that you are on the **Courses** page of the Admin role.

2. Click the **Advanced IT Security** course to open the course details.

3. Click the **Learners** link located in the **Manage** section of the left sidebar.

4. Use the **Select Instance** dropdown to select the instance you enrolled learners in throughout this chapter.

5. Expand the **Individuals** and **Self Enrolled** sections to reveal the list of learners enrolled in the course.

This gives you access to the list of learners currently enrolled in the selected instance. This is the same list that *Manager 01* has access to, except that *Learner 03* is visible in the **Self Enrolled** category.

6. Take some time to inspect the available tools.

    Notice the **Search learners** field in the upper-right corner of the list, the **Actions** link just next to it, and the **Enroll** link, which allows you to enroll even more learners in the selected instance.

    These tools are depicted in the following screenshot:

Figure 6.20 – Tools available to the administrator for managing learners enrolled in a course

7. Use the checkboxes available to select any learner from the list.

8. Click the **Actions** link located above the list of enrolled learners.

9. Inspect the available actions, making sure you do *not* click any of them.

This gives you an overview of the actions available to an administrator for managing the learners enrolled in a course. Note that the very same actions are also available to managers, but only for their team members.

There is one more situation to inspect. Remember that in the *Enrollment by Managers* section, earlier in this chapter, *Manager 01* had enrolled *Learner 02* in the course, but unfortunately, the chosen course instance was already full and *Learner 02* has been added to the waitlist. It is time to check this out!

10. Click the **Waitlist** link located in the **Manage** section of the left sidebar.

11. Use the **Select Instance** dropdown to select the instance you enrolled learners in throughout this chapter.

    And…. here is *Learner 02*!

12. Use the checkbox to select *Learner 02*.

Notice the **Allocate Seats** button that appears in the upper-right corner of the screen. This allows the administrator to override the **Seat Limit** of the course instance and enroll learners anyway (make sure you do *not* click this button in this example).

Also, notice the **Actions** button, which allows you to unenroll the selected user(s).

With these tools, administrators and managers have everything they need to manage the list of users enrolled in a given course instance, as well as to deal with learners on the waitlist.

Summary

Now that you've completed this chapter, learners can finally enroll in courses and learning can start to happen on your Learning Manager account.

In this chapter, you have given the coup de grace to the popular belief that learners enroll in courses. In Adobe Learning Manager, learners enroll in *Course Instances*, *Learning Paths*, and *Certifications*, never in courses, per se.

You created instances to address the time-bound nature of the synchronous activities included in some of the courses. You also grouped courses into Learning Paths, and you created an internal Certification that learners must obtain within 30 days of enrollment.

With these learning objects available in the course catalog, you have reviewed many workflows that allow users to enroll themselves, which is the preferred way of taking a course in Adobe Learning Manager. But administrators and managers can also enroll learners in courses without them asking. The platform itself can also automatically enroll lesarners when some kind of event occurs, as defined in *Learning Plans*.

With that, everything is in place for the miracle of learning to occur! In the next chapter, you will take on the learner role and explore the unique learning experience offered by Adobe Learning Manager.

7

Reviewing the Learner Experience

In this chapter, learning will finally start on your Learning Manager account. After all, this is the primary purpose of Adobe Learning Manager and the main reason your organization implements an LMS in the first place.

Adobe Learning Manager pays particular attention to providing an exceptional learning experience. As a matter of fact, the learner experience is one of the landmark features of Learning Manager. It is centered around a critical component known as the **Fluidic Player.** The Fluidic Player is the component that delivers the learning content. It has been designed to support a wide range of content types, including video, PDF, and Word documents, PowerPoint presentations, and interactive content in AICC, SCORM, or xAPI format.

Learners can also use the Adobe Learning Manager mobile app for iOS and Android to take courses on their mobile devices. A key feature of the mobile app is the ability to download the course content and review it offline. The course tracking data is uploaded to the server the next time the mobile device has access to the internet.

These are the features you will explore in this chapter. To do this, you will log into your account as a learner and take the courses you created in *Chapter 4, Creating Skills and Courses.* By the end of this chapter, you will have reviewed the basic learner experience using both your computer and a mobile device.

To achieve this goal, this chapter contains the following sections:

- Touring the default learner experience
- Discovering the Fluidic Player
- Using the Learning Manager mobile app
- Customizing the Fluidic Player

As you read this chapter, keep in mind that the features discussed here are those used by most users. This is the experience that your efforts as an administrator or author are geared toward.

Also, keep in mind that you are working on a trial account with only a few users and a few courses available. Some of the features discussed in this chapter only make sense on a bigger account with more users and courses.

Technical requirements

In order to perform the exercises described in this chapter, you need to meet the following requirements:

- You must have Administrator and Author access to a working Learning Manager account (trial accounts are OK).
- You must also be able to access your ALM account with at least two different learner profiles.
- These learners must both be enrolled in the same courses.
- You should have access to a mobile device (tablet or smartphone) with the Adobe Learning Manager app installed. The app is available for iOS from the Apple App Store and for Android from the Google Play Store.

If you have completed the exercises in the previous chapters, you are ready to begin! If not, you can use your own course content and users to complete the exercises in this chapter.

Touring the Default Learner Experience

The learner experience is the most carefully crafted area of Adobe Learning Manager. Only a few users will ever access one of the administrative areas of your account, while all the users are learners using the Learner experience.

In this section, you will log in to your account as *Learner 01* and take a deep dive into the default Learner experience:

1. Log in to your account as *Learner 01*. Since you did not assign a specific role to this user, you should be automatically redirected to the learner experience.

2. Click the **Notification** icon located in the upper-right corner of the screen. As shown in the following screenshot, you should see a notification telling you that an administrator has enrolled *Learner 01* in a course:

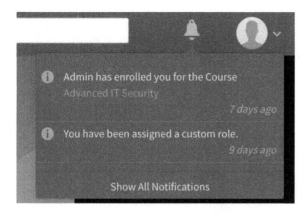

Figure 7.1 – An admin has enrolled Learner 01 in a course

Now that you are connected as a learner, you will review the learner experience in more detail, starting with the learner home page in the next section.

Reviewing the Learner home page

You reviewed the options related to the learner home page from an administrator perspective in *Chapter 2*, *Customizing the Look and Feel of Adobe Learning Manager*. These options are available from the **Branding/Learner** home page of the Administrator role.

> **Note**
> The screenshots and instructions provided in this chapter assume the default *immersive* experience.

It is now time to review the various sections of the learner home page in more detail:

- At the very top, the **masthead** spans the entire page. It should currently invite you to **Learn something new today**. This area is where various messages and recommendations are displayed. You'll learn how to configure masthead messages in *Chapter 15*, *Working with Messages and Announcements*.

- Under the masthead, you find the **My Learning List** section. This is where the courses you are currently taking are displayed. This section of the home page is a summary of the **My Learning** page that you will review later in this chapter.

- Under the **My Learning List** section, you find a row containing various items. The **Levels** item is related to the **gamification** features of Adobe Learning Manager, which will be covered in *Chapter 11*, *Badges and Gamification*.

- Another item is a calendar where the day's activities are displayed. If you select the date of one of *Learner 01*'s scheduled live classes, you will see the class activity listed in the calendar with a direct access link, as illustrated in the following screenshot:

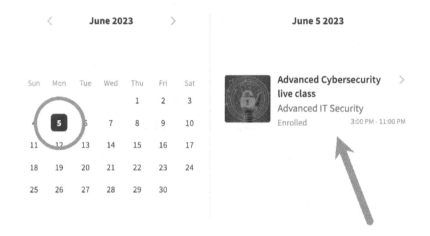

Figure 7.2 – The calendar section on the default learner home page

- The **Social Feed** item relates to the **social learning** features of Adobe Learning Manager. You will review these features in *Chapter 12, Enabling and Managing Social Learning*.

- Further down the page, you find the **Recommended based on your areas of interest** section. This section is related to the **skills** defined in Learning Manager, as discussed in *Chapter 4, Creating Skills and Courses*. In Adobe Learning Manager, the term *areas of interest* is just another word for *Skills*. These can be skills associated with courses you are enrolled in, skills that have been assigned to you by an administrator, or skills that you can handpick using the **Skills** page of the learner experience, which you will review later in this chapter.

- Finally, the **Recommended based on peer activity** section is where the artificial intelligence of Learning Manager kicks in! The content in this section is different for each user and depends on a variety of factors that you will examine in more detail in *Chapter 13, AI-Powered Recommendations for Learners*.

As you can see, the **Learner** home page is designed around three main goals: provide all important information at a glance, provide highly personalized recommendations, and offer quick access to the other pages of the learner experience.

As discussed in *Chapter 2, Customizing the Look and Feel of Adobe Learning Manager*, remember that the administrator can add, remove, and rearrange the sections of the learner home page.

You will now review each page of the learner experience one by one, starting with the **My Learning** page in the following section.

Exploring the My Learning page

The **My Learning** page lists all Courses, Learning Paths, and Certifications in which the learner is enrolled. This page gives learners a complete overview of all the training resources they are taking or have taken.

Use the following steps to access the **My Learning** page:

1. From the learner home page click the **Go to My Learning** link located in the **My Learning List** section at the top of the home page.

When you're on the **My Learning** page, you see a list of all the Courses, Learning Paths, and Certifications *Learner 01* is enrolled in. The **job aids** that can be accessed by this learner (if any) are also displayed here. Notice the **Sort By** dropdown in the upper-right corner of the screen, as well as the checkboxes in the left column, which are used to filter the learning content displayed on the page:

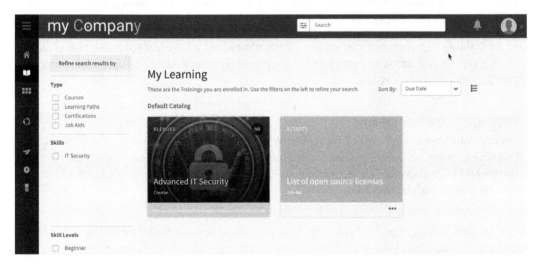

Figure 7.3 – The My Learning page of the learner experience

By default, the courses on this page are sorted by **Due Date**. This allows learners to focus their immediate attention on the courses with the closest due date.

The **My Learning** page is a great tool, especially for long-time learners who have a lot of past, present, and future learning activities under their belt. In the next section, you will briefly review the **Catalog** page of the learning experience.

Exploring the Catalog Page

The primary purpose of the **Catalog** page is to allow learners to self-enroll in courses. Indeed, as already discussed in *Chapter 6, Enrolling Users in Courses*, the primary means for a learner to register for a course is through self-enrollment.

To access the **Catalog** page, you must click the **Catalog** icon, which is the third icon from the top in the left sidebar. Alternatively, from the **Learner** home page, you can use the **Go To Catalog** link located in the **Recommended based on your areas of interest** section.

The tools on the **Catalog** page are mostly the same as those available on the **My Learning** page:

- There are checkboxes on the left-hand side to filter the list of visible learning objects.
- You can use the **Sort By** dropdown in the upper-right corner of the page to sort the visible items. The default sort order is **Recently Published**, which displays the latest addition to the catalog at the top of the list.

The best way to explain the difference between these two pages is to say that the **My Learning** page is a list of *Must-take* courses the learner is already enrolled in, whereas the **Catalog** is a list of *Could-take* courses that the learner can self-enroll in.

From the **Catalog** page, learners can review information about all the learning objects they have access to. They can also enroll in courses or send approval requests to their manager, depending on the enrollment option of the course.

> **Working with multiple catalogs**
>
> You currently have a single catalog that contains all the learning objects hosted in your Adobe Learning Manager account. By default, this catalog is available to all learners. In *Chapter 14, Working with Catalogs and Peer Accounts*, you will create additional catalogs to control which learning objects each learner has access to.

That's it for the **Catalog** page! In the next section, you will review the **Social Learning** page of the Learner experience.

Reviewing the Social Learning page

The next page of the Learner experience is the **Social Learning** page. To access this page, click the **Social Learning** icon, which is the fourth icon from the top in the left sidebar.

This page is the social network aspect of Adobe Learning Manager. The social learning features will be discussed in *Chapter 12, Enabling and Managing Social Learning*. Note that administrators can choose to completely turn off **Social Learning** in their Adobe Learning Manager account. This removes the **Social Learning** icon from the left sidebar and hides the **Social Learning** page from learners.

Reviewing the Skills Page

Following the list of icons on the left sidebar, the next icon takes you to the **Skills** page. The **Skills** page (also known as the **My Areas of Interest** page) lists the skills related to the courses you are enrolled in:

Figure 7.4 – The Skills page, also known as the My Areas of Interest page

In the preceding screenshot, the **IT Security** skill is the only one listed for *Learner 01*. This is because *Learner 01* is enrolled in the *Advanced IT Security* course, which is linked to this particular skill. In addition, each learner can handpick their areas of interest by doing the following:

1. Click the **Add Interest** link to open the **Add to My Areas of Interest** page, which lists all the skills available in your Learning Manager account.

2. Click a few skills to add them to the selection. You can also click a selected skill to remove it from the selection.

3. When you're done, click the **Add** button to return to the previous page.

You should now see additional skills on the **My Areas of Interest** page. Remember that the skills you select influence the course recommendations displayed on the Learner home page. Also, keep in mind that administrators can assign skills to learners, as discussed in *Chapter 4, Creating Skills and Courses*. Administrator-assigned skills also appear on the **My Areas of Interest** page.

Asking users to handpick areas of interest

With skills management and home page personalization being such important concepts in Adobe Learning Manager, administrators can ask learners to handpick their *areas of interest* (aka *Skills*) the first time they log into their account. Let's review this feature using the following steps:

1. Use another browser or a new private window of the same browser to log into your account as an Administrator.

2. From the **Administrator** home page, click the **Branding** link in the **Configure** section of the left sidebar. This takes you to the **Branding** page of the Administrator role.

3. Scroll down the page until you see the **Homepage Experience** section, as depicted in the following screenshot:

Tell Adobe Learning Manager how you want to drive training experiences for this account. This automatically tunes recommendation algorithms and other smart features for your use case. You can always change your inputs later. Learn more.

			Edit
Homepage Experience	○ Classic	● Immersive	
Training Type	● Custom	○ Industry Aligned	
Identify Learners as Peers based on these fields	To consider all users as peers of each other, leave this selection blank else select any 1 field.		
	Internal ⌄	External ⌄	
Enable Learner to Explore Areas of Interest (Skills)	● Yes	○ No	
Prompt Learner to choose Areas of Interest (Skills)	○ Yes	● No	

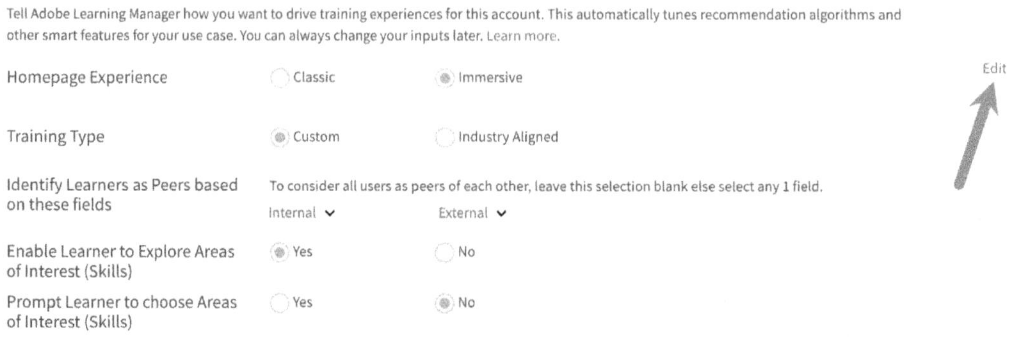

Figure 7.5 – The Hompage Experience section of the Admin role

In the preceding screenshot, notice the **Enable Learner to Explore Areas of Interest (Skills)** option, which is currently set to **Yes**. Setting this option to **No** would remove the **Skills** icon from the left sidebar in the learner experience and hide the corresponding page from learners. Hiding this page from learners simply removes their ability to access and edit their **Areas of interest**, but it is important to understand that those skills continue to exist in the system and continue to impact other aspects of the Learner experience (such as the **Recommended Based on Your Areas of Interest** section of the home page).

The **Prompt Learner to choose Areas of Interest (Skills)** option is currently set to **No**. Let's change that using the following steps:

4. Click the **Edit** link identified by the arrow in the preceding screenshot.

5. Switch the **Prompt Learner to choose Areas of Interest (Skills)** option to **Yes**.

6. Click the **Save** button located in the lower-right corner of the page.

You will now switch to the *Learner* role to test out this new option:

7. Click the **User** icon located in the upper-right corner of the page to switch to the Learner role of your user profile.

As shown in the following screenshot, as soon as the page reloads (and provided the learner has not already chosen his/her areas of interest), the system automatically prompts the learner to select areas of interest:

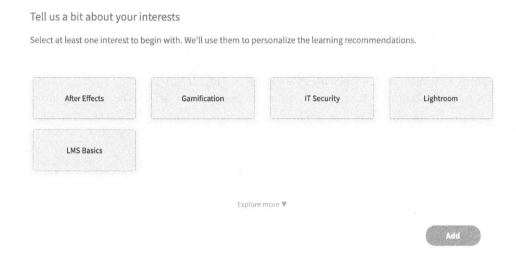

Figure 7.6 – The system prompts the user for their areas of interest

Adobe Learning Manager keeps redirecting the learner to this page at each login until the learner has made a choice.

8.   Select some skills and click the **Add** button.

9.   Back on the home page, scroll down until you see the **Recommended based on your areas of interest** section.

Since you did not choose the same *Areas of interest (skills)* as *Learner 01*, you won't see the same recommendations as when you were logged in as *Learner 01* earlier in this chapter.

In this section, you reviewed the **Skills** page of the Learner experience. You have seen how learners can select their *Areas of interest* and how this affects the recommendations that Learning Manager displays on the home page. As an administrator, you have also enabled an option that prompts learners to select their areas of interest the first time they log into your Learning Manager account.

Reviewing the Badges page

The next icon available in the left sidebar is the **Badges** icon, which takes you to the **Badges** page:

1.   Return to the browser window in which you are logged in as *Learner 01*.

2.   Click the **Badges** icon located in the left sidebar of the Learner role.

The more learners use the features of Learning Manager, the more **badges** they can earn. These are displayed on the **Badges** page in the Learner experience. From here, learners can download their badges in PDF and/or image format. Note that *Learner 01* does not have any badges at the moment.

> **Badgr**
>
> Badgr is an open online service that implements the Open Badge standard. The idea is to allow learners to centrally store all the digital badges they have earned on various compliant learning platforms (including Adobe Learning Manager) and share them on social networks and other compliant platforms. You can find more information on Badgr at `https://badgr.com/` and on digital badges in general at `https://en.wikipedia.org/wiki/Digital_badge`.

Badges will be discussed further in *Chapter 11, Badges and Gamification*.

Reviewing the Leaderboard page

The next icon of the left sidebar takes you to the **Leaderboard** page, which relates to the **gamification** features of Adobe Learning Manager. This feature will be discussed in more detail in *Chapter 11, Badges and Gamification*.

Note that an administrator can decide to completely turn off gamification for your Learning Manager account. In such a case, the **Leaderboard** icon does *not* appear on the left sidebar, and the corresponding page is hidden from learners.

Discussing the Content Marketplace page

The last icon on the left sidebar of the Learner experience provides access to the **Content Marketplace** page.

The Adobe Learning Manager **Content Marketplace** area contains over 86,000 courses available for purchase. Using the **Content Marketplace** page, learners can express their interest in courses available in the Adobe Content Marketplace. Administrators can then download a *report of interest*, which is designed to help them make a purchase decision for additional courses that are made available to learners through this Adobe Learning Manager account.

By default, all learners have access to this page and can express their interest in these additional courses. Administrators can limit the number of users who have access to this page or even disable this feature altogether.

The **Content Marketplace** page will be discussed in more detail in *Chapter 14, Working with Catalogs and Peer Accounts*.

Recap

In the previous few sections, you went through all the pages of the learner experience, one by one. Here is a summary:

- The **Learner** home page serves both as a personal summary and an area for personalized recommendations.

- The **My Learning** page is where learners have access to a complete overview of their interactions with the learning resources hosted on the platform.

- The **Catalog** page is a very important element of the learner experience. This is where learners can browse the available learning resources and enroll in courses.

- The **Skills** page allows learners to handpick their areas of interest. This selection of **Skills** influences the personal recommendations displayed on the home page.

- Users can also see their **Badges**, participate in **Social Learning** interactions with their peers, and use the **Leaderboard** area to see how they compare to their colleagues.

- Finally, learners can use the **Content Marketplace** page to express their interest in additional courses available for purchase.

You should now have a better understanding of the features available to learners and the corresponding administrative options.

In the next section, you will dive deeper into the learner experience by enrolling in and then taking a course.

Taking a course

Now that you have a better idea of what the default Learner experience looks like, it is time to do justice to the Learner role by actually taking a course using Adobe Learning Manager!

Taking a self-paced course

In this section, you will enroll in and take a *self-paced* course. Such a course comprises only self-paced modules that can be delivered by Adobe Learning Manager in a completely automatic way without any human intervention.

You will now log into your account as *Learner 01* and enroll in the *Fundamentals of IT security* course you created in *Chapter 4, Creating Skills and Course*. Perform the following steps to do so:

1. Log in to your account as *Learner 01*.

2. Open the **Catalog** page of the Learner experience using the third icon from the top in the left sidebar.

3. Click the **Fundamentals of IT security** course card.

4. Click the **Enroll** button located in the upper-right area of the course overview page.

This action takes *Learner 01* straight to the **Fluidic Player**, which is the component that delivers the content to learners. The Fluidic Player is such an important aspect of the learner experience that it will be discussed in more detail in the next section.

Discovering the Fluidic Player

The **Fluidic Player** is a key component and a landmark feature of Adobe Learning Manager. What makes it unique is its ability to deliver a wide variety of learning content. This allows learners to remain in the same learning environment regardless of the module being reviewed.

You will now review the features of the Fluidic Player in more detail. This exercise picks up where the previous section left off. You should be in the Fluidic Player with the first module of the course being displayed.

If you have used the files included in the download associated with this book, this first module is a PowerPoint presentation. Notice the icons located in the center section of the Fluidic Player, as shown in the following screenshot:

Figure 7.7 – The Fluidic Player when displaying a PowerPoint presentation

The icons identified as **1** in the preceding screenshot allow you to move from one slide to the next within the PowerPoint presentation. These controls *are specific to PowerPoint presentations and documents:*

5. Use these controls to review the PowerPoint presentation.

6. When you're done, click the icon identified as **2** in the preceding screenshot to move on to the next module of the course.

The next module is a Word document. Note that the Word document of the second module is viewed in the same Fluidic Player as the PowerPoint presentation of the first module. As a learner, you did not have to leave the Fluidic Player to switch from one type of content (a PowerPoint presentation) to the next (a Word document). This is very different from most other LMS solutions that use different media players, depending on the type of content being served:.

7. Scroll to the end of the document and use the right arrow to proceed to the next module.

   The next module is a PDF file. Again, this type of content is displayed in the same Fluidic Player as the previous two modules, without the learner being routed to a content type-specific media player.

8. Now, click the **Close** icon located in the upper-right corner of the screen.

This action closes the Fluidic Player and takes you back to the course overview page. As shown in the following screenshot, a progress bar displays your overall progress in the course (see the arrow in the following screenshot):

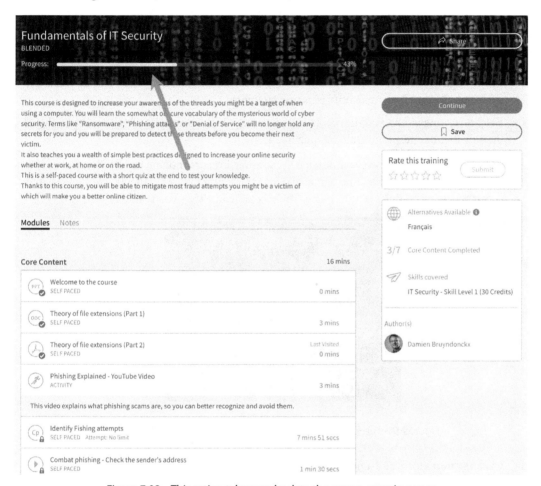

Figure 7.08 – This action takes you back to the course overview page

Also, notice that the first three modules of the course are marked as complete, the fourth module of the course is available, and all the other modules are still locked. This is because this is an *ordered* course, as defined in *Chapter 4, Creating Skills and Courses*.

9. Click the **Continue** button in the upper-right corner of the page to resume the course where you left off. This action reopens the Fluidic Player with the third module (the PDF file) being displayed

10. Click the right arrow to move on to the next module.

11. The fourth module is an external URL activity. Click the **Go to Activity URL** button to visit the external link. When you're done, return to Adobe Learning Manager and click the **Mark as complete** button.

Clicking the **Mark as complete** button automatically takes you to the next module, which is an interactive SCORM activity. Once again, this interactive SCORM content opens in the same Fuidic Player as before.

12. Go through the interactive SCORM content as a learner would. Along the way, you will learn a few things about how to identify phishing attempts.

13. Keep reviewing all the modules of this course until it is fully complete. Make sure you do all the activities and respond to all the quiz questions.

As you do so, notice the two icons located in the lower-left corner of the Fluidic Player, as shown in the following screenshot. The first icon opens the course table of contents. You can use it to access the other modules of the course. The second icon allows you to add notes:

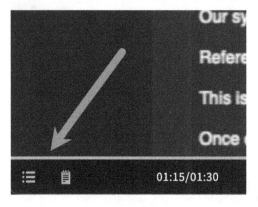

Figure 7.9 – The icons in the lower-left corner of the Fluidic Player

14. Click the **notes** icon, add a new note, and click the **Add** button. The added note is attached to your exact position in the course at the time you created the note.

15. After you have completed all the modules, click the **Close** icon in the upper-right corner of the Fluidic Player to return to the course overview page.

16. Back on the course overview page, notice the **Notes** tab next to the **Modules** tab. Use it to access the personal notes you created during the course.

Now that you have reviewed all the modules, there are a few changes on the course overview page, as shown in the following screenshot:

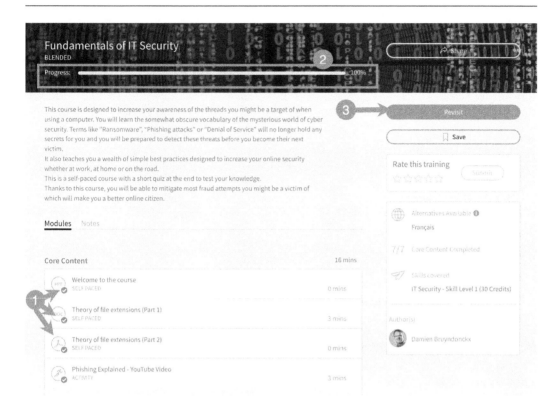

Figure 7.10 – The course overview page after completing all the modules

You should see a green checkmark next to each module (see **1** in the preceding screenshot), the progress bar at the top of the page indicates that the course is 100% complete (see **2**), and the button in the upper-right corner is now labeled **Revisit** (see **3**).

By going through this self-paced course, you have experienced the real magic of the Fluidic Player: when a module is finished, the next module is automatically loaded into the same Fluidic Player, without leaving the learning environment. This allows learners to stay focused on learning while moving seamlessly from one module to the next, regardless of the type of content being served.

The course you just reviewed as *Learner 01* is self-paced. *Learner 01* was able to complete the entire course and review all the modules without any human intervention. In the next section, you will act as *Learner 01* to take the **Advanced IT Security** course, which is centered around a face-to-face instructor-led class.

Taking an instructor-led synchronous course

In this section, you will continue touring the Learner experience by attempting to take a completely different type of course. Perform the following steps to try it out:

1. Log into your Learning Manager account as *Learner 01* and make sure you are on the **Learner** home page.

2. Click the **Advanced IT Security** course card located in the **My Learning List** section of the home page. You can also use the **My Learning** page, which can be accessed via the second icon on the left sidebar.

This action takes you to the **Advanced IT Security** course overview page. Take some time to review the information contained on this page:

*   Note the **Prerequisite Course** section at the top of the page

*   Also, note that the **Start** button in the upper-right corner of the page is currently disabled, preventing *Learner 01* from starting this course

The first module of this course is an instructor-led classroom module. Completion of this module must be reported by an instructor. Because this is an ordered course (a course in which all modules must be completed in the order defined when the course was created), the other modules of the course are also not accessible. In *Chapter 8, Exploring the Instructor Role*, you will learn how instructors can report class attendance to Learning Manager, which, in turn, will unlock the rest of this course:

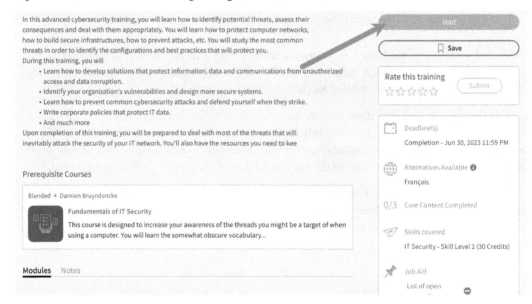

Figure 7.11 – The Start button is disabled, preventing Learner 01 from starting the course

You should now have a solid understanding of what it is like for a learner to take self-paced courses in your Learning Manager account using a web browser. In the next section, you will examine the learner experience once again, but this time using the Adobe Learning Manager app installed on your mobile device, rather than the web browser installed on your laptop or desktop computer.

Using the Learning Manager mobile app

In the previous section, you logged in as *Learner 01* to your Learning Manager account using your web browser. However, a growing number of learners want to take courses using their mobile devices, which raises a whole new set of challenges:

- The screen of a mobile device is typically much smaller than the screen of a laptop or desktop computer, which implies the creation of a specific user experience.

- Interacting with fingers on a touchscreen is very different from using a mouse on a desktop or laptop computer, so interactions need to be redesigned for touch.

- The quality and stability of the network and the available bandwidth are not guaranteed on a mobile device. Users can be connected to a fast and reliable Wi-Fi network, as well as to a slow and unpredictable 3G connection.

- How does your HR and IT departments support mobile devices for learning?

To help overcome these challenges, the Adobe Learning Manager team has developed a dedicated mobile app available for iOS and Android. The mobile app is available for smartphones and tablets alike. Use the Apple App Store or the Google Play Store to download and install the Adobe Learning Manager app on your mobile device.

The Adobe Learning Manager mobile app only reproduces the learner role. The other roles (administrator, instructor, manager, author, and integration admin) are only accessible through a web browser.

In this section, you will use the Adobe Learning Manager mobile app to log into your account as *Learner 03*, review the learner experience provided by the mobile app, and take a few courses using your mobile device.

Connecting to Learning Manager using the mobile app

First, you will use the Learning Manager mobile app to log into your account:

1. Use either the Apple App Store (iOS) or the Google Play Store (Android) to install the Adobe Learning Manager mobile app on your mobile device (Smartphone or Tablet). Once installed, tap the Learning Manager icon to open the application.

2. Enter the email address of *Learner 03* and click the **Proceed** button.

If the email address is used on multiple accounts, choose the account you want to connect to using the **Associated Accounts** page that appears on the screen.

3. Since *Learner 03* is an *external* user, you are redirected to a special login page where you must enter the email ID and password of this learner profile. Note that *internal* users go through a slightly different authentication process.

> **Internal and external users**
>
> The differences between internal and external users were discussed in *Chapter 5, Managing Users*.

Once you've logged in, you should see a screen similar to the immersive learner home page you reviewed earlier in this chapter, as shown in the following screenshot:

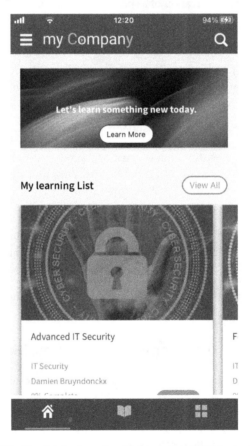

Figure 7.12 – The Adobe Learning Manager mobile app on an iPhone

Now that you are connected using the mobile app, let's review the learner experience provided by the app.

Exploring the mobile learner experience

The learner experience provided by the mobile app is very similar to the experience you reviewed in the *Touring the Default Learner Experience* section earlier in this chapter. Let's check this out:

1. Make sure you are connected as *Learner 03* using the mobile app.

2. Scroll the home page up and down and take the necessary time to identify all the sections. You should recognize the sections discussed earlier in this chapter.

3. At the bottom of the screen, tap the **My Learning** icon. This takes you to the **My Learning** page, where you can see all the Courses, Learning Paths, and Certifications *Learner 03* is currently enrolled in.

    Note the **My Learning** and **My Job Aids** tabs at the top of the page. *Job aids* were discussed in *Chapter 4, Creating Skills and Courses*.

4. The next item at the bottom of the screen is the **Catalog** icon. Tapping this icon takes you to the course catalog, where all the courses available on the platform are displayed.

5. Tap the hamburger icon (the icon with the three horizontal bars) located in the upper-left corner of the screen to reveal a side panel with additional options.

As shown in the following screenshot, the side panel allows you to view your **Profile**, review your **Notifications**, access the general **Settings** of the application, get **Help**, and **Sign out** of the Adobe Learning Manager mobile app:

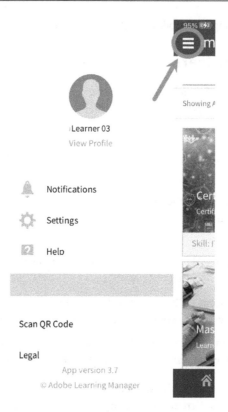

Figure 7.13 – The side panel of the Learning Manager mobile app

This gives you a quick overview of the features available in the Adobe Learning Manager mobile app. Note that a few pages that are available when using a web browser (such as the **Skills** and **Leaderboard** pages) are *not* available when using the mobile app.

In the next section, you will use the mobile app to browse the course catalog, enroll in the **Mastering Photo Editing** Learning Path, and take all the associated courses.

Enrolling in Courses using the Mobile App

In this section, you will use the mobile app to search the course catalog, enroll *Learner 03* in the **Mastering Photo Editing** Learning Path, and review the courses included in this Learning Path. Use the following steps to do so:

1. Make sure you are logged in as *Learner 03* using the Learning Manager mobile app.

2. Tap the **Catalog** icon located at the bottom of the screen.

3. Browse the Catalog until you find the **Mastering Photo Editing** Learning Path. You can also use the search icon in the upper-right corner of the screen. When found, tap the Learning Path card to open the overview page.

4. Take some time to review the information available on the overview page. When you're ready, tap the **Enroll** button. The **Enroll** button turns into a **Start** button.

5. Tap the **Start** button to begin the first course contained in the Learning Path. This opens the Fluidic Player embedded in the mobile app.

6. While reviewing the video, take some time to examine the features of the Fluidic Player. You should find the same icons that you would when you took a self-paced course on your desktop or laptop computer earlier in this chapter.

7. Review all the modules of all the courses contained in the **Mastering Photo Editing** Learning Path.

You will see that the experience provided by the mobile app is very similar to the one provided by the web browser. This is another highlight of the Fluidic Player: it can be embedded in a mobile application or even on your website. This ability will be discussed further in *Chapter 16, Exploring the Integration Admin Role*.

Enrolling using a QR code

Another way to enroll in a course using the mobile app is by scanning a QR code. An administrator must print the QR code using the course **Instances** page of the Admin role. Posting these QR codes around the organization's premises allows the learner to scan these codes using their mobile device and automatically enroll in the corresponding course. The **Scan QR Code** feature can be accessed using the hamburger icon located in the upper-left corner of the mobile app.

Taking a course while offline using the mobile app

In the previous section, you had your first look at the process of taking courses using the mobile app. In this section, you will download a course and review it offline using the mobile app. The course tracking data will be transferred to Learning Manager the next time you connect to the internet:

1. Make sure you are logged in as *Learner 03* using the mobile app.

2. In the **My Learning List** section of the home page, tap the course card of the **Fundamentals of IT Security** course. You can also use the **Catalog** page if needed.

3. On the course overview page, tap the **Download** icon identified by the arrow in the following screenshot:

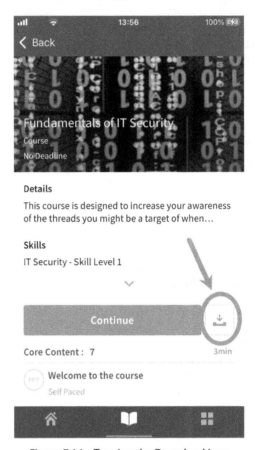

Figure 7.14 – Tapping the Download icon

4.   Confirm your intention of downloading the course and wait for the download to complete.

5.   Put your mobile device in airplane mode to mimic an offline situation.

6.   Return to the Learning Manager app and start taking the course. Notice that even though you are offline, you can review the self-paced modules as if you were connected. This is because you are using the offline copy of the content that you downloaded earlier.

Note

The SCORM content created by Adobe Captivate has not been made responsive. As a result, this content could generate horizontal and/or vertical scroll bars when viewed using a mobile device. Here, the eLearning developer (myself, in this case) is to blame, not Learning Manager! This illustrates that although Learning Manager is mobile-friendly, the content hosted on the platform must also be made responsive to provide a fully responsive mobile experience.

7. After you have reviewed a few self-paced modules, turn off airplane mode and reconnect to the internet. Return to the Learning Manager application and wait a few moments for the course tracking data to be uploaded to the Learning Manager backend.

    Note that this process takes place in the background and that no visual indication that the process has been completed appears on your screen.

Now that you have completed a few course modules using the mobile app, you will return to your desktop or laptop and log in as *Learner 03* to demonstrate that you can use your desktop or laptop to resume a course you started on the mobile app.

8. Return to your desktop or laptop computer and log in to your Learning Manager account as *Learner 03*.

Logging in as Learner 03

Remember that *Learner 03* is the only *external* learner that you defined in *Chapter 5, Managing Users*, so this user must use a custom login page. The URL of this login page is available in the email message that was sent to *Learner 03* when that user was created. If you no longer have access to this email message, browse to the **External Users** page of the Admin role and hover over the external registration profile to reveal the chain icon; then, copy the link to your clipboard.

9. Confirm that the course card on the **Learner** home page reflects the progress you have made while using the mobile app:

My Learning List

Figure 7.15 – The progress you've made on the mobile app is reflected in the web browser

In this section, you reviewed the main features of the Adobe Learning Manager mobile application. You used it to browse the course catalog, enroll in courses, and review a few modules of different types. You also downloaded some content for offline viewing, knowing that the course tracking data is sent to Learning Manager the next time the device connects to the internet.

Customizing the Fluidic Player

After reviewing many aspects of the Learner experience throughout this chapter, you have certainly noticed the key role of the Fluidic Player. Whether you're using a web browser or the mobile application, the Fluidic Player is at the heart of the course-taking experience. In *Chapter 16*, *Exploring the Integration Admin Role*, you will learn that the Fluidic Player can even be embedded in an external website, extending the reach of your course content even beyond the confines of Adobe Learning Manager. Since the Fluidic Player is such a key component, it is very important to tailor it perfectly to your specific needs.

In Adobe Learning Manager, both Administrators and Authors can customize the Fluidic Player. This is what you will experiment with in the next two sections.

Customizing the Fluidic Player as an Administrator

In this section, you will return to the Administrator role and review the options available in the backend to customize the Fluidic Player. Customizations made by an administrator are made at the account level and therefore have an impact on all the courses hosted on the Learning Manager account. Let's check this out by performing the following steps:

1. Log into your Learning Manager account as an **Administrator** and make sure you are on the **Administrator** home page.

2. Click the **Branding** link located in the **Configure** section of the left sidebar.

3. Click the **Edit** link associated with the **Player View** section of the **Branding** page. This is depicted in the following screenshot:

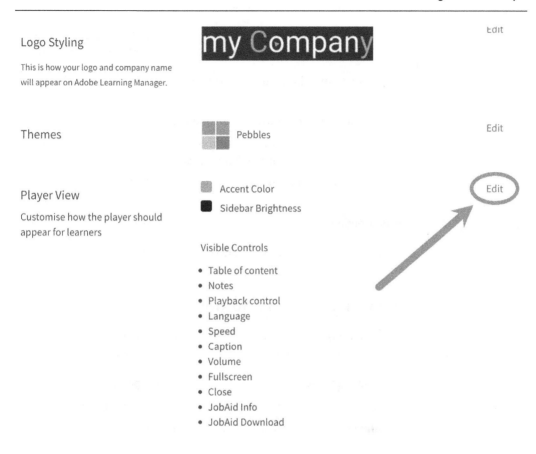

Logo Styling

This is how your logo and company name will appear on Adobe Learning Manager.

Edit

Themes

Pebbles

Edit

Player View

Customise how the player should appear for learners

Accent Color
Sidebar Brightness

Edit

Visible Controls

- Table of content
- Notes
- Playback control
- Language
- Speed
- Caption
- Volume
- Fullscreen
- Close
- JobAid Info
- JobAid Download

Figure 7.16 – Clicking the Edit link associated with the Player View option

From here, you can customize the color of various elements of the Fluidic Player and decide which icons should be visible to learners taking courses on your Learning Manager account.

4.   For this demonstration, hide a few random icons and click the **Save** button in the lower-left corner of the screen when you're done.

You now have an idea of the options available to administrators for customizing the Fluidic Player. Remember that the decisions made here by administrators affect all the learners and all the courses throughout your Learning Manager account.

Enabling Authors to customize the Fluidic Player

Authors can also customize the Fluidic Player in pretty much the same way. The main difference is that the choices made by authors only impact the course they are working on, while the choices made by administrators impact the entire Learning Manager account.

This can lead to an inconsistent learning experience across courses, which is why this feature is disabled by default. In this section, you will see how administrators can give Authors access to the Player Settings:

1. Make sure you are logged in as an Administrator and that you are on the **Administrator** home page.

2. Click the **Settings** link located in the **Configure** section of the left sidebar.

3. Next, click the **General** link located in the **Basics** section of the left sidebar. This takes you to the **General** settings page of your Adobe Learning Manager account.

4. Scroll down the page until you see the **Player settings** option. By default, this option should be disabled.

5. Enable the **Player settings** option.

Now, Authors can further customize the Fluidic Player for each course hosted on your account. We'll take a look at this in the next section.

Customizing the Fluidic Player as an Author

Now that an administrator has given authors access to the **Player settings** options, let's switch to the Author role and see how authors can customize the Fluidic Player of their courses:

1. Switch to the Author role and make sure you are on the **Author** home page.

2. Click the **Courses** link located in the **Learning** section of the left sidebar to open the **Courses** page.

3. When you're on the **Course** page, click any course card to open the **Overview** page of the chosen course.

4. Click the **Settings** link located in the left column.

5. When you're on the **Settings** page of the chosen course, click the **Edit** button located in the upper-right corner of the screen.

6. Scroll down the **Settings** page until you see the **Player Controls** section.

From here, authors can customize the Fluidic Player for that particular course using the same options as those used by administrators earlier in this chapter.

Note that authors can only set the visibility of the player controls; they cannot change the color of those controls as administrators can.

Also, note that the controls that were disabled by the administrator earlier in this chapter are also disabled here, although authors can override this choice and enable these controls anyway.

Should authors be allowed to customize the Fluidic Player for their courses?

Be very careful when allowing authors to customize the Fluidic Player for their courses, as this can lead to an inconsistent and confusing Learning experience across courses. If the ability for authors to customize the Fluidic Player in this way is disabled by default, it is for a good reason! Before moving on to the next chapter, take the necessary time to re-enable all Fluidic Player controls and disable the **Player Settings** option so that authors no longer have access to this feature.

Summary

Congratulations! With learners taking courses, your Adobe Learning Manager account has finally come to life.

In this chapter, you reviewed the default Learner Experience. You visited all the pages of the learner role using a web browser, enrolled in courses, and took a self-paced course from start to finish.

Then, you did the same on your mobile device using the Adobe Learning Manager mobile app. You even downloaded an entire course so that you can enjoy the learning content even when your mobile device is not connected to the internet.

At the heart of the learner experience is the Fluidic Player, which allows learners to move seamlessly through courses, regardless of the type of learning content being used. Because the Fluidic Player is such an important aspect of Adobe Learning Manager, you must be able to tailor it to your specific needs. That's why administrators can choose to enable or disable the features of the Fluidic Player for the entire Learning Manager account. Authors can do the same for each course, although this capability is disabled by default as it can lead to an inconsistent learning experience from course to course.

Now that you have active learners on your account, a new challenge arises: tracking your learners' progress on a daily basis. This includes preparing for instructor-led courses, managing waitlists, reviewing learner assignments, and completing checklists. These are the main tasks of the Instructor role, which you will review in the next chapter.

Exploring the Instructor Role

In the previous chapter, you achieved an important milestone – learners are now busy taking self-paced courses on your Adobe Learning Manager account. Because these courses only contain self-paced modules, they can be delivered automatically by Adobe Learning Manager with little to no human intervention.

But not all courses are self-paced, and some types of activities do require human intervention. First, instructor-led courses (face-to-face or virtual) obviously require an instructor, but that's not all. *File submission* and *checklist* activities also require human intervention to be marked as complete.

In this chapter, you will explore these non-automated activities both from the learner's and the instructor's perspectives.

First, you will log in as an *Instructor* to explore the tools and features available for managing and delivering *live* classes (face-to-face or virtual). Next, you will return to the *Learner* role and submit an assignment using the *File Submission* activity, before returning to the *Instructor* role and reviewing the submitted work. Finally, you will use the *Instructor* role again, to fill out a *Checklist* activity. By the end of this chapter, thanks to the actions performed by Instructors, learners will be able to complete the **Advanced IT Security** course that you created in *Chapter 4, Creating Skills and Courses*. You will also have reviewed the tools and features available in the *Instructor* role.

To achieve these objectives, this chapter takes you through the following sections:

- Managing instructor-led (face-to-face and virtual) classes
- Working with file submission activities
- Filling out checklist activities

Instructors are responsible for many of the day-to-day operations on your Learning Manager account. As such, they play a crucial role in the quality of the learning experience delivered by your organization. Let's dive right into the Instructor role!

Technical requirements

In order to perform the exercises described in this chapter, you need to meet the following requirements:

- You must have Instructor access to a working Learning Manager account, which can be a trial account

- The logged-in instructor must be defined as the instructor for at least one (live or virtual) class activity, one file submission activity, and one checklist activity

- Students must be enrolled for the instructor-led class, and you must have at least one additional student on the waitlist

If you have completed the exercises in the previous chapters, you meet the aforementioned requirements! If not, you can use your own course content and users to complete the exercises in this chapter. However, the instructions are based on the exercises from the previous chapters, so you may need to adapt them to your personal situation.

Managing instructor-led Classes

In the previous chapter, you experienced taking a self-paced course as a learner. This course contained only *asynchronous* self-paced modules, such as video files, PDF documents, and SCORM packages. Learners can review these modules at their own convenience with little to no human intervention. Quizzes are automatically graded, results and completion statuses are automatically reported to Learning Manager, badges and credits are automatically awarded, and so on.

Instructor-led courses, on the other end, involve a lot more logistics. Whether face-to-face or virtual, these *synchronous* activities require instructors and learners to be present at the same time, whether in a classroom or online. This obviously raises scheduling challenges, but that's not all:

- Typical classrooms and lecture halls have limited seating. If enrollment is too high, you must be ready to manage a waitlist, move the session to a larger venue, or create another instance of the session to accommodate everyone. Of course, your decisions must be communicated to learners in a professional and timely fashion. Such a follow-up is an integral part of a successful learning experience.

- A registered student may be unable to attend and decide to withdraw. In such cases, a seat is made available for the next person on the waitlist who must be duly contacted and registered for the session.

- The classroom or lecture hall may require secure access, so you need to ensure that each learner has access to the facility on the day of the session. This can include sending participants a personal access badges, a site map, or a security procedure. If the class is virtual, you must send the participants the link to the virtual class, ensure they meet the technical requirements, and assist them with installing and configuring the virtual class software and other technical issues.

- Preliminary work may be required before the class begins. This means that someone must ensure that this preparatory work is actually completed and, if necessary, send reminders to students who have not completed their preparatory work on time.

- On class day, attendance must be properly recorded and reported to Adobe Learning Manager.

- Attending a class may not be sufficient to make it a success. In many cases, *successfully* attending a class means participating in activities, answering questions, taking part in discussions, or turning in assignments. The synchronous nature of a live class makes it impossible for a computer system to gauge the participation of each learner. This is another instance where human intervention remains essential.

- Reminders must be sent to students in advance so that everyone is on the same page when the date of the class finally arrives.

In Adobe Learning Manager, these are the main tasks of the *Instructor* role. They must be performed in a timely and professional manner so as to provide an optimal learner experience. This is what you will review in this section.

Now that you have a high-level understanding of the duties devoted to and *Instructor*, let's log into Adobe Learning Manager as **Instructor 01** and review the *Instructor* role hands-on. Use the following steps to get started:

1. Log into your Learning Manager account as **Instructor 01**. When logged in, use the icon in the upper-right corner of the screen to switch to the **Instructor** role.

When Learning Manager reloads, you should be on the instructor home page, as shown in the following screenshot:

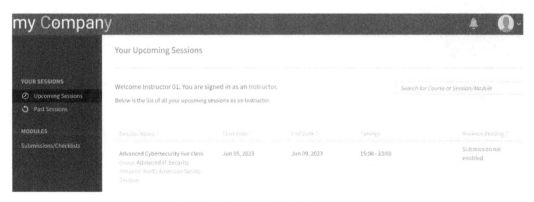

Figure 8.1 – The Instructor home page

Note

The **Instructor 01** user was created back in *Chapter 5, Managing Users*. If you did not create that user, feel free to use any suitable user available.

The Instructor home page lists all upcoming sessions assigned to the logged-in instructor. In the preceding screenshot, the logged-in user has been designated as the instructor for the live class related to the **Advanced IT Security** course you created in *Chapter 4, Creating Skills and Courses*. In the next section, let's see how Instructors can access their session details and modify them if necessary.

Reviewing session details

When instructors are designated for a class, the first thing they want to check out is the practical details of the session, such as the location, the subject matter, and the number of learners already enrolled. This information is just one click away from the Instructor home page. Let's take a look at it using the following steps:

1. Make sure you are on the instructor home page.

2. Click the session pertaining to the **Advanced IT Security** course created in *Chapter 4, Creating Skills and Courses*.

As shown in the following screenshot, this action opens the **Session Overview** page, where Instructors can review information such as **Session Name**, **Session Timings**, **Duration**, and **Venue**.

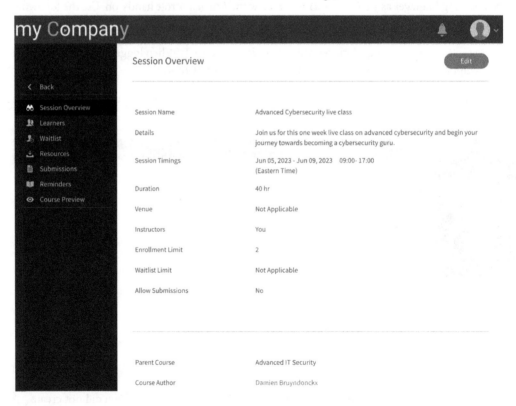

Figure 8.2 – The Session Overview page

As an instructor, you have the ability to change some of these session details. For example, you can change the date, modify the venue, and change the enrollment limit.

3. Click the **Edit** button located in the upper-right corner of the screen.

4. Type 5 in the **Waitlist Limit** field. This limits the maximum number of students that can be on a waitlist. When the waitlist is full, no additional registration can be taken for that class.

5. Switch the **Allow Submissions** field to **Yes**.

This allows learners to upload files such as assignments, reports, and assessments. Instructors can then use this material as per their instructional design.

Note that the ability for learners to upload files to the session begins to take effect on the day the session starts. In other words, if the session starts on June 15, students cannot upload their session work before June 15.

6. Take some time to examine the other session details that can be modified by an instructor.

7. Click the **Save** button located in the upper-right corner of the screen.

When modifying details in such a way, every attendee gets notified by email, as shown in the following screenshot:

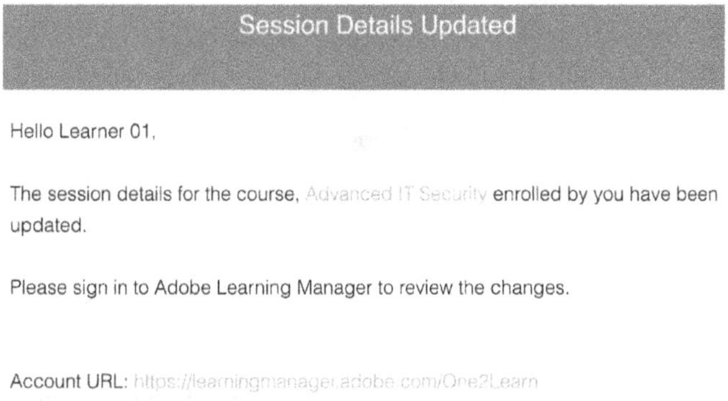

Figure 8.3 – The email notification received by attendees upon a class update

---

Customizing the Email Messages

The preceding screenshot shows the default email message sent by Learning Manager. In *Chapter 15, Working with Messages and Announcements*, you will learn how to modify the email messages sent by the platform.

Another aspect of the session that instructors want to look at is whether or not students have registered for a class. Let's review that in the next section.

Reviewing the participants list

In Adobe Learning Manager, the attendee list serves several purposes. Let's discover it hands-on using the following steps:

1. Make sure you are logged in as an instructor.

2. From the instructor home page, click the session pertaining to the **Advanced IT Security** course to open the **Session Overview** page.

3. Click the **Learners** link located on the left sidebar of the **Session Overview** page.

As shown in the following screenshot, this action takes you to the **Learners** page, where you can see basic information about your session at the top of the page as well as a list of currently registered learners.

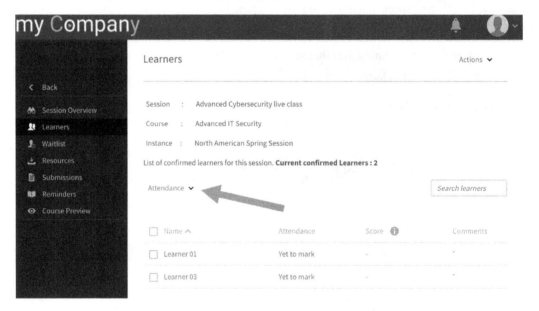

Figure 8.4 – The Learners page of a session, as seen by an instructor

In the preceding screenshot, two learners are currently confirmed for the class – **Learner 01** and **Learner 03**. Since the session has not yet started, their attendance status is **Yet to mark**.

Before going any further, note the **Attendance** dropdown (identified by the arrow in the preceding screenshot), which allows you to filter the list by attendance status, as well as the **Search learners** field in the upper-right corner of the list.

4. Click the **Actions** button located in the upper-right corner of the screen.

5. Take some time to inspect the available options.

Because you did not select any learner, some of these actions are currently unavailable, as shown in the following screenshot:

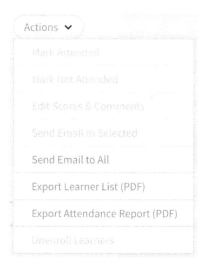

Figure 8.5 – Some actions are not available

You will now experiment with some of the available actions using the following steps:

6. Click the **Send Email to All** action.

    This opens a box containing a comma-separated list of the email addresses of all currently confirmed learners. You need to copy and paste these email addresses into your preferred email client to send these learners an email.

7. Click the **Close** button to close the **Copy Learners List** box.

8. Click the **Actions** button one more time.

9. Click the **Export Learner List (PDF)** action.

10. Save the file to your computer, and then open it in your preferred PDF reader.

This is an important document each instructor should print out before the session. Instructors can use it during the session to mark attendance. A very interesting and highly popular feature of this document is the QR code in the upper-right corner. Attendees can use the Adobe Learning Manager mobile app to scan the QR code, which automatically reports their attendance to Learning Manager.

> **The Adobe Learning Manager mobile app**
>
> The Adobe Learning Manager mobile app is available for iOS and Android. It can be downloaded either from the Apple App Store (iOS) or from the Google Play Store (Android). The mobile app was discussed in *Chapter 7, Reviewing the Learner Experience*.

It is possible that the generated PDF contains two pages – one page with the list of confirmed learners and a second page with learners on the waitlist. This is useful when a confirmed learner does not show up for a session. The seat can be reassigned to a learner on the waitlist who took the chance to show up at the beginning of the session.

Speaking of the waitlist, this is another area of interest for an Instructor. Let's review it in detail in the next section.

Managing the waitlist

When you created the course instance back in *Chapter 6, Enrolling Users to Courses*, you defined the **Seat Limit** for this session. The seat limit of a session depends on a number of factors, including the following:

- The capacity of the venue where the session takes place

- The nature of the topic taught – for example, practical courses usually require a smaller audience

- In the case of a virtual classroom, the licensing model of your preferred video conferencing solution may also be a factor in determining the **Seat Limit**

By limiting the audience in this way, you inevitably run into the problem of having more registrations than seats available. This is where a **Waitlist** comes in handy. In this section, you will review the tools and features available in Learning Manager to maintain and manage your session waitlists. Before you begin, remember the following:

- You purposely defined a ridiculously low **Seat Limit** when creating your course instance in *Chapter 6, Enrolling Users to Courses*

- In the same chapter, you tried to enroll *Learner 02* in the course, but because the **Seat Limit** had already been reached, *Learner 02* was added to the waitlist

- In the *Reviewing session details* section earlier in this chapter, you added a **Waitlist Limit** to your session to prevent the waitlist from growing too long and giving false hope to too many learners

With that in mind, it is time to head back to the Instructor role and experiment with waitlist management using the following steps:

1. Make sure you are logged in as an instructor.

2. From the instructor home page, click the session pertaining to the **Advanced IT Security** course to open the **Session Overview** page.

3. Click the **Waitlist** link located in the left sidebar of the **Session Overview** page.

This opens the **Waitlist** page of the current session, where you can see the list of learners currently on the waitlist along with their **Waitlist Number**.

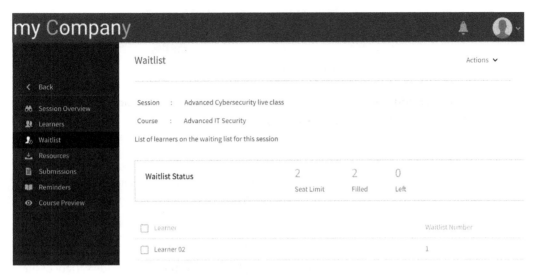

Figure 8.6 – The Waitlist page of a session

In the preceding screenshot, you can see that this particular session has a **Seat Limit** of **2** and that both seats are already **Filled**. You also see that **Learner 02** is currently the only learner on the waitlist.

4. Use the checkbox to select **Learner 02** in the list.

5. Click the **Actions** button located in the upper-right corner of the screen and take some time to review the available actions.

    The **Send Email to All** action is the only action available when no learner is selected.

    The **Unenroll Learners** action removes the selected learner(s) from the waitlist without enrolling them in the course. Conversely, the **Confirm Learners** action enrolls the learner(s) in the course. In both cases, Learning Manager automatically sends an email notification to the affected learner(s).

6. In this example, click the **Confirm Learners** action. Click **Yes** to confirm your intention. When the page reloads, **Learner 02** is no longer on the waitlist.

7. Click the **Learners** link located in the left sidebar.

When the **Learners** page reopens, make sure **Learner 02** has been added to the list of confirmed learners. This illustrates the ability to allocate a seat to someone on the waitlist even if the **Seat Limit** has been reached. In other words, instructors have the authority to override the defined **Seat Limit**.

This is one of two ways a learner can be cleared from the waitlist and enrolled in the course. The other way is to unenroll a confirmed learner so that the next learner on the waitlist is *automatically* confirmed for the session.

This concludes the tour of the tools and features available on the **Waitlist** page. In the next section, you will discover how instructors can upload resources to their sessions.

Uploading resources to a session

Instructors can upload additional resources for a session. This can be educational materials, but it can also be anything that helps with the practical organization of the event, such as an access map, a parking reservation form, or the schedule of the day. Let's review the process of uploading resources to a session using the following steps:

1. Make sure you are logged in as an Instructor. From the instructor home page, click the session pertaining to the **Advanced IT Security** course to open the **Session Overview** page.

2. Click the **Resources** link located on the left sidebar to open the **Resources** page.

3. Click the **Add** button located in the upper-right corner of the screen.

4. Browse your computer for the file you want to upload. You can upload a wide variety of file types, including text files, spreadsheets, presentations, video files, audio files, and documents.

    If you don't have any suitable file available, you can use the `liveClass/liveClass_practicalDetails.pdf` file provided in the downloads associated with this book.

When done, the uploaded file appears in the list of available **Resources**, as shown in the following screenshot:

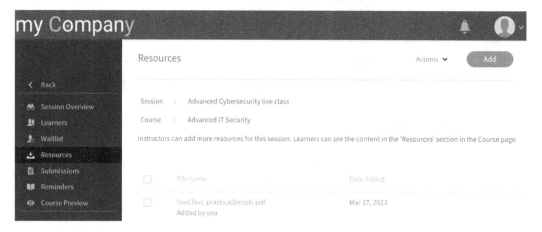

Figure 8.7 – The Resources page after a file has been uploaded

You can add as many files as needed. As for Learners, they can access these additional resources using the **Resources** section of the course overview page. Let's take a look at it in the next section.

Accessing session resources as learners

Learners can access session resources uploaded by instructors using the following steps:

1. Use another browser or a private browser window to log in as **Learner 01**. This is one of the confirmed learners of the session to which you uploaded a resource in the previous section.

2. Once logged in, click the **Advanced IT Security** course card located in the **My Learning List** section of the home page to open the course overview page.

3. As shown in the following screenshot, the course **Resources** are available at the bottom of the right column:

Figure 8.8 – Resources are available in the right column of the Course Overview page

This workflow is one way to make these resources available to learners. Another way is to simply send them as email attachments to all class attendees.

Configuring session reminders

By default, Adobe Learning Manager sends a reminder to attendees on the day of the training. As an instructor, you cannot change the content or design of this reminder, but you can decide whether or not Learning Manager sends it, as well as when and how often it is sent. Let's look at this feature in the following steps:

1. Make sure you are logged in as an Instructor. From the instructor home page, click the session pertaining to the **Advanced IT Security** course to open the **Session Overview** page.

2. Open the **Reminders** page of the session by clicking the **Reminders** link located on the left sidebar.

As shown in the following screenshot, a single reminder has already been defined:

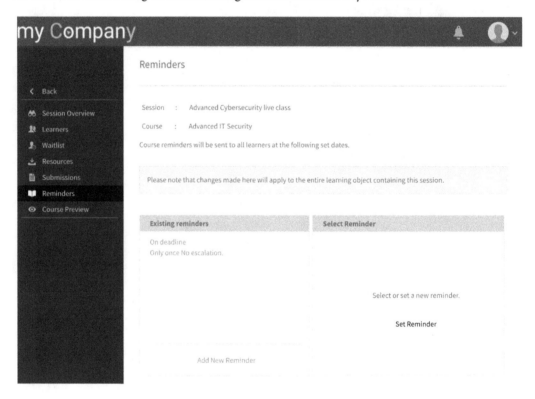

Figure 8.9 – A single reminder is defined by default

This reminder is sent **On deadline**, which means on the day of the training, and is sent **Only once**. You will now change these settings so that reminders are sent 2 days before the scheduled start of the class.

3. Click the **On deadline** link in the left column to select the existing reminder. The **Reminder Settings** appear in the right column.

If there is no reminder available for your session, you can click the **Add New Reminder** link located at the bottom of the left column.

4. Open the **When to send** dropdown and choose the **Before deadline** option.

5. Enter 2 in the **days before deadline** field.

6. Make sure the **Recurrence** field is set to **Only once**.

7. Click the blue checkmark in the lower-right corner of the **Reminders Settings** to validate the change.

Note that you can also delete the reminder using the red *trash bin* icon located next to the blue checkmark. You can also add additional reminders using the **Add New Reminder** button located at the bottom of the **Existing reminders** column.

Customizing the Session Reminder eMail

The content and design of the reminder email is defined by the platform administrators. You will review these options in *Chapter 15, Working with Messages and Announcements*.

So far in this chapter, you have reviewed the tools available to instructors to manage their sessions *before* they take place. In the next section, you will learn about the tasks Instructors should perform *during* and *after* sessions.

Marking learner attendance

During the session, the primary task of an instructor is to conduct teaching activities. However, instructors must also spend some time on administrative tasks, such as recording attendance and reporting it back to the LMS. Let's review the tools and features of Adobe Learning Manager that facilitate this aspect of the *Instructor* role.

First, remember that learners can self-report their attendance using the Adobe Learning Manager app and the QR code located in the upper-right corner of the attendance sheet generated by the system. This was already discussed in the *Reviewing the participants list* section earlier in this chapter.

However, not everyone has access to the mobile app. In such cases, instructors must manually report learners' attendance to the LMS using the following steps:

1. Make sure you are logged in as an instructor and that you are on the **Session Overview** page of the class pertaining to your **Advanced IT security** course.

    If the session has already been delivered, you need to click the **Past Sessions** link in the left sidebar to access the desired session.

2. Click the **Learners** link located in the left sidebar of the **Session Overview** page to open the **Learners** page of the chosen session.

3. Use the checkboxes to select the desired learner(s).

4. Click the **Actions** button located in the upper-right corner of the screen and select either the **Mark Attended** or **Mark Not Attended** action.

    In this example, select all three learners and mark them all as *Attended*.

Instructors would typically perform these actions either *during* or *after* the session.

> **Tip**
>
> If you are an instructor, log into Learning Manager and print out the attendee list before your session. This allows learners to scan the QR code and report their attendance themselves (thus reducing your administrative workload). It also allows you to take attendance in writing. You can then report attendance to the LMS *after* the session, so you don't have to deal with that administrative burden while you're teaching. Some organizations also require you to keep a written record of learner attendance for their archives.

Attending a session is one thing; *successfully* completing the session is another. As instructors, you may be asked to grade each learner's attendance and add comments about it in the LMS. This is what you will review in the next section.

Editing scores and comments

Sometimes, attending a class is more than just showing up. In some cases, participating in class discussions, formulating opinions, defending a case, or presenting on a topic are elements that make the class a success or a failure. In such cases, instructors can evaluate each learner by grading and commenting on their involvement in the class. Let's review this workflow hands-on using the following steps:

1. Make sure you are logged in as an instructor and that you are on the **Session Overview** page of your session. Keep in mind that if the session has already been delivered, you must click the **Past Sessions** link on the left sidebar to access the desired session.

2. Click the **Learners** link in the left sidebar.

3. Next, click the **Actions** button located in the upper-right corner of the screen.

4. Click the **Edit Scores & Comments** action to switch to score editing mode. Note that you can only enter scores and/or comments for learners that you already marked as **Attended**, as shown in the following screenshot:

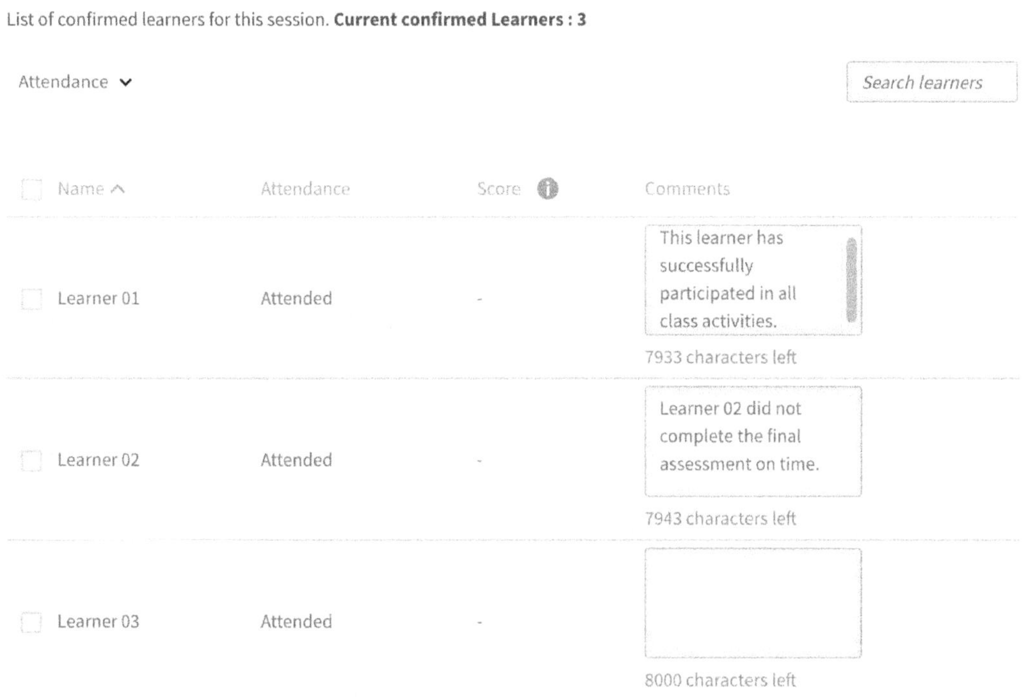

List of confirmed learners for this session. **Current confirmed Learners : 3**

	Attendance ⌄			Search learners

☐ Name ⌃	Attendance	Score ⓘ	Comments
☐ Learner 01	Attended	-	This learner has successfully participated in all class activities.
			7933 characters left
☐ Learner 02	Attended	-	Learner 02 did not complete the final assessment on time.
			7943 characters left
☐ Learner 03	Attended	-	
			8000 characters left

Figure 8.10 – Entering scores and/or comments

In the preceding screenshot, note that it is not possible to enter a **Score**. This is because, when creating the course back in *Chapter 4, Creating Skills and Courses*, you did not select the **Do you want to add quiz score for this Module** checkbox.

5.   Enter comments for each learner as per your requirements.

6.   When done, click the **Save** button in the upper-right corner of the screen.

This concludes the overview of the tools and features available to the instructor for managing live (face-to-face or virtual) training activities. Let's quickly recap what you have learned in this section:

- You learned how to log in as an instructor and reviewed the main tools of the instructor role.

- You discovered how instructors can access and edit their session details.

- You have seen how instructors manage the attendee list and how they can print out this list before the class.

- You have reviewed the tools instructors use to manage their session waitlist.

- You have seen how instructors can upload additional resources to their sessions.

- Finally, you discovered the tools instructors use to record learner attendance and to grade and comment on that attendance.

Now that an instructor has confirmed that all three learners attended the live class, they should be able to proceed with the remaining activities included in the **Advanced IT Security** course. One of these remaining activities is an assignment. In the next section, you will first return to the learner role and submit an assignment using the *File Submission* activity. Then, you will see how instructors can access the submitted assignments and grade them.

Working with the File Submission Activity

When you created the **Advanced IT Security** course in *Chapter 4, Creating Skills and Courses*, you included a *File Submission* activity in the core content of the course. This activity lets learners upload an assignment to Adobe Learning Manager. This assignment must then be reviewed by a designated instructor who either approves or rejects it.

In this section, you will log in as **Learner 01** and upload an assignment using the *File Submission* activity. Then, you will return to the *Instructor* role to review the submitted assignment.

Uploading an assignment as a Learner

Remember that in *Chapter 7, Reviewing the Learner Experience*, learners were unable to start the **Advanced IT Security** course (the **Start** button was disabled). In the previous section, by confirming that all learners have attended the live class, the instructor has in fact started the course for each of these learners. Therefore, they should now be able to proceed through the remaining activities in this course.

Let's check this out using the following steps:

1. Use another browser or a new private window of the same browser to log into your Learning Manager account as **Learner 01**.

2. Click the **Advanced IT Security** course card located in the **My Learning List** section of the home page.

3. When on the **Course Overview** page, confirm that the first module of the course is now marked as complete and that the second module is available. This situation is shown in the following screenshot:

Figure 8.11 – The first module is marked as complete

4. Click the **Upload File** link, identified by the second arrow in the preceding screenshot.

5. Select the file you want to upload. In this example, you can use the `courseContent/myAssignement.docx` file of the download associated with this book.

After your assignment is uploaded, the status changes to **Submission Awaiting Approval**. If needed, you can still change the submitted file using the **Change** link.

Now that **Learner 01** has submitted their assignment, a designated instructor has to review it and approve or reject it. Let's discuss this in the next section.

Reviewing Assignments as an Instructor

Back in *Chapter 6, Enrolling Learners in Courses, Instructor 01* was designated as the instructor responsible for receiving the assignments submitted by learners enrolled in the North American instance of the **Advanced IT Security** course.

Now that an assignment has been submitted, let's see how *Instructor 01* can access and review it by following these steps:

1. Return to the browser window in which you are logged in as *Instructor 01* and return to the Instructor homepage.

2. From the instructor home page, click the **Submissions/Checklists** link, located in the **Modules** section of the left sidebar.

This takes you to the **Modules** page of the Instructor role. From here, instructors can review their assigned *File Submission* and *Checklist* activities, as shown in the following screenshot.

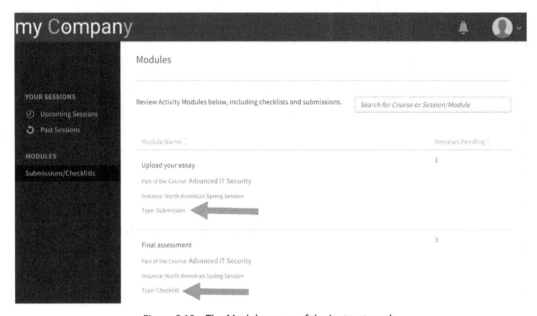

Figure 8.12 – The Modules page of the Instructor role

The activity type (**Submission** or **Checklist**) is clearly identified, as illustrated by the arrows in the preceding screenshot.

3. Click the **Submission** activity pertaining to the *North American* instance of the **Advanced IT Security** course.

This opens the **Submission** page containing a quick overview of all the documents submitted by learners. Just click a document to download it and review it.

4. Click the **Edit** button in the upper-right corner of the screen.

5. You can now enter your instructor **Comment** on the uploaded assignment.

You can make your comment visible to the learner by selecting the **Show comment** checkbox. Note that your comment is made visible to the learner only if the submission is rejected.

6. Finally, you can **Approve** or **Reject** the submission by clicking the corresponding button. In this example, **Approve** the work submitted by **Learner 01**.

   You must repeat this process for each learner who has uploaded an assignment. If the instructor rejects an assignment, the learner can upload a new version until the assignment is finally approved, which marks the file submission activity as complete.

7. When done, your screen should look like the following screenshot. You can then click the **Submit** button located in the upper-right corner of the page to commit these changes:

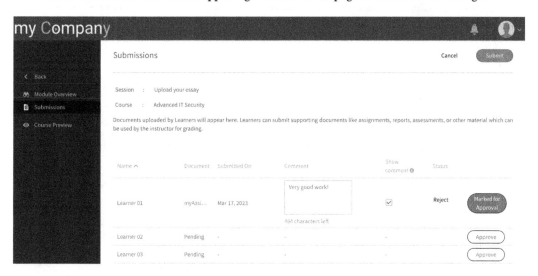

Figure 8.13 – Reviewing file submissions

This is how simple it is for instructors to access the files submitted by learners, add their comments, and accept or reject submissions. In the next section, you will review how instructors can fill out checklist activities.

Filling out checklist activities

As discussed in *Chapter 4*, *Creating Skills and Courses*, the *Checklist* activity is one of the module types that can be added to any course in Adobe Learning Manager. It allows organizations to measure the effectiveness of a course by assessing the change in learner behavior after they have completed the course.

The idea is for an instructor to visit learners at their workplace a few days or weeks after the end of the training to assess how learners are *actually* applying what they have learned.

Let's now hit the road and visit your past learners at their workplace in order to fill out the *Checklist* activities using the following steps:

1. Meet your former learners at their workplace, shake hands, and have a coffee with them! While not a mandatory step, this type of interpersonal interaction is always very helpful and enjoyable!

2. When ready, log into Adobe Learning Manager as *Instructor 01*.

3. From the instructor home page, click the **Submissions/Checklists** link, located in the **Modules** section of the left sidebar.

4. Then, click the appropriate **Checklist** activity.

5. When on the **Checklist** page, click the **Evaluate** link pertaining to the learner you are currently visiting. In this example, click the **Evaluate** link of **Learner 01**.

6. Answer the questions in the checklist and click the **Submit** button, located in the lower-right corner of the dialog box. This action is illustrated in the following screenshot:

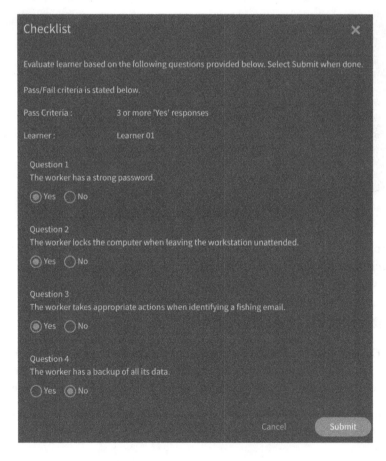

Figure 8.14 – Filling out the checklist activity

When submitting the checklist, the number of **Correct Responses** as well as the **Status** (Pass or Failed) are immediately available.

The questions included in the checklist were defined by the course author when creating the course back in *Chapter 4, Creating Skills and Courses*.

Summary

In this chapter, you have reviewed the *Instructor* role. The primary task of an instructor is to deliver the (face-to-face or virtual) classroom activities. These classroom activities are time-bound *synchronous* activities that require learners and instructors to be together either in a physical location or online.

This implies a whole new level of complexity and logistical constraints, such as scheduling courses, managing the waitlist, arranging the venue, sending practical details to learners in a timely fashion, sending reminders before the session, ensuring that everyone has the required video conferencing software installed, and reporting attendance to the LMS. Although Learning Manager cannot accomplish all of these tasks on its own, it provides instructors with features designed to help them manage the logistical, administrative, and pedagogical aspects of these synchronous activities.

Instructors are also responsible for reviewing the material submitted by learners when using the *File Submission* activity, and for completing the *Checklist* activities a few days or weeks after the course has been delivered.

Using these tools, you can use Adobe Learning Manager to deliver all kinds of training, including courses that are composed entirely of self-paced asynchronous modules, courses that are entirely instructor-led (live or online), and courses that combine both synchronous and asynchronous activities. The latter type of course is known as a *Blended* course. It is particularly powerful because it combines the advantages of both synchronous and asynchronous teaching techniques. This blended learning format is very popular among learners, trainers, and organizations.

Your efforts to implement Adobe Learning Manager, publish learning content, create courses, and deliver them online are starting to pay off. Your account has come to life, as learners and instructors are now able to interact in many ways.

However, there is still an essential missing piece to go full circle and have a solution that can truly be considered an enterprise solution. All these learning activities and interactions generate a lot of data. In addition, organizations want to ensure that learners are satisfied with the learning experience they provide and that their investment in training is meaningful and effective.

In the next two chapters, you'll explore the data collected by Adobe Learning Manager, gather feedback from students, and see how organizations can leverage this information to generate meaningful reports.

9

Configuring and Using Feedback

Thanks to the work done in previous chapters, your **Adobe Learning Manager** (**ALM**) account is now fully operational. Learners are taking courses, managers are reviewing enrollment requests, instructors are teaching and reviewing learner submissions, and authors are updating modules and creating new courses. Everything seems to be going well in the best of all possible worlds.

But is this really the case? Do learners enjoy the courses? Are they *actually* acquiring new skills? How effective is the learning? Do managers notice changes in the behavior and productivity of their team members after the training? What is the return on investment of this training effort for the organization? The truth is... you don't know!

As the enterprise **Learning Management System** (**LMS**) of choice, Adobe Learning Manager understands that such insight is critical to your organization. So in the next two chapters, you will review the extensive feedback and reporting features built into the platform. These features are based on a theoretical model called the *Four Levels of Learning Evaluation* developed by Donald Kirkpatrick (1924-2014) in the 1950s.

This chapter starts with a quick theoretical overview of Kirkpatrick's *Four Levels of Learning Evaluation* model. You will then review how the four levels are implemented in ALM.

To achieve these objectives, this chapter contains the following main sections:

- A quick look at Kirkpatrick's *Four Levels of Learning Evaluation* model
- Implementing L1 and L3 feedback
- Retrieving L1, L2, and L3 feedback
- Understanding the Course Effectiveness score
- Working with ratings

These are important capabilities that help make ALM one of the leading enterprise LMSs on the market. But enough chit-chat! It is now time to jump right in!

Technical requirements

To follow along with the exercises of this chapter, you need to meet the following requirements:

- You must have administrator access to a working Learning Manager account (it can be a trial account)

- You must have a custom course with enrolled learners, and at least one of those learners has already completed the course

- You must have manager access to your ALM account using the profile of the manager of the learners enrolled in the custom course mentioned previously

If you have completed the exercises of the previous chapters, you should be good to go! If you have not gone through the exercises of the previous chapters, feel free to use your own course material and users. Just be aware that the instructions provided in this chapter are based on the exercises from previous chapters. Therefore, you may need to adapt them to your situation.

A quick look at Kirkpatrick's Four Levels of Learning Evaluation model

Dr. Donald Kirkpatrick (1924–2014) was a Professor Emeritus at the University of Wisconsin. He spent most of his professional life at the Management Institute of the university, teaching subjects such as coaching, change management, communication, leadership, and so on. He also served as president of the **American Society for Training and Development** (**ASTD**) and was a member of Training Magazine's Hall of Fame.

During the 1950s, he developed the *Four Levels of Learning Evaluation* model (also known as the *Kirkpatrick model* or the *Four Levels* model), which served as the subject of his PhD thesis in 1954. His ideas have gained worldwide attention from a book he published in 1994 entitled *Evaluating Training Programs*. Today, this model is one of the most recognized and widely used training evaluation models in the world.

> **More info**
>
> You can find more information about Dr. Donald Kirkpatrick and his *Four Levels* model at https://www.kirkpatrickpartners.com/.

The feedback and reporting features of ALM are based on Kirkpatrick's *Four levels* model. So let's take a quick look at the main ideas in this model before discussing how these are implemented in ALM.

The four levels of Kirkpatrick's evaluation model are as follows:

- **Level 1: Reaction**: This level assesses the immediate satisfaction of learners after taking a course. It typically includes questions such as "Did you find the training useful?", "Was the training relevant to your job?", "Did you enjoy your training experience?", "Did you like the trainer?", and "Would you recommend this training to others?"

- **Level 2: Learning**: This level is about measuring the acquisition of new skills or knowledge by learners. This is where grading, online quizzes, assessments, and other types of evaluation techniques come into play.

- **Level 3: Behavior**: This level assesses the extent to which participants are able to apply what they have learned during the training to their work. It is about measuring the change in the learners' behavior (such as increased productivity, better leadership, and so on) after taking a course.

- **Level 4: Results**: This level measures whether the organization achieved its goals as a result of the training effort. In other words, this level measures the impact of learning on the organization as a whole rather than focusing on each individual learner.

In practice, most teachers and trainers get stuck at levels 1 and 2, while levels 3 and 4 are where the most useful data exists from the organization's perspective. ALM attempts to bridge the gap between these four levels to bring up as much meaningful data as possible to levels 3 and 4, which, in turn, provides information about the *real* impact of learning on the organization and, therefore, on the return on investment. Thinking backward (from L4 to L1), Kirkpatrick's model can also be a way to help evaluate the quality of the training content itself. Success at L1 and L2 better prepares for success at L3 and even L4.

> **Fun fact**
>
> After his retirement in May 2011, Donald Kirkpatrick decided to use his talent for music to write songs. You can hear him singing his songs at `https://donkirkpatrick.bandcamp.com/`.

Now that you know a bit more about the theoretical aspects of Kirkpatrick's *Four Levels* model, let's look at how it is implemented in Adobe Learning Manager.

Implementing L1 and L3 feedback

In this section, you will review the tools and options that allow you to enable and manage L1 and L3 feedback on your Learning Manager account.

> **What about L2 feedback?**
>
> L2 feedback corresponds to the *Learning* level of Kirkpatrick's model. In Learning Manager, L2 feedback is mostly automatic and does not require any action from an administrator to enable or customize it. This is the reason why L2 feedback is not discussed in this section. It will be discussed in the *Retrieving L1, L2, and L3 feedback* section later in this chapter.

L1 feedback refers to the *Reaction* level of Kirkpatrick's *Four Levels of Learning Evaluation*. As a reminder, the *Reaction* level tries to measure the overall learner satisfaction immediately after taking a course. In Learning Manager, L1 feedback is a form that each learner must complete at the end of a course.

L3 feedback refers to the *Behavioral* level of Kirkpatrick's *Four Levels of Learning Evaluation*, which attempts to measure the extent to which the behavior of a learner has changed after completing training. In Learning Manager, it is a form that the learner's manager fills in, usually a few days or weeks after the learner has completed training.

> **Courses and learning paths**
>
> Keep in mind that although the next few sections discuss L1 and L3 feedback for courses, most of these features can also be applied to learning paths. The specifics of L1 and L3 feedback for learning paths are discussed in the *L1 and L3 feedback for learning paths* section later in this chapter.

By default, L1 and L3 feedback are *disabled* on any new ALM account, but you can override this setting and enable feedback for each individual course. This is what you will examine in the next section.

Enabling L1 and L3 Feedback for a Course Instance

By default, L1 and L3 feedback is disabled at the account level. Indeed, this approach to feedback may be new to many trainers and HR managers who are not familiar with Kirkpatrick's model or who have never used an LMS that offers such feedback functionality. Administrators can override this account default by enabling L1 and/or L3 feedback for each individual course instance.

Feedback is enabled or disabled for each individual *course instance*. It means that you can enable feedback for some instances and leave feedback disabled for other instances of the same course. You can also customize L1 and L3 feedback for each individual course instance.

Also, keep in mind that L1 and L3 feedback is triggered after a learner completes a course. Therefore, changing the feedback options only affects future learners as well as current learners who have not yet completed the course. Learners who have already completed the course when the feedback options are modified are not affected by the change.

You will now turn L1 and L3 feedback on for one of the courses available in your ALM trial account using the following steps:

1. Log in to your Learning Manager account as an administrator.

2. From the admin home page, click the **Courses** link located in the **Learning** section of the left sidebar.

3. Click the course you want to enable feedback for.

   For this example, choose any (short) course available in your account. The courses provided at account creation are ideal!

4. When the chosen course is open, click the **Instances** link located in the **Manage** section of the left sidebar.

There should only be a single default instance available for that course. As discussed in *Chapter 4, Creating Skills and Courses*, this default instance is automatically created whenever you create a new course. Most of the time, this is all you need.

Feedback is not enabled for this course instance, as indicated by the dash that appears in the **Feedback Enabled** section of the course instance (see the arrow in the following screenshot):

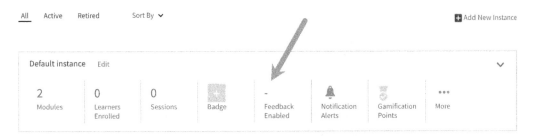

Figure 9.1 – The default instances of the course with no feedback enabled

You will now enable L1 and L3 feedback for this course instance.

5. Click the **Feedback Enabled** link, identified by the arrow in the preceding screenshot. This opens the feedback options for this course instance.

6. Toggle **L1 Reaction Feedback** on. This action displays a few additional options on the screen.

7. Type Do you have any other comments or suggestions about this course? in the **Question 1** field.

8. Take some time to examine the other available options, but don't change any of them at this time.

9. Scroll down the page and also toggle **L3 Behavior Change Feedback** on.

   Take the necessary time to examine the available L3 feedback options. Notice the question stem that is already present in the **Question 1** field as well as the **Answer Format**, which is set to **Likert Scale**. Also, note that the **Question 2** field is empty by default. Make sure you don't change any of these options at this time.

10. When ready, click the blue checkmark in the bottom-right corner to validate your changes (see the arrow in the following screenshot):

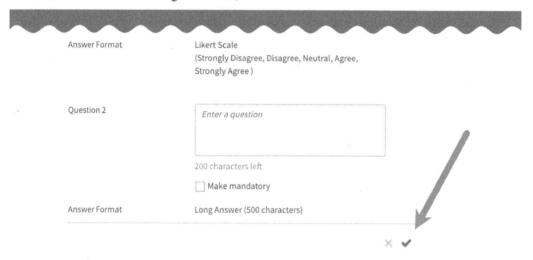

Figure 9.2 – Click the blue checkmark to validate your changes

After clicking the blue checkmark, you should see that L1 and L3 feedback has been enabled for the default course instance. From now on, each time a learner completes this course, this learner will be asked to provide L1 feedback, and the learner's manager will be asked to provide L3 feedback. This is what you will examine in the next two sections.

Providing L1 Feedback as a Learner

Now that L1 feedback has been enabled for a course (actually, a *course instance*), you will log into your ALM account as a learner, enroll in that course, and take it. If everything goes well, the system should prompt you to provide L1 feedback once you complete the course. Let's check this out by using the following steps:

1. Open a new private window of your web browser (or use another browser altogether) and log in to your account as *Learner 01*.

2. Once logged in, click the **Go To Catalog** link located in the **My Learning List** section of the home page.

3. Use the catalog features as described in *Chapter 6, Enrolling Users in Courses*, to enroll in the course for which you enabled L1 and L3 feedback in the previous section.

4. Once enrolled, the Fluidic Player opens, and the course starts. Take the necessary time to review all the modules. For most of the courses automatically available in your account, there should be no more than one or two videos to review.

5. When you have reviewed all the course material, close the Fluidic Player to return to the course overview page.

Now that you have completed the course as a student, it is time to provide L1 feedback. A few minutes after completing the course, *Learner 01* should receive an email asking to provide L1 feedback. A notification is also available in ALM.

6. Click the notification icon located in the upper-right corner of the screen (remember to allow ALM a few minutes before displaying this notification).

7. Click the **Provide Feedback** link for the course you just completed.

Clicking this link opens the **Course Feedback** form with six predefined questions, as shown in the following screenshot:

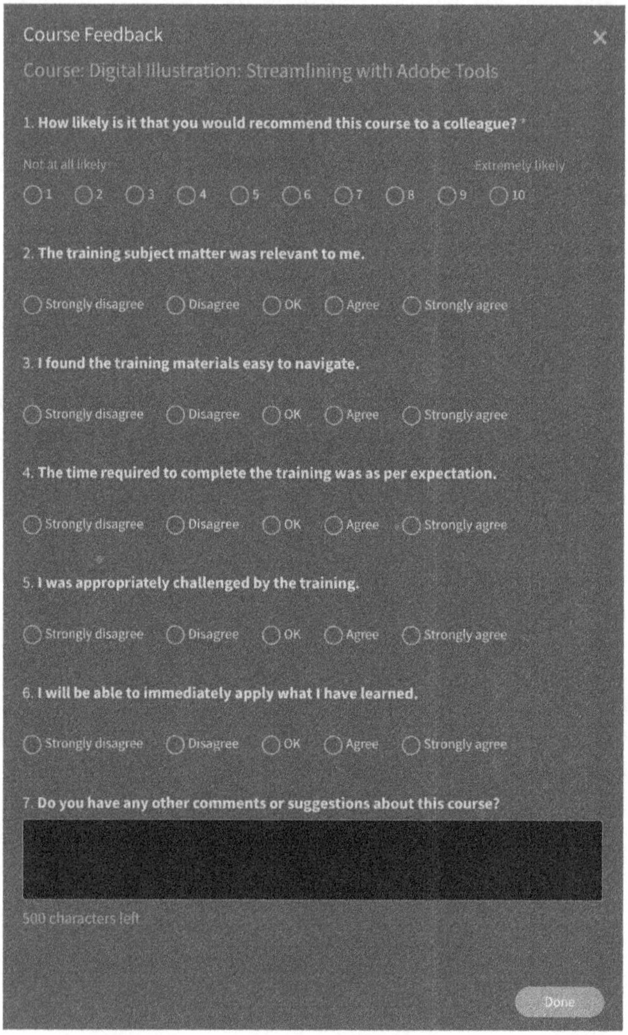

Figure 9.3 – The L1 Course Feedback form

These questions refer to the *Reaction* level of Kirkpatrick's model, where students are asked to report their overall satisfaction with their learning experience.

8. Answer the questions and click the **Done** button located in the lower-right corner of the **Course Feedback** form.

As you do so, pay very close attention to the six predefined questions. Also, notice the custom question you have defined for this course instance that appears at the end of the form. In a later section, you will learn how to customize the content of this form.

In this section, you have examined how learners provide L1 feedback after completing a course. But remember that you have also enabled L3 feedback for this course instance. Providing L3 feedback is discussed in the next section.

Providing L3 Feedback as a Manager

L3 feedback corresponds to the *Behavior* level of Kirkpatrick's *Four Levels* model, which aims to measure whether the training induces a change in the learner's behavior once back in the workplace.

In ALM, *managers* are responsible for submitting L3 feedback. After all, who better to measure a change in behavior after training than the employee's direct manager? Typically, L3 feedback should be submitted a few weeks after an employee has completed training.

By default, Learning Manager sends an email to the learner's manager 45 days after the course is complete. This is why you will not be able to experiment with providing L3 feedback right away. The following screenshot illustrates the default L3 feedback form. You should recognize the default question you examined in the *Enabling L1 and L3 feedback for a course instance* section earlier in this chapter:

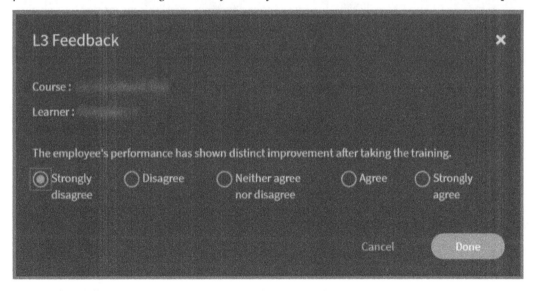

Figure 9.4 – The default L3 feedback form

To provide L3 feedback after a team member has completed training, managers must perform the following steps:

1. Log in to your ALM account as a manager.

2. From the manager home page, click the **Notifications** link located in the **View** section of the left sidebar.

3. Once on the **Notifications** page, click the **Pending Tasks** tab.

   The pending L3 feedback this manager must provide would be listed in the **Provide Feedback** section of the **Pending Tasks** page.

Now, let's be honest! We all know that very few managers log into the corporate LMS at the beginning of each workday to check whether there are some L3 feedback forms to fill out. That's why ALM also sends a reminder email to managers with a direct link to the appropriate L3 feedback form. This is how most L3 feedback is submitted.

In the previous few sections, you reviewed the main principles behind L1 and L3 feedback. Let's make a quick summary of what you have learned so far:

- L1 and L3 feedback is disabled by default on any new ALM account.

- Activating L1 and L3 feedback is done at the course instance level. This means that for a single course, you can have some course instances with feedback enabled and other course instances with feedback disabled.

- By default, the L1 feedback form contains six predefined questions. You can add up to two custom questions for each course instance. This allows you to define instance-specific questions, such as questions about the instructor or the venue.

- L1 feedback is provided by learners after course completion. L3 feedback is provided by the learner's manager. By default, L3 feedback is available to managers 45 days after a member of their team has completed training.

Setting feedback options for each course instance separately quickly becomes tedious and is error-prone. So in the next section, you will look at the **instance defaults**, which allow you to define default values for all the course instances of a given course.

Customizing Course Instance Defaults

Back in *Chapter 6, Enrolling Users to Courses*, you learned about course instances. Let's have a brief recap of what course instances are and what they allow you to do:

- Learners enroll in course instances rather than enrolling in courses.

- When creating a course, a default course instance is created automatically. This default instance is what learners actually enroll in. In most cases, this default course instance is sufficient.

- When the course includes time-bound synchronous activities (such as live or virtual instructor-led sessions), course instances allow you to schedule multiple occurrences of the same course on different dates, with different instructors, in different locations, or in different languages. This is the primary use case for multiple course instances in a single course.

In previous sections, you also learned that L1 and L3 feedback is configured at the course instance level.

In this section, you will discover how to change the default values for course instances. These defaults apply to all future instances of a given course. Let's go through this workflow using the following steps:

1. Log in to your ALM account as an administrator.

2. From the administrator home page, click the **Courses** link located in the **Learning** section of the left sidebar.

3. Click the course for which you want to edit the default instance properties.

4. When the selected course is open, click the **Instance Defaults** link located in the **Configure** section of the left sidebar.

   This is where you can modify the default values that will be applied to all future course instances of the chosen course.

5. Toggle **L1 Reaction Feedback** on.

6. Type Do you have any other comments or suggestions about this course? in the **Question 1** field.

7. Scroll down the page and also enable **L3 Behavior Change Feedback**.

8. Take some time to examine the other available options. Notice that you can also enable or disable badges by default.

   (Badges will be discussed in *Chapter 11, Badges and Gamification*).

9. When ready, click the **Save** button located in the upper-right corner of the screen.

From now on, any new course instance you create for this particular course will inherit the default values you just defined.

This is very useful for ensuring that each course instance follows a basic set of rules and best practices. It also streamlines the creation of new course instances. Keep in mind that these are only default values, which can be overridden for each new instance.

Also, the default values you just defined only apply to *future* course instances. Existing course instances are not affected by these changes unless you explicitly apply the default settings to existing instances by following these steps:

10. Click the **Instances** link located in the **Manage** section of the left sidebar.

11. Click the down arrow located in the upper-right corner of the **Default instance**.

12. In the menu that opens, locate the **Apply Default Settings** option, but make sure you do not click it in this example.

Clicking this option would apply the values defined in **Instance Defaults** to this existing course instance. The process is depicted in the following screenshot:

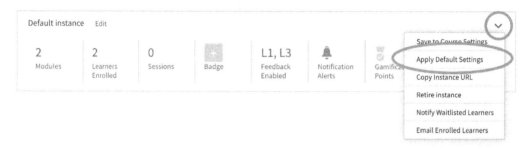

Figure 9.5 – Apply defaults to an existing course instance

So far in this chapter, you have enabled L1 and L3 feedback for a single instance of one specific course. In the next section, you will review how you can activate and configure L1 and L3 feedback for your entire account.

Configuring L1 and L3 feedback at the account level

By default, L1 and L3 feedback is disabled on your ALM account. In previous sections, you learned how to enable L1 and L3 feedback for a single instance of a specific course. You will now review the L1 and L3 feedback options available at the account level. This allows you to do the following:

- Turn L1 and/or L3 feedback on by default for any new course you create on your account
- Modify the questions displayed on the L1 feedback form
- Modify when reminders are sent to learners (for L1 feedback) and managers (for L3 feedback)

Let's now review these items one by one in the following few sections.

Turning L1 feedback on by default

Let's start by enabling L1 feedback by default on your account using the following steps:

1. Log in to your account as an administrator.
2. From the administrator home page, click the **Settings** link located at the end of the **Configure** section in the left sidebar.
3. Then, click the **Feedback** link located in the **Basics** section of the left sidebar.

As shown in the following screenshot, this takes you to the **L1 Feedback** tab of the **Feedback Settings** page:

Feedback Settings   Edit

L1 Feedback   L3 Feedback

Enable L1 Feedback for newly created Course and Learning Path

Language   English (United States)   ∨

Create a questionnaire to get feedback from learners after completing a Course. Questions should be worded as statements that learners would then respond to on a scale of 1-5.

Figure 9.6 – The L1 Feedback tab of the Feedback Settings page

4. Click the **Edit** link located in the upper-right corner of the screen.

5. Toggle the **Enable L1 Feedback for newly created Course and Learning Path** option on.

6. Click the **Save** button located in the upper-right corner of the screen.

From now on, new courses and learning paths will have L1 feedback enabled by default. It is important to keep in mind that this only affects *future* courses and learning paths. Existing training items are not affected by this change.

Note

Like any other important change you make to your account, it is important to communicate it properly to learners. After all, this additional feedback step is new to them as well. So, it is very important to tell learners that this feedback step is mandatory because many learners will ignore it if they have not been properly informed of the change.

Now that L1 feedback has been enabled by default, you will review how you can customize the content of the L1 and L3 feedback forms.

Modifying the content of L1 and L3 feedback forms

When you experienced filling out the L1 feedback form as a learner in the *Providing L1 feedback as a learner* section earlier in this chapter, there were six predefined questions in addition to the custom questions you defined at the instance level. In this section, you will learn how to modify these predefined questions.

Note that this is done at the account level, so the questions defined here are used by all the course instances available on your account.

Use the following steps to customize the content of the L1 feedback form:

1. Log into your ALM account as an administrator.

2. From the administrator home page, click the **Settings** link located at the end of the **Configure** section in the left sidebar.

3. Then, click the **Feedback** link located in the **Basics** section of the left sidebar.

4. Click the **Edit** button located in the upper-right corner of the screen.

5. Scroll down the page until you see the list of questions.

As shown in the following screenshot, you can use the toggle buttons to enable or disable each question.

You can also modify the question stem and add additional questions using the **Add More** link at the bottom of the list (see the arrow in the following screenshot).

Also, notice the **Language** drop-down menu in the upper-right corner of the page, which allows you to localize the L1 feedback form in multiple languages:

Figure 9.7 – Modifying the questions of the L1 feedback form

Before going any further, note that there is one mandatory question (**How likely is it that you would recommend this course to a colleague?**) visible at the top of the page. You cannot edit or disable this question. Also, notice that there is a separate set of questions labeled **Questions (For Self Paced Courses)** and **Questions (For Classroom Courses)**; A *classroom course* is a course that only contains instructor-led (live or virtual) activities.

6. Scroll down the page until you see the **L1 Feedback Reminders** section.

7. Click the existing reminder in the left column to see its properties in the right column.

As shown in the following screenshot, the L1 feedback reminder is sent to the learner directly on course completion. If the learner does not fill out the form, the reminder recurs every week for 4 weeks:

L1 Feedback Reminders

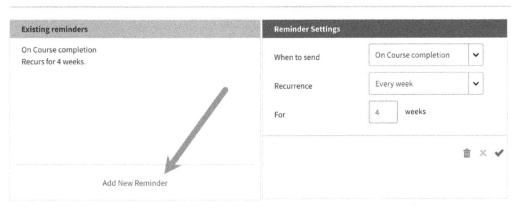

Figure 9.8 – L1 Feedback Reminders

You can, of course, modify this default reminder and/or add additional reminders using the **Add New Reminder** link at the end of the left column (see the arrow in the preceding screenshot).

8. Take the necessary time to inspect the other options available on this page. When ready, click the **Cancel** button in the upper-right corner of the page to discard any changes you may have made.

9. Click the **L3 Feedback** tab located in the upper-left corner of the page to access the options pertaining to L3 feedback.

10. Take the necessary time to review the available options.

Note that the default L3 feedback reminder is triggered 45 days after course completion and **Recurs for 4 weeks**. You can, of course, modify these settings using the very same process as the one described for L1 feedback earlier in this section.

You now have a good idea of the feedback options available at the account level. Keep in mind that these options apply to every *future* course instance. Also, remember that you can define up to two additional L1 questions and one additional L3 question at the course instance level.

In the next section, we will quickly discuss L1 and L3 feedback when applied to learning paths.

L1 and L3 feedback for Learning Paths

All the L1 and L3 feedback features discussed so far in this chapter also apply to learning paths. As a reminder, a *learning path* is a set of related courses. When learners enroll in a learning path, they actually enroll in all the courses included in that learning path. Creating learning paths was discussed in *Chapter 6, Enrolling Users in Courses*.

Let's quickly review the options pertaining to L1 and L3 feedback for learning paths using the following steps:

1. Log in to your ALM account as an administrator.

2. From the administrator home page, click the **Learning Paths** link located in the **Learning** section of the left sidebar.

3. Click any learning path available in the list.

4. When the learning path details page opens, click the **Instances** link located in the **Manage** section of the left sidebar.

Just as for courses, learning paths also have instances, and a **Default instance** is automatically created for any new learning path.

5. Click the **Feedback Enabled** link of the default learning path instance to open the L1 and L3 feedback options

The available options are similar to those available for course instances, with a few important differences.

Since learning paths are made up of several courses, it is quite possible that some (or all) of the courses included in the learning path already have L1 and/or L3 feedback enabled. In order to provide an optimal learning experience, it is important to make sure that the feedback process for the courses does not interfere with the feedback process for the learning path as a whole:

*   When toggling the **Enable for Learning Path** button on, you activate L1 feedback at the learning path level. This means that learners will be asked to fill out *a single L1 feedback form* after completing *all the courses* included in the learning path.

*   If you want to also enforce the L1 feedback options for each course included in the learning path, you must also toggle on the **Enable for Each Course** button. In this case, learners will *also* be prompted to fill out the L1 feedback form for the courses *in addition to* the L1 feedback form for the learning path. Note that if the courses included in the learning path do not have L1

feedback enabled, this button *has no effect*. It is important to understand that this button does *not* activate L1 feedback for each course. It simply applies whatever L1 feedback settings are defined at the course level *in addition to* the L1 feedback options defined at the learning path level. It is also worth mentioning that this button only applies to L1 feedback, not to L3 feedback.

- Toggling on **L3 Behavior Change Feedback** enables L3 feedback for the learning path as a whole. Note that if a course contained in the learning path already has L3 feedback enabled, Learning Manager does *not* honor course-level L3 feedback. Only the L3 feedback of the learning path is observed. This is to prevent busy managers from receiving too many L3 feedback requests when their team members enroll in learning paths.

So far in this chapter, we have discussed the options pertaining to *collecting* L1 and L3 feedback. In the next section, let's discuss how administrators can *retrieve* and use this data.

Retrieving L1, L2, and L3 Feedback

Collecting data is only the first step. It is equally important to be able to access the data so as to generate meaningful reports and make informed business decisions.

To review L1, L2, and L3 feedback data, you must be either an administrator or a manager. The difference between these two roles is that administrators have access to all the data available on the platform, while managers only have access to the data pertaining to their team members.

In this section, you will log in as an administrator and review how you can access the L1, L2, and L3 feedback data.

Accessing L1 and L3 feedback data

Remember that L1 and L3 feedback is collected at the course or the learning path level. So to access this data, you need to access the course or learning path whose data you want to view. Let's review this workflow hands-on using the following steps:

1. Log in to your account as an administrator.
2. From the administrator home page, click the **Courses** link located in the **Learning** section of the left sidebar.
3. Click the course card of the course whose data you want to review.

   In this example, choose the course for which you provided L1 feedback earlier in this chapter.
4. Click the **L1 Feedback** link located in the **Reports** section of the left sidebar.
5. If the course has multiple instances, use the **Select Instance** drop-down list to select the appropriate course instance.

This opens the course **L1 Feedback** page, as shown in the following screenshot:

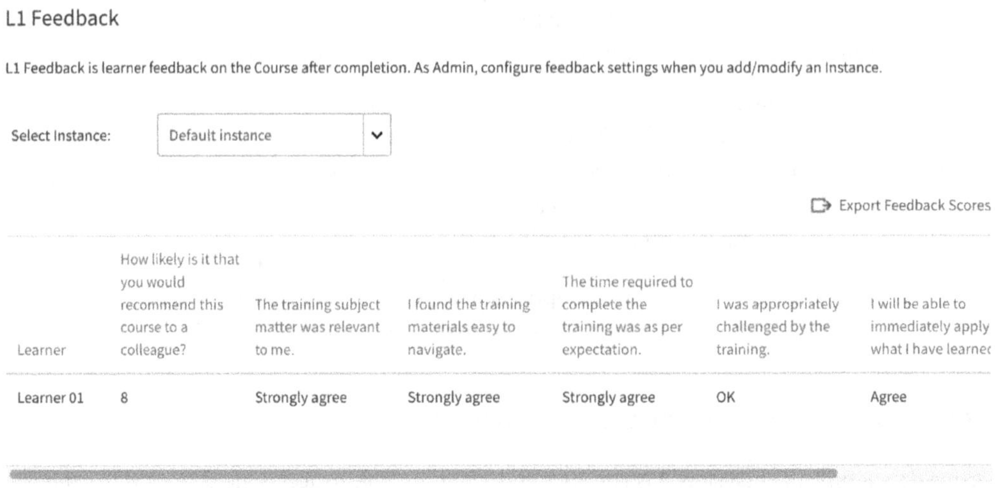

L1 Feedback

L1 Feedback is learner feedback on the Course after completion. As Admin, configure feedback settings when you add/modify an Instance.

Select Instance: Default instance   ⌄

⤴ Export Feedback Scores

Learner	How likely is it that you would recommend this course to a colleague?	The training subject matter was relevant to me.	I found the training materials easy to navigate.	The time required to complete the training was as per expectation.	I was appropriately challenged by the training.	I will be able to immediately apply what I have learnec
Learner 01	8	Strongly agree	Strongly agree	Strongly agree	OK	Agree

Figure 9.09 – The L1 Feedback page of a course as seen by an administrator

In the preceding screenshot, only **Learner 01** has provided L1 feedback so far. You should recognize the questions displayed on the L1 feedback form as well as the answers you provided in the *Providing L1 feedback as a learner* section earlier in this chapter.

Also notice the **Export Feedback Scores** link located in the upper-right corner of the page, which allows you to export an Excel file containing all the L1 feedback data.

Access to the L3 feedback is done in exactly the same way.

6. Click the **L3 Feedback** link located in the **Reports** section of the left sidebar to open the **L3 Feedback** page of the chosen course.

This page displays the L3 feedback provided by managers. Remember that by default, managers can provide L3 feedback 45 days after a learner has completed training. This is why no L3 feedback is available on this page yet.

Before wrapping up this section, remember that the very same L1 and L3 feedback pages are also available for learning paths and that the same tools are available to managers for reviewing data pertaining to their team members.

In this section, you have reviewed how administrators can access the L1 and L3 feedback data. It is now time to discuss L2 feedback in the next section.

Accessing L2 Feedback Data

L2 feedback refers to the *Learning* level of Kirkpatrick's *Four Levels* model. As a reminder, the *Learning* level examines learners' performance on quizzes, as well as the grades obtained on various assignments.

In Adobe Learning Manager these grades come from the quizzes included in interactive course modules, the assignments graded by instructors, grades obtained from checklist activities, and so on.

As such, L2 feedback is mostly automatic in Adobe Learning Manager. There is nothing to do on your end to enable L2 feedback and have Adobe Learning Manager collect this data. As long as a course or learning path contains at least one graded activity or quiz, L2 feedback data is automatically collected and made available. However, keep in mind that for some activities (such as file submissions and checklists), grades must be manually entered into the system by an instructor, as discussed in *Chapter 8, Exploring the Instructor Role*.

When you created the *Fundamentals of IT Security* course back in *Chapter 4, Creating Skills and Courses*, you included a **SCORM**compliant activity containing a quiz. This activity was built using the *Adobe Captivate* authoring tool and was uploaded to the Content Library of your ALM account as a SCORM-compliant module.

> **AICC, SCORM, and xAPI**
>
> AICC, SCORM, and xAPI are the three standards used in the eLearning industry to transmit data between interactive course modules and the LMS. Adobe Learning Manager supports all three standards, so it can host the content created by virtually any eLearning authoring tool. For more information on AICC, SCORM, and xAPI, refer to *Chapter 3, Uploading Learning Content and Managing the Content Library*.

The SCORM specification takes care of communicating the quiz results to ALM, which stores them as L2 feedback data. Let's now look at how administrators and managers can access this data using the following steps:

1. Log into your account as an administrator.
2. From the administrator home page, click the **Courses** link located in the **Learning** section of the left sidebar.
3. Open the **Fundamentals of IT Security** course you created in *Chapter 4, Creating Skills and Courses*.
4. Click the **L2 Quiz Score** link located in the **Reports** section of the left sidebar.
5. If the chosen course contains multiple instances, use the **Select Instance** drop-down menu to select the appropriate course instance.

This is how you can access the L2 data for a given course, as shown in the following screenshot:

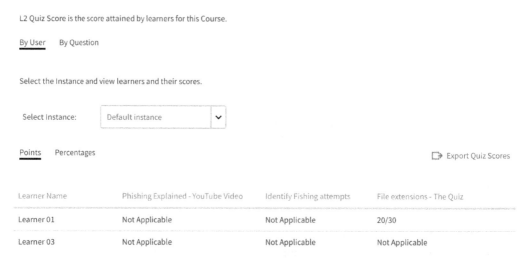

Figure 9.10 – The L2 feedback page of a course as seen by an administrator

In the preceding screenshot, only the **File extensions - The Quiz** module is a graded module containing a quiz whose score is reported to Learning Manager using SCORM. Note the **Export Quiz Scores** link located in the upper-right corner of the page, which allows you to generate an Excel file containing all the available quiz scores for the chosen course instance.

> **Note**
> The Excel report corresponding to the preceding screenshot is available in the downloads associated with this book in the `reports/L2QuizScores.xlsx` file.

You will now continue to experiment with the L2 feedback data using the tools available in Adobe Learning Manager:

1. Click the **Percentages** tab located above the data table to see the scores using percentages instead of points.

2. Next, click the **By Question** tab located in the upper-left corner of the page.

    This allows you to have a detailed overview of all the quiz questions contained in the various graded modules of the course.

> **Note**
>
> When it comes to AICC, SCORM, or xAPI modules, keep in mind that ALM is only one of two parties involved, the other party being each individual interactive module generated by a wide variety of authoring tools. The detailed data displayed in the **By Question** tab is only available if the corresponding data is transmitted by the course modules to the LMS. This has to be defined in the authoring tool used to generate the AICC, SCORM, or xAPI package. Some authoring tools support this functionality, while others do not. Also, this detailed reporting may be enabled for some course modules and not for others. In other words, don't be too quick to blame Learning Manager for the lack of data, and also make sure that reporting is properly configured in whatever authoring tool is used to build the course module.

Take some time to review the available data and relate it to the experience you had in *Chapter 7, Reviewing the Learner Experience*, while taking the course.

In this section, you learned about L2 feedback in ALM. Remember that collecting L2 data is mostly automatic. The data either comes from the AICC, SCORM, or xAPI reports sent to the LMS by the interactive learning modules or is manually entered into the system by an instructor.

The L1, L2, and L3 data is also used by the system to automatically calculate the course effectiveness score, which will be discussed in the next section.

Understanding the Course Effectiveness Score

The course effectiveness score is automatically calculated by Adobe Learning Manager and is obtained by combining the results from L1, L2, and L3 feedback. Let's review this hands-on using the following steps:

1. Log into your account as an administrator.

2. From the administrator home page, click the **Courses** link located in the **Learning** section of the left sidebar to access the list of courses currently available on your account.

3. Open the **Sort By** drop-down menu and choose to sort the list by **Course Effectiveness** (see the arrow in the following screenshot).

This last action is not mandatory, but it makes it easier to review the course effectiveness scores. As shown in the following screenshot, the course effectiveness score is displayed near the upper-right corner of each course card:

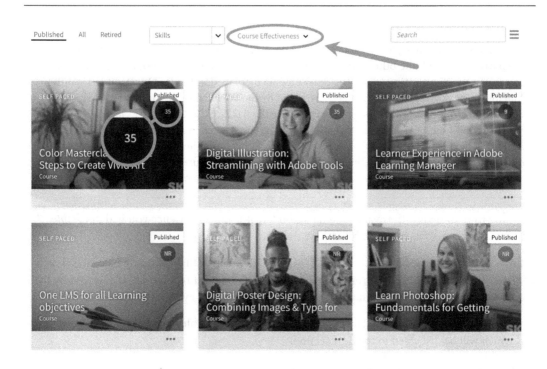

Figure 9.11 – The course effectiveness score as seen by an administrator

If Learning Manager does not have enough data to calculate the course effectiveness, the corresponding course is *not rated*, as indicated by the **NR** label visible in the second row of courses on the preceding screenshot.

It is possible to view the breakdown of each course effectiveness score by clicking the score on the course card. This gives you a better understanding of how ALM calculates the score for each course.

4.   Click the score of the first course in the list to open the **Course Effectiveness** dialog of this course.

5.   Also, click the **How Course Effectiveness is calculated** link to get additional insight on how ALM calculates the course effectiveness score.

As shown in the following screenshot, ALM takes the L1, L2, and L3 feedback data into account when calculating the course effectiveness score:

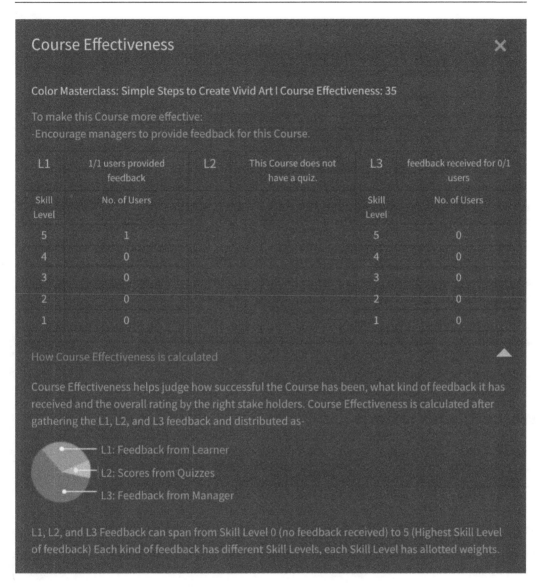

Figure 9.12 – The Course Effectiveness dialog box

Take some time to read the lower portion of the **Course Effectiveness** dialog box. Note that two-thirds of the score is based on L3 feedback from managers. Keep in mind that managers typically enter L3 feedback at least 45 days after a learner completes the course. If the L3 data is not yet available, ALM cannot take it into account when calculating the course effectiveness score, which explains the somewhat low scores for the courses currently hosted on your trial account.

If you feel like this is important information, it is possible to display the course effectiveness score to learners using the following steps:

6.   Return to the Administrator home page of your ALM account.

7.   Click the **Settings** link located in the **Configure** section at the end of the left sidebar.

8.   Next, click the **General** link located in the **Basics** section of the left sidebar.

9.   Scroll down the page until you see the **Show Ratings** section.

By default, this option is enabled but displays **Star Rating** rather than the **Course Effectiveness** score. The star rating will be discussed in the *Working with Ratings* section later in this chapter. Note that this option only affects the Learner role. Administrators always see the course effectiveness score when browsing the course section of the Admin role, regardless of the choices you make here.

In this section, you discovered that ALM automatically assigns a score for each course based on the L1, L2, and L3 feedback received. This *Course Effectiveness Score* is visible in the upper-right corner of each course card when logged in as an Administrator. It can also be made visible to learners, although that option is disabled by default.

The course effectiveness score can be useful to get a rough indication of the effectiveness of a course but be careful not to judge a course on this sole basis, as the course effectiveness score can be misleading in many situations. This is why you probably want to hide it from learners and display the star rating instead, which will be discussed in the next section.

Working with ratings

Nowadays, almost every online service has some kind of customer rating and reviewing system. For many consumers, these ratings and reviews are an essential part of the purchasing decision. It may even be these reviews that convinced you to buy this very book in the first place!

What holds true on Amazon, Booking.com, Netflix, and others, also holds true in the ALM course catalog. This is why learners have the ability to rate the courses they are taking using a five-star rating scale.

By default, the star rating feature is enabled on any new ALM account. Let's check this out using the following steps:

1.   Log in to your account as an administrator.

2.   From the administrator home page, click the **Settings** link located in the **Configure** section of the left sidebar.

3.   Then, click the **General** link located in the **Basics** section of the left sidebar.

4.   Scroll down the page until you see the **Show Ratings** section.

By default, the **Show Ratings** option should be enabled and set to the **Star rating** mode, as shown in the following screenshot:

Show Ratings   ☑ Enable   ○ Course Effectiveness ⓘ   ⦿ Star rating ⓘ

Figure 9.13 – The Show Ratings option is enabled by default

You will now log into your ALM account as *Learner 01* and take a look at how these ratings affect the learner experience.

5.   Log in to your account as *Learner 01*.

6.   Once logged in as a learner, select the **Catalog** icon on the left sidebar to go to the course catalog.

Notice that some courses have an **NR** label visible in the upper-right corner of their course card. Remember that **NR** stands for not rated. It is what ALM uses when there is not enough information to display the star rating for a course.

You will now visit the **My Learning** page of *Learner 01*. Remember that this page lists all the training items *Learner 01* is currently enrolled in or has recently completed.

7.   Click the **My Learning** icon on the left sidebar to open the **My Learning** page of *Learner 01*.

8.   Open any of the courses visible on the **My Learning** page of *Learner 01*.

9.   When on the course overview page, use the **Rate this training** section of the left sidebar to submit *Learner 01*'s rating for this course.

10.   When done, return to the **Catalog** page of the learner experience using the **Catalog** icon of the left sidebar.

11.   Confirm that the star rating you just submitted is now visible on the corresponding course card, as shown in the following screenshot:

Figure 9.14 – The star rating is visible on the course card in the catalog

This feature makes it very easy for learners taking courses to quickly submit their ratings and for learners browsing the course catalog to identify courses and learning paths that have received the highest ratings from previous learners.

Summary

In this chapter, you reviewed the extensive feedback capabilities available in Adobe Learning Manager. These capabilities are essential to any modern enterprise LMS because they allow the organization to collect valuable learning data and analyze it to document the effectiveness of the learning efforts and the worthiness of the investments being made.

In ALM, these features are based on a well-known theoretical model named the *Four Levels of Learning Evaluation* that was developed by *Dr. Donald Kirkpatrick* in the *1950s*. Level 1 is the *Reaction* level, level 2 is the *Learning* level, and Level 3 is the *Behavior* level.

L1 and L3 feedback are disabled by default in Adobe Learning Manager. You can enable them either at the course instance level or the account level. Also, remember that these feedback features also apply to learning paths.

But there is a fourth level to Kirkpatrick's Learning Evaluation model. It is the *Results* level. This is where organizations leverage the collected data to measure the impact of learning on the organization as a whole. This is the subject of the next chapter, in which you will review the extensive reporting capabilities available in ALM.

10
Reporting in Adobe Learning Manager

In the previous chapter, we discussed L1, L2, and L3 feedback for courses and learning paths. Remember that these feedback features are based on Donald Kirkpatrick's *Four-Levels of Learning Evaluation* model. *Four levels, did you say?* That's right! You only covered the first three levels in the previous chapter.

This chapter is entirely dedicated to the fourth level of Kirkpatrick's model. This is the **Results** level, which aims to measure the impact of the training strategy on the organization. It is at this stage that the focus shifts from the individual learner to the organization as a whole. For organizations, such insight is critical to identify areas for improvement, continually refine the organization's **Learning and Development (L&D)** strategy, and ultimately make informed business decisions.

Technically speaking, generating reports requires two distinct steps. First, you need to collect the data, and then you leverage that data to generate all kinds of reports. In **Adobe Learning Manager (ALM)**, data collection is automatic. You don't have to do anything to enable or configure any data collection mechanism on the platform. As for data mining, Adobe Learning Manager comes with a handful of predefined **reports**, but you can also create your own **custom reports**, share them with other users, and even export the data to another tool (such as Microsoft Excel) for further analysis.

These reports are arranged into **dashboards**. Some of these dashboards are available out of the box on every ALM account, but you can also create your own **custom dashboard** where you can arrange your custom reports as you see fit.

This chapter begins by exploring the default dashboards available in the system and discussing the reports they contain. You will then create your own custom reports and dashboards. Finally, you will examine extra options allowing you to subscribe to reports and discuss the reporting features available to managers. To achieve these objectives, this chapter contains the following main sections:

- Reviewing the default reports
- Creating custom reports and dashboards

- Subscribing to reports
- Reporting features for managers

These reporting features are instrumental in making ALM one of the leading enterprise **Learning Management Systems** (**LMSs**) on the market. There's a lot to discover, so let's get started!

Technical requirements

To follow along with the exercises in this chapter, you need to meet the following requirements:

- You must have administrator access to a working Learning Manager account (it can be a trial account)
- You must have a custom course with enrolled learners, and at least one of these learners should have completed the course
- You must have Manager access to your ALM account using the profile of the manager of the learners enrolled in the custom course mentioned in the previous item

This chapter picks up where the previous chapter left off. So, if you have completed the exercises of the previous chapter, you are ready to begin this one. If you have not, feel free to use your own course material and users. Just be aware that the instructions provided in this chapter are based on the exercises from previous chapters. Therefore, you may need to adapt them to your situation.

> **Note**
>
> Currently, your ALM trial account probably has only a few learners and a few courses. That's enough to get through this book and take your first steps with the platform, but it's too little data to experience the full power of ALM's extensive reporting capabilities. Keep that in mind when experimenting with the features documented in this chapter.

Reviewing the default reports

Most of the reporting capabilities of ALM are available to both administrators and managers. In this section, you will log in to your account as an administrator and explore the available default reports using the following steps:

1. Log in to your account as an administrator.
2. From the administrator home page, click the **Reports** link located in the **Manage** section of the left sidebar.

This takes you to the **Reports** section of the admin role. From here, you can use the links available in the left sidebar to review the automatically generated reports or to create your own **Custom Reports**:

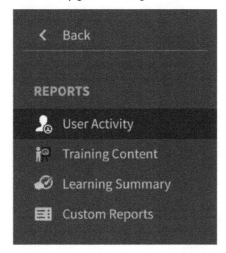

Figure 10.01 – The links available in the REPORTS section

You will now review each of these links one by one. Let's start by reviewing the **User Activity** dashboard in the next section.

Reviewing the User Activity dashboard

The **User Activity** dashboard is the page that opens by default when you access the **Reporting** section of the Admin role. It contains three important reports that are available out of the box in every ALM account. These reports give you an overview of user activity within your account and help you answer questions such as the following:

- How many registered users do you have, and how does that number evolve over time? Keep in mind that ALM is charged by the seat, so keeping an eye on this metric is critical to controlling your costs.

- How many learners access the platform on a daily basis? How does the number of visits change over time? These metrics are important to help you assess learner engagement.

- How many learners are using the Learning Manager mobile app to access training content from their mobile devices?

- How much time do learners spend on your ALM account? How does this number evolve? This metric allows you to answer questions such as: are learners spending enough time learning? Does the time spent learning meet the organization's expectations? How do promotional campaigns affect the time spent learning?

The first report available on the **User Activity** dashboard is **Registered Users Report**, shown in the following screenshot:

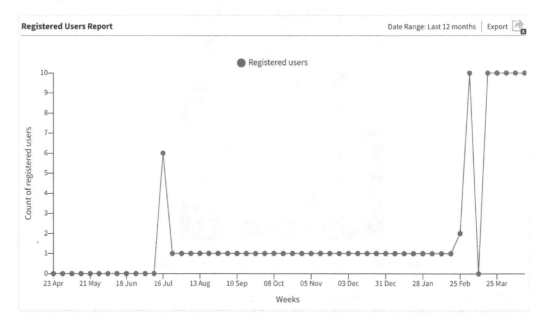

Figure 10.02 – Registered Users Report

This report tracks the number of registered users in your account on a weekly basis. In the preceding screenshot, notice that the number of registered users suddenly drops at the end of February. This is because the external registration profile created in *Chapter 5*, *Managing Users*, was disabled, so the seats used by that external profile were released on that date, and the users registered through this external registration profile lost their access to your ALM account.

For organizations using the **Monthly Active Users** (**MAU**) licensing model, this report shows the count of active learners on a monthly basis.

> **Adobe Learning Manager licensing models**
>
> There are two main licensing models available for Adobe Learning Manager: the **Registered User** model and the **Monthly Active Users** model. These two models were discussed in *Chapter 1*, *Introduction to Adobe Learning Manager*, in the *Getting access to Adobe Learning Manager* section.

Note that it is possible to export this data to a **Comma-Separated Values** (**CSV**) file using the following steps:

1. Make sure you are on the **User Activity** page of the admin role.

2. Click the **Export** button located in the upper-right corner of the **Registered Users Report**.

3. Take some time to read the message in the **Generating Report Request** dialog before clicking the **OK** button.

4. When the report is available, click the notification icon (the bell icon in the upper-right corner of the screen) to download the report. The downloaded .csv file can be opened with any spreadsheet application.

The **Registered Users Report** is only the first report available on the **User Activity** page. The next available report is the **User Visits** report. Let's explore it using the following steps:

5. Scroll down the **User Activity** page until you see the **User Visits Report**.

The **User Visits Report** shows the number of visits made to the platform over a given period of time. Note that each login is considered an access, even if the logged-in user just browses the system without actually viewing any course content.

By default, the report is configured to show data for all users in your account over the last 30 days, but you can change this by using the drop-down lists available above the report.

6. Open the **Date Range** drop-down list.

7. Choose any available date range. The report is immediately updated for the chosen date range.

    Note that if you choose a different value than the *Last 30 Days*, the report displays the data on a month-to-month basis rather than on a day-to-day basis.

8. Open the **Date Range** drop-down menu and return to the default value.

You can also filter the report by *User Groups*. As discussed in *Chapter 5, Managing Users*, remember that Adobe Learning Manager automatically generates a large number of user groups based on various user information. Custom groups are also possible. To use these groups as filters for the **User Visits Report**, you must first configure this feature using the following steps:

9. Click the **Configure** link located above the **User Visits Report**.

10. Take some time to read the message displayed in the **Configure User Group Filters** dialog.

    When done, type the name of a user group in the **Search User Groups** field. Click the desired group when it appears in the list. Repeat this action with up to 10 user groups.

The ability to filter this report by user group is very useful for comparing how various groups use the platform.

Note that ALM only records data for configured user groups. This means that if the user group configuration changes, ALM can only display data for the newly configured group from the date the group was added to the drop-down list.

Finally, note that the report distinguishes between visits made from the mobile app and visits made from other sources. Other sources are desktop and laptop computers, as well as headless access made through the Adobe Learning Manager API from external applications.

Scrolling down the **User Activity** page, there is one last report available. Let's explore it now:

11. Scroll down the **User Activity** page until you see **Learning Time Spent Report**.

This report shows the total learning time spent on the platform in blue and the median time spent by individual learners in green. This is a good indication of learner engagement: the more time learners spend learning on the platform, the more engaged they are.

Learning Manager calculates the time spent learning based on the amount of time users spend actually taking courses on the platform. In other words, the time spent browsing the course catalog is not included in this report.

Note that the **User Group** and **Date Range** drop-down fields discussed earlier also apply to this report. Also, notice the **Export** button available in the upper-right corner of the report, which allows you to export this data as a CSV file.

This concludes your overview of the **User Activity** report page, where three basic reports are available to ALM administrators. In the next section, you will explore the reports available on the **Training Content** page.

Reviewing the Training Content dashboard

The second default dashboard available in the left column of the **Reports** section is the **Training Content** dashboard. It contains two reports designed to give you an overview of the courses available in your Adobe Learning Manager account. These reports allow you to answer questions such as the following:

- How many courses are available on the account, and how does this number evolve? You can use this data to analyze whether this matches the organization's ambitions in terms of course offerings, whether an increase in the number of courses available translates into an increase in time spent learning on the platform, and so on.

- What are the courses that are most successful in terms of enrollment, views, and completion? This allows you to verify that the courses promoted by the organization are effectively being taken by learners. You can also use this information to determine what makes these courses so successful and use that data to improve the other courses hosted on your account.

Let's now explore this dashboard hands-on using the following steps:

1. Log in to your account as an administrator.

2. From the administrator home page, click the **Reports** link located in the **Manage** section of the left sidebar.

3. Next, click the **Training Content** link in the left sidebar to open the **Training Content** dashboard.

The first report available on the **Training Content** dashboard is the **Trainings Report**, illustrated in the following screenshot.

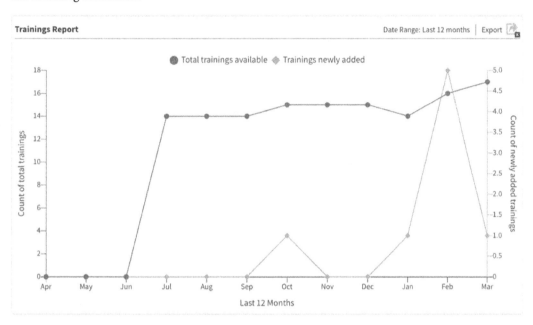

Figure 10.03 – The Trainings Report

This report shows the evolution of the number of training available on your platform over the last 12 months.

Note that this particular graph has two vertical axes (also called *y* axes). The vertical axis on the left is used for the **Count of total trainings** and generates the blue line of the graph. The vertical axis on the right is used for the **Count of newly added trainings** and generates the green line. It is possible for these two axes to not use the same scale. For example, in the preceding screenshot, the *total trainings* axis on the left goes from 0 to 18, while the *newly added* axis on the right goes from 0 to 5, which explains why the two lines do not reach the same height.

Also, note the **Export** button in the upper-right corner of the graph, which allows you to generate a CSV file of the corresponding dataset.

4.   Scroll down the **Training Content** dashboard until you see the **Active Trainings Report**.

This report provides information on the training content considered *active*. Active content is courses that have newly enrolled learners, have been viewed in the Fluidic Player, or have been completed within a given timeframe. By default, the **Active Trainings Report** shows data pertaining to the current month, but this can be changed using the **Date Range** drop-down menu:

5.   Open the **Date Range** drop-down menu located above **Active Trainings Report**.

6.   Choose any date range available and see how the report is immediately updated.

7.   Open the **Date Range** drop-down menu again and select the current month, which is the default value.

Note that you can also filter this report by **User Group** using the very same technique as for the reports included in the **User Activity** dashboard discussed earlier.

The following screenshot shows the **Active Trainings Report** with the default **User Group** option (**All Internal Learners**) and **Date Range** (**This Month**) selected:

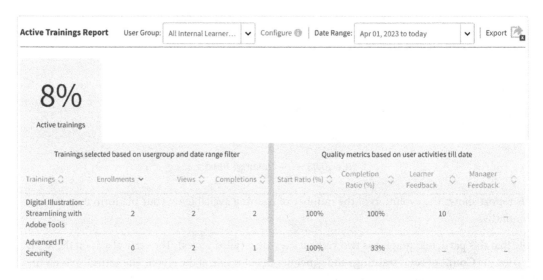

Figure 10.04 – Active Trainings Report

In the preceding screenshot, you can see that **8%** of all training available on my account are considered *active*. Also, notice that **Active Trainings Report** is divided into two columns:

- The left column shows the list of *active* training based on enrollment, view, and completion data for the selected **User Group** in the given **Date Range**.

- The right column shows the quality metrics of the selected courses.

    Start Ratio represents the percentage of learners that effectively started the training after enrollment.

    Completion Ratio shows the percentage of learners that started the course and effectively completed it. In the preceding screenshot, for instance, only one-third of the learners that started the **Advanced IT Security** course completed it.

    The **Learner Feedback** column is the average of all L1 feedback on a scale from 1 to 10. Remember that L1 feedback is provided by the learners at the end of the course.

    The **Manager Feedback** column is the average of all the L3 feedback on a scale from 1 to 5. As discussed earlier, L3 feedback is provided by managers sometime after the end of the training. By default, managers should provide L3 feedback 45 days after the end of training. This explains why the **Manager Feedback** column is empty in the preceding screenshot.

This report is a great way to get a quick overview of all active training and their respective quality metrics. It allows organizations to quickly identify the most successful training courses and those that need improvement.

This concludes the overview of the **Training Content** dashboard, which is one of the default dashboards available out of the box in Adobe Learning Manager. There is one last default dashboard to explore, which is what we will do in the next section.

Exploring the Learning Summary dashboard

For learning to occur on your account, you need learners on one end and learning content on the other end. The **User Activity** dashboard discussed earlier focused on the *learner* aspect, while the **Training Content** dashboard, discussed in the previous section, focused on the *learning content* aspect.

In this section, you will explore the **Learning Summary** dashboard, which focuses on the interactions between learners and learning. From that perspective, the reports in this dashboard measure the *liveliness* of your account. They allow you to answer questions such as these:

- How many enrollments, views, and course completions have taken place on the account? How many learners are actually involved in these statistics?

- What are the skills acquired by the learners in a given period of time? This helps you figure out whether the skills available in the workforce match the needs and targets of the organization.

- How are learners doing with the deadlines? Are they taking their assigned courses on time? Do they remain compliant? This is especially useful in organizations using Learning Manager for compliance training.

Let's now take a look at the **Learning Summary** dashboard and at the reports it contains using the following steps:

1. Log in to your account as an administrator.

2. From the administrator home page, click the **Reports** link located in the **Manage** section of the left sidebar.

3. Next, click the **Learning Summary** link in the left sidebar.

This last action takes you to the **Learning Summary** dashboard. From top to bottom, this dashboard contains three reports: the **Summary** report, the **Skills Status** report, and the **Compliance Dashboard**.

This dashboard is a little different than those discussed in the previous two sections. First, notice that there is no **Export** button on this dashboard. There is also a **Showing Data For** drop-down menu in the upper-right corner of the page. This drop-down menu affects all three reports on the dashboard:

4. Open the **Showing Data For** drop-down menu located in the upper-right corner of the **Learning Summary** dashboard to examine its content.

The options available in the **Showing Data For** drop-down menu include all the *root users* as well as all the *external profiles*:

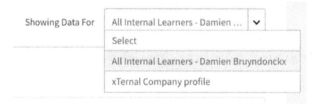

Figure 10.05 – The Showing Data For drop-down menu

As discussed in *Chapter 5*, *Managing Users*, external profiles allow you to define external users. External users are individuals who need access to your account without being part of your organization. This typically includes partners, suppliers, subcontractors, consultants, or franchisees. In the preceding screenshot, the **xTernal Company profile** option corresponds to the external profile that was defined in the *Creating external users* section of *Chapter 5*, *Managing Users*.

Root users are the users of your account that meet the following two requirements:

- Root users must be managers
- Root users do not report to any manager

In other words, root users are at the top of the user hierarchy. By default, the primary administrator of your account is the only available root user. In the preceding screenshot, my user profile (**Damien Bruyndonckx**) is the only root user available. Typical root users are the top executives of your organization or someone in your organization that manages external users/partners.

> **Listing root users**
>
> ALM maintains a list of all root users in the **Root Level Learners** user group. This is one of the automatically created user groups in ALM. From the administrator home page, go to **Users | User Groups** and look for the **Root Level Learners** group.

You will now explore the reports available on the **Learning Summary** dashboard using the following steps:

5. Choose any root user available in the **Showing Data For** drop-down menu.

6. Take some time to inspect the **Summary** report at the top of the page. It gives you a quick overview of what happened on your account in terms of enrollments, views, and completion for the current month by default.

7. Open the drop-down menu located in the upper-right corner of the **Summary** report to change the time range.

    Take some time to review the available time range options. When ready, return to the default date range.

8. Click the **Learning Summary Details** link located in the bottom-right corner of the **Summary** report.

As shown in the following screenshot, this operation opens a data table containing a breakdown of all teams and sub-teams that make up the user hierarchy under the selected root user:

Learning Summary   Actions ⌄

		Damien Bruyndonckx	Apr 01, 2023 to today
	Team Size (4)		

Team View

Team & Members	Enrollments	Views	Completions
☐ Damien Bruyndonckx's Team(4)	2	4	3
☐ Damien Bruyndonckx's Direct Team (2)	0	0	0
☐ Manager 01'S Team (2)	2	4	3

Figure 10.06 – A table view of the Enrollment data available in the Summary report

In the preceding screenshot, *Damien Bruyndonckx* is the selected root user. Looking at the table, you learn that Damien Bruyndonckx is the direct manager of two users. You also learn that one of these two users is *Manager 01*, who is the head of a team of two. So Damien Bruyndonckx has a team of four people but a direct team of only two people:

9. Use the checkboxes in the first column of the table to select one or more of the available teams.

10. When a team is selected, click the **Actions** button located in the upper-right corner of the screen.

11. Click the **Exports** link to generate CSV exports of the selected data.

    As usual, Learning Manager displays the **Generating Report Request** dialog box, letting you know that the report is being generated and that it takes a little bit of time before it is available.

    Click the **OK** button to dismiss the dialog box and wait for the report availability notification.

This is how you can export the data pertaining to this report even though there is no **Export** button directly available on the **Learning Summary** dashboard.

The data table also allows you to drill deeper down into the data. This is what you will now experiment with using the following steps:

12. Click the name of a team in the **Team & Members** column of the table to open a similar data table showing only the data pertaining to the selected team.

    Depending on the depth of the user hierarchy, you can keep drilling down into the data by clicking the names of the teams shown in the table as you navigate through the levels of the user hierarchy.

    Use the *Back* link in the upper-left corner of the page to go back up the user hierarchy.

13. Click the **Learning Summary** link in the left sidebar to return to the **Learning Summary** dashboard.

14. Scroll down the page until you see the **Skills Status** report.

The **Skills Status** report is the second report available on the **Learning Summary** dashboard. It is a bar chart showing the skills that are in progress and the skills that have been achieved by the selected group of learners.

Skills were discussed in *Chapter 4, Creating Skills and Courses*. As a reminder, you can create skills and skill levels within your account and link those skills to courses. As learners take courses, they accumulate points toward acquiring the skills related to the courses they have taken.

Just like for the **Summary** report discussed earlier, you can click the **Team Skills Details** link located in the bottom-right corner of the **Skills Status** report to display the same data in a table:

15. Click the **Team Skills Details** link located in the bottom-right corner of the **Skills Status** report.

16. Choose a **Skill** and a **Level** using the drop-down list available at the top of the page.

17. Take some time to explore the data table displayed on the second half of the page. Notice the **Actions** menu, which allows you to export the data as a CSV file.

18. When ready, click the **Learning Summary** link in the left sidebar to return to the **Learning Summary** dashboard and scroll down the page until you see the **Skills Status** report again.

You can also choose the skills you want to display using the link located in the upper-right corner of the **Skills Status** report.

19. When ready, scroll down the page until you see the **Compliance Dashboard** report.

This report allows you to check the compliance status of learners enrolled in various courses. This is an important report for many organizations using Adobe Learning Manager for compliance training. From here, you get an overview of the level of compliance achieved by learners on the platform. Just like the other reports available on this dashboard, you can view the data in a table format and drill down for further analysis.

This concludes our exploration of the dashboards and reports available by default in Adobe Learning Manager. These reports are designed to give you a general overview of what is happening on your account:

- The **User Activity** dashboard gives you an overview of the users. You can use it to get information about the number of registered users, the number of visits, and the learning time spent on your account.

- The **Training Content** dashboard gives you information about the content hosted on your ALM account. You can see the total number of training courses available, the number of newly added training courses, as well as information about active training.

- Finally, the **Learning Summary** dashboard gives you information about how users interact with the training content. You can see a basic summary of enrollments, views, and completions, as well as the **Skills Status** report and the **Compliance Dashboard** report.

Various filters and links provide a lot of meaningful variations on these basic reports. Remember that to take full advantage of these reporting capabilities, you need to give your learners enough time to interact with learning content and complete courses. You also need to give Learning Manager some time to generate meaningful daily, weekly, and monthly datasets.

These default reports already contain a lot of useful information. But that may not be the exact data your organization is looking for. Fortunately, you can also create your own custom reports and arrange them within your own custom dashboards. This is what you will review in the next section.

Creating Custom Reports and Dashboards

In most organizations, most administrators are very interested in the metrics provided by the default reports discussed in the previous section. In some rare cases, these reports provide exactly the type of information they are looking for. But more often than not, organizations define goals and outcomes that are unique to them. Therefore, they look for additional indicators and reports that help them document these specific requirements.

This is why Adobe Learning Manager allows you to define a wide range of custom reports, each with a multitude of variations and nuances. The possibilities are virtually endless, so every organization should find a way to extract the exact data they are looking for.

Just like the default reports, custom reports are also arranged into dashboards. By default, ALM comes with an empty default dashboard where you can arrange your custom reports as you see fit. But you can also create additional custom dashboards and even share them with other users. These are the features that you will explore in this section.

To access the custom reports, take the following steps:

1. Log in to your account as an administrator.
2. From the administrator home page, click the **Reports** link located in the **Manage** section of the left sidebar.
3. Finally, click the **Custom Reports** link in the left sidebar.

When the page opens, notice the four tabs at the top of the main content section, as illustrated in the following screenshot:

Figure 10.07 – The tabs of the custom reports page

You will review these four tabs one by one in the next few sections:

4. Make sure you are on the **Sample Reports** tab, as illustrated in the preceding screenshot.
5. Take some time to examine the three sample reports provided.

The purpose of these three sample reports is to give you a sense of what custom reports look like in Adobe Learning Manager. They use *dummy data* that is the same in every account. In other words, they do *not* use the actual data available in *your* account. These three sample reports are arranged in a single **Sample Dashboard**. You will now use them to examine the basic capabilities of custom reports and custom dashboards:

6. Hover over the bars in the different reports to reveal various types of tooltips.

7. Click the – icon located in the upper-right corner of each report to collapse the corresponding report.

8. Click the + icon to expand the collapsed reports.

9. You can also move the reports around to rearrange them within the sample dashboard.

10. Scroll down the page until you see the **Skills Vs Managers** report. Notice that this report spans the entire second row of the sample dashboard.

    Because this particular report contains a lot of data, only part of the data is visible by default.

11. Use the mouse wheel to zoom in and out. Use the bottom area of the **Skills Vs Managers** report to move the gray rectangle from left to right so as to select the portion of the graph you wish to view. This action is depicted in the following screenshot:

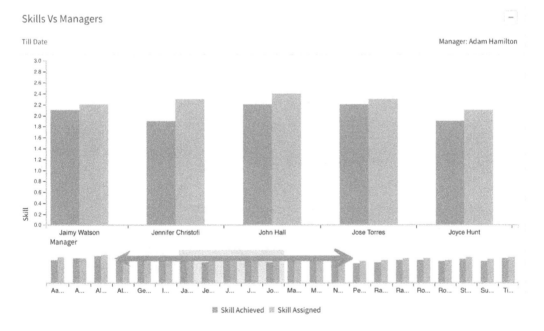

Figure 10.08 – Zooming and panning on a custom report

Now that you have a better idea of what custom reports look like and how they can be arranged within a custom dashboard, let's create a few of those in the next section.

Creating custom reports

There are so many custom reports that can be created in ALM that it is impossible to cover them all in this book. So, to prepare for this section, we contacted some ALM customers and partners and asked them what their top three custom reports are. The three reports that received the most votes are the following:

- The number of courses followed per profile
- The time spent learning per user
- The course effectiveness, by course

In this section, you will explore the available options by building these three custom reports.

> **The right account**
>
> In doing so, keep in mind that you are using a trial account with very few users and courses available, so there is very little data to populate these reports. If you have access to another ALM account with more users and courses, feel free to use that other account to experiment with creating custom reports. These reports would then be based on a larger set of data and would therefore be more relevant.

Out of the box, ALM contains a single dashboard, which is empty by default. Use the following steps to access this default dashboard:

1. Make sure you are logged in as an administrator.
2. From the administrator home page, click the **Reports** link located in the **Manage** section of the left sidebar.
3. Next, click the **Custom Reports** link in the left sidebar.
4. Finally, open the **Dashboard Reports** tab, which is the second tab available at the top of the page.

This opens the default dashboard, which is empty by default, as shown in the following screenshot:

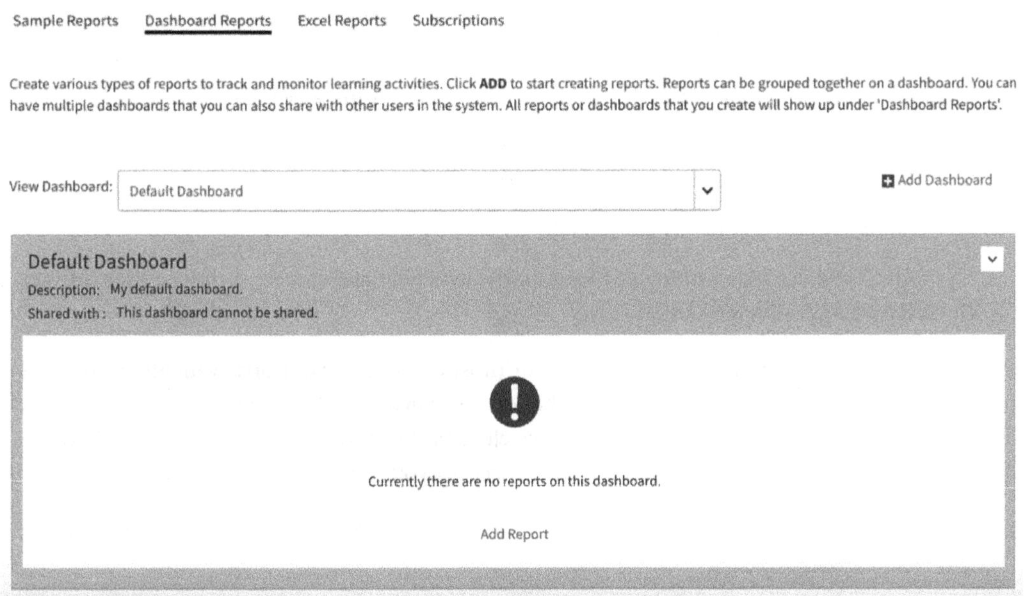

Sample Reports   Dashboard Reports   Excel Reports   Subscriptions

Create various types of reports to track and monitor learning activities. Click **ADD** to start creating reports. Reports can be grouped together on a dashboard. You can have multiple dashboards that you can also share with other users in the system. All reports or dashboards that you create will show up under 'Dashboard Reports'.

View Dashboard: | Default Dashboard | ∨ | ➕ Add Dashboard

Default Dashboard   ∨
Description: My default dashboard.
Shared with : This dashboard cannot be shared.

!

Currently there are no reports on this dashboard.

Add Report

Figure 10.09 – The default dashboard is empty by default

If you do not explicitly create your own custom dashboard, any custom report you create in Learning Manager is automatically added to this default dashboard.

In the next section, you will build your first custom report and add it to this default dashboard.

The number of courses followed per profile report

The first report you will build will allow you to examine the number of courses followed by each profile. As discussed in *Chapter 5, Managing Users*, *profile* is one of the fields available when creating new users in Adobe Learnig Manager. Depending on how your organization is structured, the *profile* field may have different meanings, but most of the time, the *profile* of a person corresponds to the job title or the department of the person.

This report will allow you to determine how the learning activities are distributed across profiles and to answer questions such as the following:

- Are all the profiles learning in the same way?
- Are there profiles that take more courses than others? Does that translate to these profiles being more performant?

- What are the profiles that learn less than others? How does that affect their performance? How can we explain that some profiles learn more and others learn less?

Follow these steps to build this first custom report:

1. Make sure you are on the empty default dashboard page, as discussed in the previous section.

2. Click the **Add Report** link located in the middle of the default dashboard. You can also click the **Add** button located in the upper-right corner of the page.

    This action opens the **Add Report** dialog.

3. Open the **Type** drop-down menu. Examine the available options, then choose the **Courses Enrolled and Completed** option.

Choosing a report type generates default values for most of the other options available in the **Add Report** dialog. These *Report Types* can therefore be seen as *templates* to help you build custom reports quickly. In this example, these defaults get you very close to the report you want to create. There are only a few parameters left to adjust to get exactly the report you want:

4. Open the **For (X-axis)** drop-down menu and examine the available options. When ready, choose the **Profile** option.

5. Open the **Time Span** section and confirm that the **Date** drop-down option is currently set to **YTD** (year to date). Take some time to examine the other options, but make sure you do not make any changes.

6. Open the **Filters** section. Notice that you can filter the report by **Manager**, **Profile**, **User Group**, and **Content**. By default, there are no filters defined, which is exactly what you need for this example.

7. Make sure the **Add Report** dialog looks like the following screenshot, and click the **Save** button:

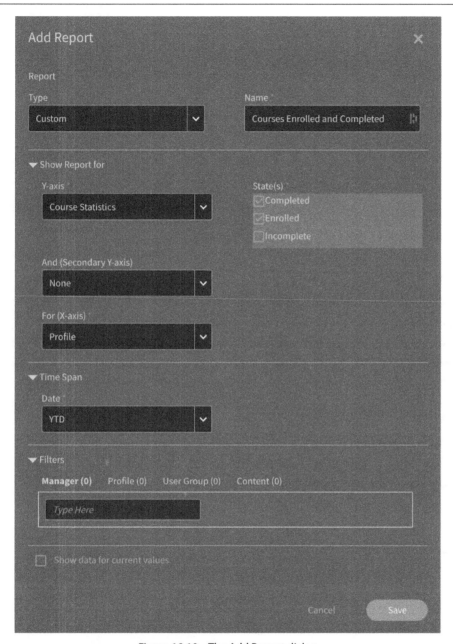

Figure 10.10 – The Add Report dialog

After clicking the **Save** button, the **Courses Enrolled and Completed** report is added to the default dashboard.

8. Take some time to examine the generated report. Hover your mouse over the bars to reveal tooltips with the value of each of the data points.

Also, notice the two filters available at the top of the report, as shown in the following screenshot:

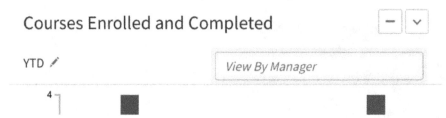

Figure 10.11 – Filters available on your first custom graph

These two fields provide similar options to the **Time Span** and **Filters** sections of the **Add Report** dialog discussed earlier. Let's now experiment with those two filters:

9. Click the pencil icon next to the **YTD** (Year To Date) label.

10. Open the drop-down menu and choose another date range. Notice how the report is immediately updated to reflect the new date range. Make sure to return to the default value (**YTD**) before continuing with this exercise.

11. Enter the name of a manager in the **View By Manager** field and notice how this action immediately updates the report. Make sure you clear the **View By Manager** field before continuing with this exercise.

These few experiments illustrate the flexibility of these custom reports. You will now finalize this first report using the following steps:

12. Click the down arrow located in the upper-right corner of the **Courses Enrolled and Completed** report.

13. Take some time to inspect the available options. When ready, click the **Edit Report** link.

14. Type Number of courses followed per profile in the **Report Name** field.

15. Open the **And (Secondary Y-axis)** drop-down menu and choose the **Learning Time Spent** option.

16. Leave the other options as is and click the **Save** button.

Your report should now look like the following screenshot:

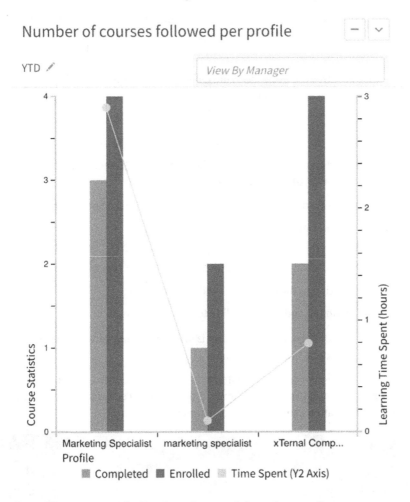

Figure 10.12 – The Number of courses followed per profile report

Notice that this chart now has two *y* (vertical) axes. The vertical axis on the left corresponds to the **Y-axis** drop-down menu when defining the report. Remember that this option is *mandatory* when building a report. The vertical axis on the right corresponds to the **And (Secondary Y-axis)** option. It allows you to add additional data points to the chart (basically, you can make two charts into one!). It is not mandatory to supply a secondary *y* axis when building a chart, but it is a very powerful option that allows you to quickly compare two values.

Building this first graph allowed you to discover the basic tools and features available in ALM for generating custom reports. In the next section, we will examine even more features by creating the **Time spent to learn per user** report.

The Time spent to learn per user report

The second custom report you will create is the **Time spent to learn per user** report. This custom report will help you identify the most active users and compare the user activity per profile, content, manager, and so on.

Because you may have hundreds or even thousands of users on your account, the ability to filter this report is paramount. To illustrate the filtering capabilities, we will only consider internal users in this example. Let's get started by following these steps:

1. Make sure you are on the **Custom Reports** page of the **Reports** section of the admin role.

2. Go to the **Dashboard Reports** tab and click the **Add** button located in the upper-right corner of the screen to open the **Add Report** dialog.

3. Open the **Type** drop-down menu and select the **Learning Time Spent per Course** report.

4. In the **Name** field, change the name of the report to Learning Time Spent per Internal User.

5. Open the **For (X-axis)** drop-down menu and select the **User** option.

6. Open the **Filters** section at the end of the **Add Report** dialog.

7. Click the **User Group** tab and add the **All Internal Users** group.

   Remember that the **All Internal Users** group is one of the groups that is automatically created and maintained by Adobe Learning manager.

   Note that you can add multiple user groups to the filter as well as any combination of **Manager**, **Profile**, **User Group**, and **Content**, as shown in the following screenshot. This allows for a very large number of variations and nuances for your custom reports:

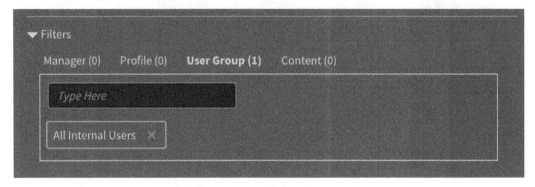

Figure 10.13 – The Filters section of the Add Report dialog

8. Click the **Save** button located in the bottom-right corner of the **Add Report** dialog to add the new report to the default dashboard.

Thanks to the preceding steps, you have created an additional custom report that has been added to the default dashboard. As with the report created in the previous section, you can use the *date range* and *manager* filters to further filter the dataset used to generate the report.

You will now create the same report but for *external users*. The **Learning Time Spent per External User** report will be very similar to the report you just created. So instead of starting from scratch, you will duplicate the **Learning Time Spent per Internal User** report and adjust a few options. Use the following steps to do so:

9. Click the drop-down arrow located in the upper-right corner of the **Learning Time Spent per Internal User** report.

10. Click the **Create a Copy** option to open the **Copy Report** dialog.

    The **Copy Report** dialog allows you to choose the dashboard you want to copy the report to. Since you have not yet created a custom dashboard, the only option available is to copy the report to the **Default Dashboard**.

11. Select the **Default Dashboard** option and click the **Copy** button.

    A new custom report named **Copy of Learning Time Spent per Internal User** appears on the default dashboard.

12. Click the drop-down arrow located in the upper-right corner of the **Copy of Learning Time Spent per Internal User** report. Choose the **Edit Report** option.

13. Type Learning Time Spent per External User in the **Report Name** field.

14. Open the **Filters** section and go to the **User Group (1)** tab.

15. Remove the **All Internal Users** group from the filter and replace it with the **All External Users** group.

16. Click the **Save** button to close the edit form and generate the new report.

You should now have two additional custom reports on the default dashboards: one showing **Learning Time Spent per External User** and the other one showing **Learning Time Spent per Internal User**, as illustrated in the following screenshot:

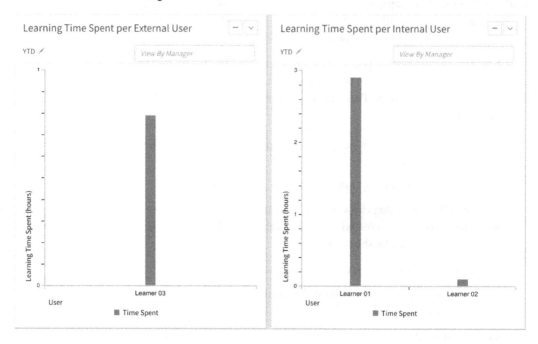

Figure 10.14 – Two additional custom reports appear on the default dashboard

You can also export the data of the chosen report as a CSV file. This allows you to open the data table in an external tool (such as Microsoft Excel) and use the features of that external application to further analyze the data. Let's review this feature hands-on using the following steps:

17. Click the drop-down arrow located in the upper-right corner of the report whose data you want to export.

18. Click the **Download Report** option.

19. Take some time to read the **Generating Report Request** message. When ready, click the **OK** button.

20. Sometime later (depending on the amount of data to be exported), you are notified that the report is ready to be downloaded.

In this section, you have created the **Learning Time Spent by User** custom report. In addition to creating the report, you have learned how to duplicate an existing report and adjust the copy to create another report. You have also used the **User Group** filter, which is similar to the **Manager**, **Profile**, and **Content** filters. Finally, you exported the data pertaining to a custom report as a CSV file that you can open in any spreadsheet application for further analysis.

In the next section, you will create the course effectiveness by course report.

The course effectiveness by course report

For this third report, remember that ALM automatically calculates a *Course Effectiveness Score* based on the L1, L2, and L3 feedback of each course. Thanks to this report, you will be able to quickly identify the courses with the highest/lowest course effectiveness.

To build this third report, you will not use any of the predefined templates available in the **Type** drop-down menu. Instead, you will build your report from scratch using the following steps:

1. Make sure you are on the **Custom Reports** page of the **Reports** section of the admin role.

2. Go to the **Dashboard Reports** tab and click the **Add** button located in the upper-right corner of the screen to open the **Add Report** dialog.

3. Open the **Type** drop-down menu and choose **Custom**.

   Notice that the **Custom** report type does not provide any default values for the other fields of the **Add Report** dialog.

4. Type `Course effectiveness by course` in the **Name** field.

5. Open the **Y-axis** drop-down menu and choose the **Course Effectiveness** option.

6. Open the **And (Secondary Y-axis)** drop-down option and choose the **Learning Time Spent** option.

7. Open the **For (X-axis)** drop-down menu and select the **Course** option.

8. Leave the other options at their default values and click the **Save** button to add this new custom report to the default dashboard.

It is possible that the Course Effectiveness Score is not yet available for some courses (remember that L3 feedback is typically provided 45 days after course completion), so don't be surprised to see a mostly empty graph.

In this section, you created a custom report from scratch using the **Custom** type. This concludes your first overview of creating custom reports in Adobe learning Manager. Don't hesitate to keep exploring the many variations available, as it is virtually impossible to document them all in this book. Also, remember that you need a much bigger dataset in order to take full advantage of ALM's reporting capabilities. Therefore, the primary goal of this section was to show you as many options as possible to get you started.

In this section, you learned the following:

- Adobe Learning Manager has one empty default dashboard. Unless otherwise stated, any new custom report is automatically added to this default dashboard.

- There are several predefined report **Types** available. Use them as templates to speed up the creation of your custom reports.

- Each report must contain a horizontal (x) axis and a vertical (y) axis, which is displayed on the left side of the report. Optionally, you can add a secondary y axis, which is displayed on the right side of the report.

- Each report includes a quick *date range* filter in the upper-left corner and a quick *manager* filter in the upper-right corner.

- Many additional filters are available when building the report. These include a **Date Range** filter, a **Manager** filter, a **User Group** filter, and so on.

- You can copy an existing report to any available dashboard. Use this feature to quickly create several variations of the same report.

- You can edit an existing report after its initial creation.

- You can export the data of a custom report as a CSV file that can be opened in any spreadsheet application for further analysis.

In the next section, you will create custom dashboards and arrange your custom reports within these dashboards, discovering even more features along the way.

Creating custom dashboards

The custom reports you have created so far in this chapter have been added to the default dashboard, which is available out of the box in every ALM account. This default dashboard is unique to your user account. It means that other administrators have their own default dashboard where they can define their own custom reports. In other words, the custom reports you have defined so far are only visible to you.

Sometimes, this default dashboard is all you need, but there are lots of circumstances where additional custom dashboards are very useful:

- Custom dashboards allow you to group your custom reports so you can better organize them, which helps you analyze the data and make sense of it.

- Custom dashboards can be shared with other managers. This feature allows administrators to define reports that can be used by managers throughout the organization. This allows busy managers to access meaningful data without having to create their own custom reports. It also helps you standardize the reports used in the organization. Of course, each manager can add their own custom reports and dashboards in addition to those shared by administrators.

You will now create a custom dashboard that you will share with all the managers in the organization using the following steps:

1. Make sure you are logged in as an administrator.

2. From the administrator home page, click the **Reports** link located in the **Manage** section of the left sidebar.

3. Then, click the **Custom Reports** link in the left sidebar and go to the **Dashboard Reports** tab.

4. Click the **Add Dashboard** link located to the right of the **View Dashboard** drop-down menu. This action opens the **Add Dashboard** dialog.

5. Type `All Managers dashboard` in the **Name** field.

    As a best practice, also add a short description in the **Description** field.

6. Type `All Managers` in the **Share With** field and select this user group when it becomes available in the list.

7. When the **Add Dashboard** dialog looks like the following screenshot, click the **Save** button.

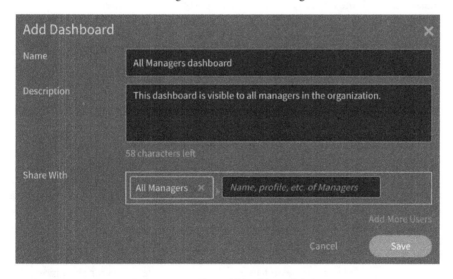

Figure 10.15 – The Add Dashboard dialog

Thanks to the preceding actions, you have created a new empty dashboard. You can now add custom reports to this new dashboard using the techniques described in the previous section. You can also copy or move custom reports from other dashboards to this one using the following steps:

8. Use the **View Dashboard** drop-down menu to return to **Default Dashboard**.

9. Click the drop-down arrow located in the upper-right corner of the report you want to move/copy. For this example, I used the **Learning Time Spent per Internal User** report created in the previous section.

10. Click the **Move to Dashboard** option to open the **Move Report** dialog.

11. Select the dashboard you want to move the report to (in this example, choose **All Managers Dashboard** that was created earlier) and click the **Move** button.

    Repeat these actions with the **Number of courses followed per profile** report.

12. Use the **View Dashboard** drop-down menu to return to the **All Managers Dashboard** created earlier and confirm that the two custom reports you just moved to this dashboard are visible.

13. Click the drop-down arrow located in the upper right corner of one of these two custom reports.

14. Choose the **Resize to 1×2** option to have the report span one entire row. This illustrates yet another option available to arrange reports on dashboards.

    Feel free to further arrange this dashboard using drag-and-drop actions and the **Resize to 1×2** option.

15. Finally, click the drop-down arrow located in the upper-right corner of your custom **All Managers dashboard**. Take good note of the available options allowing you to *add a report* to this dashboard, *edit* the dashboard, or *delete* the dashboard altogether.

In this section, you have created a custom dashboard, and you have moved two of your custom reports to it. You've also learned how a custom dashboard can be shared with other managers, which helps the organization streamline the use of custom reports. Finally, you arranged these reports on your custom dashboard.

Later in this chapter, you will log in as a manager and confirm that managers have access to this custom dashboard. But for now, let's review how you can use Excel reports in the next section.

Exporting Excel Reports

In addition to the reports created in the previous section and displayed as graphs in Adobe Learning Manager, there is a full set of additional reports that you can export as CSV files for further analysis in any compatible application or for archival purposes. That's what you will explore in this section.

Once again, there are so many reports and variations available that we will not be able to cover them all in this book. We will only concentrate on three of the most popular Excel reports among the ALM customers and partners we are in touch with.

Use the following steps to access the Excel reports available in Adobe Learning Manager:

1. Make sure you are logged in as an administrator.

2. From the administrator home page, click the **Reports** link located in the **Manage** section of the left sidebar.

3. Then, click the **Custom Reports** link on the left sidebar and go to the **Excel Reports** tab.

This takes you to the long list of Excel reports available in ALM.

> **Excel or not Excel...**
>
> ... that's the question! Although Learning Manager calls them *Excel* reports, all exports are done in CSV format. A CSV file can be opened in many applications, not just spreadsheets, and you can use any spreadsheet application, not just Microsoft Excel. Excel is simply the most popular spreadsheet software, and that's probably why it's called **Excel Reports** in ALM. Feel free to try this feature with whatever spreadsheet application you use and take advantage of the unique charting and data analysis features available in your specific software package.

You will now export three Excel reports, starting with the **Learner Transcripts** report in the next section.

Exporting the Learner Transcripts report

The first Excel report you will explore is the **Learner Transcripts** report. This report contains a comprehensive overview of all the learning activities of a learner or a group of learners. This type of report is very useful for human resources departments as it helps grasp the full picture of all the learning activities performed by learners on your account.

In this section, you will generate a **Learner Transcripts** report for your team of learners using the following steps:

1. From the **Excel Reports** tab of the **Custom Reports** section of the administrator, click the **Learner Transcripts** link to open the **Learner Transcripts** page.

    If you have generated learner transcripts previously, these will be listed on this page with the ability to download them again.

2. Click the **Generate New** button located in the upper-right corner of the page to open the **Learner Transcripts** dialog.

3. Open the **Select Range** drop-down menu and inspect the available options.

    In this example, I chose the **Last One Month** option but feel free to choose any option that suits your needs.

4. Use the **Select Learners** section to select the users or user groups you want to generate the learner transcript for.

    You can use any number of individual users, user groups, or any combination of both. In this example, I chose my team's user group (**Damien Bruyndonckx's Team**).

5. Take some time to inspect the other available options but don't change any of them at this time.

You have now entered all the basic information needed to generate the **Learner Transcripts** report. You could stop here and click the **Generate** button, but before doing that, let's explore the available advanced options:

6. Click the **Advanced Options** link located in the bottom-left corner of the **Learner Transcripts** dialog.

7. Take some time to explore the available options.

    When ready, select the **Include Module information** checkbox.

8. Click the **Generate** button located in the bottom-right corner of the **Learner Transcripts** dialog. Read the message and click the **Generate** button again.

9. When the report is ready, the newly created report is added to the list of available learner transcripts, as shown in the following screenshot:

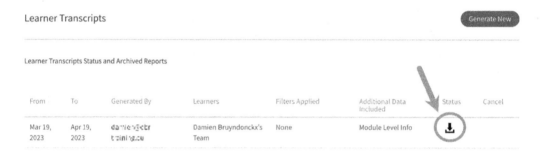

Figure 10.16 – The new Learner Transcripts report is added to the list

10. Click the download icon (see the arrow in the preceding screenshot) to download the generated learner transcript in CSV format, then open it in your favorite spreadsheet application and inspect the available data.

> **Personal learner transcript**
>
> In addition to the learner transcript generated in this section, each learner can export their personal learner transcript. To do so, click the user icon in the upper-right corner of the screen and choose the **Profile Settings** option. Scroll all the way down to find the **Download My Learning Transcript (XLS)** link.

In this section, you have explored the **Learner Transcripts** Excel reports available to administrators. In the next section, you will explore another Excel report and its associated options.

Exporting the Login/Access report

You will now explore the **Login/Access report** available as an Excel report. This report contains detailed information about user logins and access to the account. It is used by organizations to answer questions such as these:

- Who are the most active users on the platform?

- When do users typically connect to the account?

- What is the profile, location, department, and so on of the most active users?

- Is there a correlation between user activity and their profile, manager, location, and so on?

Use the following steps to generate and explore the **Login/Access report**:

1. From the **Excel Reports** tab of the **Custom Reports** section of the administrator, click the **Login/Access report** link to open the **Login/Access report** dialog.

2. Open the **Select Range** drop-down menu and explore the available options. For this example, choose **Last One Month**.

3. Click the **Generate** button and read the **Generating Report Request** message. Then, click the **OK** button to proceed.

4. When the report is ready, a notification appears under the bell icon in the upper-right corner of the screen. Click the notification to download the **Login/Access report** in CSV format.

5. Open the downloaded CSV file in your favorite spreadsheet application and inspect the available data. An example is shown in the following screenshot:

Figure 10.17 – The Login/Access report generated as seen in Apple Numbers

In this section, you have explored the **Login/Access report** available in ALM. You will explore one last report in the next section.

Exporting the Feedback report

In the previous chapter, we discussed L1 feedback and L3 feedback. As a reminder, L1 feedback is provided by learners directly upon course completion, while L3 feedback is provided by the learner's manager after the training has ended. In the *Retrieving L1, L2, and L3 feedback* section of *Chapter 9, Configuring and Using Feedback*, you could access this data for one training course at a time.

You will now explore another way of accessing L1 and L3 feedback with the added benefit of being able to consolidate the data of several different courses into a single report:

1. From the **Excel Reports** tab of the **Custom Reports** section of the admin role, click the **Feedback Report** link to open the **Feedback Report** dialog.

2. Take some time to examine the available options.

    In this example, choose to download feedback for **All Trainings** and choose a **Feedback Date Range** option of at least one month to have enough data to export.

3. When ready, click the **Download** button, read the **Generating Report Request** message, and click **OK**.

4. When the report is ready, a notification appears under the bell icon in the upper-right corner of the screen. Click the notification to download the **Login/Access report** in CSV format.

5. Open the downloaded CSV file in your favorite spreadsheet application and inspect the available data.

You have now looked at three of the available Excel reports. This has given you an idea of how Excel reports work and of the wealth of options available. Of course, there are other reports, each containing a myriad of options. We can't possibly cover them all in this book, so feel free to continue exploring the available reports on your own in search of the exact information your organization is looking for.

Subscribing to reports

In the *Creating custom reports and dashboards* section earlier in this chapter, you learned how to create a wide variety of meaningful reports. But these reports are only useful if you visit them from time to time and examine how the figures evolve.

Adobe Learning Manager understands that administrators and managers are very busy with their day-to-day tasks and do not always have the opportunity to log in to the corporate LMS to review stats and reports. Fortunately, you can have Learning Manager email your favorite reports to you on a regular basis.

Note that this is only possible with your own custom reports or with the custom reports that are shared with you.

Let's see how you can subscribe to such custom reports using the following steps:

1. From the **Custom Reports** section of the administrator, click the **Dashboard Reports** tab to return to the custom reports you created earlier in this chapter.

2. Choose the report you want to subscribe to. Keep in mind that you may have additional reports available on custom dashboards. These are also eligible for subscription.

    In this example, I choose the **Learning Time Spent per External User** report we created earlier.

3. Switch to the **Subscription** tab available at the top of the page.

4. Enter the name of the report you want to subscribe to in the **Reports** field. Click the chosen report when it appears in the list.

5. Open the **Frequency** drop-down menu and choose the most appropriate option.

6. If needed, you can customize the **Subject of the e-mail** in the corresponding field.

7. You can also customize the email address(es) the report should be sent to in the **Alternate email** field. If you leave this field empty, the report is sent to the email address associated with your ALM user profile.

8. Click the blue check icon at the end of the row to validate your new subscription.

As shown in the following screenshot, you should now have one subscription listed on this page:

Figure 10.18 – One subscription is listed on the page

You can add as many subscriptions as needed. You can also update and delete these subscriptions using the icons visible at the end of each row.

Keep in mind that these subscriptions are only possible with your own custom reports or with custom reports that are shared with you. This is yet another great reason to create custom reports in the first place!

Reporting Features for Managers

So far, you have experienced the reporting features of ALM when logged in as an administrator. In this section, you will discover that most of these features are also available to managers. The main difference is that administrators have access to all the data, while managers only have access to the data pertaining to their team.

You will now log in as *Manager 01* and explore the reporting features from a manager's perspective:

1. Log in to your account as *Manager 01*.

2. Once logged in, switch to the **Manager** role using the icon located in the upper-right corner of the screen.

Take some time to examine the manager home page. Notice that it is very similar to the **Learning Dashboard** available to administrators and that we discussed earlier in this chapter:

3. Click the **Details** link located in the bottom-right corner of the **Learning Summary** section of the manager home page.

    This action takes you to the **Learning Summary** page, where *Manager 01* can see additional information pertaining to the members of the team.

4. Click the **Compliance Dashboard** link located in the **My Team View** section of the left sidebar. Notice that it is very similar to the **Compliance Dashboard** reports located on the **Learning Summary** page available to administrators, as discussed earlier in this chapter.

5. Click the **Team Skills** link located in the **My Team View** section of the left sidebar. Notice that it is very similar to the **Skills Status** reports located on the **Learning Summary** page available to administrators.

6. Click the **Reports** link located in the **View** section of the left sidebar.

7. Take some time to examine each of the four tabs available across the top of the **Reports** page.

Going through these tabs from left to right, you should see the following:

*   The **Sample Reports** tab is exactly the same as in the admin role.

*   The **Dashboard Reports** tab allows managers to create their own custom reports using the exact same techniques as those available to administrators. The only difference is that the dashboards created by managers cannot be shared with other users.

*   The **Shared Reports** tab contains the dashboards created by administrators and shared with *Manager 01*. This tab should contain the **All Managers dashboard** created earlier in this chapter.

*   The **Subscriptions** tab allows managers to subscribe to any of the custom reports available to them using the same technique as those used by administrators.

As you can see, managers have access to pretty much the same reporting features as administrators. The main difference is that managers only see the data pertaining to their team members, while administrators have access to all the data available on the account.

Summary

In this chapter, you reviewed the extensive reporting capabilities of ALM. These features can be seen as the fourth level of Kirkpatrick's *Four Levels of Learning Evaluation* model. It is the **results** level where organizations leverage available data to measure the impact of learning on the organization as a whole.

A handful of reports are available by default, but you can also create your own custom reports, export various datasets as CSV files, and subscribe to reports so that Learning Manager emails you the data pertaining to your custom reports on a regular basis.

Reports are organized into dashboards, and you can create your own custom dashboards in addition to the dashboards available by default. Administrators can even share their customized dashboards with managers to help them access relevant information and to standardize the reports used throughout the organization.

These very powerful reporting features contribute to establishing Adobe Learning Manager as one of the leading modern enterprise LMSs on the market.

But Adobe Learning Manager has a lot more to offer. In the next few chapters, you will discover how you can use the **Gamification** and **Social Learning** features to enhance the Learner experience, increase engagement, and ultimately, increase the retention and effectiveness of learning throughout the organization.

Let's start by exploring the gamification features in the next chapter.

Part 3 – Enhancing the Learner Experience

In this third part, we will focus on enhancing the learner experience through the use of the Gamification, Social Learning, and AI-powered features of Adobe Learning Manager.

This section comprises the following chapters:

- *Chapter 11, Badges and Gamification*
- *Chapter 12, Enabling and Managing Social Learning*
- *Chapter 13, AI-Powered Recommendations for Learners*

Badges and Gamification

People learn best when they have fun! This is something teachers and instructors have known for thousands of years. There is historical evidence that games and game-based learning were well-known educational ideas in ancient Greece and during the Roman Empire. The earliest African board games used to teach mathematics, logic, and strategy were designed over 5,000 years ago!

Despite this long and rich history, the term **gamification** first appeared in online education around 2008 and gained popularity as of 2010. A widely accepted definition of gamification is *the use of game-design elements and game principles in non-game contexts.*

This definition is not specific to education. In fact, gamification is present in many aspects of our daily lives. For example, we earn miles when we fly and redeem them for free upgrades, and we earn points and stamps when we shop and redeem them for all sorts of gifts, and so on. In the corporate world, many organizations use employee honor rolls to increase engagement and productivity and to recognize achievements.

Regardless of the area of application, game design elements are the basic building blocks of gamification. Points, badges, leaderboards, scenario-based training, and avatars are some of the typical game design elements being used. Many of these are available in Adobe Learning Manager.

In this chapter, you will first learn about **badges** and discover how they are used within Adobe Learning Manager. Then, you will explore the gamification feature, which awards points to learners when they interact with the learning content hosted on your account. You will first explore these features from the administrator's perspective before reviewing how they affect the learner experience.

To achieve these objectives, this chapter contains the following main sections:

- Creating and using badges
- Enabling and configuring gamification
- Experiencing gamification from the learner's perspective

By the end of this chapter, you will have reviewed yet another range of features that will help you increase learner engagement by making learning more fun. This will further help your organization promote a learning culture among employees.

Technical requirements

To perform the exercises of this chapter, you need to meet the following technical requirements:

- You must have administrator and learner access to a working Learning Manager account (which can be a trial account).

- You must have at least one skill, one course, one learning path, and one certification available on your account. This can be custom training content or content that was made available by default when you created your trial account.

If you have completed the exercises in the previous chapters, you are good to go! If you did not go through the previous chapters, feel free to use whatever course content and users are available on your account. Just be aware that the instructions provided in this chapter are based on the exercises of the previous chapters, so you will need to adapt them to your situation.

Creating and Using Badges

Badges are one of the most commonly used game design elements in online education. They symbolize the learner's achievements, help add credibility to the learner's credentials, and are a source of pride.

In Adobe Learning Manager, learners earn badges by achieving skills, completing courses and learning paths, or achieving certifications. To use badges, you must first define them in the system. Then, you need to link those badges to courses, learning paths, skills, and certifications.

In this section, you will learn how to create custom badges using the following steps:

1. Make sure you are logged in as an administrator.
2. From the administrator home page, click the **Badges** link located in the **Configure** section of the left sidebar.

This opens the **Badges** page. As shown in the following screenshot, a handful of badges are already defined on your ALM trial account:

Active   Retired   Sort By ∨

CAPTAIN   CERTIFIED   GURU   HERO   NINJA   SCHOLAR

SUPERSTAR   ROCKSTAR

Figure 11.1 – A handful of badges are already defined in your ALM trial account

Take some time to examine the **Badges** page. Notice the **Sort By** drop-down menu, which allows you to sort the badges either by name or date updated. You can also create your own custom badges using the following steps:

3. Click the **Add** button located in the upper-right corner of the screen to open the **Add Badge** dialog.

4. Type Cybersecurity Fighter in the **Badge Name** field.

5. Upload the badges/cyberSecurity_fighter.png image available in the download associated with this book in the **Badge Image** field.

   Note that the badge image must be a square of at least 250 pixels by 250 pixels. If the image provided is not a square, Learning Manager automatically resizes it to a square. You can use any popular image format, including JPG and PNG files.

6. When ready, click the **Save** button to generate your first custom badge.

7. Repeat the preceding steps to create three additional badges. Use the images provided in the badges/ folder of the download associated with this book:

   • **Badge Name**: Cybersecurity Specialist; **Badge Image**: cyberSecurity_specialist.png.

   • **Badge Name**: Photo Editing Master; **Badge Image**: photoEditingMaster.png

   • **Badge Name**: Certified IT Professional; **Badge Image**: certifiedITPro.png

At the end of this process, you should have four additional badges available on the **Bages** page of the Admin role.

Creating badge images

The badge images that are available in the `badges/` folder of the download associated with this book have been created with Adobe Express (formerly Adobe Spark). Adobe Express is an online service designed to help you create great-looking graphics for your social media posts. It is available in the browser or as a mobile app for iOS and Android. Adobe Express is available for free to anyone with an Adobe ID. Premium features are available for a fee. You can find more information about Adobe Express at `https://www.adobe.com/express/`.

Now that you have custom badges, you need to tell Learning Manager what to do with them. That's what you'll explore in the next few sections.

Assigning Badges to Skills

One of the many ways learners can acquire badges is by achieving skills. Creating skills and linking them to courses was discussed in *Chapter 4, Creating Skills and Courses*. As a reminder, Adobe Learning Manager lets you define skills and levels within those skills. When learners take courses, they receive points toward achieving the skill(s) to which the course is linked.

You will now return to the custom **IT Security** skill you created in *Chapter 4, Creating Skills and Courses*, and associate a badge with each of the two levels you have defined for this skill. These badges will help learners publicize their new skills and add credibility to their achievements:

1. Make sure you are logged in as an administrator.

2. From the administrator home page, click the **Skills** link located in the **Manage** section of the left sidebar to open the **Skills** page.

3. Click the **IT Security** skill you created in *Chapter 4, Creating Skills and Courses*, to open the **Edit Skill** dialog. Remember that you have defined two levels for this particular skill.

4. If necessary, expand the **Level 1** section located in the lower portion of the **Edit Skill** dialog.

5. Open the **Choose from the following Badges** drop-down menu and select the **Cybersecurity Fighter** badge defined in the previous section.

6. Repeat the preceding steps to assign the **Cybersecurity Specialist** badge to **Level 2** of the **Cybersecurity** skill. This action is illustrated in the following screenshot:

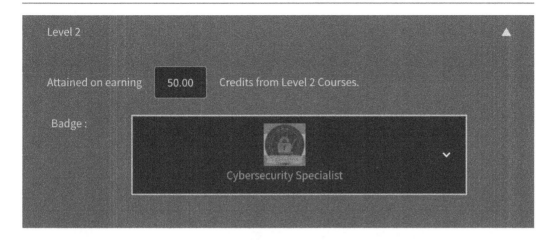

Figure 11.2 – Assigning a badge to a Skill Level

7. When ready, click the **Save** button located in the lower-right corner of the **Edit Skill** dialog.

From now on, when learners achieve the *IT Security – Level 1* skill, they automatically receive the **Cybersecurity Fighter** badge. They also receive the **Cybersecurity Specialist** badge when they reach *Level 2* of the same skill.

In this section, you learned how to link badges to skills. In the next section, you will explore how to link badges to courses and learning paths.

Assigning Badges to Courses and Learning Paths

Another way to earn badges is by completing courses and learning paths. To do this, administrators must first link badges to these learning objects. To be more exact, you must link badges to course *instances* and learning paths *instances*. This allows you to have different badges for each course instance.

You will now assign a badge to the *Mastering Photo Editing* learning path you created in *Chapter 6, Enrolling Users to Courses*, using the following steps:

1. From the administrator home page, click the **Learning Paths** link located in the **Learning** section of the left sidebar.

2. Click the **Mastering Photo Editing** learning path (or any other available learning path).

3. When the chosen learning path opens, click the **Instances** link located in the **Manage** section of the left sidebar.

4. Click the **Badges** link associated with the instance you want to modify.

5. Toggle the **Enable Badge** switch on.

6. Open the **Choose from the following Badges** drop-down menu and choose the **Photo Editing Master** badge you created earlier in this section.

This process is depicted in the following screenshot:

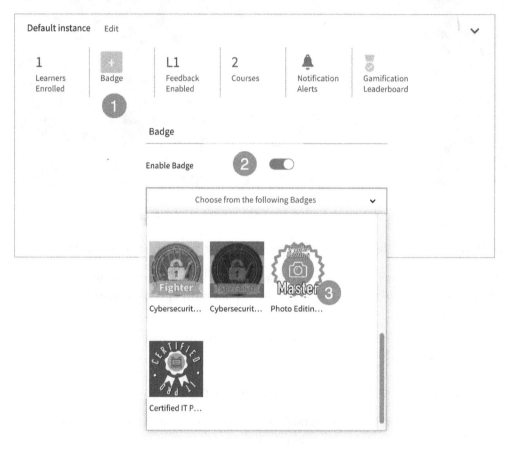

Figure 11.3 – Assigning a badge to a Learning Path instance

7.   When ready, click the blue checkmark in the lower right corner of the screen to validate your changes.

From now on, every learner that completes the *Mastering Photo Editing* learning program will be awarded the *Photo Editing Master* badge.

Using the instance defaults

As discussed in the *Customizing course instance defaults* section of *Chapter 9, Configuring and Using Feedback*, you can use the **Instant Defaults** link in the **Configure** section of the chosen course or learning path to assign the same badge to every *future* course or learning path instance by default.

In this section, you learned how to assign a badge to a learning path instance. The process is exactly the same for assigning a badge to a course instance.

In the next section, you will assign a badge to a certification using a very similar process.

Assigning badges to certifications

Completing a certification is yet another way of acquiring a badge in Adobe Learning Manager. Let's review this feature hands-on by linking a badge to the *Certified IT Pro* certification you created in *Chapter 6, Enrolling Users in Courses*. Use the following steps to do so:

1. From the administrator home page, click the **Certifications** link located in the **Learning** section of the left sidebar.

2. Click the **Certified IT Pro** certification you created back in *Chapter 6, Enrolling Users in Courses* (or any other available certification).

3. When the certification opens, click the **Edit** button located in the upper-right corner of the screen.

4. Scroll down the page until you see the **Badge** option.

5. Open the **Choose from the following Badges** drop-down menu and choose the **Certified IT Pro** badge created earlier in this chapter:

Figure 11.4 – Assigning a badge to a Certification

6. Finally, click the **Republish** button in the upper-right corner of the screen to validate your changes.

In this section, you have explored how to link a badge to a certification. Remember that you can link badges to skills, courses, and learning paths as well. In the next section, you will return to the **Badges** page of the admin role and explore how you manage badges in the long run.

Retiring and Deleting Badges

As the learning content in your ALM account evolves, so do the badges. In this section, you will learn how to retire and delete old badges using the following steps:

1. From the administrator home page, click the **Badges** link located in the **Configure** section of the left sidebar to open the **Badges** page.

2. Use the checkboxes in the upper-left corner of each badge to select one or more of the available badges (in this example, make sure you do not select any of the custom badges you created earlier in this chapter).

3. Open the **Actions** drop-down menu located in the upper-right corner of the screen.

4. Click **Retire** to retire the selected badges.

A *retired* badge can no longer be linked to any skill, course, learning path, or certification, but it remains available in the skills, courses, learning paths, and certifications to which it is already linked. In addition, learners who have been awarded these badges retain them and can continue to use them as usual.

5. Click the **Retired** tab located in the upper-left corner of the page to open the list of retired badges.

6. Again, use the checkboxes to select one or more of the retired badges.

7. Open the **Actions** drop-down menu located in the upper-right corner of the screen and inspect the available options.

    Clicking the **Republish** option puts the selected badges back in the *active* state.

    Clicking the **Delete** button definitively deletes the selected badges from the system.

8. In this example, select all the retired badges and use the **Republish** action to restore the initial situation.

In this section, you learned how to *retire* and *delete* existing badges, which concludes your exploration of badges in Adobe Learning Manager.

Note that there is absolutely no obligation to use badges in Adobe Learning Manager. In fact, no badges are issued by default. You must explicitly link badges to skills, courses, learning paths, or certifications for ALM to start distributing badges to learners. This allows organizations that are new to badges to assess how they are perceived by their staff before deciding whether or not to roll them out.

Badgr

In some scenarios (such as in customer education, where organizations want to give their customers the ability to share their badges as widely as possible), it makes sense to give learners the opportunity to display their badges outside of Adobe Learning Manager. This is made very easy through the integration with **Badgr**, a global platform that implements the **Open Badges** standard for storing and sharing badges. In Adobe Learning Manager, administrators can enable the Badgr integration using the **Badgr Integration** option on the **Settings | General** page of the Administrator role. More information about Badgr and the Open Badges standard can be found at `https://community.canvaslms.com/t5/Canvas-Badges/tkb-p/canvas_badges`.

In the next section, you will review the gamification feature of Adobe Learning Manager, which allows you to award points to learners when they interact with the learning content hosted on your account.

Enabling and configuring Gamification

In the previous section, you learned about *badges*, which are one of the most popular game design elements used in eLearning. In this section, you will learn about *points*, which is another widely used game design element in online learning.

The idea is quite simple: learners get points whenever they interact with the learning content hosted on your account. The more they learn, the more points they get. These points are visible on the **Leaderboard** page of the Learner role, where learners can view their score and see how they compare with their peers. The goal is to promote positive competition among employees, which in turn increases learning and engagement.

Avoid confusion

Most users are unfamiliar with the term *gamification* and refer to this feature as *the leaderboard*. Communication is a key aspect of implementing these types of features, so be sure to use terms and expressions that everyone understands when communicating about these gamification features.

Let's begin our discovery of gamification in Adobe Learning Manager by looking at how learners earn points. Follow these steps to do so:

1. Make sure you are logged in as an administrator.
2. From the administrator home page, click the **Gamification** link located in the **Configure** section of the left sidebar.

   At the top of the **Gamification** page, notice the four levels available. When learners reach a certain threshold, they are awarded the corresponding level.

3. Click the **Edit** link located in the upper-right corner of the **Levels** section.

As shown in the following screenshot, this allows you to modify the point threshold for each level. Also notice the **Revert to Original** link, which allows you to restore the default values:

Figure 11.5 – Setting up the points threshold for each level

4. In this example, click the **Cancel** button to leave the current values in place.

The rest of the **Gamification** page describes the events that award points to learners. For example, the first section describes how *fast learners* can get extra points. As illustrated by the following screenshot, a learner that completes one course per month gets 50 points, completing two courses per month awards 100 points, completing five courses per month awards 400 points, and so on:

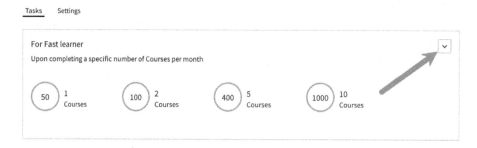

Figure 11.6 – Fast learners get extra points when completing courses

You can, of course, change the default values using the following steps:

5. Click the drop-down arrow associated with the **For Fast learner** section at the top of the **Gamification** page (see the arrow in the preceding screenshot).

6. Click the **Edit** button and take some time to review the available options.

7. When ready, click the **Cancel** button to keep the current values.

There are a dozen of these sections available on the **Gamification** page, each describing a set of events that award points to learners. Each of these sections can be modified or even completely disabled using the preceding steps.

8. Take the necessary time to inspect the other available sections and the options they contain. This should give you a better understanding of how learners acquire points in Adobe Learning Manager.

In this section, you have reviewed the basic options for configuring gamification on your ALM account. In the next section, you will discover more advanced options pertaining to gamification in Adobe Learning Manager.

Configuring Advanced Gamification Options

In the previous section, you discovered the basic configuration options for gamification in Adobe Learning Manager. In this section, you will dig a little deeper and discover the advanced gamification options. Follow these steps to access these options:

1. Make sure you are logged in as an administrator.

2. From the administrator home page, click the **Gamification** link located in the **Configure** section of the left sidebar.

3. Click the **Settings** tab located just below the **Levels** section, as shown in the following screenshot:

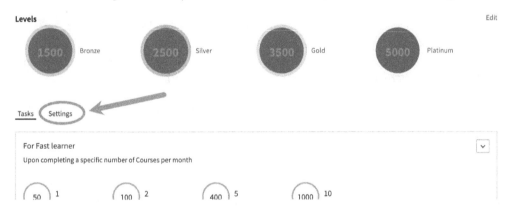

Figure 11.7 – Accessing the advanced gamification settings

This takes you to the advanced gamification settings, which you will review one by one in the following few sections.

Enabling and disabling gamification

By default, gamification is enabled for internal users only. This is what most organizations want. That being said, this default is not adequate in all situations:

- Gamification raises concerns about privacy as learners can see each other's scores on the leaderboard. This is the main reason why some organizations want to turn off gamification altogether.

- If your organization trains a lot of external users, you may want to turn gamification on for external users as well.

These are some of the reasons why you may want to enable or disable gamification on your account. Let's review how this can be done by following these steps:

1. From the **Settings** tab of the **Gamification** page, click the **Edit** link associated with the **Gamification Feature** option.

2. As shown in the following screenshot, gamification is enabled for internal learners and disabled for external learners by default:

Figure 11.8 – Enabling and disabling gamification for internal and external learners

3. Make sure you don't make any changes to the current settings and click the **Cancel** button in the lower-right corner to close the **Gamification Feature** section.

In this section, you learned how to enable and disable gamification both for internal and external learners. When Gamification is disabled, the **Leaderboard** page is removed from the Learner experience.

Modifying the Gamification Scope

When gamification is enabled, all learners compete against each other by default. This is great when you have a small number of learners (up to a few hundred), but for larger organizations with several thousand learners, this default may not be optimal:

- You may have some profiles (job titles) for whom training is a critical part of their job description, while other profiles have fewer training requirements and opportunities. Does it really make sense to have these very different profiles compete against each other in gamification?

- Multinational companies operating in different countries need to take cultural variations into account. In some cultures, gamification is taken very seriously, while in other cultures, it is not as much of a concern. In this case, it makes sense to group people by location and let them compete only against other individuals in the same group.

- Some special profiles, such as top-level executives, should be removed from gamification as they probably have no interest in competing against their own employees for points in the corporate **LMS**.

These are some of the reasons why you may want to restrict the scope of gamification, which can be done using the following steps:

1. From the **Settings** tab of the **Gamification** page, click the **Edit** link associated with the **Scope Settings** option.

2. Select the **Limit Gamification to certain Learners and Learner groups** checkbox.

3. Open the **User characteristic** drop-down menu and review the available options. In this example, choose the **profile** option.

   Remember, most of the time the profile of a learner is a synonym for the job title or department.

4. Open the **Value** drop-down menu and inspect the available options. In this example, deselect the **Profile (ceo)** option to remove users with this profile from gamification.

With this configuration, users with the *CEO* profile are removed from gamification. Other profiles are considered gamification scopes. Thus, the *Marketing Manager* profile defines a gamification scope with the corresponding learners competing against each other, while the *Marketing Specialist* profile defines another gamification scope and thus another gamification competition among the corresponding learners.

5. Since you have just a few learners on your account, click the **Cancel** button to keep the default configuration active.

In this section, you have reviewed the *scope* settings of gamification, which allows you to split your learners into multiple gamification competitions based on a user characteristic of your choosing (typically, the user profile or the location).

Modify the Confidentiality Settings

Say you have enabled gamification, and learners are competing against each other. It works so well that you see a significant increase in learner engagement. But not all learners are equal in the face of gamification! Employees begin to notice that their managers (or, even worse, the top executives in the organization) don't have as many points as they do. So when the same managers try to motivate their team members to take courses, their credibility may be at stake!

Hopefully, the confidentiality settings allow you to hide the scores of specific learners from others. Let's review this feature hands-on by following these steps:

1. From the **Settings** tab of the **Gamification** page, click the **Edit** link associated with the **Confidentiality Settings** option.

2. Use the **Find Learners by Name, Profile etc.** field to search for learners. In this example, search for the **All Managers** group.

3. Use the checkboxes to select all the listed managers.

4. Click the **Hide** button to hide the selected users from gamification.

With this option in place, the selected managers continue to take part in gamification. They are still awarded points whenever they complete training or acquire a new skill, but their score is no longer displayed to the other learners on the leaderboard.

You will now return to the initial situation by following these steps:

5. From the **Settings** tab of the **Gamification** page, click the **Edit** link associated with the **Confidentiality Settings** option.

6. Switch to the **Confidential Learners** tab to reveal the list of learners whose score is currently hidden from other learners. This operation is illustrated in the following screenshot:

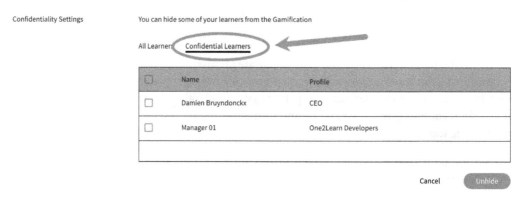

Figure 11.9 – The list of Confidential Learners for Gamification

7. Use the checkboxes to select all the confidential learners.

8. Click the **Unhide** button in the lower-right corner of the page.

You are now back to the initial situation where all learners are part of a single gamification scope.

Resetting gamification

John, a new employee, joins your company in June. This is also when he gains access to your Adobe Learning Manager account. John starts taking courses and quickly earns a few certifications. John is a competitor and enjoys the gamification features of ALM. But John started earning points in June when most of the colleagues he competes against had been on the LMS for much longer, so they had a head start in earning points, and that's not fair!

This is one of those situations where it's a good idea to reset gamification from time to time. In most organizations, gamification is reset at the beginning of each new year to prevent longer serving employees from accumulating so many points that new employees are discouraged from competing in the first place, which would defeat the very purpose of gamification.

Follow these steps to reset gamification on your ALM account:

1. From the **Settings** tab of the **Gamification** page, click the **Reset Settings** link associated with the **Reset Gamification** option.

2. Take some time to review the available options. When ready, select the **Reset Learners Scores only** option.

3. Click the **Reset** button in the lower-right corner of the screen.

4. Read the **Resetting Gamification** warning message and click the **yes** button to reset the learner scores to 0!

In this section, you learned how to reset gamification. This concludes your review of the advanced gamification settings. You now have a much better understanding of what gamification is and how it is implemented in Adobe Learning Manager.

In the next section, you will change hats and experience gamification from the learner's perspective.

Experiencing gamification from the learner's perspective

Don't forget that most of the users accessing your account are *Learners* that will never see any of the Admin screens and settings discussed so far in this chapter. In this section, you will log in to your account as a learner and focus on how learners experience badges and gamification:

1. Log in to your account as *Learner 01*.

2. Once logged in, open the **Badges** page of the learner experience.

This page lists the badges acquired or in the process of being acquired by the logged-in learner. In the following screenshot, you can see that the **Cybersecurity Fighter** and **Cybersecurity Specialist** badges are both **In Progress** for *Learner 01*. These two badges were defined and configured earlier in this chapter:

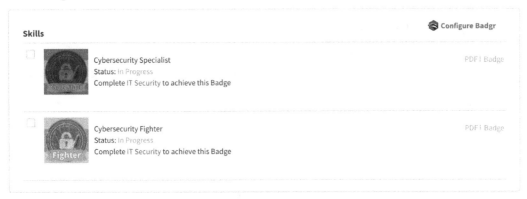

Figure 11.10 – The Cybersecurity Fighter badge currently in progress

Remember that *Learner 01* completed the **Fundamentals of IT Security** course you created in *Chapter 4, Creating Skills and Courses*. This awarded Learner 01 30 points towards the *IT Security – Level 1* skill. Learner 01 needs an additional 20 points to achieve that skill and be awarded the **Cybersecurity Fighter** badge. Displaying in-progress badges in this manner is a way to encourage learners to continue their learning and acquire more skills.

> **Configure Badgr**
> The **Configure Badgr** link, visible in the preceding screenshot, is only displayed if you have enabled Badgr integration in the **Settings | General** page of the administrator role.

Now, let's review the leaderboard page of the learner experience.

3. Browse to the **Leaderboard** page of the learner experience. Since you have reset gamification at the end of the previous section, all scores should be 0.

    Notice the list of events that allow learners to earn points visible in the right column of the page.

You will now enroll *Learner 01* in the *Mastering Photo Editing* learning path and complete all the courses of that learning path. After completing the learning path, you will return to the **Badges** and **Leaderboard** pages to check on the badge and gamification points acquired.

4. Browse to the **Catalog** page of the learner experience and use the features described in *Chapter 7, Reviewing the Learner Experience*, to search for the **Mastering Photo Editing** learning path.

5. When found, click the learning path card to open the overview page. This particular learning path includes two short courses.

    (If you did not perform the exercises of *Chapter 6, Enrolling Users in Courses*, choose any available (short) Learning Path.)

6. Click the **Enroll** button located in the upper-right corner of the page.

7. Review the content of both courses in the Fluidic Player, just like a regular learner would.

8. When you have completed all the courses of the *Mastering Photo Editing* learning path, return to the **Badges** page of the learner role.

As shown in the following screenshot, *Learner 01* should have achieved the **Photo Editing Master** badge:

Figure 11.11 – Learner 01 has achieved the Photo Editing Master badge

Notice the **PDF** and **Badge** links that Learner 01 can use to download the badges.

9.   When ready, browse to the **Leaderboard** page of the learner experience.

Once on the **Leaderboard** page, you should notice that *Learner 01* has gained a few points by completing the two courses included in the *Mastering Photo Editing* learning path and by acquiring a new skill.

10.   Hover the mouse over the number of points to see the breakdown of the score. This action is illustrated in the following screenshot:

Figure 11.12 – Hover over the number of points to display the score breakdown

By reviewing the **Badges** and **Leaderboard** pages of the learner role, you have come full circle and seen how the badges and gamification features you have configured as an Administrator influence how learners interact with Adobe Learning Manager.

Summary

With badges and gamification, you've made learning on your ALM account fun and added a touch of positive competition among learners.

First, you reviewed badges. Badges are one of the most popular game design elements used in eLearning. They are a visual representation of a learner's achievements and merits. Adobe Learning Manager comes with a handful of predefined badges, but it is very easy to add your own to the system. You can then link these badges to skills, courses, learning paths, and certifications so that learners are awarded the corresponding badge when they complete the training.

The gamification feature allows learners to get points when they interact with the content available on your ALM account. These points are visible on the **Leaderboard** page of the learner role, where learners can review their own score and see how they compare with their colleagues. The goal is to promote a learning culture within the organization by creating positive competition among learners.

But making learning fun is not the only way to increase learning engagement and efficiency. Numerous research also indicates that people learn best when they learn *together*. So, in the next chapter, you'll review the social learning features of Adobe Learning Manager. These will help you make the learner experience even more appealing.

12
Enabling and Managing Social Learning

When taking face-to-face classes with an instructor, there is the *formal* training time, during which participants attend the instructor's lecture. Then there is the *informal* learning that occurs during casual discussions, group work, while reading a book or an article recommended by someone else, or just when hanging out with your classmates. Some research even suggests that we retain more information from informal discussions and interactions than from traditional learning.

Teachers know how to take advantage of our natural desire for social interaction to facilitate learning and increase retention, as evidenced by the repeated use of pedagogical techniques such as group work, peer review, or presentations.

At first glance, one might think that distance learning complicates or even prevents these social and informal interactions. But this is without counting on the insatiable need for social contact (as well as the ingenuity) of mankind. Let's take the example of younger generations, who create private discussions on social networks to discuss their courses and share learning materials (parents and teachers are, of course, completely excluded from these groups).

Learning management systems also strive to allow learners to interact casually and informally. Many learning platforms offer features such as live chats, discussion forums, and collaboration areas designed to encourage learners to engage with each other on a variety of topics and share their content with each other.

Adobe Learning Manager (**ALM**) is no exception. It contains a fully featured social learning engine where users can share content with their peers, participate in conversations, follow other users, upvote and downvote content posted by others, and more. Organizations can leverage this power to encourage interaction among learners and foster a true corporate learning culture.

Allowing any user to upload content to the LMS raises concerns about the relevance of the uploaded content. Fortunately, ALM also comes with a built-in AI-powered content curation engine that administrators can use to ensure that the content posted on the platform is of the highest quality.

These are the main features that you will review in this chapter. To achieve these objectives, this chapter covers the following topics:

- Activating and using course discussions
- Enabling social learning
- Sharing content as a user
- Content moderation and curation
- Reviewing the social learning options of the administrator

This makes for another great chapter packed with features that will help you take the learner experience provided by your ALM account to the next level.

Technical requirements

To follow along with the exercises in this chapter, you need to meet the following requirements:

- You must have administrator access to a working ALM account (it can be a trial account)
- In addition to the administrator account mentioned previously, you must have access to at least two internal learner accounts, one external learner account, and one manager account

If you have completed the exercises in the previous chapters, you are ready to go! If you haven't, feel free to use your own material and users. Just be aware that the instructions provided in this chapter are based on the exercises from previous chapters. Therefore, you may need to adapt them to your situation.

Activating and using course discussions

When you take a face-to-face course, informal interactions naturally occur between participants (learners and instructors). Breaks and lunchtimes lend themselves particularly well to these casual encounters. More often than not, discussions that began during the class continue during these breaks, and relevant aspects of the subject matter are often discussed or expanded upon over a coffee, tea, or sandwich.

The ALM equivalent of these informal discussions is the **Course Discussions**. Each discussion relates to a specific course and is only available to learners enrolled in that course.

To take a closer look at this feature, it is necessary to log in to your account twice: once as an administrator and once as a learner. Follow these steps to do so:

1. Open a first browser window and log in to your account as an administrator.
2. Open a private browser window (or another browser altogether) and log in to the same account as *Learner 01*.
3. Make sure you keep both browser windows open throughout this entire section.

You are now ready to start exploring the course discussion feature of Adobe Learning Manager.

Activating, using, and managing course discussions for a single course

By default, course discussions are disabled across your entire account. In this section, you will override this general account setting and enable discussions for a single course.

First, you will quickly review the current learner experience by performing the following steps:

1. Use the browser window where you are logged in as *Learner 01*.

2. From the learner home page, click the **My Learning List** link or use the **My Learning** icon to access the **My Learning** page.

3. Click any of the courses available on the **My Learning** page.

As shown in the following screenshot, *Learner 01* currently has access to the **Modules** and **Notes** tabs of the course overview page:

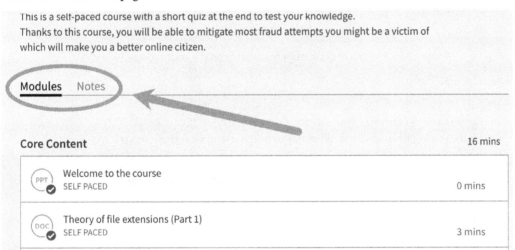

Figure 12.1 – Learner 01 has access to the Modules and Notes tabs

You will now return to the admin role and enable discussion for that course using the following steps:

4. Switch to the browser window where you are logged in as an administrator.

5. From the administrator home page, click the **Courses** link located in the **Learning** section of the left column.

6. Click the same course as the one you reviewed as a learner.

7. When on the course overview page, click the **Settings** link located in the **Configure** section of the left sidebar.

8. Select the **Enable** checkbox associated with the **Discussion Board** setting.

9. Now that the course discussion has been activated for that specific course, return to the learner experience, refresh the page, and confirm that a **Discussions** tab is now available next to the **Modules** and **Notes** tabs as shown in the following screenshot.

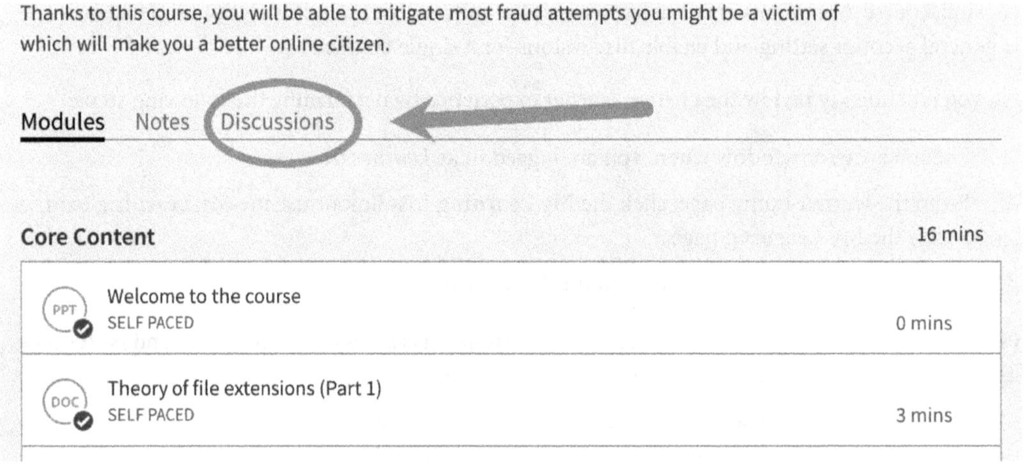

Thanks to this course, you will be able to mitigate most fraud attempts you might be a victim of which will make you a better online citizen.

Modules   Notes   Discussions   ⬅

Core Content   16 mins

PPT	Welcome to the course	
	SELF PACED	0 mins

DOC	Theory of file extensions (Part 1)	
	SELF PACED	3 mins

Figure 12.2 – The Discussions tab is now visible on the course overview page

> **Note**
> Course discussions are only available for internal learners. If you are using your own users, make sure you log in as an internal learner to follow along with this exercise.

10. Click the **Discussions** tab (identified by the arrow in the preceding screenshot) to open the newly activated discussions.

11. Type a short message in the **Say something about this Course** field and click the **Post** button.

Your message has been posted on the course's **Discussions** tab. It is now visible to the other learners enrolled in this course. Let's check this out.

12. Sign out as *Learner 01*, then sign back in as *Learner 02*.

13. If *Learner 02* is already enrolled in the course *Learner 01* added a message to, use the **My Learning** page of *Learner 02* to access that course.

    If *Learner 02* is not enrolled in the course yet, use the **Catalog** to self-enroll *Learner 02*.

14. When on the course overview page, switch to the **Discussions** tab.

As shown in the following screenshot, the message posted by *Learner 01* can be seen by *Learner 02*:

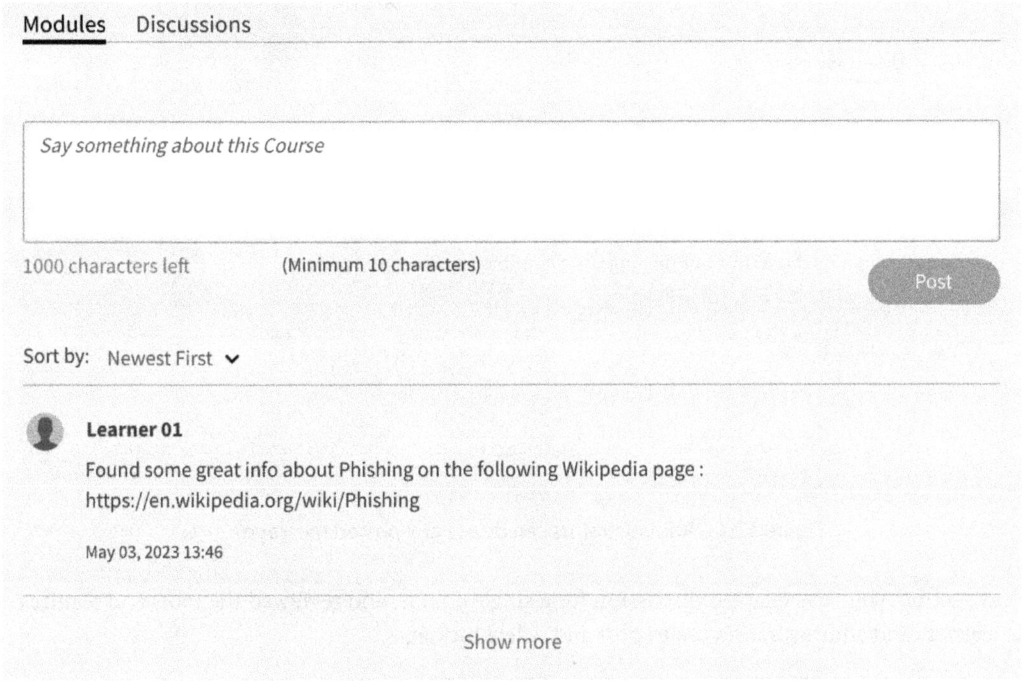

Figure 12.3 – Learner 02 sees the message posted by Learner 01

Note that a course discussions board is a very simple messaging application. It does not offer any mechanism to reply to another person's message or to like/dislike a message. That said, *Learner 02* has the opportunity to keep the conversation going by posting another message.

This raises the issue of moderating such discussion. What happens if participants start arguing? Or if the content being posted has nothing to do with the subject matter or is of poor quality? Or when older messages are no longer relevant and need to be deleted? These are a few of the circumstances where messages should be deleted from the discussion.

This task is the responsibility of the platform administrator. Let's take a closer look at this workflow using the following steps:

15. Return to the browser window where you are logged in as an administrator.

16. Use the icon located in the upper-right corner of the screen to switch to the **Learner** role.

17. When in the learner experience, go to the learning catalog and open the course in which *Learner 01* and *Learner 02* have posted messages.

18. When on the course overview page, click the **Discussions** tab.

As shown in the following screenshot, Administrators can access the **Discussions** tab of the course without being enrolled. They can also delete any of the messages:

Figure 12.4 – Administrators can delete any posted message

In this section, you have enabled discussion for a single course, and reviewed the tools and features that learners and administrators use to post and delete messages.

> **Tip**
>
> Remember that instructors are, first and foremost, ordinary learners. Therefore, instructors can browse the catalog as learners and self-enroll on their courses to participate in these discussions with learners. Also, some administrators like to enroll on the courses they moderate as it helps them keep a better eye on the course discussions.

In the next section, you will modify the general account settings and enable discussion by default on your ALM account.

Enabling Course Discussions by default

Course discussions are disabled by default at the account level. In the previous section, you learned how to override this setting to enable discussions for a particular course. In this section, you will return to the administrator role and enable course discussions by default at the account level using the following steps:

1. Make sure you are logged in as an administrator.

2. From the administrator home page, click the **Settings** link located in the **Configure** section of the left sidebar. This action opens the **Basic Info** page.

3. When on the **Basic Info** page, click the **General** link located in the **Basics** section of the left sidebar. This action opens the **General** page of the settings.

4. Locate the **Discussion Board** option, which is disabled by default.

5. Select the **Enable** checkbox associated with the **Discussion Board** option, as illustrated in the following screenshot:

Discussion Board   ☑ Enable

Enable to allow learners to see the Discussion Board. As Admin, you have the ability to delete any comments. Know more.

Figure 12.5 – Enabling course discussion by default at the account level

This action enables discussions by default for all the courses available in your account. However, if discussions are disabled at the course level, the course setting takes precedence. In other words, courses that are already available in your account retain their current setting, while future courses will have their **Discussion Board** enabled by default.

This concludes your exploration of course discussions in Adobe Learning Manager. This feature attempts to mimic the informal conversations that occur naturally alongside any face-to-face training. It is very simple to implement and use, but its capabilities are limited. Let's quickly recap what has been discussed in this section:

- Course discussions are disabled by default at the account level, but administrators can override this general account setting and enable discussions on a course-to-course basis.

- When course discussion is enabled for a course, any enrolled learner can post messages. However, there is no built-in mechanism to answer someone else's post or to like/dislike a message.

- Users can delete their own messages, but not those messages posted by other users. Administrators can delete any message, even if they are not enrolled in the course.

- When you enable the **Discussion Board** option at the account level, all *future* courses will have their discussion boards enabled by default. Existing courses keep their current settings.

In the next section, you will review the **Social Learning** engine of Adobe Learning Manager.

Working with Social Learning

In addition to the course discussions discussed in the previous section, Adobe Learning Manager also contains a full-fledged social learning engine. When activated, it provides an experience that bears many similarities to the most popular social networks:

- Learners can follow each other so they get notifications when someone they follow publishes something.

- Social learning posts are published on **boards**. The concept of *boards* is very similar to the concept of *walls* or *stories*, which are used by most mainstream social networks.

- Users can upvote (like) or downvote (dislike) any content posted.

- In addition to text-based posts, users can also publish multimedia content (such as audio files, videos, and images), files of different types, and URLs.

One of the main differences between the course discussion covered in the previous section and the social learning boards discussed here is that the latter is *skill-related* rather than *course-related*. This means that anyone interested in a skill is welcome to join a discussion board related to that particular skill, regardless of which courses that learner is enrolled in.

> **Skills**
>
> Skills were discussed in *Chapter 4, Creating Skills and Courses*. Please refer to that chapter for more information about creating and managing skills in Adobe Learning Manager.

Enabling and Disabling Social Learning

By default, social learning is enabled for all learners on your ALM account. But, as with any social network, social learning involves direct interactions between individual learners. This means that learners have access to each other's profiles, which raises privacy concerns for many organizations. This is especially true if your organization uses Adobe Learning Manager to deliver training mostly to external users.

In addition, some organizations have rules about using social media during business hours. Some ALM customers choose to not use social learning because it might send a conflicting message to their staff.

These are some of the many reasons why organizations may want to completely or partially disable social learning on their ALM account.

> **Internal and external users**
>
> Internal and external users were discussed in *Chapter 5, Managing Users*. In a nutshell, internal users are employees of your organization, while external users are employees of other organizations (such as customers, suppliers, partners, and franchisees).

In this section, you will first examine the learner experience when the default settings are applied (i.e., when social learning is enabled for everyone). Next, you will disable social learning for external users and examine how this affects their learner experience.

Use the following steps to review the default learner experience:

1.   Log in to your account as *Learner 01*.

2.   Click the hamburger icon located in the upper-left corner of the screen to reveal the pages currently available to learners.

3.   Confirm that a **Social Learning** button is present in the left sidebar:

Figure 12.6 – The Social Learning button is visible in the left sidebar of the Learner experience

4.   Also confirm that the **Social Feed** widget is visible on the learner home page.

By default, every learner has access to these features.

You will now log in to your account as an administrator and disable social learning for external users.

5.   Log in to your account as an administrator.

6.   From the administrator home page, click the **Social Learning** link located in the **Manage** section of the left sidebar.

7.   At the top of the page, switch to the **Settings** tab.

As shown in the following screenshot, the first option available on this page allows you to completely disable Social Learning on your account:

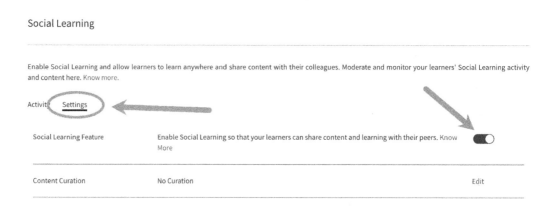

Figure 12.7 – The Settings tab of the Social Learning page

8.   Further down the page, click the **Edit** link associated with the **Scope Settings** option.

9.   Deselect the **Enable for External learners** checkbox.

10. Click the **Save** button when done.

11. Read the **Confirmation Required** message and click the **Proceed** button.

You will now log in to your account as an external learner and confirm that this learner no longer has access to social learning.

12. Log in to your account as *Learner 03* (or any other available *external* learner).

> **Logging in as Learner 03**
>
> *Learner 03* is an external learner that was defined in *Chapter 5, Managing Users*. Remember that external learners use a dedicated URL to log in to your account. If you don't remember this URL, return to the **External Users** page of the admin role, hover over the external registration profile, and click the link icon to copy the URL to your clipboard.

13. Once logged in as *Learner 03*, confirm that the **Social Learning** button is *not* visible in the left sidebar of the Learner experience.

14. Also confirm that the **Social Feed** widget is *not* available on *Learner 03*'s home page.

In this section, you have enabled social learning on your ALM account, but for internal users only. These users see the **Social Learning** button in the left sidebar of the learner experience, as well as the **Social Feed** widget on the learner home page.

In the next section, you will log back in as *Learner 01* and experiment with **Social Learning** as a learner.

Creating and following discussion boards

Just like any social network, social learning in Adobe Learning Manager is all about discussing with others and sharing content. In ALM, content posted by users is organized into **discussion boards**. These **boards** are similar to the *walls* or *stories* found in mainstream social networks.

What makes boards particularly interesting is that they are connected to skills. As discussed in *Chapter 4, Creating Skills and Courses*, a single skill can be used in many different courses. So you can have different learners enrolled in (or interested in) many different courses and at different proficiency levels all on the same board. In fact, any learner interested in a given skill is welcome to join a board dedicated to that skill, even if they are not yet enrolled in a course related to that skill.

To experiment with these features, you will log in to your account twice: once as *Learner 01* and once as *Learner 02*. These are both internal learners, so they both have access to social learning. Use the following steps:

1. Open a browser window and log in to your account as *Learner 01*.

2. Open a *private* browser window (or another browser altogether) and log in to the same account as *Learner 02*.

3. Make sure you keep both browser windows open for this entire section.

Now that everything is in place, you can create your first discussion board and post your first message.

Creating a new board

Since you have just activated social learning, there shouldn't be any board available to host your first post, so you have to create a board in addition to posting a message. Use the following steps to do so:

1. Use the browser window where you are logged in as *Learner 01*.

2. From the learner home page, click the **Social Learning** icon of the left sidebar to open the **Social Learning** page.

3. Click the **New Post** button to start sharing something.

4. Type a small message in the **Write or paste something here...** field.

When done, notice that the **Post** button is still disabled. That's because you need to choose the discussion board you want to post your message on. But wait! There is no discussion board available yet. So, let's create one right now.

5. Click the **Create a New Board** link located just below the **Type here to search a board** field. This action opens the **New Board** dialog.

6. Type IT Security in the organization in the **Board Name** field.

7. As a best practice, also supply a short description in the **Description** field.

8.   Use the **Board Skills** field to search for the **IT Security** skill you created in *Chapter 4, Creating Skills and Courses*.

Note that you can link a single discussion board to several skills.

9.   By default, the user that creates a board (*Learner 01*, in this example) is automatically defined as the board moderator. If needed, use the **Moderators** field to add additional moderators. In this example, though, leave it empty for now.

10. Take some time to review the three **Visibility** options available at the bottom of the **New Board** dialog. In this example, you will create a **Public** board.

11. Make sure the **New Board** dialog looks as follows. Then, click the **Create** button:

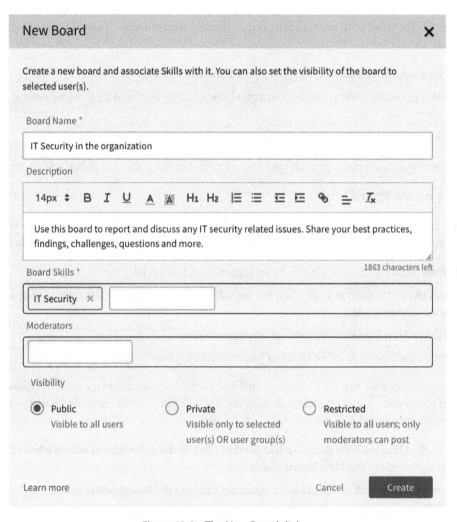

Figure 12.8 – The New Board dialog

12. Creating a new board earns you five points! Click the **Awesome** button to acknowledge this message.

13. Now that the board is available, you can click the **Post** button to publish your first message on the newly created discussion board.

14. Posting a message earns you five additional points! Click the **Awesome** button to acknowledge this message.

15. Confirm that your post appears on the **IT Security in the organization** discussion board, as shown in the following screenshot:

Figure 12.9 – Your first post has been correctly published on the new discussion board

Social learning points and gamification points

The points earned by creating boards and posting messages are different from the gamification points discussed in the previous chapter. The points discussed in this section are specific to social learning. They are used to define the **subject matter experts** (**SMEs**) for the various discussion boards. This will be discussed in more detail in the *Content moderation and curation* section later in this chapter.

In this section, you created a new discussion board and posted your first message. Before going any further, let's take a moment to reflect on what just happened, keeping in mind that you are currently using the default social learning options:

- A post cannot exist outside of a discussion board. If no discussion board is available, you are required to create one when posting your first message.

- By default, every learner is allowed to create a new discussion board. In the *Reviewing the social learning options of the administrator* section later in this chapter, you will learn how to limit the users allowed to create new discussion boards.

- In this example, you created a new *public* board. Public boards are visible to all users, and everyone can participate in the discussion. You can also create *private* boards. These are only visible to selected users. Finally, you can create *restricted* boards, which are visible to all users, but only moderators can post messages. This option is very useful when you want to allow only selected instructors or subject matter experts to post on the discussion board.

These are the basic options used to create boards and post messages. Now, let's see how other users can follow the board and participate in the conversation.

Finding and following boards

A board is only useful when several learners follow it and participate in the discussion. In this section, you will see how *Learner 02* can access the newly created board and add to the discussion.

In Adobe Learning Manager, there are several ways for a learner to join a discussion board:

- First, the user who creates a board automatically follows it
- Second, users automatically follow any board they add comments to
- Finally, users can also decide to explicitly follow a board without posting a message

Let's do some hands-on experimentation with these features using the following steps:

1. Switch to the browser window where you are logged in as *Learner 02*.
2. Use the icons on the left sidebar to open the **Social Learning** page.

By default, the **Social Learning** page opens on the **My Boards** tab visible in the left column of the page. Since *Learner 02* has not participated in any discussions or created any new board, the **My Boards** tab of the **Social Learning** page of *Learner 02* is currently empty.

3. Click the **All Boards** tab located in the left column of the page. You can also use the the **Explore All Boards** link located in the middle of the **Social Learning** page.

In this example the list is quite short as you only have one board defined on your account. Of course, this number is bound to increase as more learners create additional boards and participate in multiple discussions. So, let's take a look at the tools available to search for boards and filter the list.

4. In the upper-left corner of the list, open the **Sort by** dropdown. By default, the list is sorted by **Date**, but you can also sort it by **Relevance**.

5. In the upper-right corner of the list, notice two icons that allow you to toggle between **Post View** and **Board View**. By default, you are in **Post View**, as shown in the following screenshot:

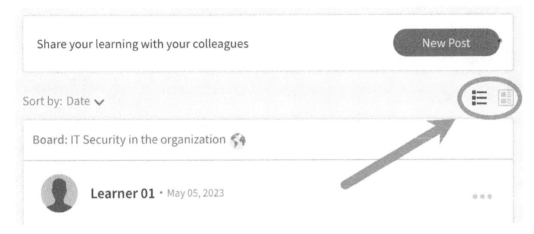

Figure 12.10 – By default, you are in Post View

6. Switch to **Board View** using the icon highlighted in the previous screenshot.

When you're in **Board View**, two additional dropdowns are available atop the list. They allow you to filter the list of boards by **Skills** and **Activity**:

• Remember that a discussion board is directly related to one or more skills. This makes the **Skills** filter very useful as it allows you to see only the boards related to the selected skill(s).

• The **Activity** filter refers to how active the board is. You want to follow the most active boards.

Also, notice the main search field, which is visible in the upper-right corner of the page, next to the user and notification icons. This field also allows you to search for discussion boards using keywords.

Now that you know how to search for discussion boards, you will have *Learner 02* follow the **IT Security in the organization** board created by *Learner 01* in the previous section.

7. While in **Board View**, click the circle icon with the three little dots associated with the **IT Security in the organization** board.

8. In the menu that opens, click the **Follow Board** option. This is how learners can follow a board without posting a message.

These last actions are illustrated in the following screenshot:

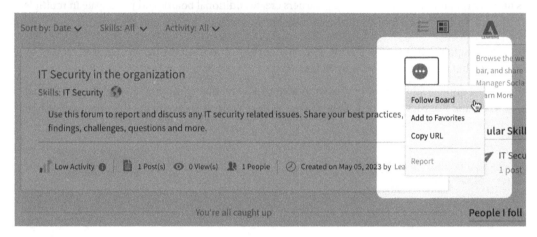

Figure 12.11 – How to explicitly follow a board

9. Return to the **My Boards** tab by clicking the corresponding button in the left column.

    Confirm that the **IT Security in the organization** board is now visible in the **My Boards** tab of *Learner 02*.

From here, *Learner 02* can post additional content, respond to existing messages, upvote (like) or downvote (dislike) any post, and more.

10. Click the **Go to Board** link to open the **IT Security in the organization** board.

11. Click the circle icon with the three dots located in the upper-right corner of the **IT Security in the organization** heading.

12. Choose **Add to favorites** from the menu that opens.

13. Finally, click the **My Boards** tab located in the **Boards** section of the left column to return to the default **Social Learning** page of *Learner 02*.

In the **Favorites** section of the left column, notice a direct link to the **IT Security in the organization** board, as shown in the following screenshot:

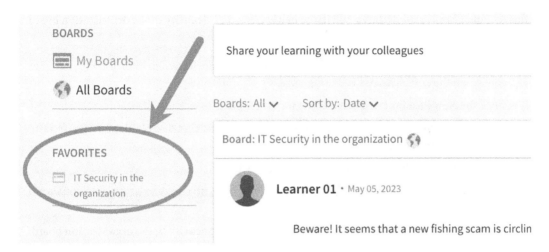

Figure 12.12 – The Favorites section of the Social Learning page

In this section, you discovered how learners can use the tools available on the **Social Learning** page to search for discussion boards, follow discussion boards, and add discussion boards to their favorites.

You now have one discussion board available and two learners following that board. In the next section, you will concentrate on the various types of content that can be shared on these discussion boards.

Sharing content on Discussion Boards

Now that you have a discussion board available, learners want to use it to share different types of content with their peers. In the previous section, you added some simple text messages to the discussion board and saw how learners can respond to these messages and how they can upvote (like) or downvote (dislike) them.

In this section, you will post different types of content to the newly created discussion board. This includes sharing web pages, documents, images, videos, and so on. Let's start by creating polls and questions.

Creating Polls and Questions

In addition to the simple text-based posts discussed in the previous section, learners can also generate simple polls and questions. These are a great way to increase learner engagement with the social learning feature. It is also a great way for instructors to extend their class discussions or prepare their audience for the next class.

In this section, *Learner 02* will start a poll in the newly created **IT Security in the organization** board using the following steps:

1. Make sure you are using the browser window where you are logged in as *Learner 02*, and that you are on the default **Social Learning** page.

2. Click the **New Post** button located at the top of the page.

3. Type Which security threat are you most afraid of? in the **Write or paste something here...** field.

4. Click the **Add Poll** button located below the text field.

5. Enter the following four options for the poll responses: Phishing, Viruses, Ransomware, and Other.

6. Use the **Type here to search a board** field to select the **IT Security in the organization** board.

7. Click the **Post** button when done. This action publishes the new poll on the **IT Security in the organization** board.

8. Still logged in as *Learner 02*, provide your response to the poll. Don't forget to click the **Submit Choice** link when done.

9. Return to the browser window where you are logged in as *Learner 01* and browse to (or refresh, if already open) the **Social Learning** page.

10. Confirm that the poll created by *Learner 02* is visible on the **Social Learning** page of *Learner 01*.

11. Answer the poll as *Learner 01*.

After *Learner 01* has entered their choice, the results of the poll are immediately visible, as shown in the following screenshot:

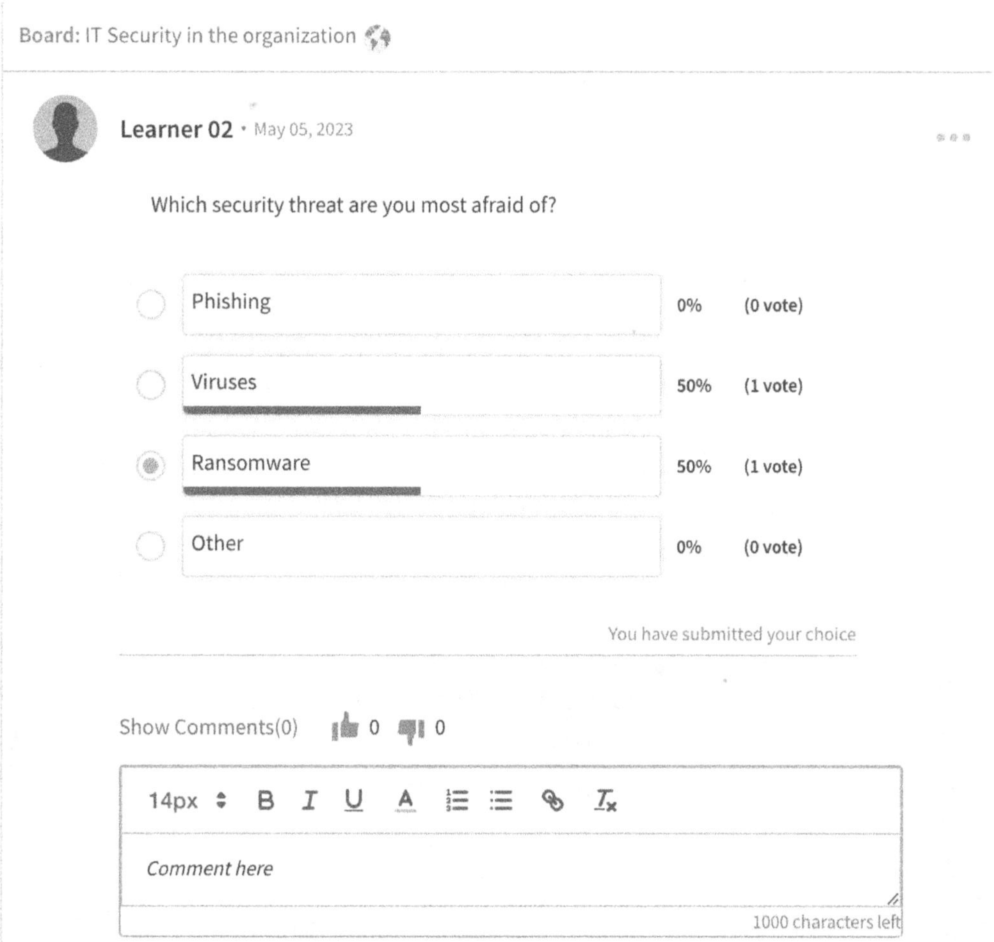

Board: IT Security in the organization 🌐

Learner 02 · May 05, 2023   ● ● ●

Which security threat are you most afraid of?

○ Phishing   0%   (0 vote)

○ Viruses   50%   (1 vote)

◉ Ransomware   50%   (1 vote)

○ Other   0%   (0 vote)

You have submitted your choice

Show Comments(0)   👍 0 👎 0

| 14px ⬍ | **B** | *I* | <u>U</u> | A | ⯇ | ⯇ | 🔗 | T𝗑 |

Comment here

1000 characters left

Figure 12.13 – The result of the poll is visible to all learners that have submitted an answer

You can use the same technique to create questions. In such a case, you would use the **Mark Question** button instead of the **Add Poll** button. This allows you to mark one of the comments as the right answer to the question.

Creating polls is a simple way to engage learners in an ongoing conversation, while creating questions and marking the correct answer help learners quickly identify relevant information in the discussion thread.

In the next section, you will explore a unique way of sharing web pages on Adobe Learning Manager's discussion boards.

Sharing Web pages

While browsing the internet, a learner comes across the Wikipedia page on computer security. It is so insightful that they want to share the link with the other learners following the **IT Security in the organization** board.

This is such a common situation that Adobe Learning Manager provides a unique mechanism for users to quickly post any URL to any available discussion board.

In this section, you will put this mechanism in place and use it to post a web page on the **IT Security in the organization** board. Perform the following steps to do so:

1. Make sure you are still on the default **Social Learning** page of *Learner 01*.

2. Also, make sure that the bookmark bar of your browser is currently visible.

3. On the right-hand side of the **Social Learning** page, locate the **Share to Social** widget at the top of the right column.

4. Click and drag the **Adobe Learning Manager** icon to the bookmark bar of your browser. After this process, you have one additional bookmark available in your bookmark bar, as shown in the following screenshot:

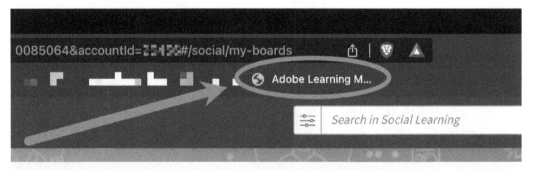

Figure 12.14 – The Adobe Learning Manager bookmark is visible in the bookmark bar

5. Now that the URL sharing mechanism is in place, browse the Wikipedia page on computer security at `https://en.wikipedia.org/wiki/Computer_security`.

6. Once the page opens, click the new **Adobe Learning Manager** bookmark.

   If necessary, follow the on-screen instructions to log in as *Learner 01*.

7. Fill in the form that appears in the right pane and click the **Post** button. This action is shown in the following screenshot:

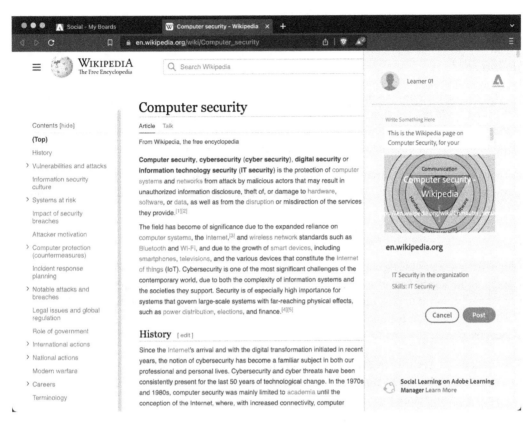

Figure 12.15 – A pane appears on the right-hand side of the browser window

Sharing web pages this way awards *Learner 01* five additional points!

8. Click the **Go to post** button to return to the **Social Learning** page of *Learner 01* and see the URL that has just been posted.

The widget you incuded in the bookmark bar of your browser is called a **bookmarklet**. It makes the process of sharing web pages so simple that learners have no excuse not to start sharing!

Tip

This bookmarklet requires that you allow popups in your browser. Also, be aware that some browsers (such as Firefox and Brave) block most of these bookmarklets by default. You may have to adjust the security settings of your browser to allow the bookmarklet to work. More information can be found in the official ALM user guide at `https://helpx.adobe.com/in/learning-manager/learners/feature-summary/share-to-social.html`.

Sharing web pages on discussion boards is a very common use case. Sharing files is another very common situation, which you will examine in the next section.

Sharing files

After completing the **Fundamentals of IT Security** course, *Learner 01* has put together a document summarizing the *10 best practices for increasing IT security within the organization. Learner 01* has already shared this document with their direct team and has received tremendous feedback! This encourages *Learner 01* to share the document with a wider audience using one of the available discussion boards.

This is just one of the many circumstances in which users may want to upload a document to one of the available discussion boards. In this section, you will review how that can be done by performing the following steps:

1. Make sure you are still on the default **Social Learning** page of *Learner 01.*

As discussed in the previous sections, you can start a new post by clicking the **New Post** button available at the top of the **Social Learning** page. When using that technique, you must choose the discussion board where you want to post the new message in addition to writing the post itself. In this section, you will explore another technique by first going to the chosen discussion board and then starting a new post from there.

2. Click the **IT Security in the organization** link located at the top of the list of recent posts. You can also use the **Go to Board** link located further down the page. This opens the **IT Security in the organization** board page.

3. Click the **New Post** button located at the top of the page, below the header.

4. Click the **Upload file** icon located right above the **Write or paste something here…** field. This operation is illustrated in the following screenshot:

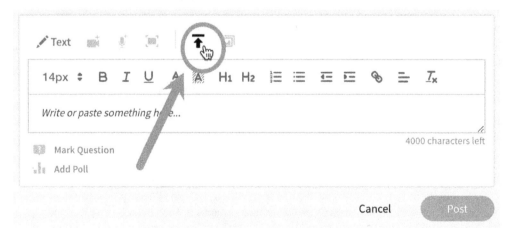

Figure 12.16 – Clicking the Upload File icon

5. Type a small message in the **Write or paste something here…** field to accompany your file submission.

6. Use the upload area just below the text field to upload the `socialLearning/10Best PracticesITSecurity.pdf` file of the download associated with this book.

7. Click the **Post** button when ready.

After some time, your submitted document is visible on the discussion board. Other learners can now comment on your file submission, upvote (like) or downvote (dislike) it, and even download a copy of the submitted file.

In this example, you uploaded a PDF document, but Adobe Learning Manager supports a wide range of video, audio, document, and image files. Refer to the official ALM documentation for an up-to-date list of supported content types and formats: `https://helpx.adobe.com/ learning-manager/learners/feature-summary/social-learning-web-user. html#Supportedcontentformats`.

The ability to share such a wide variety of files with other learners is a very powerful and engaging way of sharing knowledge. For example, instructors can use it to entice learners into social learning by posting training slides, course handouts, and more.

Sharing with the Adobe Learning Manager Desktop App

Adobe Learning Manager has gone the extra mile by removing as many obstacles as possible between a mere interest in sharing something and the action of actually doing it! In addition to sharing text-based content, web pages, and files, you can use the Adobe Learning Manager desktop application to create multimedia content to be shared on the discussion boards.

> **Desktop application availability**
>
> At the time of writing, the Adobe Learning Manager desktop application still uses the old *Captivate Prime* branding. It is available for both Windows and Mac More info on the Adobe Learning Manager desktop app and its system requirements is available at `https://helpx.adobe. com/learning-manager/learners/adobe-captivate-prime-app-for- desktop/adobe-captivate-prime-desktop-app-system-requirements. html`.

The Adobe Learning Manager desktop application allows you to create the following three types of content:

*   You can record simple videos from your computer screen and/or webcam. This allows you to use video to give feedback, expose a problem, share a process, or even create a quick tutorial.

*   Recording a quick audio message is sometimes faster and more effective than a written description. That's why the desktop application also lets you quickly create and share voice recordings.

- Finally, the desktop application allows you to create and annotate screenshots that you can then share on all available discussion boards.

Installing the application on your computer also allows you to get notifications from Adobe Learning Manager even if you are not browsing the account, and even if you are not logged in.

The following screenshot shows the welcome screen of the Adobe Learning Manager desktop application with all the available options.

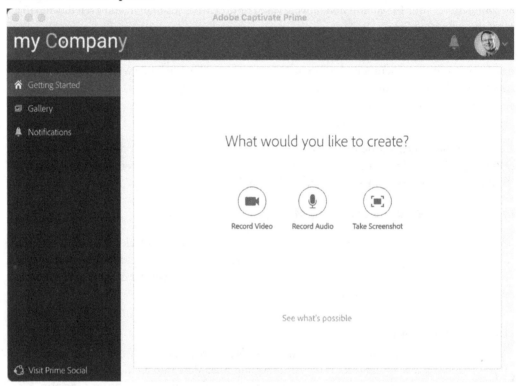

Figure 12.17 – The Adobe Captivate Prime desktop application welcome screen

An in-depth discussion of all the features of the Adobe Learning Manager desktop application is beyond the scope of this book. You can find more information on the following page of the official ALM user guide: https://helpx.adobe.com/learning-manager/learners/adobe-captivate-prime-app-for-desktop.html.

Thanks to the features described in the last sections, learners are now able to share a lot of content of different types on the discussion boards of Adobe Learning Manager. This raises the question of how to moderate and curate this content. This is precisely what is discussed in the next section.

Content moderation and curation

Allowing users to post content online and participate in discussions certainly has a lot of potential. But it also opens the doors to all sorts of arguments, disputes, and even verbal assaults from learners, not to mention the varying quality of the content being shared. This problem is not specific to Adobe Learning Manager. Just take a quick look at most social networks and you'll see these problems occur whenever people engage in discussions.

Thankfully, Adobe Learning Manager includes powerful content moderation and curation features:

- **Content moderation** refers to the ability to edit and/or delete any content that is deemed inappropriate. This can be done directly by moderators, or after a learner has reported a post as inappropriate.

- **Content curation** is the process of checking the quality and relevance of the content being shared by learners. For example, when someone posts information that is outdated, irrelevant, or even false, it must be removed (or at least flagged as such), even if the person who posted it did so in a perfectly honest and polite manner.

This is what you will review in this section. First, let's discuss how one can become a discussion board moderator.

Designating board moderators

In the *Creating and following discussion boards* section, earlier in this chapter, *Learner 01* created the **IT Security in the organization** discussion board. This makes *Learner 01* the owner of this specific discussion board. As the owner, *Learner 01* can delete every post available on the discussion board, even if they are not the author of the post. Let's review this ability hands-on by performing the following steps:

1. Log in to your account as *Learner 01*.

2. Go to the **Social Learning** page, and then to the **IT Security in the organization** board.

3. Find a post created by *Learner 02* and click the three dots located in the upper-right corner of that post.

As shown in the following screenshot, *Learner 01* can delete this post, even though it was created by *Learner 02*:

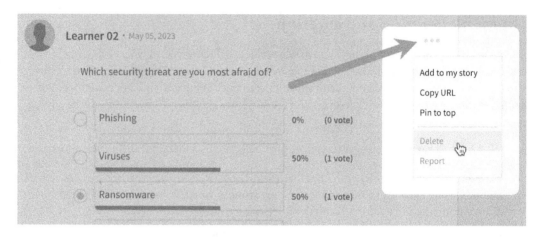

Figure 12.18 – Learner 01 can delete the posts created by Learner 02

Indeed, *Learner 01* is the owner of this discussion board, which automatically makes that learner a board moderator.

4. Use another browser or a private window of the same browser to log in to your account as *Learner 02*.

5. While logged in, go to the **Social Learning** page, and then to the **IT Security in the organization** board.

6. Find one of the posts created by *Learner 01* and click the three dots icon located in the upper-right corner of that post. Notice that the **Delete** option is *not* available to *Learner 02*.

7. Now, find one of the posts created by *Learner 02* and click the three dots icon associated with that post. Notice that *Learner 02* can delete their own posts.

Through these little experiments, you've learned that every learner has the right to delete their own posts. You also learned that the owner of the board is also a board moderator. As such, that learner has the right to delete any content posted on the board.

Now, let's return to the browser window where you are logged in as *Learner 01* to modify the board settings and add additional moderators.

8. Return to the browser window where you are logged in as *Learner 01*.

9. Make sure you are still on the **IT Security in the organization** board page.

10. Scroll back to the very top of the page and click the circle icon with the three little dots located in the upper-right corner of the board's header.

11. In the menu that opens, click the **Edit** button to open the **Board Settings** form.

From here, you can modify many options, including **Board Name**, **Description**, **Board Skills**, and **Visibility**:

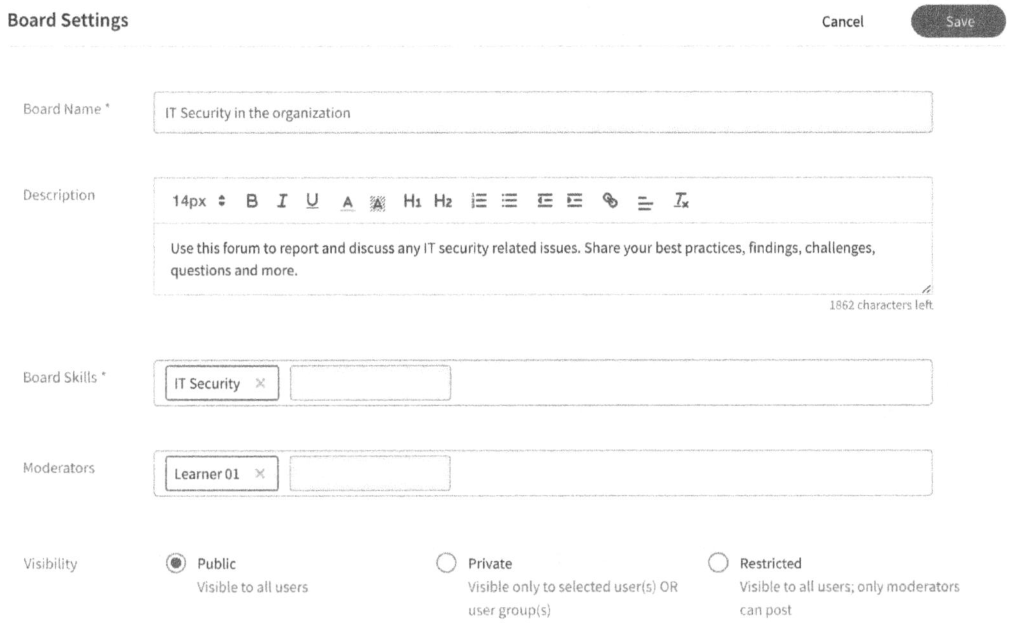

Board Settings   Cancel   Save

Board Name *   IT Security in the organization

Description   14px ⇕ **B** *I* U̲ A 🖍 H₁ H₂ ⋮≡ ≡ ⧉ ⧉ 🔗 ≡ Tₓ

                    Use this forum to report and discuss any IT security related issues. Share your best practices, findings, challenges,
                    questions and more.

                                                                                      1862 characters left

Board Skills *   IT Security ×

Moderators   Learner 01 ×

Visibility   ◉ Public   ○ Private   ○ Restricted
                      Visible to all users   Visible only to selected user(s) OR   Visible to all users; only moderators
                                                  user group(s)   can post

Figure 12.19 – The Board Settings form

12. Add *Learner 02* to the list of **Moderators**. Then, click the **Save** button in the upper-right corner of the form.

13. Return to the browser window where you are logged in as *Learner 02* and refresh the **IT Security in the organization** board page.

14. Find something posted by *Learner 01* and click the three dots icon. Confirm that the **Delete** option is now available to *Learner 02*.

Now that *Learner 02* has been designated as a moderator, they have the same permissions as *Learner 01*, including the ability to edit the board settings and remove *Learner 01* from the list of board **Moderators**.

It is also important to know that the administrators have the same abilities as the board owner: they can delete any post and they can edit (and even delete) the board itself. This is very important when, for example, the owner of a board leaves the organization. In such a case, any administrator can take over the board's moderation, designate new moderators, or even completely delete the board.

In this section, you have learned how to edit an existing board. This includes changing the list of board moderators. You also learned that moderators can delete any post in the board they moderate. But that's not all moderators can do. In the next section, you will examine one of the other responsibilities of board moderators.

Reporting inappropriate posts

In Adobe Learning Manager, any learner has the ability to report a message that seems inappropriate. In such a case, a board moderator must review the report and decide on a course of action.

That's what you're going to look at in this section. First, you will log in to your account as *Manager 01* and report a post. To do this, follow these steps:

1. Use another browser or another private window of the same browser to log in to your account as *Manager 01*.

2. Go to the **Social Learning** page of *Manager 01* and switch to the **All Boards** tab.

3. Click the three dots icon associated with any of the content published on the **IT Security in the organization** board.

4. In the menu that opens, click the red **report** link. Take some time to read the **Confirmation Required** message and click the **Report** button.

This illustrates how a user can report a post. Notice that *Manager 01* did not have to follow the board or participate in the discussion to report a post.

Now, let's return to the browser window where you are logged in as a board moderator (this can be either *Learner 01* or *Learner 02*) and see how to follow up on such a report.

5. Return to a browser window where you are logged in as a board moderator (*Learner 01* or *Learner 02*).

6. Click the notification icon located in the upper-right corner of the screen. There should be a notification telling you that **Manager 01 has reported abuse on a Post**.

7. Click the **Post** link in the notification to open the reported post in a dedicated dialog box.

From here, you can review the post and decide what to do. Because you are a board moderator, you can decide to delete the post or leave it alone.

In this section, you learned how learners can report messages they feel are inappropriate and how moderators can follow up on these reports.

This concludes your overview of discussion board moderation. By default, the owner of a board is also the primary moderator, but they can designate additional moderators, not to mention that any administrator also has moderation rights on all the discussion boards available on the account.

Moderating a board is about keeping the discussion courteous, but it does not guarantee the accuracy or worthiness of the content being shared. That's what content curation is for, and that's what you'll examine in the next section.

Activating Content curation

In the previous section, you discussed content moderation. Moderators do not have to be subject matter experts; their only responsibility is to make sure that the discussion remains courteous.

Content curation, on the other hand, is meant to ensure the quality of the content posted on discussion boards. As such, content curation requires the analysis of posted content for accuracy, relevance, and timeliness. Therefore, content curation is the responsibility of individuals considered experts in the subject matter.

Remember that learners receive points each time they participate in a social learning activity. These points are used to identify **Subject Matter Experts** (**SMEs**) for the various boards. These SMEs are in charge of manual content curation in the discussion board(s) for the topics they are experts on.

These are the features that you will explore in this section. But before you start your exploration, it is necessary to activate content curation, which is disabled by default on any new account.

You will now return to the administrator role and enable content curation on your account using the following steps:

1. Log in to your account as an administrator.
2. From the administrator home page, click the **Social Learning** link located in the **Manage** section of the left sidebar and switch to the **Settings** tab.
3. Click the **Edit** link associated with the **Content Curation** option.

As shown in the following screenshot, **No Curation** is the default value:

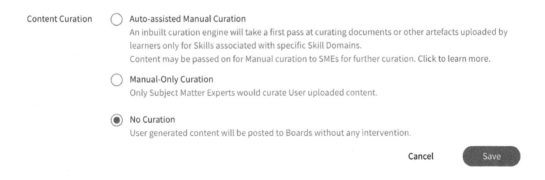

Figure 12.20 – By default, the No Curation option is enabled

Take some time to read the descriptions associated with each available option:

*   When **Manual-Only Curation** is enabled, only the designated SMEs can curate the content uploaded by learners to the discussion boards.

- When **Auto-assisted Manual Curation** is enabled, the built-in AI-powered curation engine tries to automatically check the quality of the uploaded content. If it fails, the content is then passed on to designated SMEs for manual curation.

Note that when **Auto-assisted Manual Curation** is enabled, you must map the skills defined on your account to specific **skill domains** known to the AI-powered curation engine. This is what you will do in the next section, but first, let's enable content curation:

4. Select the **Auto-assisted Manual Curation** option.

5. Click the **Save** button to confirm.

Auto-assisted Manual Curation is now enabled on your account.

In the next section, you will provide the AI-powered curation engine with a mapping between the custom skills defined on your account and the skill domains known to the artificial intelligence.

Mapping Skills to Skill Domains

Although a very powerful technology, artificial intelligence still needs some input from actual humans to perform effectively.

When it comes to the built-in curation engine of Adobe Learning Manager, the engineering team at Adobe has defined a set of **Skill Domains** and has trained the artificial intelligence in those skill domains. So, by default, the AI only knows about these predefined skill domains and has no idea what the custom skills you defined on your account are all about.

This is the reason why you must map the skills available on your account to one or more of these predefined skill domains. This is what you will do in this section by performing the following steps:

1. Make sure you are logged in to your account as an administrator.

2. From the administrator home page, click the **Skills** link located in the **Manage** section of the left column.

Back in *Chapter 4, Creating Skills and Courses,* you created the **IT Security** skill, which you will now map to one or more of the predefined skill domains known to the artificial intellignece baked into Adobe Learning Manager.

3. Click the **IT Security** skill you created in *Chapter 4, Creating Skills and Courses*, to open the **Edit Skill** dialog. (If you did not perform the exercises of *Chapter 4*, choose any skill available.).

4. In the middle of the dialog, spot the **Skill Domain** option and click the associated **Know More** link.

This action opens a page in the official ALM user guide containing the current list of skill domains known to Adobe Learning Manager. Browse the list and take note of the skill domains that apply to the skill you clicked on. In this example, you will link your custom **IT Security** skill to the **Computer security** and **Information technology** skill domains.

5. Return to the browser window/tab where the **Edit Skill** dialog is visible.

6. Use the **Skill Domain** field to link your custom **IT Security** skill to the **Computer Security** and the **Information technology** skill domains.

7. When the **Edit Skill** dialog looks as follows, click the **Save** button:

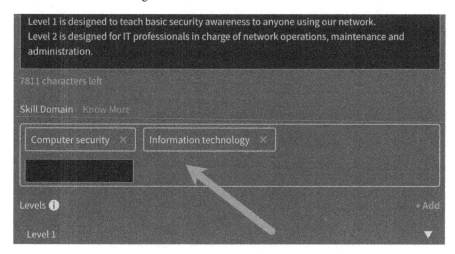

Figure 12.21 – Mapping skills to skill domains

Thanks to this process, you informed the artificial intelligence powering the built-in curation engine that your custom **IT Security** skill relates to the **Computer security** and **Information technology** skill domains the AI knows about.

The built-in curation engine is now ready to analyze the content uploaded by learners on the discussion boards related to the **IT Security** skill. But even the most sophisticated artificial intelligence technology is not foolproof. If automatic curation fails, remember that manual curation by an SME made of flesh and blood is required.

Therefore, before you give content curation a try, you still need to review how one becomes an SME and how administrators can manage the list of SMEs for each of the available skills.

> **Adobe Sensei**
>
> Adobe Sensei is the name of Adobe's artificial intelligence technology. It powers all of the AI-powered features included in any Adobe products, including the curation engine of Adobe Learning Manager. More on Adobe Sensei and the other AI-powered features of ALM will be provided in *Chapter 13, AI-Powered Recommendations for Learners*.

Managing SMEs

Content curation heavily relies on **Subject Matter Experts** (**SMEs**) reviewing content shared by learners. In this section, you'll learn how one becomes a SME and how administrators can manually refine the list of SMEs for each of the available skills.

Remember that when learners participate in social learning activities (such as creating new boards and posting content), they earn points. They also receive points when their content (or comments) are upvoted (liked), when their answer to a question is marked as the correct answer, and so on.

By default, the three users that have accumulated the most points in a given skill are considered SMEs for that skill. Note that each skill has its own list of SMEs and that a single user can serve as SME for multiple skills.

In addition to these defaults, administrators can also manually designate SMEs by awarding extra SME points to selected learners. Let's review this feature hands-on by performing the following steps:

1. Make sure you are logged in as an administrator.

2. From the administrator home page, click the **Social Learning** link located in the **Manage** section of the left sidebar.

3. Scroll down the **Activity** tab of the **Social Learning** page until you see the **Skills** section.

The **Skills** section of the **Activity** tab only shows the skills that are related to one or more of the available discussion boards. In this example, you should see the **IT Security** skill being listed, as shown in the following screenshot:

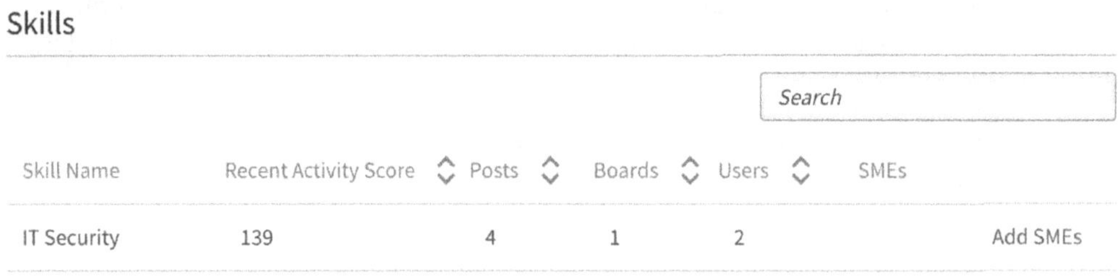

Skills

Skill Name	Recent Activity Score	Posts	Boards	Users	SMEs
IT Security	139	4	1	2	Add SMEs

Figure 12.22 – The Skills section of the Activity tab on the Social Learning page

Take some time to review the metrics available in the **Skills** section of the **Activity** tab.

4. Click the **Add SMEs** link associated with the **IT Security** skill to open the **SMEs for this Skill** dialog.

There should be no SME currently assigned to the **IT Security** skill, as shown in the following screenshot:

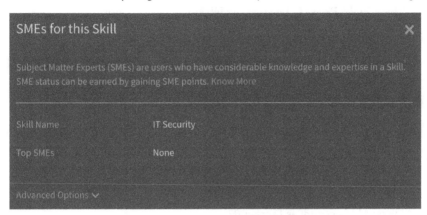

Figure 12.23 – The SMEs for this Skill dialog

This is because the **IT Security in the organization** discussion board is fairly new, with only two learners participating in the discussion. As a result, none of the board participants have yet accumulated enough points to be considered an SME.

5. Click the **Advanced Options** link located in the lower-left corner of the dialog.
6. Select the **Enable Minimum SME Points** checkbox and type 50 in the corresponding field.

This means that a minimum of **50** points is required for a learner to become an SME in the **IT Security** skill. This ensures that the learner has some insight and experience in that skill when the system makes them an SME.

However, at this time, none of the board participants have accumulated 50 points, so no one can claim SME status for the **IT Security** skill. Let's remedy this situation by manually giving *Learner 01* 100 SME points for that skill. Thanks to this little tweak, the **IT Security** skill will have an SME, and that SME will have a lot of credibility in the eyes of other learners participating in the corresponding discussion boards.

7. Type the first letters of Learner 01 in the **Type to Search for users** field. Click **Learner 01** when it appears in the list.
8. Enter **100** in the **Add Points** field for *Learner 01*.
9. Click the **Save** button when done.

With 100 SME points in the **IT Security** skill, *Learner 01* is now an undisputed expert in IT security, so the organization can rely on this user for content curation when the AI-powered automatic curation falls short. Let's explore that workflow in the next section.

Manual content curation by an SME

This section is where all the pieces fit together! So far, you have the following:

- You have enabled **Auto-assisted Manual Curation** on your account
- You have mapped the **IT Security** skill to predefined skill domains known to the built-in AI-powered curation engine
- You have defined *Learner 01* as an SME in **IT Security**

You will now log in as *Learner 02* and upload a PDF document to the **IT Security in the organization** discussion board. This document contains only *Lorem Ipsum* placeholder text, so the automatic curation engine will not be able to give this content a good rating and will forward the curation decision to *Learner 01*. Let's get started:

1. Log in to your ALM account as *Learner 02*.

2. Return to the **Social Learning** page of *Learner 02*, and then to the **IT Security in the organization** discussion board.

3. Click the **New Post** button and upload the `socialLearning/fakeDocument.pdf` file included in the download associated with this book to the **IT Security in the organization** board.

4. When posting the document, notice that the notification has changed! It now states that *the post has been sent for curation.* Click the **OK** button to dismiss the notification.

The document uploaded by *Learner 02* is being reviewed by the built-in curation engine. In fact, the AI is currently assigning a relevance score to this content. If the score is higher than 50%, the content is considered relevant and is immediately published on the discussion board. If the score is lower than or equal to 50%, the curation decision is passed on to the SMEs of that skill. In this case, since the PDF file contains only placeholder text, the automatic curation should fail, and *Learner 01* should be prompted to review the content manually. Let's check this out using the following steps:

5. Log out as *Learner 02*, and then log back in as *Learner 01*.

6. Click the notification icon in the upper-right corner of the screen. As shown in the following screenshot, a post is awaiting curation:

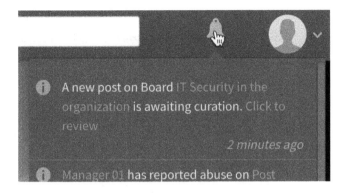

Figure 12.24 – A post is awaiting manual curation

7. Click the **Click to review** link of the notification.

This opens a page where *Learner 01* can review the submitted file. At the end of the page, *Learner 01* can estimate the relevance of the content and optionally add comments.

8. Give the content a very low relevance score and add a small comment. When your screen looks as follows, click the **Submit** button:

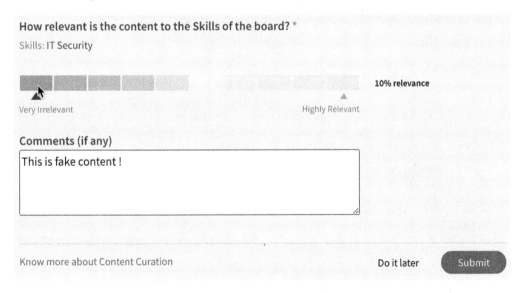

Figure 12.25 – Manual content curation by an SME

Note that this curation effort awards *Learner 01* five more SME points in the **IT Security** skill!

With such a low relevance score, the submitted PDF file has been rejected. It will not appear on the **IT Security in the organization** discussion board, and *Learner 02* will be notified of this decision at the next login.

In this section, you have reviewed the auto-assisted manual curation workflow. This concludes your exploration of content curation in Adobe Learning Manager. For more information on content curation, please refer to the official user guide at `https://helpx.adobe.com/learning-manager/administrators/feature-summary/social-learning-configurations-as-an-admin.html#Contentcuration`.

In the next section, we will review the options available to administrators for managing Social Learning on your ALM account.

Reviewing the Social learning Options of the Administrator

So far in this chapter, you have reviewed the social learning features of Adobe Learning Manager using, for the most part, the default settings. There are only two general options that you have modified in previous exercises:

- You have turned off social learning for external learners
- You have activated the auto-assisted manual curation workflow

All the other settings are still at their respective defaults.

In this section, you will explore the general social learning options of Adobe Learning Manager available to administrators. Perform the following steps to start your hands-on exploration of these settings:

1. Log in to your account as an administrator.
2. From the administrator home page, click the **Social Learning** link located in the **Manage** section of the left sidebar.
3. At the top of the page, switch to the **Settings** tab.

Now that you are at the right place, let's review the options available on this page one by one in the next few sections.

Using Social Learning Scopes

Keep in mind that you are using a trial account with very few users. Therefore, there is not much activity on the social learning discussion boards. This is a pretty simple situation to administer and it works well for small organizations with up to a few hundred learners.

However, if you are part of a larger organization with thousands of users posting lots of messages on a large number of discussion boards, you might want to segment social learning into different scopes. You can, for example, do the following:

- Create social learning scopes based on language, so that learners can only access the discussion boards created in their own language

- Base social learning scopes on job roles, so that learners in the marketing department have a different social learning scope than learners in other departments of the organization

- Link social learning scopes to learners' locations, so learners located in North America have their own social learning scope separate from learners located in Europe

Being able to segment social learning activities in this way is even more critical when dealing with external users. As a reminder, external users do not belong to your organization. These are individuals working for partners, vendors, and customers, among others, who have access to your ALM account. You probably want to confine these users to their own social learning spaces, depending on the organization they are from.

Perform the following steps to define social learning scopes:

1. Make sure you are on the **Settings** tab of the **Social Learning** page of the administrator application.

2. Click the **Edit** link associated with the **Scope Settings** option.

3. Open the **User characteristic** drop-down menu associated with internal learners.

As shown in the following screenshot, the default value for this drop-down menu is **All Internal Users**. This means that all the users share the same social learning space by default.

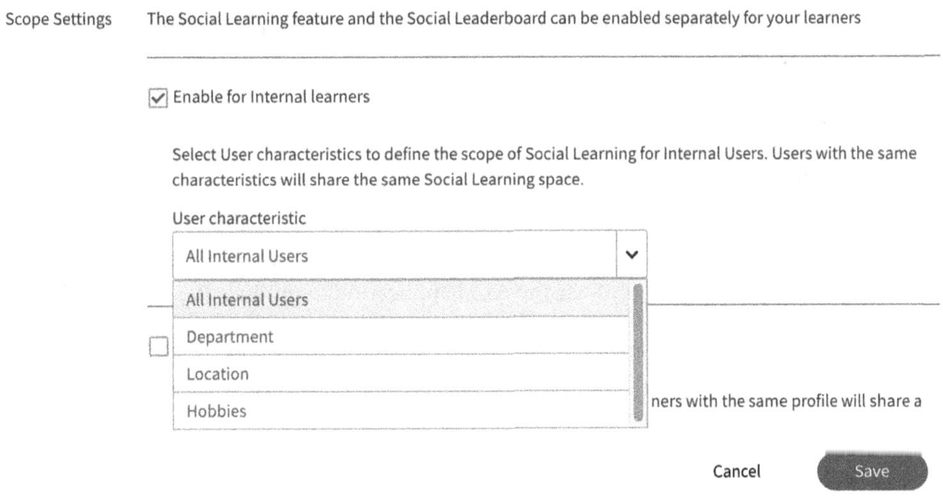

| Scope Settings | The Social Learning feature and the Social Leaderboard can be enabled separately for your learners |

☑ Enable for Internal learners

Select User characteristics to define the scope of Social Learning for Internal Users. Users with the same characteristics will share the same Social Learning space.

User characteristic

| All Internal Users | ⌄ |

All Internal Users

☐ Department

Location

Hobbies

ners with the same profile will share a

Cancel   Save

Figure 12.26 – The default social learning scope is All Internal Users

When choosing another option in this list – say, for example, the **Department** option – you define different social learning scopes based on the learner's department so that learners can only interact with other learners from their own department. In this example, though, since you have very few learners, leave this option at the default value.

4. Click the **Cancel** button to close the **Scope Settings** options without saving any changes.

Thanks to social learning scopes, administrators can segment learners so that they only interact in social learning activities with other learners in the same scope.

Modifying the download Configuration

Moving down the list, the next option is **Download Configuration**. This refers to where users download the Adobe Learning Manager Desktop application from. By default, the application is downloaded from the Adobe servers.

However, for obvious security reasons, many organizations restrict where users can download from. In such a case, you can host the desktop app installers somewhere on your corporate network, and have Adobe Learning Manager redirect learners to that custom location when downloading or updating the ALM desktop app.

Let's review this feature hands-on by performing the following steps:

1. Make sure you are on the **Settings** tab of the **Social Learning** page of the administrator application.

2. Click the **Edit** link associated with the **Download Configuration** option.

From here, you can choose any of the following three options:

- **Adobe servers**: This is the default value; when enabled, the desktop application is downloaded from the Adobe servers.

- **Enterprise servers**: When choosing this value, the desktop app installers are hosted on your corporate network. For this to work, you have to provide the URL of the installers, as well as the version that your company is hosting.

- **Disable downloads for learner**: When this option is enabled, users cannot download the ALM desktop application. This does not mean that they cannot share images, videos, or audio recordings, only that they cannot use the ALM application to produce these resources.

Also, notice the two links at the bottom of the **Download Configuration** section. Use them to download the installation files and save them somewhere on the corporate network. In this example, you will completely disable the ALM Desktop application.

3. Select the **Disable downloads for Learners** option and click the **Save** button.

Let's now continue your exploration of the general settings of social learning in the next section.

Modifying the Board Creation Permission

By default, any learner can create an unlimited number of discussion boards on your account. This default is consistent with the information sharing and informal discussion behavior that social learning aims to promote. But it also causes problems, especially on large accounts with several thousand learners or if hot topics (e.g., those related to major corporate training initiatives) arise within the organization. In such circumstances, you can end up with so many discussion boards on the same topic that social learning quickly becomes a nightmare to administer. In addition, relevant discussions can be scattered across so many boards that it becomes difficult for learners to access this information, which defeats the very purpose of social learning.

These are some of the reasons why you want to limit the number of people allowed to create new discussion boards. You can do so by performing the following steps:

1. Make sure you are on the **Settings** tab of the **Social Learning** page of the administrator application.

2. Click the **Edit** link associated with the **Board Creation Permissions** option.

3. Select the **A group of learners** radio button.

4. Finally, use the search field to search for the relevent user group(s).

You can choose any built-in or custom group. Users who do not belong to any of the selected groups will not be able to create new discussion boards. That said, they retain all their abilities to participate in the discussions taking place on any available boards.

> **Note**
>
> Built-in and custom groups were discussed in *Chapter 5, Managing Users*.

In this example, you will stick to the default and allow all learners to create new discussion boards.

5. Switch back to the **All Learners** option and click the **Save** button.

In the next section, you will learn about the **Special Users** option.

Defining Special Users for Social Learning

The next option is the **Special Users** option. This option is most useful when combined with the *Scope Settings* option described earlier in this chapter.

As a reminder, social learning scopes allow you to segment your learners by a chosen user characteristic so that they can only interact with the other learners in the same scope.

This means that nobody in the organization has a comprehensive overview of all the social learning activities taking place on your account across the different scopes. Fortunately, administrators can grant the *Special User* privilege to a user group, so that Adobe Learning Manager bypasses all scope restrictions and grants these special users access to all the available discussion boards.

Let's take a look at this feature by performing the following steps:

1. Make sure you are on the **Settings** tab of the **Social Learning** page of the administrator application.
2. Click the **Edit** link associated with the **Special Users** option.
3. Use the search field to search for the appropriate user group.

   Note that you can only select a single user group. This can be either a built-in or custom group.

4. In this example, though, since you have not enabled any social learning scope, the **Special Users** option is not relevant.

   Click the **Cancel** button to close the **Special Users** option without saving any changes.

The last setting on this page is the **Customize** setting, which you will review in the next section.

Customizing the Social Learning page

In this section, you will explore the **Customize** option. It allows you to customize the look and feel of the **Social Learning** page of the learner experience. Let's take a quick look at it by performing the following steps:

1. Make sure you are on the **Settings** tab of the **Social Learning** page of the administrator application.
2. Click the **Edit** link associated with the **Customize** option.

From here, you can customize various aspects of the **Social Learning** page of the learner experience, including the banner image, the page header, the support text, and more. Note that you can do so for each language by using the **Language** dropdown, highlighted by the arrow in the following screenshot:

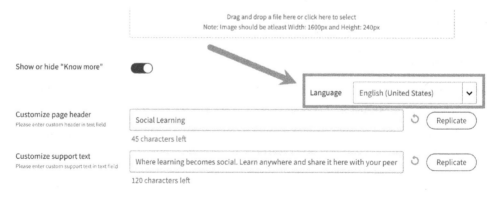

Figure 12.27 – The options available to customize the look and feel of the Social Learning page

Feel free to customize these options as you wish. Don't forget to click the **Save** button when you are done.

This concludes your overview of the general **Social Learning** settings available in the admin role. Thanks to these options, you can fine-tune how social learning works on your Adobe Learning Manager account so that it matches the specific requirements of your organization.

Summary

In ancient times, Aristotle said, "*Man is, by nature, a social animal.*"

This is why, despite all the technological tools at our disposal to communicate remotely, we still like to travel, attend conferences, and take live face-to-face classes conducted by instructors made of flesh and blood. The added value of these live events comes from the countless informal conversations we have with our classmates, instructors, and other conference attendees. In fact, a lot happens during these informal conversations: people get to know each other, business cards are exchanged, and use cases are discussed. Profitable business partnerships and even true friendships are often born out of these conversations. Believe me, this is a true story! The very book you are reading is a perfect illustration of this phenomenon (hi, Sean!).

Some say that distance learning complicates or even prevents these social interactions. While it is true that LMSs and distance learning will never completely replace our dire need for social contact, learning platforms have developed a wide variety of tools to facilitate discussion, information sharing, positive competition, collaboration, engagement, and more. These tools not only complement formal (live or online) learning; used properly, they can even become an integral part of an organization's learning and development strategy by fostering a true culture of learning, sharing, and collaboration.

Adobe Learning Manager is no exception! First, you can enable the **Discussions** tab in any of the available courses. This allows any learner enrolled in that course to participate in a discussion with other learners. This feature is disabled by default, but you can easily enable it either separately for each course or at the account level.

Adobe Learning Manager also includes a full-fledged social learning platform. This functionality is based on skill-related discussion boards, where learners can post a wide variety of content. The URL-sharing bookmarklet and the Adobe Learning Manager desktop application make it so easy to create and share content that there is little to no barrier between a mere interest in participating in social learning activities and the action of actually sharing content. In addition, advanced content moderation and curation capabilities, including an integrated AI-powered curation engine, make the day-to-day administration of these discussion boards a breeze!

But the curation engine is not the only feature of Adobe Learning Manager that relies on artificial intelligence. Remember that ALM allows each learner to enroll in any course available in the catalog. Unfortunately, it is not always easy to find one's way through a vast catalog of courses. This is where the artificial intelligence of Adobe Learning Manager comes into play by providing personalized recommendations to each learner. This is what you will explore in the next chapter.

AI-Powered Recommendations for Learners

In **Adobe Learning Manager** (**ALM**), the primary way for learners to take courses is to browse the course catalog and enroll *themselves* in the courses that they are interested in. However, Adobe Learning Manager is also an enterprise LMS. As such, it should enable organizations of all sizes to implement their learning strategy, which in turn derives from many factors, including compliance training as well as local and international regulations. So, Adobe Learning Manager is on a mission to bridge the gap between the courses available in the course catalog, the requirements of the organization, and the interests of individual learners.

Another important aspect to consider is that Adobe Learning Manager has been designed to handle large deployments with thousands of learners and huge course catalogs, containing tens of thousands of courses provided by a mix of in-house instructors and third-party vendors. This huge amount of content provides a myriad of learning opportunities, which is precisely what makes things both interesting and complicated. Learners need to be guided through these huge catalogs to find the exact course they need based on their profile, job description, past activities, peer activities, and personal interests, all while keeping an eye on the organization's strategy, industry developments, regulatory environment, and more.

This is not easy. How can you maintain the list of skills available on your account when your course catalog is mostly made of third-party off-the-shelf content? How can you recommend courses to each learner when the size of your organization implies that you have a wide variety of profiles to train? How can you ensure that the skills available within your organization are aligned with the ever-changing demands of your industry? How can you tweak the course recommendations made to learners in order to implement the learning and development strategy specific to your organization? Those are the main problems that the **artificial intelligence** (**AI**) and **machine learning** (**ML**) algorithms built into ALM help you address.

In this chapter, we will revisit the learner home page and discuss the various types of recommendations available. You will then discover the inputs that the artificial intelligence considers when providing recommendations specific to each learner. Some of these inputs are automatically curated by the artificial intelligence without any administrator contribution; these are called *implicit inputs*. Others are manually entered into the system by administrators or even by the learners themselves. These are called *explicit inputs*.

To discuss these features and processes, this chapter is made up of the following main sections:

- A word on Adobe Sensei
- Revisiting the learner home page
- Using industry-aligned skills
- Recommendations based on peer activity
- Using manual recommendations

While reviewing the exercises of this chapter, keep in mind that AI needs a very large quantity of data to be efficient. In other words, the features discussed in this chapter are most useful in large accounts with hundreds of learners taking thousands of courses. This is probably not the case with the trial account you're using for the exercises in this book.

Technical requirements

To review the exercises of this chapter, you need to meet the following technical requirement:

- You must have administrator and learner access to a working ALM account (this can be a trial account) using two different user profiles

If you have completed the exercises in the previous chapters, you are good to go. If not, don't worry. You can use your own course content and user accounts. Just remember that the instructions provided in this chapter are based on the exercises from previous chapters, so you might need to adapt them to your specific situation.

A Word on Adobe Sensei

Adobe Sensei is Adobe's in-house Artificial Intelligence (AI) and Machine Learning (ML) technology. It was first introduced in November 2016 and was developed in order to compete with other large technology players (such as Amazon, IBM, Microsoft, and Apple) who have also developed their own AI/ML solutions. Adobe developed Sensei with specific use cases in mind so that it can be embedded in a wide variety of Adobe-branded applications and services.

> **Note**
> *Sensei* is the Japanese word for a respected teacher or leader.

Nowadays, Adobe Sensei powers dozens of features in a wide range of Adobe products:

- Adobe Sensei is used in many **Adobe Creative Cloud** applications, powering features such as Content-Aware Fill in Adobe Photoshop, enhanced search capabilities in Adobe Stock, the color-matching algorithm in Adobe Color, and advanced video effects in Adobe Premiere Pro and After Effects.

- Adobe Sensei is at the core of **Adobe Experience Cloud**, powering features such as predictive analytics, advertisement targeting, personalized content, recommendations, and search engines.

- Adobe Sensei is also present in **Adobe Document Cloud** to improve the accuracy of PDF document scanning, simplify PDF form filling, and assist in signing PDF documents with Adobe Sign

As you can see, Sensei has become a key technology used in some of Adobe's most renowned products, powering some of their most remarkable and advanced features.

When it comes to Learning Manager, Adobe Sensei is the behind-the-scenes technology that powers the automatic curation process (discussed in *Chapter 12, Enabling and Managing Social Learning*), as well as the powerful recommendation engine, which is the subject of this chapter.

More information on Adobe Sensei can be found on the official Adobe website at `https://www.adobe.com/sensei.html`.

Revisiting the learner home page

Always bear in mind that Adobe Learning Manager is a learner-centric LMS, where the primary way to enroll in a course is through self-registration. Each learner can log in to the account, browse the course catalog, and enroll in the course that they find most relevant. How learners determine which course is relevant depends on many factors, such as personal interests, career plan, position in the organization, recommendations from peers, and training history.

The built-in artificial intelligence and machine learning (AI/ML) algorithm is meant to assist learners and organizations in discovering the most relevant courses based on a wide range of factors.

These recommendations are displayed on the learner home page using various widgets that the administrator can arrange in many ways. In this section, let's review the learner home page along with the administrator options that allow you to customize it. To do so, you need to log in to your account twice: once as an administrator and once as a learner. Use the following steps to do so:

1. Open a browser window and log in to your account as an administrator.

2. Open another browser, or a private window of the same browser, and log in to the same account as *Learner 01*.

Make sure you keep both browser windows open for this entire chapter.

Reviewing the Administrator options

Back in *Chapter 2, Customizing the Look and Feel of Adobe Learning Manager*, we discussed the differences between the **Classic** learner experience and the **Immersive** learner experience, and you customized the content that was available on the learner home page. Let's quickly review these options and make sure that you are ready for the exercises of this chapter:

1. Use the browser window in which you are logged in as an administrator.

2. From the administrator home page, click the **Branding** link located in the **Configure** section of the left sidebar.

3. Scroll down the **General** page until you see the **Homepage Experience** option.

4. Click the **Edit** link associated with the **Homepage Experience** option. This enables all the options located at the bottom of the **General** page, as shown in the following screenshot:

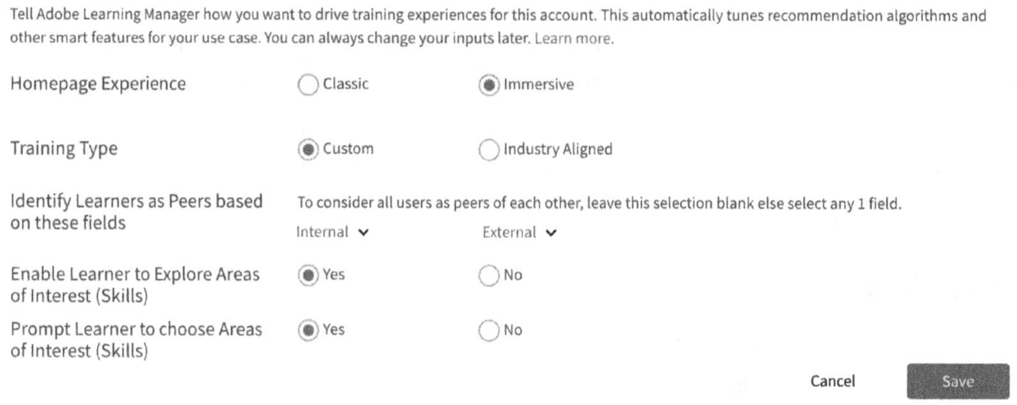

Tell Adobe Learning Manager how you want to drive training experiences for this account. This automatically tunes recommendation algorithms and other smart features for your use case. You can always change your inputs later. Learn more.

Homepage Experience	◯ Classic	⦿ Immersive
Training Type	⦿ Custom	◯ Industry Aligned
Identify Learners as Peers based on these fields	To consider all users as peers of each other, leave this selection blank else select any 1 field. Internal ⌄	External ⌄
Enable Learner to Explore Areas of Interest (Skills)	⦿ Yes	◯ No
Prompt Learner to choose Areas of Interest (Skills)	⦿ Yes	◯ No
	Cancel	Save

Figure 13.01 – The Homepage Experience section of the Branding page

5. Make sure **Homepage Experience** is set to **Immersive**.

6. Make sure the **Training Type** option is set to **Custom**.

This last action tells Adobe Learning Manager that the catalog contains mostly custom courses created by in-house instructors or external providers commissioned by your organization. This works well for smaller course catalogs containing very few (if any) third-party off-the-shelf contents. Therefore, the AI-driven recommendation engine only needs to consider the skills linked to your custom courses to generate recommendations. Remember that you have explicitly defined these skills and manually linked them to your courses using the features discussed in *Chapter 4, Creating Skills and Courses*.

7. Make sure the **Enable Learner to Explore Areas of Interest (Skills)** and **Prompt Learner to choose Areas of Interest (Skills)** options are both set to **Yes** (more on these two options later in this chapter).

8. Click the **Save** button to save and apply these options.

9. Click the **Learner Homepage** link located at the top of the left sidebar to open the **Learner Homepage Settings** page.

   As discussed in *Chapter 2, Customizing the Look and Feel of Adobe Learning Manager*, this is where administrators can modify the content of the learner home page.

10. At the top of the page, make sure the **Immersive** switch is turned on.

11. Then, click the **Reset to Default** link located in the upper-right corner of the page.

12. Scroll through the whole page from top to bottom and review the applied settings. Most of them should be self-explanatory. Make sure you keep them in mind for the next section.

13. When ready, click the **Save** button located in the upper-right corner of the page.

These options and switches are now in their correct configurations for the exercises of the next section, where you will review the current learner experience.

Reviewing the Learner Experience

You will now switch to the browser window in which you are logged in as *Learner 01* to review the areas of the learner experience influenced by the options you manipulated in the previous section. Perform the following steps to do so:

1. Use the browser window in which you are logged in as *Learner 01* and make sure you refresh the page to apply the changes you made in the previous section.

2. Scroll down the learner home page, paying special attention to the content of the **Recommended based on your areas of interest** and **Recommended based on peer activity** sections.

These are the two sections of the learner home page where the effects of the AI-powered recommendation engine are visible. The content in these two sections has been carefully selected by the AI and is specific to the logged-in learner.

In ALM, *areas of interest* is a synonym of *skills*, so the content of the **Recommended based on your areas of interest** widget directly depends on *Learner 01*'s skills. These skills are determined using a variety of methods:

- First, there are the skills related to the courses that *Learner 01* has enrolled in. For example, the **Fundamentals of IT Security** course is linked to the **IT Security level 1** skill. So, when *Learner 01* enrolled in the **Fundamentals of IT Security** course, that skill was automatically linked to *Learner 01*'s profile. Any other courses related to the same skill are therefore taken into consideration by the AI when generating recommendations in the **Recommended based on your areas of interest** section of the learner home page.

- Additionally, administrators can assign skills to individual learners and/or user groups. This allows organizations to promote the skills they want their employees to focus on.

- Because you have set the **Enable Learner to Explore Areas of Interest (Skills)** option to **Yes**, learners can also handpick their *areas of interest* using the **Skills** section of the learner experience.

Let's quickly review the **Skills** page used by learners to modify their *areas of interest* (that is, the list of skills they are interested in):

3. Click the **Skills** icon located in the left column of the learner experience to open the skills page of *Learner 01*.

As shown in the following screenshot, this page lists the *Skills* (aka **Areas of Interest**) linked to *Learner 01*'s profile:

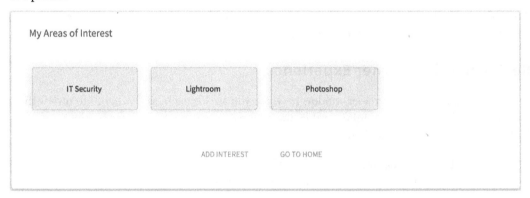

Figure 13.02 – The skills related to Learner 01's profile

These are the skills that the AI considers when generating the contents of the **Recommended based on your areas of interest** section of the home page:

4. Use your mouse to hover over any of these skills. This reveals a cross icon that you can use to remove the skill from the list.

5. Click the **Add Interest** link to open the **Add to my Areas of Interest** page. This page lists all the other skills available on the account as defined on the **Skills** page of the Admin role.

6. Click any skills to add them to *Learner 01*'s interests. Then, click the **Add** button located in the lower-right corner of the page.

This action adds the selected skill(s) to *Learner 01*'s interests. From now on, the AI will consider these additional skills when generating personalized recommendations for *Learner 01*.

In the last two sections, you reviewed the default learner experience provided by your ALM trial account and the corresponding administrator options. In addition, you have rediscovered the concept of **Skills** and the important role that it plays when the AI generates each learner's unique home page.

Generating the **Recommended based on your areas of interest** section of the learner home page is an example of a process that takes place automatically behind the scenes but is deeply influenced by the choices made by both administrators and learners.

In the next section, you will continue this discussion on skills by exploring **Industry-Aligned Skills**.

Using industry-aligned skills

The current learner experience works well when you have a somewhat limited course catalog containing mostly courses defined internally by in-house authors or contractors. However, most large organizations also include third-party off-the-shelf content in their course catalog.

Adobe Learning Manager is able to integrate this external content into its own course catalogs through either dedicated integrations (as discussed in *Chapter 16, Exploring the Integration Admin Role*), the ALM Content Marketplace (as discussed in *Chapter 14, Working with Catalogs and Peer Accounts*), or some kind of custom development.

Using this capability, you greatly expand the list of skills covered by the courses available on your account. This is great news for your learners and the organization as a whole, but it makes administering and tracking these skills a lot more complicated! Consider the following questions:

- How do you maintain the list of skills available on your account when most courses come from external libraries? Not to mention that these libraries are constantly being updated by their respective owners.

- How do you map the skills covered by these massive course catalogs to the skills your company and employees need the most?

- How do you mine these huge course catalogs to make relevant course recommendations in an ever-changing world where industries and regulations are in constant motion?

These are some of the questions you need to address to ensure that both the learners and the organization get the most out of this massive course offering.

Hopefully, the built-in AI does the heavy lifting for you based on a few simple options available in the admin role. Let's review these options, hands-on, by following these steps:

1. Use the browser window in which you are logged in as an administrator.

2. From the administrator home page, click the **Branding** link located in the **Configure** section of the left sidebar.

3. Scroll down the **Branding** page until you see the **Homepage Experience** section.

4. Click the **Edit** link associated with the **Homepage Experience** option.

5.   Switch the **Training Type** option to **Industry Aligned**, as shown in the following screenshot:

Tell Adobe Learning Manager how you want to drive training experiences for this account. This automatically tunes recommendation algorithms and other smart features for your use case. You can always change your inputs later. Learn more.

Homepage Experience	◯ Classic	◉ Immersive
Training Type	◯ Custom	◉ Industry Aligned
Identify Learners as Peers based on these fields	Select any 5 fields. Internal ⌄	External ⌄
Enable Learner to Explore Areas of Interest (Skills)	◉ Yes	◯ No
Prompt Learner to choose Areas of Interest (Skills)	◉ Yes	◯ No

Cancel   [Save]

Figure 13.3 – Switching Training Type to Industry Aligned

This is how you tell ALM that your course catalog includes off-the-shelf content. This content is provided either by third-party providers (such as LinkedIn Learning, getAbstract, and Pluralsight) or through a purchase from the built-in Content Marketplace. As a result, when generating recommendations for learners, the AI must take into account thousands of industry-aligned skills, in addition to the custom skills defined in your account.

These industry-aligned skills are curated by Adobe by constantly monitoring hundreds of industries, thousands of courses, millions of resumes and job descriptions, and more. This data is used by the ALM engineering team to train the built-in AI.

Before saving the changes and examining how they impact the learner experience, there is one more important step to complete in the administrator area. This step must be completed now in order for ALM to allow you to save the changes. However, it will be discussed in more detail in the next section:

6.   Open the **Internal** drop-down menu associated with the **Identify Learners as Peers based on these fields** option and select the **profile** checkbox.

7.   Now, open the **External** drop-down menu associated with the **Identify Learners as Peers based on these fields** option and also select the **profile** checkbox.

8.   Finally, click the **Save** button located in the lower-right corner of the page.

These simple steps are all it takes for the administrator to start using industry-aligned skills. From now on, over 50,000 new skills are available in your account! Best of all, the built-in AI automatically maps these skills to the thousands of courses available in your course catalog, thus helping your learners browse the catalog and enroll in the courses that are most relevant to them.

Speaking of learners, let's return to the learner experience and explore how it is affected by these changes.

Industry-aligned skills in the learner experience

In this section, you will return to the browser window in which you are logged in as *Learner 01* and examine how **Industry Aligned** skills affect the learner experience.

> **Note**
>
> As you read through this section, bear in mind that industry-aligned skills are typically used with larger course catalogs, which primarily comprise third-party content. This means that you will not see the immediate benefits of this feature with the very small course catalog currently available on your trial account.

Use the following steps to browse industry-aligned skills as a learner:

1. Use the browser window in which you are logged in as *Learner 01*.

2. From the learner home page, click the **Skills** icon in the left sidebar to open the **My Areas of Interest** page.

    If you are already on that page, make sure you refresh the browser window so that the changes made in the previous section are applied.

Now that you have activated the industry-aligned skills in the admin role, notice that a new **Industry Aligned Skills** tab is available on the **My Areas of Interest** page:

Figure 13.4 – The Industry Aligned Skills tab is available from the My Areas of Interest page

The **Admin Defined Skills** tab contains the custom skills defined on the **Skills** page of the admin role. These skills are specific to your organization, and you must manually link them to your custom courses.

The **Industry Aligned Skills** are provided by the built-in AI. They are automatically mapped to any third-party content available in your course catalog.

3. Click the **Add Interest** link at the bottom of the page to open the **Add to my Areas of Interest** page.

4. Switch to the **Industry Aligned Skills** tab of the **Add to my Areas of Interest** page.

And that's where the magic of AI kicks in! You are presented with a giant **Skill Map** containing thousands of skills known to the AI.

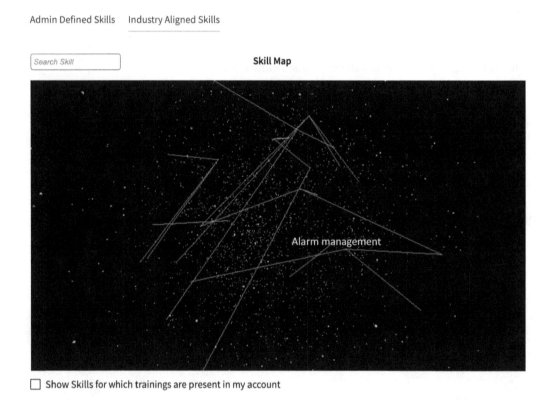

Figure 13.5 – You are presented with a giant Skill Map

5. Use the **Search Skill** field in the upper-left corner of the **Skill Map** to search for a skill of your choosing.

6. Upon choosing a skill in the **Search Skill** field, the **Skill Map** zooms into the selected skill and the skills it connects to.

7. Keep browsing the **Skill Map** using these tools. Each time you click a skill (that is, a dot on the map), it is added to the **Selected Skills** section below the **Skill Map**.

8. You can remove skills from your selection by hovering your mouse over a selected skill and clicking the cross icon in the upper-right corner of the skill.

9. Finally, click the **Add** button located in the lower-right corner of the page to save your changes.

From now on, the AI will consider the chosen **Industry Aligned Skills** in addition to the chosen **Admin Defined Skills** when generating the contents of the **Recommended based on your areas of interest** section of the learner home page. In other words, the AI now includes any available third-party content in the generated recommendations.

Thanks to these two sets of skills (*Admin Defined* and *Industry Aligned*), learners can select skills related to their personal interests, while organizations can still assign skills to their employees to keep some control over the skills available in the organization.

However, the **Recommended based on your areas of interest** section of the learner home page is not the only one providing personalized recommendations:

10. Click the logo in the upper-left corner of the screen or the **Home** icon of the left sidebar to return to the learner home page.

11. Scroll down the page until you see the **Recommended based on peer activity** section.

The **Recommended based on peer activity** section of the learner home page is yet another widget providing personalized recommendations generated by the built-in AI. Let's take a closer look at it in the next section.

Recommendations Based on Peer Activity

The default learner home page of Adobe Learning Manager contains several widgets whose content is provided by the built-in AI. In the previous section, you discovered the **Recommended based on your areas of interest** widget.

In this section, you will explore the **Recommended based on peer activity** widget and the admin options that affect the recommendations it produces.

To come up with these recommendations, the artificial intelligence must analyze how you and your peers behave on the account. This includes analyzing the courses learners have enrolled in, the skills covered by those courses, the L1 and L3 feedback received, whether or not new courses published on the platform are successful, current industry trends, and more. All this data is fed into the artificial intelligence that generates the content of the **Recommended based on peer activity** widget.

This complex process is mostly automatic and takes place behind the scenes without any input from the administrator. However, there is one critical aspect of this process that the administrator can (and should) interfere with. The AI must know what *your* definition of "peers" is.

You will now return to the admin role and discover how you can inform the AI about the properties used to determine peer groups within the users defined on your account:

1. Use the browser window in which you are logged in as an administrator.

2. From the administrator home page, click the **Branding** link located in the **Configure** section of the left sidebar.

3. Scroll down the **Branding** page until you see the **Homepage Experience** section.

4. Click the **Edit** link associated with the **Homepage Experience** option.

5. Open the **Internal** drop-down menu associated with the **Identify Learners as Peers based on these fields** option.

As shown in the following screenshot, the **profile** option should currently be the only one selected in this drop-down menu. This means that learners with the same *profile* are considered *peers*. Remember that each organization is free to decide what *profile* means, but most of the time, *profile* is a synonym of *position*, *role*, *rank*, or *job description*.

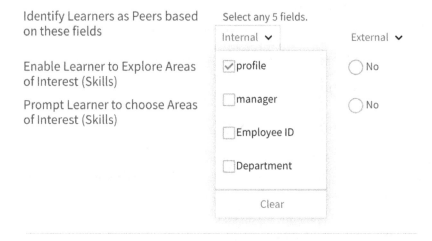

Figure 13.6 – The only selected option of the Internal drop-down menu should be profile

Note that you can choose up to five of these fields from the list, which allows each organization to precisely define who should be considered as *peers* by the AI. Also, note that Adobe Learning Manager differentiates between internal and external users when defining peer groups.

> **Important note**
>
> This only applies to accounts containing more than 1,000 users. If your account has less than 1,000 users, the AI does not have enough data to split your learners into peer groups. In such scenarios, all the users are part of the same peer group regardless of the options selected here.

It is very difficult to experience the full power of this feature on a trial account containing only a few users and courses. Feel free to experiment further with this feature as your account grows larger, in terms of both the number of users and the number of available courses:

6. Click the **Cancel** button in the lower-right corner of the page to close these options without saving any changes.

In this section, you reviewed how the **Recommended based on peer activity** section of the learner home page works and how you, as an administrator, can define the way Learning Manager divides your users into peer groups.

There is one more type of recommendation available in Adobe Learning Manager. In the next section, you will explore manual recommendations made by administrators.

Using Manual Recommendations

The recommendations you've explored so far in this chapter are all powered by the artificial intelligence built into Adobe Learning Manager. Learners and administrators can influence how recommendations are generated, but the process is, for the most part, entirely automatic. These recommendations serve learners well and deliver on ALM's promise of being a learner-centric LMS.

But Adobe Learning Manager is also an enterprise LMS, and organizations want to have a say in what courses the platform recommends to learners. For example, consider the following:

*   You want your employees to have an opportunity to be trained on a new product before an official product launch
*   You need to train your workforce on a new tool your organization is implementing or on a new version of a business-critical enterprise solution used in your organization
*   You want to advertise courses related to skills that are not sufficiently available in your organization
*   You must provide compliance and regulatory training to certain user groups

These are just a few of the many circumstances in which manually recommending courses to specific target audiences is very helpful. Hopefully, Adobe Learning Manager has you covered! Let's review this feature hands-on, using the following steps:

1. Use the browser window in which you are logged in as an administrator.
2. From the admin home page, click the **Announcements** link located in the **Manage** section of the left sidebar to open the **Announcements** page of the administrator.

From this page, you can create and broadcast several types of announcements. This section only covers course recommendations. The other types of announcements will be discussed in *Chapter 15, Working with Messages and Announcements*:

3. Click the **Add** button located in the upper-right corner of the page to open the **Create Announcement** dialog.

4. Open the **Type** drop-down menu located at the top of the **Create Announcement** dialog and select **As Recommendation**.

5. Type in the first few letters of the name of the training you want to recommend in the **Trainings** section of the **Create Announcement** dialog.

    For this example, take any course available in your account that *Learner 01* has *not* yet enrolled in.

    As you type in the name of the training you want to recommend, note that you can use this type of announcement to recommend not only courses but also job aids, learning paths, and certifications.

    Finally, note that you can include multiple trainings of different types in the same announcement.

6. Enter the first few letters of the target user group in the **User Groups** section of the **Create Announcement** dialog.

    In this example, choose the **All Internal Users** group. Note that you can choose multiple user groups if needed.

7. Click the **Advanced Settings** link located in the lower-left corner of the **Create Announcement** dialog. Take some time to review the available options, but don't change any at this time.

8. When the **Create Announcement** dialog looks similar to the following screenshot, click the **Save** button located in the lower-right corner of the box:

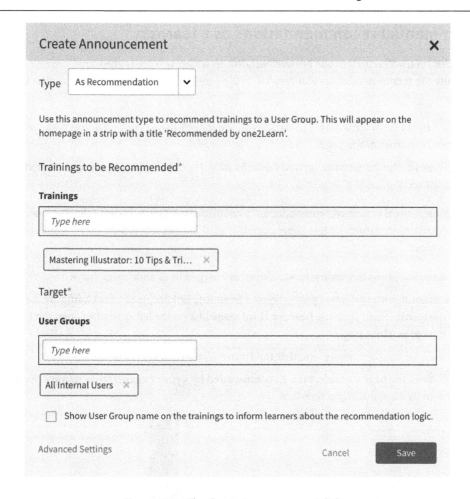

Figure 13.7 – The Create Announcement dialog

9. Finally, click the **Publish Now** button located in the lower-right corner of the **Announcement created successfully** message box.

10. Switch to the **Published** tab of the **Announcements** page and confirm that the new recommendation is visible.

In this section, you learned how you, as an administrator, can manually create a course recommendation using the **Announcements** section of the admin role. In the next section, you will switch to the learner role and explore how that recommendation is displayed in the learner experience.

Viewing manual recommendations as a learner

In this section, you will return to the browser window in which you are logged in as *Learner 01* and examine how the recommendation you created in the previous section is displayed on the learner home page:

1. Return to the browser window in which you are logged in as *Learner 01* and make sure you are on the learner home page.

2. Scroll the learner home page up and down looking for the announcement you created in the previous section.

Bad news! Your manual course recommendation is *not* displayed. This is because the **Recommended by <your organization name>** widget is not currently enabled. So, let's return to the admin role and enable that widget:

3. Return to the browser window in which you are logged in as an administrator.

4. From the administrator home page, click the **Branding** link located in the **Configure** section of the left sidebar. Then, click the **Learner Homepage** link on the left sidebar to open the **Learner Homepage Settings** page.

5. At the top of the page, make sure that the **Immersive** switch is turned on.

6. Scroll down the page and select the **Recommended by <your organization name>** checkbox, as shown in the following screenshot:

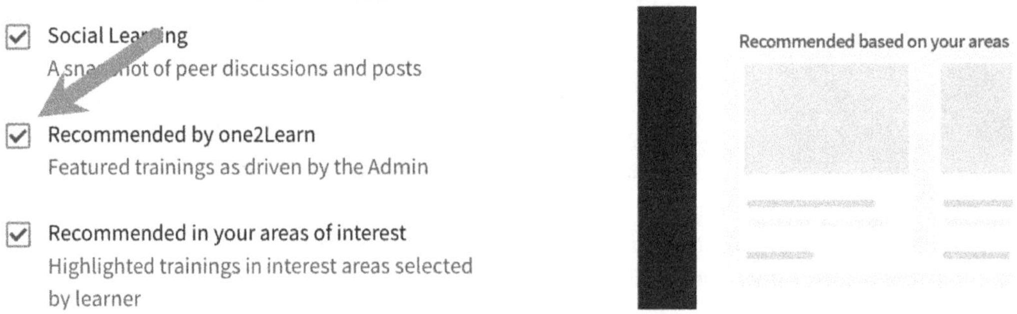

Figure 13.8 – Selecting the Recommended by <your organization name> checkbox

7. Finally, click the **Save** button located in the upper-right corner of the page.

Now that you have enabled the **Recommended by <your organization name>** widget, you will return to the browser window in which you are logged in as *Learner 01* to check it out!

8. Return to the browser window in which you are logged in as *Learner 01* and refresh the home page.

9. Scroll down the learner home page and confirm that the **Recommended by <your organization name>** widget is visible and that it displays the course you manually recommended in the previous section.

In this section, you activated the **Recommended by <your organization name>** widget in the admin role so your manual recommendations can be displayed on the learner home page. This demonstrates how administrators can manually recommend different types of training content (courses, job aids, certifications, and learning paths) to specific target audiences.

Summary

The way you will use the features presented in this chapter on your ALM account will primarily depend on the nature of the courses available in your course catalog and on the size of your account (in terms of both courses and learners). If you primarily have custom courses created by internal authors or contractors, you should use the **Custom** course type. In this case, only the skills you have defined in the admin role and manually linked to your custom courses are taken into account by the artificial intelligence to generate personalized recommendations for learners.

On the other hand, if your course catalog is primarily made of external content libraries provided by third-party vendors, you should choose the **Industry Aligned** course type. This enables thousands of industry-aligned skills in your ALM account. These skills have been carefully curated by the Adobe Learning Manager engineering team and integrated into Adobe Sensei, which is Adobe's own artificial intelligence technology that powers all these features behind the scenes. As a result, the course content provided by these huge external libraries is taken into account by the AI to generate personalized recommendations.

In addition to skills, the artificial intelligence also generates recommendations based on peer activity. This feature is fully functional on larger deployments with at least 1,000 learners. Indeed, keep in mind that Adobe Learning Manager is designed for large deployments with several thousand learners. All these users have a wide variety of roles and functions within the organization. They have such different expectations and interests that it makes little sense to consider them all as a single peer group. That's why Adobe Learning Manager allows you to split your users into different peer groups based on up to five user characteristics of your choosing. This allows the artificial intelligence to generate more accurate recommendations based on peer activity.

Finally, organizations also have a say in what courses are recommended to their employees. Therefore, administrators can manually assign skills to learners and manually recommend courses to specific target audiences.

Remember that these powerful features rely on a gigantic and constant flow of data to deliver their promise, so give your ALM account enough time to grow before you take full advantage of this technology. This is especially true for small and mid-sized organizations using Adobe Learning Manager, as these accounts generate less data than larger deployments.

So far, in this book, you have worked with the default training catalog that is available in any Learning Manager account. This catalog is visible to all internal and external users. So, currently, all users have access to all the content hosted on your account. In the next chapter, you will create additional catalogs and learn how to make them available to certain learners only. This will allow you to tailor your course offerings to the different user groups using your ALM account.

Part 4 –
Administering the Platform

Now that you have a much better understanding of how Adobe Learning Manager works, it is time to focus on the general administration of the platform and its integration within the IT ecosystem used in your organization.

This section comprises the following chapters:

14

Working with Catalogs and Peer Accounts

Currently, all the users defined on your account have access to all of the courses available in your course catalog. This is the default situation, and it might very well meet your needs. However, more often than not, organizations need precise control over who can access which courses or need to segment content and reporting data for certain user groups. For example, courses available to internal users might be different from courses available to external users, and courses that contain sensitive or confidential information might only be made available to specific audiences within the organization. These are just two of the many situations where not all learners should have access to the same set of courses. In Adobe Learning Manager, such access control is achieved by creating multiple catalogs.

Besides allowing you to define who can access which courses, creating catalogs also allows you to share your courses with other ALM accounts, which is very useful in many situations, such as when you sell courses to other organizations or when the headquarters of a multinational corporation wants to share courses with local offices from around the world.

You can also use the built-in **Content Marketplace** to purchase third-party content that is made available to your account as additional course catalogs, all without leaving the administrator role of your Adobe Learning Manager account.

In addition to sharing learning content, Adobe Learning Manager also allows you to share user licenses with other accounts using the **Peer Accounts** feature. With Peer Accounts, organizations can purchase a large number of seats and distribute them among multiple ALM accounts. This is very useful for large organizations with multiple subsidiaries around the world, or to fund training for partners or franchisees.

These are the features you will explore in this chapter, which includes the following main sections:

- Working with multiple catalogs
- Sharing catalogs

- Enabling and disabling catalogs

- Catalogs in the learner experience

- Exploring Content Marketplace

- Working with peer accounts

Using these features, you can tailor your ALM deployment so that it exactly matches the needs of your organization, regardless of its size, industry, strategy, or internal operations.

Technical requirements

To complete the exercises of this chapter, you need to meet the following technical requirements:

- You must have administrator access to a working ALM account (this can be a trial account)

- You must be able to access the same account using an internal learner account and an external learner account

- You should have at least a dozen courses available in your account (the default courses made available with each new account work just fine)

- Optionally, administrator access to another ALM account will allow you to further experiment with some of the features discussed in this chapter

If you have followed the exercises of the previous chapters, you are good to go. If not, feel free to use the course content and the users available on your account. Note that the instructions provided in this chapter build upon the exercises from previous chapters, so you may need to adapt them to your specific situation.

Working With Multiple Catalogs

In Adobe Learning Manager, a catalog is a collection of learning objects. So far, all the content available on your account is part of the default catalog that was automatically created along with your account. This default catalog has the following characteristics:

- It cannot be deleted (but it can be disabled; as discussed in the *Enabling and Disabling Catalogs* section later in this chapter)

- All the courses, learning paths, certifications, and job aids that you create on your account are automatically included in the default catalog

- By default, all the learners (including internal *and* external learners) have access to the default catalog

This default situation is very simple to understand and administer, and it may well correspond to your needs. There is nothing wrong with using it in production. However, there are also many situations where not all learners should have access to the same set of courses:

- For example, courses on enterprise solutions used internally should only be available to your organization's employees (internal users), but not to external partners, vendors, or customers (external users).

- Courses on future products being developed within your company should only be accessible to the R&D department. Indeed, these courses may contain confidential information currently under embargo.

- Subscribing to external course libraries provided by third-party vendors comes at a cost. Most of the time, this cost depends on the number of users accessing these libraries. For this reason, you may want to limit the number of users with access to these external courses.

- Some courses (such as courses on local regulations, for example) might only be relevant in certain parts of the world. Only users in the corresponding regions should have access to these courses.

These are just a few of the situations where it is useful to control which learners have access to which courses.

Adobe Learning Manager addresses this problem through the use of catalogs. A **catalog** is a collection of courses, learning paths, certifications, and job aids:

- Administrators can create an unlimited number of custom catalogs

- You can add an unlimited number of training items to each catalog and a single training item can be part of multiple catalogs

- It is by granting access to these catalogs to various user groups that administrators control who has access to what content

Now that you have a high-level understanding of what catalogs are and why you might want to use them, let's return to the administrator role to explore this feature hands-on in the next few sections.

Creating custom catalogs

In this section, you will log in to your account as an administrator and create two new catalogs. The first one will be accessible to internal users only and the second one to external users only. Follow these steps to create these two course catalogs:

1. Log in to your account as an administrator.

2. From the administrator home page, click the **Catalogs** link located in the **Learning** section of the left sidebar. This opens the **Catalogs** page of the administrator.

As shown in the following screenshot, **Default Catalog** is the only one currently available in your account:

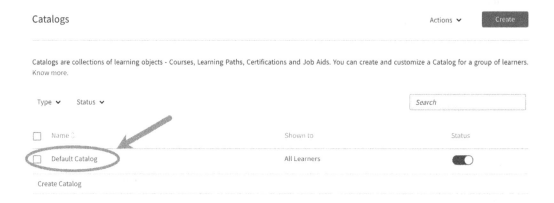

Figure 14.01 – The Default Catalog is the only one available by default

3. Click the **Create Catalog** link or the **Create** button located in the upper-right corner of the page to open the **Create Catalog** page.

4. Type `Internal catalog` into the **Catalog Name** field. Note that this is the only information required at this stage of creating a new catalog.

> **Tip**
> It's a good idea to establish clear naming conventions in the early stages of your ALM deployment. This is true not only for naming catalogs, but also for any other element of Adobe Learning Manager that you can name. This ensures consistency and, therefore, ease of use for learners and administrators alike, right from day one.

5. As a best practice, take some time to provide a **Cover Image** and type a small description into the **Description** field.

    If you do not have a suitable image, you can use the `catalogs/internal.jpg` image in the downloadable files associated with this book.

6. When the **Create Catalog** page looks similar to the following screenshot, click the **Next** button located in the upper-right corner of the screen:

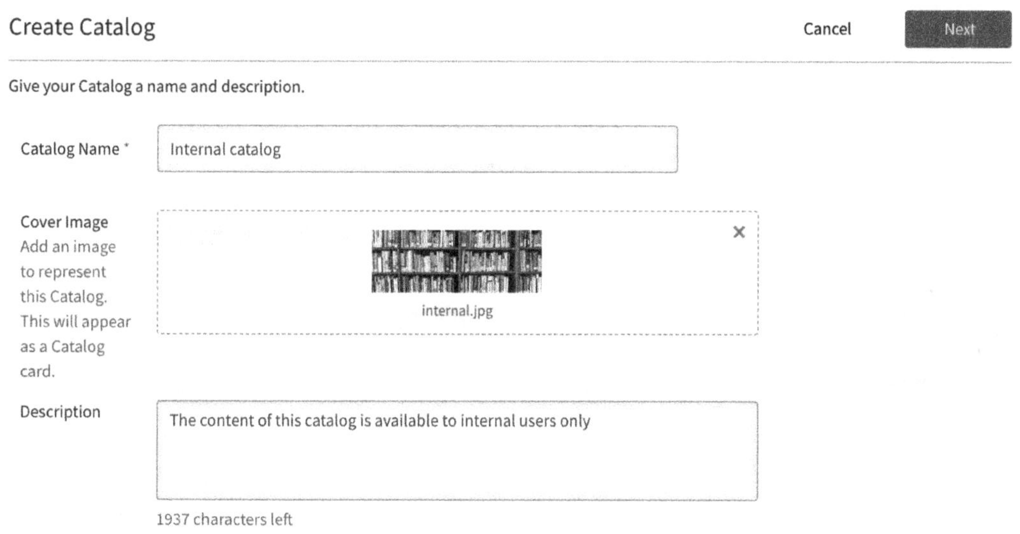

Figure 14.02 – Creating the Internal Catalog

When the page reloads, additional links are available in the left sidebar. These allow you to add content to the catalog and to share it either internally or externally. You will review them in later sections. For now, return to the **Catalogs** page of the administrator and create the **External Catalog** using the following steps:

7.   Click the **Back** link located at the top of the left sidebar.

This takes you back to the **Catalogs** page, where the newly created **Internal Catalog** should be listed. Notice that your new catalog is not yet enabled, as indicated by the **Status** switch in the last column of the table.

8.   Repeat the preceding actions to create the **External Catalog**. Use the `catalogs/external.jpg` image in the sample files associated with this book if you do not have a suitable image of your own.

9.   When done, the **Catalogs** page of the administrator should look similar to the following screenshot:

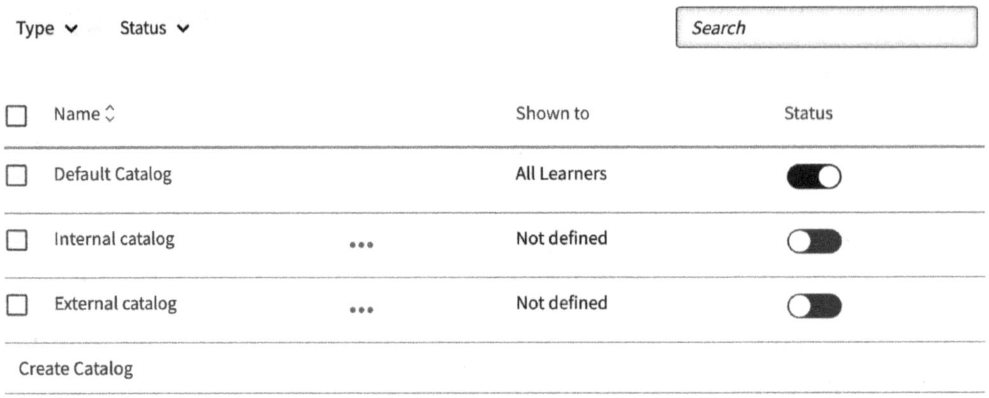

Figure 14.03 – The Catalogs page after creating your two custom catalogs

As you can see, the process of creating new catalogs is very simple. That said, there are still two things to do before you can activate your newly created catalogs. First, you need to define the content of each catalog, and second, you need to select the learners that will have access to them.

> **The catalog image**
>
> The preferred size for a catalog cover image is 280 px by 100 px. You can use any of the popular image file formats, including `.jpg` and `.png`. More information can be found in the official ALM user guide at `https://helpx.adobe.com/learning-manager/system-requirements.html`.

In the next section, you will define the content of your two newly created catalogs.

Adding content to catalogs

A catalog is a collection of learning objects. In the previous section, you created two custom catalogs. You will now add content to these course catalogs using the following steps:

1. Make sure you are logged in to your account as an administrator.

2. From the administrator home page, click the **Catalogs** link located in the **Learning** section of the left sidebar.

3. Click the **Internal Catalog** you created in the previous section.

4. Click the **Content** link located in the **Manage** section of the left sidebar.

As shown in the following screenshot, there are four tabs available at the top of the page that opens, representing the four types of content that can be included in a catalog:

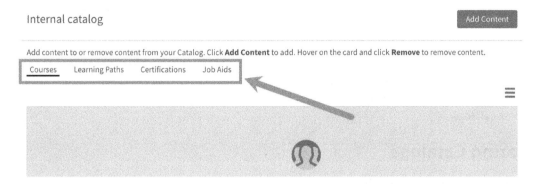

Figure 14.04 – The four types of content that can be included in a Catalog

5.   Click the **Add Content** link located in the middle of the page or on the **Add Content** button in the upper-right corner.

This takes you to a page with a list of all the courses available on your account. It features a **Skills** filter, a **Sort By** dropdown, and a **Search** field that you can use to search for courses.

6.   To add a course to the catalog, hover over the bottom of the corresponding course card and click the **Add** link.

If the course you add to the catalog has prerequisites, these are automatically added to the catalog in addition to the selected course.

Use this technique to add a few courses of your choosing to the **Internal Catalog**.

7.   If needed, you can use the tabs at the top of the page to add **Learning Paths**, **Certifications**, and **Job Aids** to the catalog using the very same techniques.

8.   When done, click the **Save** button in the upper-right corner of the page.

9.   Then, click the **Back** link at the top of the left sidebar to return to the **Catalogs** page of the administrator.

10.   Repeat the preceding operations to add training content to the **External Catalog**. Remember that the same content can be included in multiple catalogs.

To test all possible situations, be sure to add some items to both catalogs and others to only one of the two catalogs. Also, make sure that some items are not included in either catalog.

In this section, you added content to the two custom catalogs that you created in the previous section. The main takeaways of this section are as follows:

- A catalog is a collection of learning items that can contain courses, learning paths, certifications, and job aids

- The same learning item can be part of multiple catalogs

You have now completed the first of the two operations required before you can activate the catalogs and make them available to learners. In the next section, you will choose which users will have access to these catalogs.

Sharing Catalogs

In this section, you will share the catalogs created earlier with specific user groups. This is how administrators decide which users have access to which catalogs. Adobe Learning Manager distinguishes between the internal and external sharing of catalogs:

- Internal sharing refers to giving access to your catalog to learners defined within your account. These can be *both internal and external learners*. Indeed, both types of learners are defined within your ALM account, as discussed in *Chapter 5, Managing Users*.

- External sharing refers to giving access to your catalog to learners defined *in other ALM accounts*.

Let's reiterate this! Internal and external sharing *has nothing to do* with the concept of internal and external users, as described in *Chapter 5, Managing Users*. It's about the ability to share the contents hosted on your ALM account either with users defined *within your account* (internal sharing) or with users defined *in other ALM accounts* (external sharing).

Let's review these two types of sharing in the next few sections.

Internal Sharing

In our example, we want to grant internal users access to our custom **Internal Catalog**. The **External Catalog**, should only be accessible to the external users of your account. Both these situations fall under the *internal sharing* mechanism of Adobe Learning Manager.

Let's review this using the following steps:

1. Make sure you are logged in to your account as an administrator.
2. From the administrator home page, click the **Catalogs** link located in the **Learning** section of the left sidebar.
3. Click the **Internal Catalog** created earlier in this chapter.
4. Then, click the **Share Internally** link located in the left sidebar.

5. Click the **Add User Groups** link located in the middle of the page or the **Add** button in the upper-right corner.

6. Use the **Search** field to search for the `All Internal Users` group. If necessary, you can repeat this operation to select multiple user groups.

7. When your screen looks similar to the following screenshot, click the **Save** button:

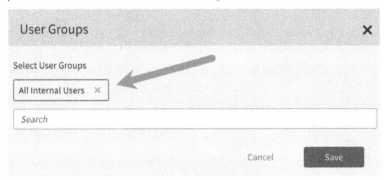

Figure 14.05 – Add the All Internal Users group to Select User Groups

You just granted all your internal users access to the **Internal Catalog**. You will now repeat the same operations to grant all your external users access to the **External Catalog**:

8. Click the **Back** link at the top of the left column to return to the **Catalogs** page.

9. This time, click the **External Catalog**, then click the **Share Internally** link in the left sidebar (remember that your external users are defined *within your ALM account*, so you must use the *internal* sharing mechanism).

10. Click the **Add User Groups** link located in the middle of the page or the **Add** button in the upper-right corner.

11. Add the **All External Users** group to the selected user groups and click the **Save** button.

12. Finally, click the **Back** link at the top of the left sidebar to return to the main **Catalogs** page of the admin role.

Despite all the steps you have taken so far in this chapter, nothing has changed for learners yet! This is because your new custom catalogs are not yet enabled. We will discuss enabling and disabling catalogs in the *Enabling and Disabling Catalogs* section later in this chapter. However, for now, let's briefly discuss external sharing in the next section.

External Sharing

Sharing a catalog externally enables you to give access to your course content to users defined on other ALM accounts. This can be very useful in many situations:

- You can sell your courses to other organizations that are also using Adobe Learning Manager as their enterprise LMS.

- If you have partners, suppliers, and customers who also use Adobe Learning Manager as their LMS, you can use external sharing rather than defining their employees as external learners on your own account. By doing this, you will not have to pay for the user seats used by these external users as this cost is covered by the other account.

- Some multinational corporations choose to use separate ALM accounts for each of their regional branches. This allows each branch to remain independent and manage its own training strategy separately from the organization's headquarters and other branches. In this scenario, the head office can use external catalog sharing to push corporate training content into the ALM accounts of its branches. This allows for the implementation of a global training strategy on top of the regional strategies.

These are just a few of the circumstances in which external catalog sharing can be very useful. Let's explore this feature, hands-on, using the following steps:

1. Make sure you are logged in to your account as an administrator.
2. From the administrator home page, click the **Catalogs** link located in the **Learning** section of the left sidebar.
3. Open your custom **Internal Catalog**.
4. Finally, click the **Share Externally** link located in the left sidebar.

As shown in the following screenshot, a message informs you that this catalog is already shared internally, so it cannot be shared externally:

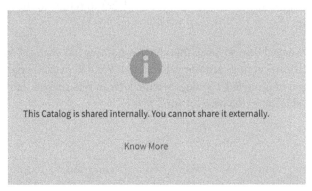

This Catalog is shared internally. You cannot share it externally.

Know More

Figure 14.6 – You cannot share the same catalog both internally and externally

Thanks to this little experiment, you discover that you cannot share the same catalog both internally and externally. So, to proceed with this exercise, it is necessary to create yet another custom catalog:

5. Click the **Back** link at the top of the left sidebar to return to the main **Catalogs** page.

6. Click the **Create Catalog** link or the **Create** button in the upper-right corner of the page.

7. Type a name of your choice into the **Catalog Name** field and click the **Next** button.

8. Click the **Share Externally** link located in the left sidebar.

9. Click the **Add External Accounts** link or the **Add** button in the upper-right corner of the screen.

This opens the **External Account** dialog, as shown in the following screenshot:

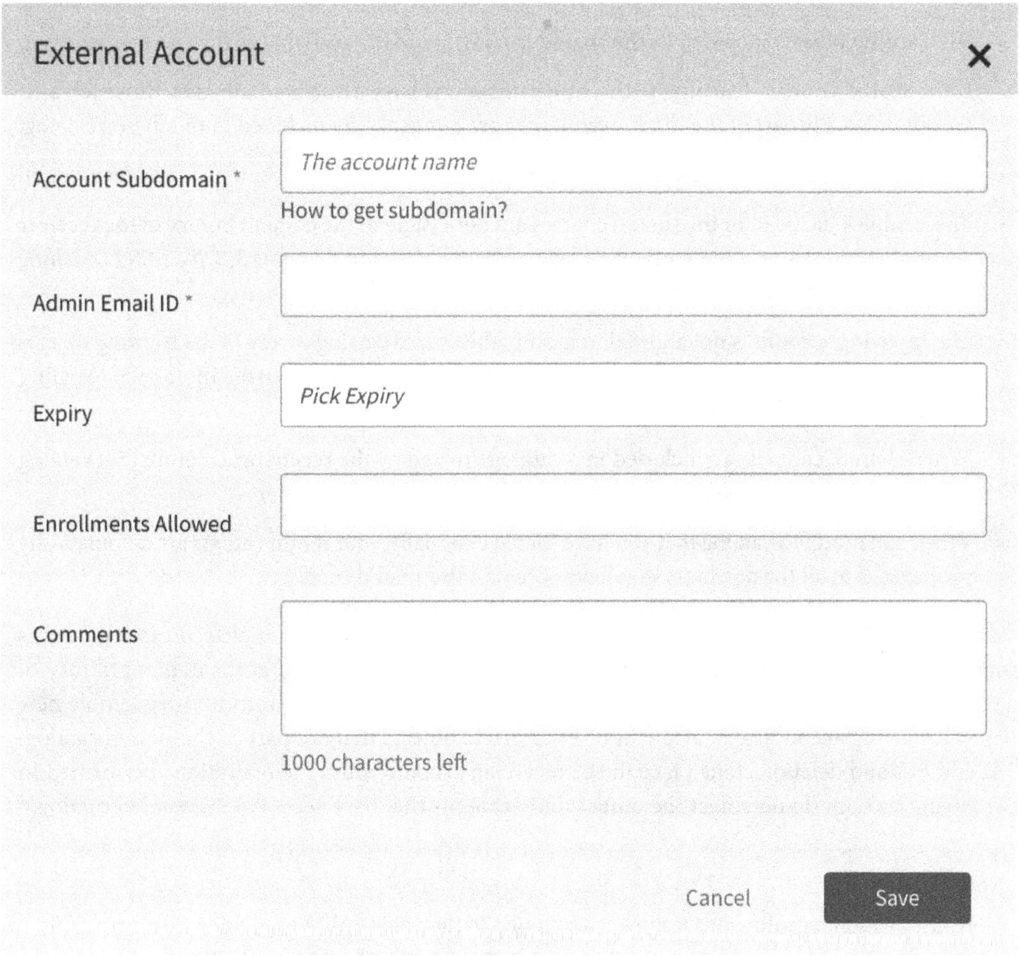

Figure 14.07 – The External Account dialog

Most of the fields in the **External Account** dialog are self-explanatory. Notice that there are only two required fields in this form:

- In the **Account Subdomain** field, enter the URL of the external ALM account you want to share this catalog with

- You also need to type the email address of the external account administrator into the **Admin Email ID** field

After completing this form, the external account administrator receives an email with a unique URL that must be visited in order to accept or reject the shared catalog.

By default, accepting the shared catalog has the following consequences:

- All learning objects included in the shared catalog are made available to the receiver account.

- If the shared courses, learning paths, or certifications have associated job aids, those job aids are automatically part of the share, even if they are not explicitly included in the shared catalog.

- The skills associated with the shared catalog are automatically copied over to the receiver account.

- The modules included in the shared courses are not visible in the content library of the receiver account (modules and the content library were discussed in *Chapter 3, Uploading Learning Content and Managing the Content Library*).

- The receiving account is not allowed to modify the shared catalog or any of the learning objects it contains. That said, the receiving account can use the shared courses in its own learning paths, certifications, and catalogs.

- When shared, courses are included in a catalog created by the receiving account; that catalog cannot be shared externally to prevent the resharing of the shared items.

- When you modify a catalog that you have shared externally, your modifications are automatically propagated to all the accounts that have access to the shared catalog.

In addition to this default situation, you can also enable full control of your shared catalog. In this scenario, the modules included in the shared learning objects are visible in the content library of the receiving account. This means that they can be used by the receiving account to assemble new courses. Receiving accounts can also edit or even delete objects that are part of the shared catalog. These editions and deletions take place in the receiving account only. The operations performed in the receiving account do not affect the other ALM accounts that have access to this shared catalog.

> **Note**
>
> More information regarding this feature can be found in the official ALM user guide at `https://helpx.adobe.com/learning-manager/administrators/feature-summary/shared-catalog-full-control.html`.

If you happen to have access to another ALM account, don't hesitate to further experiment with this feature. That said, in the context of this book, we're going to break off the process here and delete the custom catalog you just created:

10. Click the **Cancel** button located at the bottom of the **External Account** dialog.

11. Then, click the **Back** button located at the top of the left sidebar.

12. Use your mouse to hover over the catalog that you created in this section and click the trash icon that appears to delete the catalog.

13. Confirm your intention by clicking the **Delete** button located in the **Confirmation Required** message.

> **Note**
> The default courses available in any new ALM account are, in fact, part of a course catalog created by Adobe that is pushed to your account using the **Share Externally** feature discussed in this section.

In this section, you discovered sharing catalogs either internally or externally. Remember that internal sharing allows you to grant access to your catalogs to the user groups defined within your ALM account. This includes both the internal and the external users of your account. External sharing allows you to share your custom course catalogs with other ALM accounts. These can belong to providers, suppliers, partners, and customers that are also using Adobe Learning Manager as their LMS or to local subsidiaries of your own international organization.

You now have two custom catalogs available in your account. Each contains a number of learning items, and you have defined the users who have access to these catalogs. In the next section, you will finally enable these catalogs, which will make them available to your learners.

Enabling and Disabling Catalogs

In the preceding sections, you created two custom catalogs, added learning content to them, and granted access to these catalogs to specific user groups. Now you are ready to activate these catalogs so that they become available in the learner experience.

But before doing that, remember that there is a third catalog available in your ALM account. This is the default catalog that was automatically created along with your account. This default catalog has some special characteristics of its own. Let's explore that in the next section.

Modifying the Default Catalog

Remember that the default catalog contains all of the learning objects available in your account and is accessible to all users. Let's take a look at how you can modify this default catalog using the following steps:

1. Make sure you are logged in to your account as an administrator.

2. From the administrator home page, click the **Catalogs** link located in the **Learning** section of the left sidebar.

3. Open the **Default Catalog**.

As shown in the following screenshot, the left sidebar of the default catalog contains only a small subset of the features available when a custom catalog is opened:

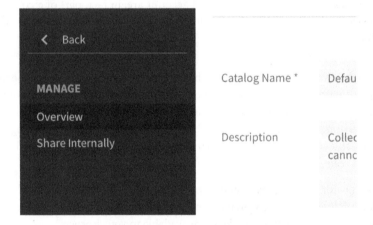

Figure 14.08 – The left sidebar of the Default Catalog

For example, there is no **Content** link available in the left sidebar of the default catalog. This means that you cannot change the content of the default catalog. In other words, every course, learning path, certification, and job aid you create in your account will *always* be part of the default catalog, no matter what!

Also, notice that there is no **Share Externally** link available. This means that your default catalog cannot be shared with other ALM accounts.

4. Click the **Share Internally** link available in the left sidebar.

This opens a page where you can modify who has access to the **Default Catalog**. Remember that, by default, all the users (both internal and external) defined on your account have access to the **Default Catalog**. However, because the content in the **Default Catalog** cannot be modified, controlling access to your learning content usually involves disabling the default catalog altogether. This is what you will do now using the following steps:

5. Click the **Back** link at the top of the left sidebar.

6. Switch the **Default Catalog** off using the associated toggle button located in the **Status** column.

7. Then, enable the **Internal Catalog** using the same technique.

8. Finally, use the checkbox to select the **External Catalog** in the list. Then, open the **Actions** drop-down menu located in the upper-right corner of the page. Take some time to examine the available actions and click **Enable** to turn the **External Catalog** on.

At the end of this process, you have disabled the **Default Catalog** and enabled the two custom catalogs you created earlier in this chapter.

Thanks to the changes implemented in this section, your custom catalogs are now available in the learner experience. Let's give it a try in the next section.

Catalogs in the learner experience

In this section, you will log in to your account as a learner and inspect how the work done in the previous sections impacts the learner experience. As you do so, remember the following:

- You have two custom catalogs enabled on your ALM account and you have disabled the Default Catalog

- One catalog is available to *all internal users*, while the other one is available to *all external users*

- Some courses are included in only one of the two catalogs, others are included in both catalogs, and some courses are not included in either catalog

- Some learners already enrolled in, started, or even completed courses before you created the custom catalogs and disabled the Default Catalog

With that in mind, let's head to the learner experience to examine the impact of the two custom catalogs built earlier in this chapter:

1. Log in to your account as *Learner 01*.

2. Once logged in, click the **Go To Catalog** link on the home page, or the **Catalog** icon of the left sidebar, to open the **Catalog** page of *Learner 01*.

3. Confirm that the courses visible to *Learner 01* are those included in the **Internal Catalog** created earlier, plus the courses in which *Learner 01* is currently enrolled.

> **Filtering by catalog**
>
> When the logged-in learner has access to multiple catalogs (which is not the case in this example), admins can enable the ability for learners to filter by catalog on the **Catalog** page of the learner experience. To do so, go to the **Settings | General** page of the admin role and look for the **Show Filter Panels** option.

4.   Click the **My Learning** icon in the left sidebar to open the **My Learning** page of *Learner 01*.

As discussed in *Chapter 7, Reviewing the Learner Experience*, the **My Learning** page lists all the courses the logged-in learner is enrolled in, including the courses already completed. This includes courses that are not part of the **Internal Catalog** but that the learner enrolled in when the **Default Catalog** was still enabled:

5.   Click the logo in the upper-right corner of the screen, or the **Home** icon of the left sidebar, to return to the learner home page.

6.   Scroll all the way down the learner home page and note that the available course recommendations (if any) only contain courses that are part of the catalog(s) currently accessible to the logged-in learner.

You will now log out as *Learner 01* and log back in as *Learner 03*, one of the external learners that you defined in *Chapter 5, Managing Users*. Also, remember that external learners use a special login page.

> **Accessing the login page of external learners**
>
> If you don't remember the URL of the login page for *Learner 03*, return to the **Users | External** page of the administrator, roll your mouse over the external learner profile, and click on the *chain* icon that appears to copy the login page URL to your clipboard.

7.   Log out as *Learner 01*, then, log back in as *Learner 03*.

8.   Once logged in as *Learner 03*, open the **Catalog** page.

9.   Confirm that the courses available on the **Catalog** page of *Learner 03* are different from those that were available when *Learner 01* was logged in.

These experiments demonstrate that *Learner 01* and *Learner 03* no longer have access to the same set of courses. This is because the two learners do not have access to the same course catalog(s) and are only able to view those courses, learning paths, certifications, and job aids included in the catalog(s) they do have access to.

> **Browsing by catalog**
>
> Using the **Branding** link in the **Configure** section of the left sidebar, admins can add the **Browse by Catalog** widget to the Learner Homepage. When enabled, the catalogs accessible by the logged-in learner are displayed on the home page. This allows the learner to browse the available training content by catalog.

This section concludes our overview of **Catalogs** in Adobe Learning Manager. It is by placing courses, learning paths, certifications, and job aids in catalogs that you can control which learners have access to which learning objects. You can also share catalogs with other accounts using the **external sharing** feature of Adobe Learning Manager.

Exploring the Content Marketplace

To make it easier to integrate third-party content into your account, Adobe has developed the **Content Marketplace**. When Content Marketplace was first introduced, it already contained over 70,000 courses covering a wide range of topics.

With this new Content Marketplace, you can do the following:

- Explore available courses and let learners express their interest.
- Purchase access to all of the content or to carefully selected playlists.

That's what you'll explore, in this section, using the following steps:

1. Make sure you're logged in to your account as an administrator.
2. From the administrator home page, click the **Content Marketplace** link located in the **Manage** section of the left sidebar to open the **Content Marketplace** page of the admin role.

The **Content Marketplace** page contains two tiles, as shown in the following screenshot:

Content Marketplace

Quality training content makes it easy for you to get your Digital Learning program on the road. Now access 70,000+ courses from leading content providers across topic areas such as Creative Cloud, Business, Sales & Marketing, Safety, Compliance and more.

Deliver a diverse bouquet of courses ranging from Compliance, Business, Marketing and more. Give your users an assortment of high-quality learning curated by world class content providers.

Master the tools you need to fully realize your creativity, with handpicked training courses to become an expert with the world's best platform for artists and dreamers.

Figure 14.9 – The main page of Content Marketplace

3. Click the **Creative Cloud Training** option.

This action opens a new page where you can browse a special course catalog containing courses on Adobe Creative Cloud applications (such as Photoshop, Illustrator, and InDesign). If you are interested in purchasing these courses, click the **Contact Adobe** button located in the upper-right corner of that page.

4. Return to the Adobe Learning Manager browser window.

5. Click the **Enterprise Training** option to open the **Enterprise Training** page of the marketplace and take some time to examine the available options.

6. When done, focus your attention on the **Invite Users** section in the lower-left corner of the page.

In this section, you can invite learners to explore the content available in the **Enterprise Learning** catalog of the **Content Marketplace**. The idea is to let them express their interest in the courses and playlists available.

By default, **All Learners** have access to **Content Marketplace**. In this example, you will only allow internal learners to browse **Content Marketplace** and express their interest:

7. Switch to the **Selected learners** option of the **Invite Users** section of the **Enterprise Training** page.

8. Click the **Invite Users** button to open the **Invite Users to Explore** dialog.

9. Use the **Search** field to select the `All Internal Users` group.

    Note that you can add as many users/user groups as needed.

10. Finally, click the **Invite Users** button located in the lower-right corner of the **Invite Users to Explore** dialog.

11. Take some time to read the **Invite Users** confirmation message and click the **Proceed** button.

From now on, all your internal users have the ability to explore the courses available in the built-in **Content Marketplace** and express their interest. Confirm that the **Invite Users** section of the **Enterprise Training** page appears similar to the following screenshot:

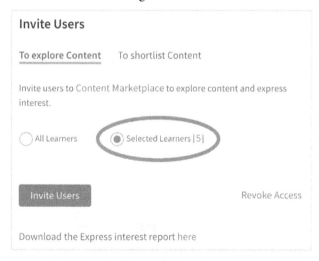

Figure 14.10 – Invite Users to Content Marketplace to express their interests

In the next section, you will log in to your account as *Learner 01* and examine how inviting users to review **Content Marketplace** affects the learner experience.

Browsing the Content Marketplace as a learner

In the previous section, you invited all your internal learners to explore the courses available in the **Content Marketplace**. These learners can now express their interest in the courses that are for sale in the built-in Content Marketplace. This is a good way for organizations to gauge interest in this additional content before purchasing access to all or part of it.

In this section, you will log in to your account as an internal learner, browse **Content Marketplace**, and express interest in some of the courses it contains. To do this, perform the following steps:

1. Log in to your account as *Learner 01*.

2. Once logged in, click the **Content Marketplace** icon at the bottom of the left sidebar.

This takes *Learner 01* to the learner version of **Content Marketplace**. From here, *Learner 01* can use the filters available in the left column, the **Search** field, and the **Sort by** drop-down menu to search for courses:

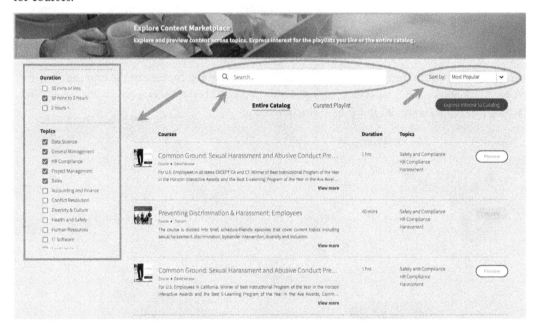

Figure 14.11 – The search tools available to browse Content Marketplace

3. Take the necessary time to browse through **Content Marketplace** using the available search tools. Note that a two-minute preview is available for some of the courses.

4. If you find the course offering interesting, click the **Express Interest to Catalog** button located in the upper-right corner of the page.

5. Click the **Curated Playlist** tab available at the top of the page. From here, you can explore the available playlists and express interest in any of them separately.

6. Make sure you express your interest in some of these playlists before moving on to the next section.

In this section, you reviewed how selected learners can browse **Content Marketplace** and express their interest either for the entire catalog or for any of the available playlists. In the next section, you will return to the admin role and download the **Express interest report** before making a purchase in **Content Marketplace**.

Reviewing the express interest report

After some time, many learners have expressed interest in the content available in **Content Marketplace**. It is now time to review this data and help your organization make an informed decision about purchasing access to all or some of this content.

In this section, you'll discover how administrators can download the **Express interest report** before making a purchase decision. To do this, perform the following steps:

1. Log in to your account as an administrator.

2. From the administrator home page, click the **Content Marketplace** link located in the **Manage** section of the left sidebar.

3. From the **Content Marketplace** page, click the **Enterprise Training** card.

4. Scroll down the **Enterprise Training** page until you see the **Invite Users** section.

5. Click the **Download the Express interest report here** link, as shown in the following screenshot:

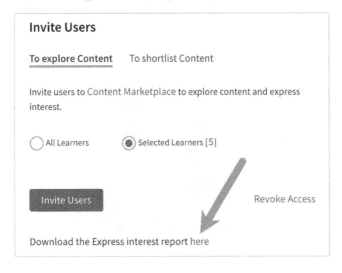

Figure 14.12 – Download the Express interest report

6. Take some time to read the **Download Express Interest Report** message, and click the **OK** button.

7. When the report is ready, a notification appears in the notification icon (the bell icon), located in the upper-right corner of the screen.

The express interest report is a .csv file that can be opened with any spreadsheet application, such as Microsoft Excel, Apple Numbers, or OpenOffice. This report gives you a first indication of how much interest learners have in the content available on Content Marketplace.

Inviting users to shortlist content

If you want more granular and informed guidance on which courses your organization should purchase access to, you can also invite selected Subject-Matter Experts to shortlist the content to be purchased. This is what you will experiment with in this section using the following steps:

1. Log in to your account as an administrator and browse to the **Content Marketplace** page of the admin role.

2. Click the **Enterprise Training** card and scroll down the page until you see the **Invite Users** section.

3. Switch to the **To shortlist content** tab of the **Invite Users** section.

4. Click the **Invite Users** button to open the **Invite Users** dialog.

5. Use the **Search** field to search for the users you wish to invite. Note that you can only select individual users; this dialog does not allow you to select User Groups.

6. Add **Learner 01** to the list of invited users and click the **Invite Users** button.

In addition to being invited to express interest in the entire catalog and in curated playlists, *Learner 01* is now one of the few experts invited to shortlist content for purchase. Let's now return to the learner experience and see how *Learner 01* can accomplish this new mission.

7. Use another browser or a private tab of the same browser to log in to your ALM account as *Learner 01*.

8. As shown in the following screenshot, *Learner 01* now has access to the **Content Hub** page.

Figure 14.13 – Learner 01 now has access to the Content Hub page

The first time *Learner 01* accesses the **Content Hub** page, ALM displays a welcome message with clear explanations on how to use **Content Hub**.

9. Take some time to browse the **Content Hub** using all the available tools. These should be self-explanatory. Along the way, make sure you add items to your personal library.

Once done, *Learner 01* should inform the administrator of their shortlisted items. Note that there is no built-in workflow in Adobe Learning Manager for this step of the process.

> **Note**
>
> In addition to selected subject-matter experts, administrators always have access to the Conent Hub page from their learner experience.

These two workflows (inviting users to explore content and inviting experts to shortlist content) are designed to provide organizations with enough insight to make an informed decision on what content to purchase from the built-in Content Marketplace. In the next section, let's see how you can initiate a purchase directly from the Admin role of Adobe Learning Manager.

Purchasing content in the Content Marketplace

If your organization decides to purchase some or all of the available content, you must return to the **Enterprise Training** page of the admin role and click the link located in the **Purchase** section of the Content Marketplace page to initiate the purchase process with the Adobe sales team. This action is illustrated in the following screenshot:

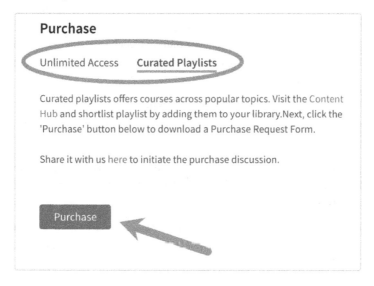

Figure 14.14 – Initiating a purchase process

The Adobe Learning Manager team will process your request and send you an activation key that you can redeem in the **Enter Activation Key** field at the bottom of the page.

This concludes your exploration of the built-in Content Marketplace of Adobe Learning Manager. More information regarding this feature can be found in the official user guide at `https://helpx.adobe.com/learning-manager/administrators/feature-summary/content-marketplace.html`.

Working With Peer Accounts

Most of the time, a single ALM account is enough for an organization to manage its entire training offering. However, it is not uncommon for large organizations to use several different ALM accounts. This provides tremendous flexibility and enables Adobe Learning Manager to be integrated into virtually any type of organization, regardless of size, complexity, and internal structure:

- Multinational organizations can use multiple ALM accounts for their various branches and regional offices.
- Multiple accounts can be used for the different brands owned by a single corporation.
- Some organizations use multiple accounts to increase the security of their training. Courses containing confidential information are hosted on a separate account, which only accredited learners have access to.

The increased flexibility offered by using multiple accounts has three distinct facets.

First, there is the content aspect. Each account has its own content library and its own set of courses, training paths, certifications, and job aids. In addition, as discussed in the *External Sharing* section earlier in this chapter, an ALM account can push content into other accounts using custom catalogs shared externally. This allows each regional office of a multinational organization to manage its course offering independently from the main office and from other branches, while still allowing the main office to push global content into the ALM accounts of its subsidiaries.

Second, there is the financial aspect; in other words, who pays for the seats used in each ALM account? Once again, the great flexibility of Adobe Learning Manager allows you to look at things from different perspectives:

- Organizations can decide to let each account pay for its own use. This is the default scenario. As far as billing is concerned, each ALM account is a different customer that purchases its own set of licenses directly from Adobe.
- Some organizations prefer to purchase all their licenses centrally and distribute them among their various ALM accounts using the **Peer Accounts** feature. In such a case, the costs are fully covered by a single ALM account (usually the global-headquarters account).

- Of course, a combination of these two models is also possible. Part of the available licenses in a specific account can be purchased directly from that account, while another part of the available seats is allocated from another ALM account.

Third, there is the branding aspect. Since each ALM account can be branded independently from each other, peer accounts are very useful for organizations that have multiple brand images with specific logos and colors on each account. This is especially useful for large organizations owning multiple brands.

It is now time to explore the **Peer Accounts** feature, hands-on, using the following steps:

1. Log in to your account as an administrator.

2. From the administrator home page, click the **Settings** link located in the **Configure** section of the left sidebar.

3. Then, click the **Peer Accounts** link located in the **Integrations** section of the left sidebar to open the **Peer Accounts** page of the administrator.

This page displays the list of seats and reports you have shared with other accounts, as well as the list of seats and reports you have received from other accounts. At this time, this page should be empty, as you have not yet shared anything with any other account.

In this example, let's pretend that you are the administrator of the headquarters account and you want to allocate some of the licenses you purchased with this account to the ALM account of one of your local branches:

4. Click the **Add** button located in the upper-right corner of the page to open the **Add Peer Information** dialog.

Notice that only two of the fields in the **Add Peer Information** dialog are required:

- The **Account Subdomain** field is the URL of the ALM account to which you want to allocate seats.

- The **Admin Email ID** field is the email address of an administrator on the receiving ALM account. After completing this form, Adobe Learning Manager sends an email to this address with instructions on how to set up this peer account on the receiving end.

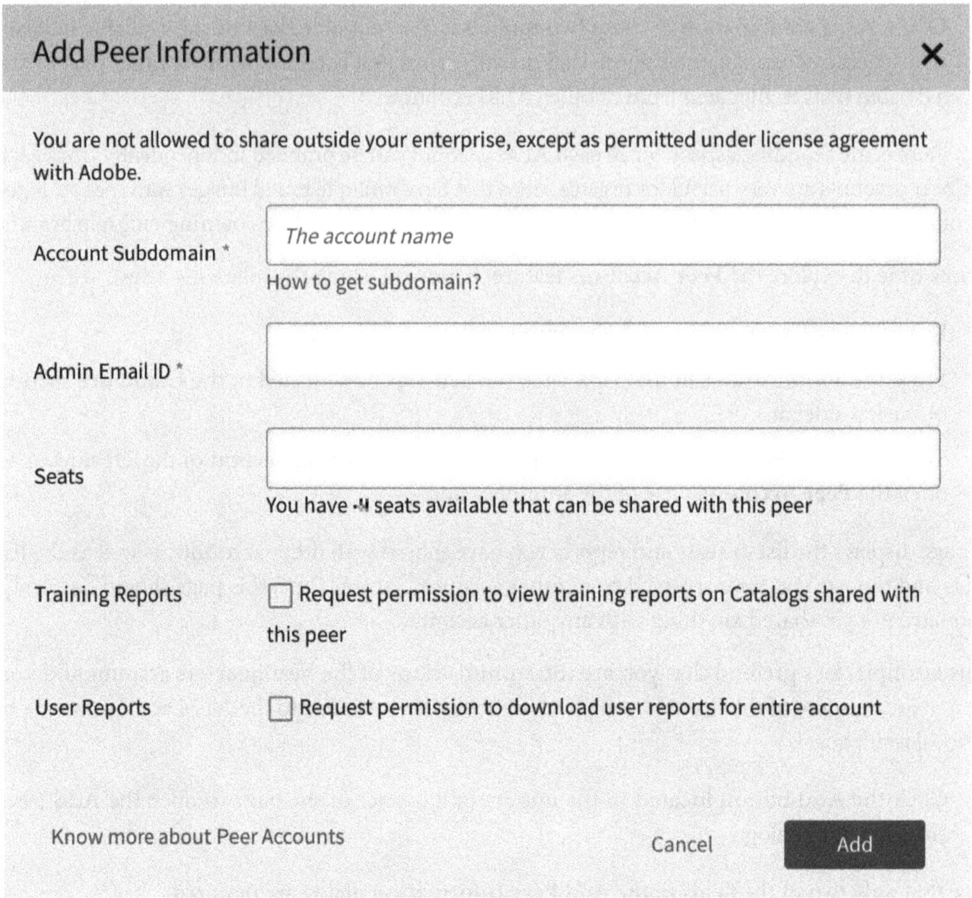

Figure 14.15 – The Add Peer Information dialog

Of course, you should also specify the number of seats you want to allocate to the other account using the **Seats** field.

Optionally, you can use the **Training Reports** and **User Reports** checkboxes to access the reports generated by the peer account you are currently creating. This feature is very useful when you want reports from peer accounts used in your organization to be available centrally (typically in the corporate headquarters ALM account). The reporting capabilities of Adobe Learning Manager were discussed in *Chapter 10, Reporting in Adobe Learning Manager.*

If you have administrator access to another ALM account, feel free to further experiment with this feature. However, in the context of this book, we have to abort the process here using the following steps:

5.   Click the **Cancel** button located in the lower-right corner of the **Add Peer Information** dialog.

This cancels the current process and takes you back to the main **Peer Accounts** page of the administrator.

> **Note**
>
> More information regarding peer accounts can be found in the official ALM user guide at `https://helpx.adobe.com/learning-manager/administrators/feature-summary/peer-account.html`.

Summary

In this chapter, you discovered three important features of Adobe Learning Manager: *Catalogs*, the *Content Marketplace*, and *Peer Accounts*.

Catalogs allow you to control which learners have access to which learning objects. Remember, you don't directly control who has access to which course, but you do control who has access to which catalog. So, by adding courses, learning paths, certifications, and job aids to the various catalogs available in your account, you effectively enforce access control on your learning content.

Catalogs can be shared internally or externally. You use internal sharing to determine which learners *defined within your ALM account* have access to what catalog. The learners defined within your account are all internal *and* external learners, as discussed in *Chapter 5, Managing Users*. You use external sharing when you want learners defined *in other ALM accounts* to access your learning content.

The **Default Catalog** is a special catalog that was created by default with your ALM account. It contains all the learning objects hosted on your account and is visible to all learners by default. While you can change the group(s) of users who have access to the **Default Catalog**, you cannot change its contents and you cannot delete it. Therefore, an effective access control policy often involves disabling the **Default Catalog** altogether.

You can also deploy additional course catalogs using the built-in **Content Marketplace**. Thanks to this feature, organizations can easily purchase access to additional course catalogs from within the Admin role of Adobe Learning Manager.

Peer accounts allow you to purchase large numbers of licenses using a single ALM account and allocate some of these licenses to other accounts. This feature is used by larger organizations that want to centrally control the cost of their ALM deployment while using multiple independent accounts for each of their regional branches.

It is easy to confuse externally shared custom catalogs with peer accounts. To differentiate them, remember that externally shared custom catalogs are intended to make *content* available to other accounts. By using this feature, you are acting on the editorial and instructional design aspects of your course offering.

In contrast, by using peer accounts, you act on the *billing* and *branding* aspects of your ALM deployment.

Since these are two different features, you can decide to use either one of them or both at the same time. This makes Adobe Learning Manager so incredibly flexible that it can fit into virtually any organization, regardless of how it is operated internally.

Throughout the many chapters of this book, you have reviewed multiple features, and Adobe Learning Manager has sent quite a few email messages and notifications. These messages play a critical role in how ALM operates and in how learners engage with the platform. In the next chapter, you'll learn about the announcement and messaging system of Adobe Learning Manager and how to customize these important messages.

15

Working with Messages and Announcements

In previous chapters, you experimented with many of the features of **Adobe Learning Manager**. Along the way, you noticed that ALM sends a lot of email messages to learners. These messages are designed to keep learners engaged in their learning process and to bring them back to the LMS as often as possible.

Let's also be realistic! While we, as instructional designers, all dream of a world where learners learn on their own and naturally engage with the content we give them access to, we must recognize that in the real world, most workers receive their assignments and training requirements in their mailbox or via messages on their phone. In short, messaging is critical to the success of any LMS deployment.

These messages extend the reach of the LMS to the mailbox of each learner and are, for most users, the starting point of many workflows. This is the reason why most organizations take great care in customizing these messages, in terms of both visual design and content.

But emails are just the tip of the iceberg. Adobe Learning Manager also gives you the ability to deliver different types of announcements to specific target audiences. You can use these announcements in a variety of situations, such as promoting new content, sending various types of reminders, and displaying platform-related announcements.

This is what you will discover in this chapter, which is made up of the following main sections:

- Working with announcements
- Configuring the messaging system
- Customizing individual email messages

By the end of this chapter, you will have the necessary tools to take full ownership of your account by customizing the user experience, both on the platform itself and through the messages sent by Adobe Learning Manager.

Technical Requirements

To complete the exercises in this chapter, you must meet the following technical requirements:

- You must have administrator and learner access to a working ALM account (which can be a trial account).

- You must have access to the mailboxes of these users in order to read emails sent by Adobe Learning Manager.

If you have completed the exercises in the previous chapters, you are ready to go. If you have not, feel free to use whatever course material and users are available in your account. However, keep in mind that the instructions in this chapter are based on the exercises from previous chapters, so you will need to adapt them to your situation.

Working With Announcements

Let's pretend that your organization has just subscribed to a new third-party content library or has purchased access to content available in the built-in Content Marketplace. Now you need to inform your learners about the availability of this new content and encourage them to check it out. This is one of the many situations in which Adobe Learning Manager's **announcements** feature comes in handy.

There are three different types of announcements available in Adobe Learning Manager:

- **Notifications** are displayed as dialog boxes and as alerts in the bell icon located in the upper-right corner of the learner experience.

- **Masthead** announcements are displayed in the *Masthead*, which is the upper section of the learner home page.

- Finally, **Recommendations** are used to manually recommend courses to specific target audiences. These manual course recommendations were discussed in *Chapter 13, AI-Powered Recommendations for Learners*, and will not be further discussed in this chapter.

In the next two sections, you will explore the remaining two types of announcements: the *notification* and *masthead* announcements.

Creating Notifications

Notifications are typically used for general platform announcements (such as the winner of a contest, a maintenance downtime, or a corporate event) or for targeted reminders (such as reminding managers to submit their L3 feedback).

In this example, you will create a notification announcing the upcoming annual reset of the gamification points. In the *Configuring Advanced Gamification Options* section of *Chapter 11, Badges and Gamification*, you enabled gamification for internal users only, so you should target your notification at this specific user group.

It is now time to head back to the admin role of your ALM account to create your first notification using the following steps:

1. Log in to your account as an administrator.

2. From the administrator home page, click the **Announcements** link located in the **Manage** section of the left sidebar to open the main **Announcements** page of the administrator.

3. Click the **Add** button located in the upper-right corner of the page to open the **Create Announcement** dialog.

4. At the top of the **Create Announcement** dialog, make sure the **Type** drop-down menu is set to **As notification**.

5. Type your notification message in the **Message** field of the form. Note that this is required information.

HTML message

The **Message** field of the **Create Announcement** form supports HTML. This allows you to enter a snippet of HTML code into the **Message** field rather than just text. This feature is very useful for inserting a hyperlink or adding formatting to the message.

---

6. Optionally, you can attach an image or a video file to your announcement. For this exercise, you can use the announcements/notification.png sample image included in the downloadable files associated with this book.

7. At the bottom of the dialog, the **Target** property is the second required element of the form. In this example, use the **Type Here** field to select the All Internal Users group.

Sending notifications to learners enrolled in a specific course

Using the **Trainings** tab of the **Target** section in the **Create Announcement** form, you can target the notification at learners enrolled in specific courses, learning paths, and certifications instead of relying on user groups.

---

8. Click the **Advanced Settings** link located in the lower-left corner of the form to reveal additional options. Take some time to examine the available options, but do not change any at this time.

9. When the **Create Announcement** dialog looks as in the following screenshot, click the **Save** button, located in the lower-right corner of the form.

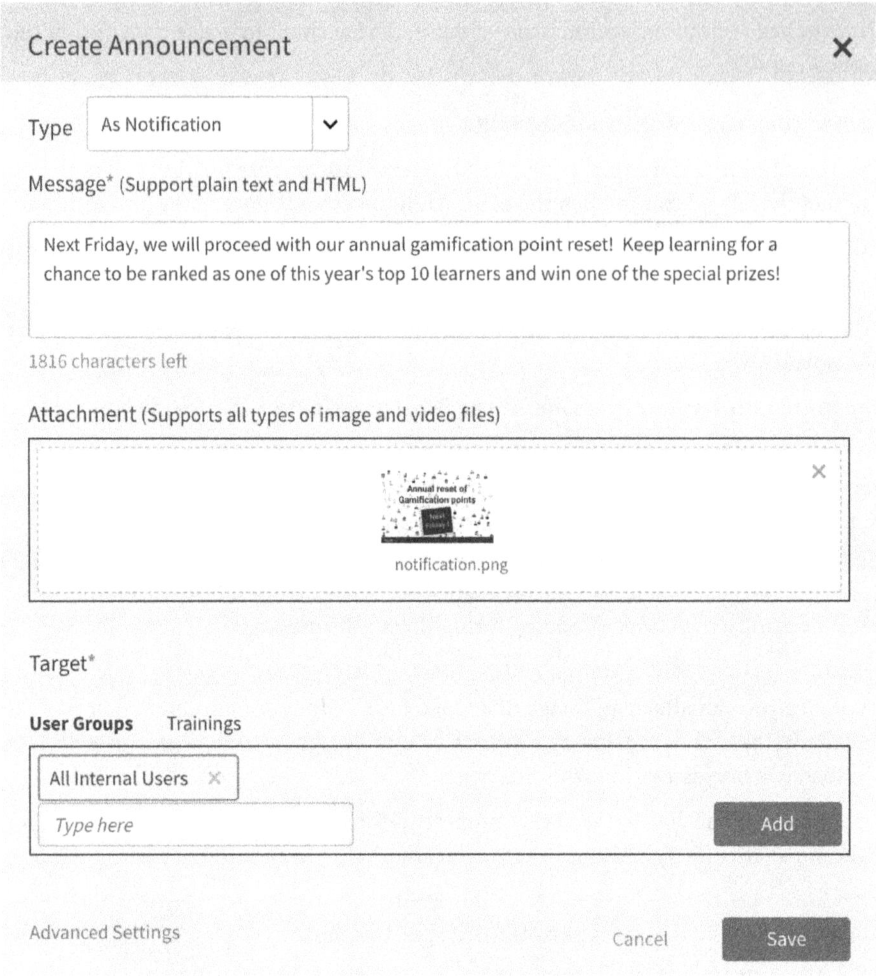

Figure 15.1 – The Create Announcement form when creating a notification

10. Read the **Announcement created successfully** message and click the **OK** button to dismiss it.

Your new notification has been created. It currently appears on the **Draft** tab of the **Announcements** page in the admin role. You still need to publish the announcement to make it visible to learners.

11. Click the *gear* icon associated with your new announcement and take some time to review the available options.

12. When ready, click **Publish**.

13. Finally, switch to the **Published** tab of the **Announcements** page to confirm that your notification is now in the *published* state.

As soon as the notification is published, an email is sent to all learners in the target audience:

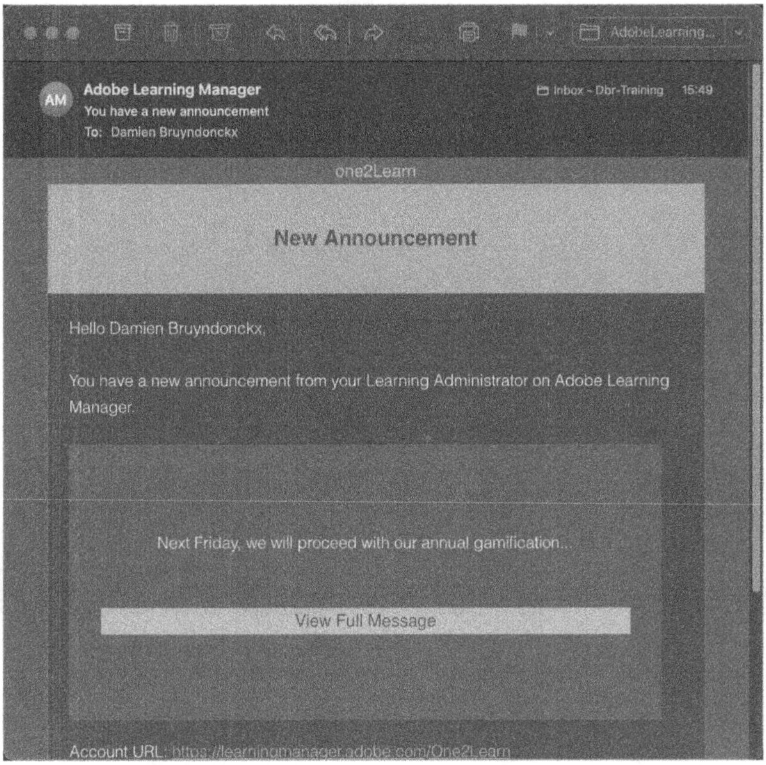

Figure 15.02 – An email is sent to all learners in the target audience

In addition to this email message, the notification is also displayed in the Learner Experience. Let's check this out in the next section.

Notifications in the Learner Experience

Now that you have a published notification, you will log in as an internal learner and see how that notification is displayed in the learner experience:

1. Log in to your account as *Learner 01*.

2. As soon as you are logged in, the notification appears in the middle of the screen. Take a moment to review it, then close it using the close button in the upper-right corner of the notification.

3. The notification is also available by clicking on the bell icon, located in the upper-right corner of the screen.

In this section, you have created a notification that has been emailed to all learners in the target group. In addition, the notification is also displayed in the Learner Experience when the learner logs in.

Keep in mind that the notification is only one of three types of announcements available in Adobe Learning Manager. Also, keep in mind that the target audience for such a notification can be one or more user groups or learners enrolled in specific courses, learning paths, or certifications. Notifications are typically used in situations such as scheduled maintenance outages, general platform or corporate announcements, and targeted reminders.

Creating Masthead Announcements

The Masthead is the big rectangular area that spans the top of the learner experience. It currently encourages learners to *learn something new today*:

Figure 15.3 – The default Masthead of Adobe Learning Manager

This is one of the preferred areas to display all kinds of announcements to learners. For example, you can use the masthead to promote new learning content, announce a corporate event, highlight a company-wide training effort, or announce the winner of the annual gamification points contest! In addition to its prominent position in the user interface, the Masthead can be used as a call to action that redirects learners to another web page.

In this exercise, you will use the masthead to announce the immediate availability of the internal catalog you created in *Chapter 14, Working with Catalogs and Peer Accounts*, providing your internal users with a direct link to this new catalog. To do so, your first task is to grab the link to the internal catalog by following these steps:

1. Make sure you are logged in to your account as an administrator.
2. From the administrator home page, click the **Catalogs** link located in the **Learning** section of the left sidebar.
3. Hover your mouse over the **Internal Catalog** you created in the previous chapter.
4. Click the *chain* icon that appears to copy the direct link to the catalog to the clipboard.

Now that you have copied this link, your next task is to configure your masthead announcement.

5. Click the **Announcements** link, located in the **Manage** section of the left sidebar, to return to the main **Announcements** page of the admin role.

6. Click the **Add** button located in the upper-right corner of the screen to open the **Create Announcement** dialog.

7. At the top of the **Create Announcement** dialog, set the **Type** dropdown to **As Masthead**.

8. For an announcement of the *masthead* type, you must supply either an image or a video file in the **Attachment** field.

    In this example, you can use the `announcements/masthead.jpg` file available in the downloads associated with this book.

Notice the **Language** drop-down menu in the upper-right corner of the **Attachment** section, which allows you to upload a different image for each language you support.

Preferred image sizes

The preferred size for a masthead image or video is 1,280 x 360 pixels. You can review the recommended size of images, as well as other system requirements, on the following page of the official ALM user guide: `https://helpx.adobe.com/learning-manager/system-requirements.html`.

---

9. Paste the link you copied earlier in the **Action Button** field.

10. Finally, add the **All Internal Users** group to the **Target** section of the form.

The ability to target **Masthead Announcements** to specific user groups is very interesting. It allows you to display a different Masthead for each user group, which is particularly useful in many situations, such as customer education scenarios.

11. When the **Create Announcement** dialog looks as follows, click the **Save** button located in the lower-right corner:

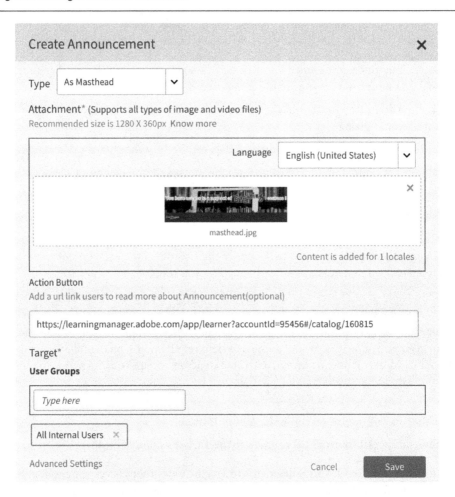

Figure 15.4 – The Create Announcement form when creating a Masthead

12. Click the **OK** button to dismiss the **Announcement created successfully** message.

When Adobe Learning Manager has finished processing the content, your new masthead announcement becomes available in the **Draft** tab of the **Announcements** page. As usual, you must now *publish* the new masthead so that it becomes visible to learners.

13. Click the *gear* icon associated with your new masthead and click **Publish**.

14. Switch to the **Published** tab of the **Announcements** page to confirm that your masthead announcement is now in the *published* state.

A new masthead should now be visible to all the internal learners logging in to your ALM account. Let's take a look at this in the next section.

Mastheads in the learner experience

In this section, you will return to the learner experience and review the masthead you created in the previous section:

1. Log in to your account as *Learner 01* or as any other internal user.

2. As soon as you are logged in, you should see the new masthead spanning the upper portion of the home page:

Figure 15.5 – The new masthead is visible at the top of the learner home page

3. Click the **Learn More** link and confirm that you are being redirected to the **Internal Catalog** page.

> **Multiple mastheads**
>
> If you have multiple Mastheat announcements published at the same time, Adobe Learning Manager displays them as an image carousel.

In this section, you have reviewed *masthead* announcements. Remember that **Mastheads** can be used as calls to action, which is what makes them different from other types of announcements.

In the next section, you will download the **Notification Announcements Report** in order to know which users have seen which announcements.

Exporting the Notification Announcement Report

Several announcements of different types have been published and are currently visible in the learner experience. But does this mean that learners will *actually* view them? What about learners who do not log in very often? Will they see important announcements in time? These are some of the reasons why it is important for administrators to have an overview of who *actually* viewed which announcement.

This is the purpose of the *Notification Announcements Report*, which can be exported from the **Announcements** page of the administrator. Let's take a look at it by performing the following steps:

1. Make sure you are logged in as an administrator.
2. From the administrator home page, click the **Announcements** link located in the **Manage** section of the left sidebar.
3. In the upper-right corner of the **Announcement** page, click the **Actions** button, then click **Export Notification Announcements Report**.
4. Take some time to read the **Generating Report Request** message and click the **OK** button.

Depending on the size of your account and the number of announcements currently being broadcast, it may take a little while for Adobe Learning Manager to generate the report. When the report is ready, a notification appears in the notification area of the administrator, as shown in the following screenshot:

Figure 15.6 – A notification appears when the report is ready

Just click the link in the notification to download the **Notification Announcements Report** in CSV format.

> **The CSV file format**
>
> **CSV** stands for **comma-separated values**. Remember that such a file can be opened in virtually any spreadsheet application, including Microsoft Excel, Apple Numbers, and OpenOffice.

Take the necessary time to open the report using the spreadsheet application available on your system. In the next section, you will review the tools available on the **Announcements** page of the administrator for viewing, editing, and deleting announcements.

Viewing, Modifying, and Deleting Announcements

When you created various types of announcements in the previous sections, you took a look at the advanced options that allow you to schedule the start and/or end date of the announcement, among other things. Since you didn't use these options, your announcements are broadcast immediately and remain visible until you manually withdraw them. Let's take a closer look at this process by following these steps:

1. Log in to your account as an administrator.

2. From the administrator home page, click the **Announcements** link located in the **Manage** section of the left sidebar.

By default, the **Announcements** page of the administrator opens on the **Draft** tab. An announcement is in a draft state when it has been saved but not yet published. Notice the two additional tabs available at the top of the **Announcements** page:

- The **Scheduled** tab displays a list of published announcements with a start date in the future. ALM automatically broadcasts these announcements and moves them to the **Published** tab when their start date is reached.

- The **Published** tab lists all the announcements currently visible to learners. After completing the exercises in the previous sections, this is where the announcements you have created should be displayed.

You can manually withdraw a published announcement using the following steps:

3. Switch to the **Published** tab of the **Announcements** page.

4. Click the *gear* icon associated with your masthead announcement.

5. Click the **Withdraw** option in the menu that opens.

From now on, this masthead is no longer displayed to any learners. Note that this does not remove the announcement from the list of published announcements. You can always modify the announcement and/or broadcast it again later. You can also decide to completely delete the announcement, which is what you will do next.

6. Click the *gear* icon associated with your masthead announcement one more time.

7. Click the **Delete** link available in the menu that opens. Note that the **Delete** option is only available for announcements that have been previously withdrawn.

Finally, let's take a look at how you can edit existing announcements:

8. Click the gear icon associated with any of the remaining published announcements.

9. Click the **Edit** option in the menu that opens to open the **Edit Announcement** dialog.

10. Click the **Advanced Settings** link located in the lower-left corner of the **Edit Announcement** dialog.

11. Try to modify the **Start Date** and/or **End Date** property.

Note that Adobe Learning Manager does not allow you to change the start or end date of a published announcement. However, you can change other options, such as the **Message** and the **Target** audience.

12. Click the **Cancel** button located in the lower-right corner of the **Edit Announcement** dialog to return to the **Published** tab of the **Announcement** page.

This concludes your overview of announcements in Adobe Learning Manager. Remember that Adobe Learning Manager provides three types of announcements: **Recommendations** (as discussed in *Chapter 13, AI-Powered Recommendations for Learners*), **Notifications**, and **Mastheads**.

In the next section, you will review the messaging system of Adobe Learning Manager and learn how to customize the email messages sent by the platform.

Configuring the Messaging System

As you completed the exercises in the previous chapters, the users you defined in *Chapter 5, Managing Users*, received a large number of emails from Adobe Learning Manager. In fact, almost every event triggers an email. Managers receive even more messages because in addition to messages about their activities as learners, they also receive messages about the activities of their team members.

This approach is intentional. These messages are designed to extend the reach of the ALM experience and are a starting point for many learner workflows. This is why many organizations pay particular attention to both the visual design and the content of these email communications.

In this section, you will review the main options used by administrators to configure your account's email system. Use the following steps to do so:

1. Log in to your account as an administrator.

2. From the administrator home page, click the **Email Templates** link located in the **Configure** section of the left sidebar.

3. At the top of the page, click the **Settings** tab, as shown in the following screenshot:

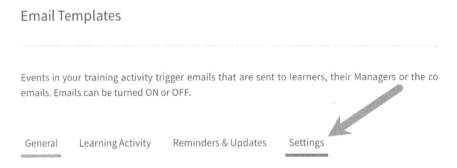

Figure 15.07 – Clicking the Settings tab of the Email Templates page

This tab contains the main configuration options for the ALM email system. Most of these options should be self-explanatory. In the next few sections, you will review the options that require a little more explanation.

Modifying the Sender's Name and Address

Until now, the sender of all the emails sent from your ALM account has been `admin@` `adobelearningmanager.com`. This is the default sender for all ALM accounts. That said, many organizations prefer to use an email address from their own email domain (i.e., an email address that looks like `<name>@<company.com>`) as the sender address.

This is perfectly possible but cannot be done within the admin role of ALM. To configure a custom sender address, it is necessary to contact the Adobe support team at `learningmanagersupport@` `adobe.com`.

Changing the sender's name and address is just the first step in customizing the email messages sent by your ALM account. In the next section, you will learn how to customize the banner and the signature of these messages.

Customizing the email banner and the email signature

All the emails sent from your ALM account start with the same *banner* and end with the same *signature*. In this section, you will customize these elements. As you do so, keep in mind that these options affect all the emails sent from your ALM account.

Perform the following steps to customize the **Email Banner** and **Email Signature**:

1. Make sure you are on the **Settings** tab of the **Email Templates** section of the admin role.

2. Click the **Edit** link associated with the **Email Banner** option.

From here, you can choose a solid background color or upload a custom banner image. In this exercise, you will upload a banner image.

3. Select the **Custom Image** radio button.

4. Upload the `announcements/emailBanner.jpg` image available in the downloads associated with this book.

    Note that the uploaded image must be either a `.jpg` or `.png` file with a size of 1,240 x 200 pixels.

5. When the image is uploaded, switch the **Show Email Text** option to **Yes** to see how the title of the email appears on top of the banner image.

6.   When your screen looks as follows, click the **Save** button to save your changes:

Figure 15.08 – When the new banner is in place, click the Save button

Now that your custom email banner is in place, you will change the email signature.

7.   Click the **Edit** link associated with the **Email Signature** option.

8.   You can now change the email signature for the different languages you support. Click the **Save** button when done.

There are currently no other options to further customize the look and feel of these email messages. For example, you cannot create your own email templates from scratch or add additional templates to your account.

In this section, you customized the look and feel of all the email messages sent from your ALM account. This is a very important step, but it does not affect the number of emails sent from your account, which can quickly become annoying for some people. We'll look at ways to solve this problem in the next two sections.

Disabling Optional Manager Emails

By default, Adobe Learning Manager sends a fairly large number of messages to your learners, but managers receive even more emails than others. First of all, managers are also learners, so they receive all emails related to their activities, just like any other learner. But managers also receive additional emails about the actions of their team members.

Hopefully, you can turn these **Optional Manager Emails** off using the following steps:

1.   Make sure you are on the **Settings** tab of the **Email Templates** section of the admin role.

2.   Deselect the **Optional Manager Emails** checkbox.

With this action, you prevent ALM from sending too many emails to the already overloaded inboxes of busy managers. They'll certainly thank you for that. But on the other hand, don't forget that managers play a critical role in your ALM account. For example, they must review the enrollment requests of their team members in a timely fashion, they must submit their L3 feedback after their team members have completed training, and so on. Now that they're getting fewer reminder emails, make sure you have other strategies in place to remind them of their duties. Targeted announcements and mastheads can help in this respect.

In addition to middle and senior managers, other top-level executives in the organization also need to be protected from receiving too many messages from the corporate LMS. Let's look at this in the next section.

Configuring Do Not Disturb

For most learners, the high number of messages sent by Adobe Learning Manager is not a problem because these emails directly relate to the actions they take on the platform. However, senior managers and other top-level executives are already overwhelmed with tons of emails and don't look forward to the prospect of receiving a bunch of extra automated messages from the corporate LMS.

This is where the **Do Not Disturb** feature of Adobe Learning Manager comes into play. You can use it to limit the number of messages sent to selected individuals, typically members of the senior management team and other top executives in the organization.

Follow these steps to configure the **Do Not Disturb** list:

1. Make sure you are on the **Settings** tab of the **Email Templates** section of the admin role.

2. Click the **Edit List** link associated with the **Do Not Disturb** option.

3. Use the **Search users to add or update** field to select the users that must be on the **Do Not Disturb** list.

   Note that you can only enter users, not user groups. In other words, you can only select one user at a time, which emphasizes the fact that this feature is designed to affect only a small number of selected individuals.

   In this exercise, add any available user to the **Do Not Disturb** list.

4. Open the **Direct Emails** drop-down menu associated with the users you just added.

   As shown in the following screenshot, this allows you to select the type of emails that should be blocked for this particular user:

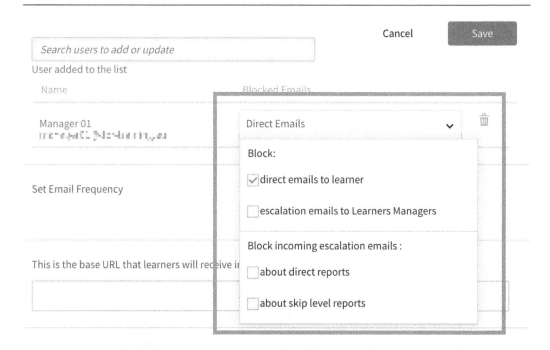

Figure 15.09 – Configuring the Do Not Disturb list

5. You can keep adding individuals to the **Do Not Disturb** list as required and click the **Save** button when done.

The **Do Not Disturb** feature should not be confused with the ability to turn individual email messages on and off. The main difference is that the **Do Not Disturb** feature only affects a small number of individuals, while enabling and disabling emails affects all users of your account.

Configuring the Digest Email Messages feature

In addition to messages triggered by events in your account, Learning Manager can also send bi-weekly (by default) digest emails to learners. However, due to the sheer number of messages sent by regular operations taking place in your account, this option is disabled by default. In this section, you will examine what a digest email looks like. Then, you will discover how to enable and configure the **Digest Email** option.

Let's get started by performing the following steps:

1. Make sure you are on the **Settings** tab of the **Email Templates** section of the administrator.

2. Scroll down the page until you see the **Digest Email Settings** option at the bottom of the page.

3. Click the **(View Email)** link to open a sample digest email message in another browser window/tab.

4. Take some time to review this sample message to get a better idea of what a digest email looks like. Return to the admin role of ALM when you're ready.

Note that the **Edit** link associated with the **Digest Email Settings** option is not available by default. This is because the option is disabled in the main settings of your ALM account. When the **Digest Email** option is enabled, this link allows you to choose the frequency of the digest email. You can choose between bi-weekly (the default) or monthly.

To enable the **Digest Email** option on your account, you need to go to the **Settings | General** page of the admin role. Unfortunately, this option is not available for trial accounts, which is why we can't experiment with it further in this book.

> **Note**
>
> More information on the **Digest Email** feature is available on the following page of the official ALM user guide: `https://helpx.adobe.com/learning-manager/administrators/feature-summary/email-templates.html#digest-email`.

This concludes your exploration of the main email system settings for your ALM account. Keep in mind that everything covered in this section applies to the entire account. In the next section, you will learn how to customize each individual email message.

Customizing individual email messages

At this point, the users you defined in *Chapter 5*, *Managing Users*, should have received a significant number of emails from ALM. Granted, by default, Adobe Learning Manager tends to go a little overboard when it comes to sending emails. Fortunately, you can enable and disable each message individually. You can also completely customize the content of these messages.

This is what you will explore in this section. You'll start by taking a detailed look at the long list of messages available in Adobe Learning Manager and see how to enable and disable them individually.

Enabling and Disabling Messages

There are many events in Adobe Learning Manager that trigger the sending of emails. These messages can be customized in various sections of the admin role:

- The **Email Templates** section of the admin role is the main place to customize the emails sent by Adobe Learning Manager. Any changes made in this section affect the entire account.
- You can override some of the messages defined at the account level for each course, learning path, and certification. This allows you to customize the content of these messages based on the learning activity from which the email originates.

Let's start by reviewing the long list of email messages available at the account level.

Account-level messages

In this section, you will review the list of email messages available in the main **Email Templates** section of the admin role using the following steps:

1. Make sure you are logged in as an administrator.
2. From the administrator home page, click the **Email Templates** link located in the **Configure** section of the left sidebar.

Earlier in this chapter, you reviewed the options available on the **Settings** tab of this page. In this section, you will examine the other three tabs: the **General** tab, the **Learning Activity** tab, and the **Reminders & Updates** tab. Each of these tabs contains a list of email messages that are broadcast whenever a specific event occurs.

3. Take the necessary time to browse the list of messages available on these three tabs.
4. Use the switches in the last column of the table to enable/disable the corresponding email message.

    Note that, by default, all the messages are enabled.

The following screenshot shows the upper portion of the **General** tab of the **Email Templates** page with the **Role Assigned - Instructor** message disabled:

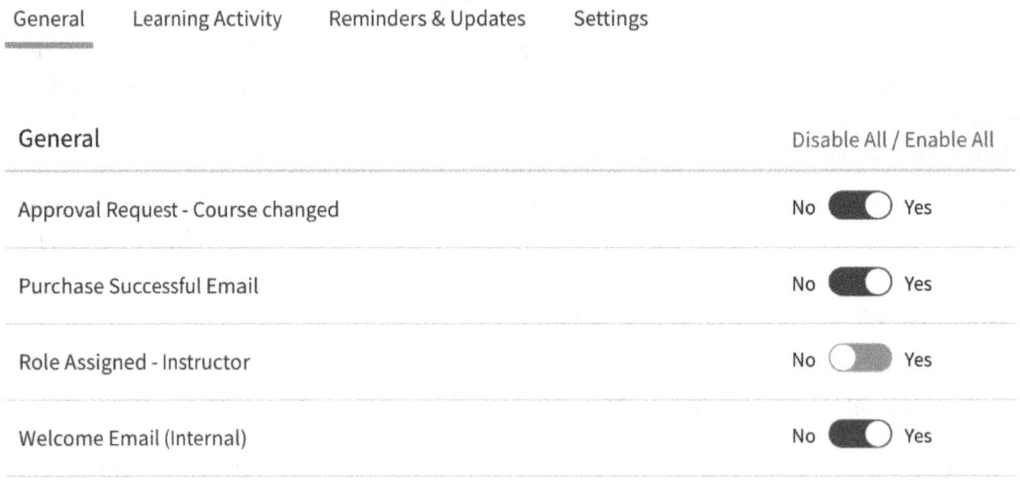

General	Learning Activity	Reminders & Updates	Settings

General	Disable All / Enable All
Approval Request - Course changed	No (Yes
Purchase Successful Email	No (Yes
Role Assigned - Instructor	No) Yes
Welcome Email (Internal)	No (Yes

Figure 15.10 – The Role Assigned - Instructor message is disabled

Now that you have a better idea of the list of messages available at the account level, let's take a look at the **Email Templates** section for courses, learning paths, and certifications.

Email templates for courses, learning paths, and certifications

Each course, learning path, and certification also has its own list of **Email Templates**. By default, these learning objects inherit the email templates defined at the account level, but you can also choose to customize the email templates for each of them. In this case, the options set at the learning object level take precedence over the options set at the account level. Perform the following steps to modify the email templates of a course:

1. Make sure you are logged in to your account as an administrator.

2. Click the **Courses** link located in the learning section of the left sidebar.

3. Click the course whose email templates you wish to modify.

4. Finally, click the **Email Templates** link located in the **Configure** section of the left sidebar.

This opens the list of email templates for that specific course. It works exactly the same way as the account **Email Templates** page you reviewed in the previous section. Just keep in mind that the changes you make here only affect this course and take precedence over account-level settings.

5. Take some time to review the list of available messages.

6. You can use the same process to review the email templates for learning paths and certifications.

By the end of this section, you should have a much better idea of all the email messages sent by ALM. It is important to remember that you cannot add your own messages to this list. However, you can modify the content of each of these messages, which is what you will discover in the next section.

Modifying the Content of Email Messages

In this section, you will learn how to modify the content of the email messages sent by the platform. You will review this process using one of the messages available in the account-level **Email Templates** section, but the process is exactly the same for all other email templates available in the various sections of the admin role.

In this example, you will customize the account-level **Course – Enrolled by Admin/Manager** message. Use the following steps to do so:

1. Make sure you are logged in to your account as an administrator.

2. From the administrator home page, click the **Email Templates** link located in the **Configure** section of the left sidebar.

3. Click the **Learning Activity** tab.

4. Finally, click the **Course – Enrolled by Admin/Manager** message.

As shown in the following screenshot, this action opens the **Template Preview** dialog, which contains all the tools you need to customize the content of the email template:

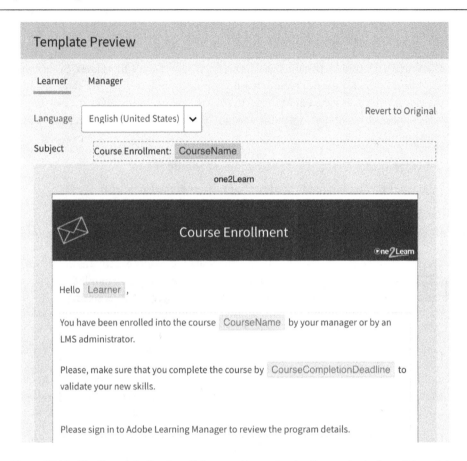

Figure 15.11 – The Template Preview dialog used to customize the content of email templates

5.   At the very top of the **Template Preview** dialog, make sure you are on the **Learner** tab.

The **Learner** tab displays the version of the message sent to learners when the corresponding event occurs. The **Manager** tab displays the version of the message sent to the learner's manager. (Remember that you can disable these manager messages by disabling the **Optional Manager Email** option, in the **Settings** tab.)

6.   Use the **Language** drop-down menu to choose the language version you want to customize.

7.   If needed, you can modify the subject of the message using the **Subject** field.

8.   You can also modify the body of the message, including the message title in the banner.

When modifying the content, there are two types of text elements you can use:

- **Static text** is the text you type using your keyboard. These portions of the text are always the same, regardless of the learner or course involved.

- **Dynamic text** refers to the content that is different each time a message based on this template is sent. For example, the learner's name or the course name are dynamic text elements.

To enter dynamic text, you must use the icons that appear in the upper-right corner of the text field you are editing. For example, in the following screenshot, we are customizing the body of the message. The icons that allow us to include dynamic text in this area are highlighted by the arrow:

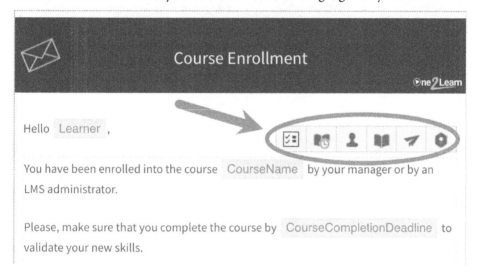

Figure 15.12 – Adding dynamic text to an email template

In the preceding screenshot, the **Learner**, **CourseName**, and **CourseCompletionDeadline** elements are pieces of dynamic content.

9. When done, click the **Save** button located in the lower-right corner of the **Template Preview** dialog.

10. Finally, make sure that the **Course – Enrolled by Admin/Manager** message is enabled (the corresponding switch is set to **Yes**).

From now on, whenever an administrator enrolls a learner in a course, Adobe Learning Manager sends your customized message to that learner. The following screenshot shows the email message received by *learner 02* after an administrator has enrolled that learner in a course.

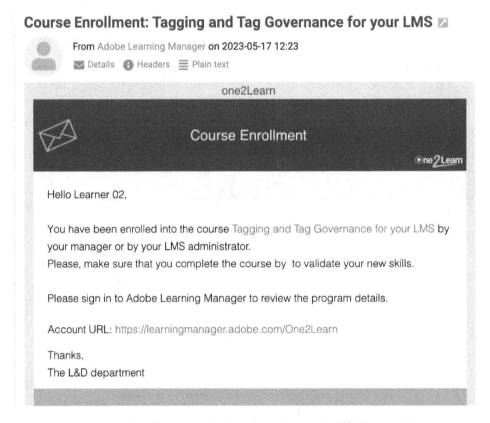

Course Enrollment: Tagging and Tag Governance for your LMS

From Adobe Learning Manager on 2023-05-17 12:23
Details   Headers   Plain text

one2Learn

Course Enrollment

One2Learn

Hello Learner 02,

You have been enrolled into the course Tagging and Tag Governance for your LMS by your manager or by your LMS administrator.
Please, make sure that you complete the course by to validate your new skills.

Please sign in to Adobe Learning Manager to review the program details.

Account URL: https://learningmanager.adobe.com/One2Learn

Thanks,
The L&D department

Figure 15.13 – The customized email message received by Learner 02

In this section, you learned how to modify the content of the email messages sent by Adobe Learning Manager. Remember the following:

- The text you type with your keyboard is considered *static* text and is the same every time the email template is used.
- The pieces you add by clicking the icons available in the **Template Preview** dialog are considered *dynamic* text elements. These elements are different each time the email template is used.
- Most of the time, the same event triggers two emails: one to the learner and one to the learner's manager. You can customize these two messages using the tabs available at the top of the **Template Preview** dialog.
- You can also customize the same message in every language you support by using the **Language** drop-down menu of the **Template Preview** dialog.

These easy-to-use tools allow you to take full ownership of the messages sent from your ALM account. Keep in mind that these messages are an important part of the experience you provide to your learners. So, be sure to personalize them as required.

Summary

One of the challenges of a platform such as Adobe Learning Manager is keeping learners actively engaged over long periods of time. This is especially true in today's hyper-connected world, where each of us is already surrounded by an increasing number of platforms of all kinds.

To overcome this challenge, almost every event occurring on the platform triggers two emails: one to the learner and one to the learner's manager. These emails are designed to extend the reach of Adobe Learning Manager so that learners are always aware of what is happening on the LMS and are constantly encouraged to log back in. Most organizations consider these emails to be an essential aspect of the experience they provide to their learners. Therefore, they spend a lot of time and attention on customizing the look and feel as well as the content of these messages.

While this technique has proven effective, it is not uncommon for learners to complain about the large number of emails they receive from Adobe Learning Manager. This is especially true for managers and other senior executives who receive even more messages than ordinary learners. Fortunately, Adobe Learning Manager allows you to disable **Optional Manager Emails** and place a small group of selected individuals (typically senior managers and other top-level executives) on the **Do Not Disturb** list. You can also customize the content of each message and even decide to enable or disable them individually.

You also reviewed the **Notification**, **Masthead**, and **Recommendation** announcements that are visible to learners when they are logged in. These notifications can be targeted to specific audiences thanks to the user groups available in your ALM account.

These announcements and messages play a key role in bringing your account to life and fostering a true culture of learning and sharing within the organization. This is an important aspect of the learning experience that is certainly worth spending the necessary time and attention on.

But the learning experience provided by the corporate LMS is just one of many elements of the overall experience your organization provides to its employees, partners, suppliers, and customers. One of the landmark features of Adobe Learning Manager is its ability to seamlessly integrate into any corporate environment and augment any existing experience with a training component. This is made possible by the many integrations available out of the box and by the Adobe Learning Manager API. This is what you will explore in the next and final chapter of this book.

16

Exploring the Integration Admin Role

Organizations that use **Adobe Learning Manager** include businesses of all sizes. While small businesses may only use the default standalone configuration of Adobe Learning Manager, most larger organizations already use lots of other enterprise applications to manage their day-to-day operations. For these organizations, the ability to seamlessly integrate with their existing infrastructure is a key factor in deciding whether or not to invest in a solution such as Adobe Learning Manager.

Fortunately, Adobe Learning Manager offers a wide range of tools and features designed to seamlessly integrate into virtually any existing enterprise ecosystem. The ultimate goal of these features is to enable all kinds of data exchange between Adobe Learning Manager and these external systems. This can include user data, course transcripts, attendance reports, and course content from external providers.

In this chapter, you will first discover the connectors available out of the box in Adobe Learning Manager. If no connector is available for the systems used in your organization, you can leverage the Learning Manager **application programming interface (API)** to develop a custom solution.

The API is also what makes Learning Manager a headless LMS. This means that developers can create a fully customized Learner Experience while using Adobe Learning Manager as the backend. Finally, we'll briefly touch on the migration service, which makes it easy to transition from your existing LMS to Adobe Learning Manager.

Configuring, monitoring, and securing these connectors is a task devoted to the **Integration Admin** role, which is the role you will explore in this chapter. To achieve this goal, this chapter is made up of the following main sections:

- Data exchange between Learning Manager and other systems
- Exploring the available connectors
- Automating user creation and updates

- Developing applications with the API
- Discovering the migration process

Thanks to these unique features, you can easily integrate Adobe Learning Manager into the existing IT infrastructure of your organization, regardless of the size or complexity of that environment.

Technical requirements

To perform the exercises in this chapter, you must meet the following technical requirements:

- You must have Administrator and Integration Admin access to a working Learning Manager account, which can be a trial account
- A basic understanding of programming and application development is helpful but not required

You are now ready to discover yet another amazing set of capabilities provided by Adobe Learning Manager.

Data Exchange Between Learning Manager and Other Systems

All the tools and features discussed in this chapter share a common goal: enabling the exchange of data between your ALM account and other IT solutions deployed within your organization. This section briefly describes the types of data that can be exchanged and discusses some typical use cases.

Automated user import

As discussed in *Chapter 5*, *Managing Users*, it is perfectly possible to define users directly within Adobe Learning manager. That being said, virtually every organization maintains some kind of centralized user directory responsible for user authentication.

LDAP-compliant directory solutions, such as Microsoft Active Directory, Azure ADFS, OpenLDAP, and ApacheDS, are among the most popular directory solutions used by organizations of any size.

> **LDAP**
>
> **LDAP** stands for **Lightweight Directory Access Protocol**. It is the most widely used industry standard for accessing and maintaining directory services within a computer network. Most enterprise directory software complies with the LDAP standard.

Since most organizations maintain their list of users in these directories, it doesn't make sense to redefine these same users in Adobe Learning Manager. A better approach is to let Adobe Learning Manager regularly query these external directories to automatically update its user list.

This use case will be discussed in more detail in the *Automating User Creation and Updates* section later in this chapter.

Automated User Skills export

As discussed in *Chapter 4, Creating Skills and Courses*, the concept of *skills* is central to the way Adobe Learning Manager works.

For many organizations, skills management is not limited to administering the training department but is part of a broader human resources management framework. For example, many organizations offer additional benefits or career opportunities to individuals who have acquired certain skills.

To facilitate this type of administration, Adobe Learning Manager allows you to automatically export learner skills reports to your preferred human resources management system.

Exporting report data from Adobe Learning Manager

Adobe Learning Manager produces a lot of data. But so do most of the other applications you use in your organization. The ability to export data from Adobe Learning Manager allows you to integrate that data into much larger datasets produced by a wide range of systems across the organization. As a result, organizations can use data mining and visualization technologies to cross-reference ALM-generated learning data with a host of other data from various sources as part of their overall business intelligence efforts.

Data exchange with virtual classroom solutions

In *Chapter 4, Creating Skills and Courses*, you learned that Adobe Learning Manager can be used to deliver instructor-led synchronous training activities, either face-to-face or using a virtual classroom solution.

> **Asynchronous versus Synchronous activities**
>
> As a reminder, *Asynchronous* modules are self-paced training content that learners access individually at their own convenience. *Synchronous* activities are live instructor-led face-to-face or virtual classes where multiple participants are together in the same physical or virtual space.

Synchronous modules are hosted in your content library, as described in *Chapter 3, Uploading Learning Content and Managing the Content Library*. But Adobe Learning Manager has no built-in solution for conducting virtual classrooms, so you must rely on external virtual classroom solutions, such as Zoom, Microsoft Teams, or Adobe Connect.

Fortunately, Adobe Learning Manager has built-in connectors for the most popular virtual classroom solutions. They allow you to automatically sync data, such as attendance, interactions, and completion statuses, with your ALM account.

Integration of external content libraries

Adobe Learning Manager can exchange data with virtually any third-party content library, either through a dedicated connector or some custom development using the API. This allows you to display the courses provided by these external libraries directly in your ALM account and track your learners' interactions with this external content.

Connecting to cloud services and FTP accounts

Finally, Adobe Learning Manager can import and export all kinds of data using an FTP connection. This allows you to define custom workflows for data exchange in CSV format between Adobe Learning Manager and virtually any enterprise solution used in your organization.

> **CSV and FTP**
>
> **CSV** stands for **comma-separated values**. A CSV file is a delimited text file that uses a separator (usually a comma, tab, or semicolon) to separate each value. The CSV file format is a very popular generic solution for exchanging data between all kinds of systems. **FTP** stands for **File Transfer Protocol**. It is a standard communication protocol used for transferring files between computers.

As an example, we will review one such workflow in detail in the *Automating User Creation and Updates* section later in this chapter. But first, let's recap what you have learned in this section.

This section has introduced you to the main types of data that can be exchanged between Adobe Learning Manager and other enterprise systems used within the organization. In essence, these data exchanges can be categorized as follows:

- **User data**: This allows ALM to retrieve user data maintained in other systems
- **Reporting data**: This allows you to export data from Adobe Learning Manager for further analysis with dedicated data mining and visualization tools
- **Learning activity data**: This allows you to sync data between Adobe Learning Manager and external virtual classroom solutions or external content libraries

The easiest way to implement these data exchanges is to use the built-in connectors available in the Integration Admin role of Adobe Learning Manager. So, in the next section, you will log in as an Integration Admin and take a first look at the available connectors.

Exploring the Available Connectors

In the previous section, you learned about the main types of data that can be exchanged to and from Adobe Learning Manager. Now it's time to look at ways to implement these connections within your account.

Use the following steps to log in as an **integration admin** and explore the connectors available out of the box in Adobe Learning Manager:

1. Log in to your account as an administrator (or as any other user that has the **Integration Admin** role assigned).

2. Click the user icon located in the upper-right corner of the screen and switch to the **Integration Admin** role.

By default, the Integration Admin role opens to the list of available connectors. Each of these connectors has a unique set of capabilities and configurable options. Let's take a look at how to learn about the capabilities of each connector.

3. Hover your mouse over the **Salesforce** connector and click the **Getting Started** link that appears on the screen.

This opens a page describing the main capabilities of the **Salesforce** connector, as shown in the following screenshot:

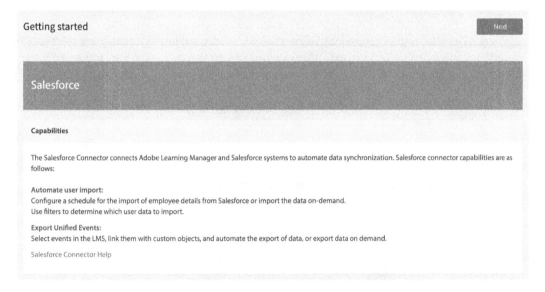

Figure 16.1 – The Getting started page of the Salesforce connector

From here, you learn that you can use the Salesforce connector for *automated user import*. In other words, all the users defined in your Salesforce account can automatically become users of your Adobe Learning Manager account as well.

You also have the ability to *export unified events*, which means that you can configure ALM to automatically send all kinds of data to Salesforce (such as learning transcripts, user reports, and skills reports) whenever an event occurs (such as training enrollment, training completion, skill completion, or a new user being added).

More information on the Salesforce connector can be found in the official ALM user guide at `https://helpx.adobe.com/learning-manager/integration-admin/feature-summary/connectors.html#connector_salesforce`.

> **About Salesforce**
>
> **Salesforce** is a popular cloud-based **Customer Relationship Management** (**CRM**) service provided by Salesforce.com, Inc., a San Francisco-based software company. More information on Salesforce can be found on the official Salesforce website at `https://www.salesforce.com/`.

4. To connect your Salesforce account to your ALM account, click the **Next** button located in the upper-right corner of the page.

First, you need to enter your organization's Salesforce URL, which requires that you have a Salesforce subscription. If you have one, feel free to further experiment with this connector, but for the purposes of this exercise, we'll go back to the list of available connectors and continue our exploration.

5. Click the **Back to Connectors** link located at the top of the left sidebar to return to the list of available connectors.

6. Hover over any of the available connectors to reveal the corresponding **Getting Started** link, which opens a page that further explains the capabilities of the chosen connector.

   Take the necessary time to repeat the preceding steps with the other connectors to have a better idea of their respective capabilities.

In this section, you have reviewed the connectors that are available out of the box with Adobe Learning Manager.

> **Note**
>
> These connectors are developed by the Adobe Learning Manager team. Adding custom connectors to the list is currently not supported.

As an example, in the following section, you will configure one of these connectors to set up a process for automatically importing and updating user data from an external system.

Automating User Creation and Updates

In the *Creating internal and external users* section of *Chapter 5, Managing Users*, you reviewed different methods for adding internal and external users to your Adobe Learning Manager account. These methods work fine and may well cover your needs, but they also have serious limitations, especially for large organizations:

- Most large organizations already have directories where the user data ALM needs to work is already available. Therefore, it makes little sense to duplicate this data in the ALM account.

- Creating users is one thing, but maintaining the user list over time is a completely different challenge. This is another instance where duplicating user data makes little sense. ALM should be able to update its user list whenever the central corporate directory is updated.

As an enterprise LMS, Adobe Learning Manager acknowledges this situation and understands that it must scale with your organization, no matter how large your business grows.

To illustrate the use of the built-in connectors, you will now configure an automated user import and update process over the next few sections. We will use generic technologies (i.e., CSV and FTP), which work with virtually any third-party directory service. That said, keep in mind that Adobe Learning Manager may have a dedicated connector for the technology you use in your organization, in which case you would use that dedicated connector rather than the workflow described here.

Configuring the ALM FTP connector

Virtually every enterprise-grade directory solution can *export* data as CSV files. It turns out that Adobe Learning Manager is particularly good at *importing* user data in CSV format, as discussed in *Chapter 5, Managing Users*. The trick is to have your corporate directory export its data to a location where Adobe Learning Manager can automatically retrieve it at regular intervals.

The first step in setting up this workflow is to configure the FTP connection that will be used to automatically upload user data to Adobe Learning Manager. If your organization already has an FTP server, you can use the **Custom FTP** connector to connect your ALM account to your existing FTP. If you do not have an FTP server available, Adobe has partnered with an external organization called **ExaVault** to provide you with the necessary FTP service. This service is available through the built-in **Adobe Learning Manager FTP** connector, which you will now configure using the following steps:

1. Make sure you are logged in as an Integration Admin and that you are on the home page of the integration admin role.

2. Hover over the **Adobe Learning Manager FTP** connector to reveal the available options.

3. Click the **Connect** link.

4. Enter your email address and click the **Connect** button located in the upper-right corner of the screen.

5. Optionally, you can choose a name for your connection in the **Connection Name** field. Click the **Save** button located in the upper-right corner of the screen to save your changes.

After a few moments, you should receive an email from the *ExaVault* company, asking you to set up your FTP password.

6. Click the link in the email message and follow the on-screen instructions to create your ExtraVault password.

> **ExaVault**
>
> *ExaVault* is the company Adobe has partnered with to offer you the Adobe Learning Manager FTP service. This service is part of your ALM subscription and comes at no extra cost. It is also available to trial accounts for the duration of the trial. Note that you can only configure a single ExaVault account for each ALM account.

Take good note of the FTP server URL (**https://primedev.exavault.com/**) and your username (**primeuser-XXXXXX**). Both pieces of information are available in the welcome email you receive from ExaVault. Along with the password you just created, these are the credentials you need to transfer the CSV files exported from your internal user directory.

After completing these steps, you have access to an FTP server. The next step is to map the columns of the exported CSV file to the fields expected by Adobe Learning Manager.

Mapping the import fields

Each organization and directory solution has its own way of naming fields and exporting CSV files. Therefore, it is important to map the columns in the exported CSV file to the fields that Adobe Learning Manager expects. To do this, you must return to the Integration Admin role and perform the following steps:

1. Make sure you are logged in as an Integration Admin.

2. From the integration admin home page, hover over the **Adobe Learning Manager FTP** connector to reveal the available options.

3. Click the **Manage Connections** link to open the **Manage Connections** page.

4. Click the name of your FTP connection to open a page listing the **Capabilities** of this FTP connection.

5. Click the **Import Internal Users** link located in the **Capabilities** section.

Now you need to import a CSV file generated by the directory service you want to synchronize ALM with. At this point, the goal is not to import users but to map the columns in this CSV file to the fields of Adobe Learning Manager. Of course, subsequent imports must all use a CSV file with the same structure, that is, a CSV file with exactly the same set of columns each time.

6. Click the **Choose CSV** link located at the end of the description message at the top of the page.

7. Use the `users/importUsers.csv` file of the download associated with this book. This CSV file contains seven columns and five rows.

8. Map the **Adobe Learning Manager** fields (in the left column) to the fields of the CSV file (in the right column), using the drop-down lists in the right column.

    Note that the **Name**, **Email**, **Profile**, and **Manager** fields are required. Make sure that you map at least those fields.

9. When your screen looks as follows, click the **Save** button located in the upper-right corner of the screen:

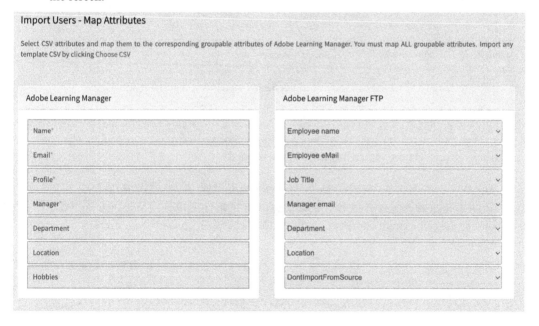

Figure 16.02 – Mapping the ALM fields to the columns of the CSV file

After completing these steps, ALM knows where to find the information it needs in the CSV files generated by your organization's user directory. In the next section, you will inspect the CSV file, prepare it for upload, and upload it to your ExaVault FTP account.

Uploading user data with the ALM FTP connector

Adobe Learning Manager is now ready to accept the CSV files exported from your central user directory. In this section, you will explore the sample CSV file, get it ready, and upload it to ExaVault FTP by performing the following steps:

1. Open the `users/importUsers.csv` file using the spreadsheet application installed on your system.

As shown in the following screenshot, the CSV file contains seven columns and five rows (in addition to the header row at the top of the file). If you have performed the exercises in *Chapter 5, Managing Users*, these users should already be defined in your ALM account:

	A	B	C	D	E	F	G
				importUsers			
1	Employee name	Employee eMail	Employee ID	Department	Job Title	Location	Manager email
2	<YOUR NAME HERE>	<YOUR EMAIL HERE>	ADMIN	ADMIN	CEO	<YOUR CITY HERE>	
3	Manager 01	<ADD EMAIL HERE>	M453379	Marketing	Marketing Manager	San Jose	<YOUR EMAIL HERE>
4	Learner 01	<ADD EMAIL HERE>	L8734	Marketing	Marketing Specialist	San Jose	<MANAGER 01 EMAIL HERE>
5	Learner 02	<ADD EMAIL HERE>	L547896	Marketing	Marketing Specialist	San Jose	<MANAGER 01 EMAIL HERE>
6	Instructor 01	<ADD EMAIL HERE>	I596321	Learning & Development	Senior Trainer	New York	<YOUR EMAIL HERE>

Figure 16.03 – The users/importUsers.csv file, as seen in a spreadsheet application

Before uploading this CSV file to ExaVault FTP, it is necessary to adjust its content. Note that these adjustments are only necessary because of the educational situation this book puts you in. When using this workflow in production, such adjustment is not needed.

2. Type your name in cell A2, your ALM admin email address in cell B2, and your city in cell F2.

3. Add the email addresses of all four remaining users in the **Employee eMail** column. Make sure you use the same email addresses as those used when you created these users in *Chapter 5, Managing Users*.

4. Enter your ALM admin email address in cells G3 and G6 to define you as the manager of both *Manager 01* and *Instructor 01*.

5. Enter the email address of *Manager 01* in cells G4 and G5 to define *Manager 01* as the manager of both *Learner 01* and *Learner 02*.

    This configuration defines a three-level hierarchy where you are the *General Manager* and where *Manager 01* manages a small team of two employees.

6. Feel free to add additional users in the CSV file using the same pattern.

> **Defining managers**
>
> When importing the file, ALM reads it from top to bottom. Therefore, it is very important to define managers at the top of the file, before defining their team members: a user must exist before being defined as someone else's manager.

7. Save the CSV file when done.

> **Double-check the CSV file before uploading it**
>
> Remember that, depending on the regional settings of your system, the separator used in the CSV file may have been replaced with something else than a comma (,). To resolve this potential problem, open the CSV file in a text editor (such as Notepad on Windows or TextEdit on Mac) and use the *Find and Replace* feature to replace the separator used by your system with commas (,).

8. Open a new browser window and browse to `https://primedev.exavault.com/`.

9. Log in to your ExaVault account using the username you received via email and the password you created earlier.

10. Once logged in, browse to the `import/user/internal` folder of your ExaVault account.

11. Use a drag-and-drop action or the **Upload** button located in the upper-right corner of the ExaVault interface to upload the `users/internalUsers.csv` file.

> **Note**
>
> When running this workflow in production, you will not upload these CSV files manually as you do here. Instead, you will use an automated process to upload the CSV file generated by your enterprise directory to ExaVault. Some directory services even have a built-in FTP upload mechanism. Consult the documentation of your directory service to know your options and choose the one that best suits your situation.

After completing this section, the CSV file exported from your corporate directory has been successfully uploaded to your ExaVault account. The final step is to have Adobe Learning Manager connect to Exavault and fetch this CSV file at regular intervals. This is what you will do in the next section.

Configuring a data source

In this section, you will return to the Admin role of your ALM account and configure the periodic data import from your ExaVault FTP account. Use the following steps to do so:

1. Make sure you are logged in as an Administrator.

2. From the Administrator home page, click the **Settings** link located in the **Configure** section of the left sidebar.

3. Now, click the **Data Sources** link located in the **Integrations** section of the left sidebar.

Once on the **Data Sources** page, you should see the ExaVault FTP connection you configured in the previous sections listed as a potential data source, as shown in the following screenshot:

Sources

Source: One2Learn Extravault Connection   Edit

Import not enabled

Sync Settings

Enable Auto Sync   ☐

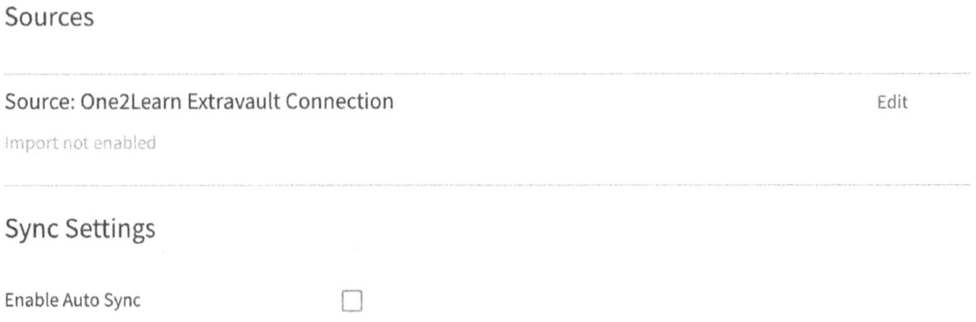

Figure 16.4 – The ExaVault FTP connection configured earlier is listed as a data source

4. Click the **Edit** link associated with your ExaVault data source.

5. Select the **Enable Import** checkbox.

6. Also, select the **Enable Auto Sync** checkbox located in the **Sync Settings** section at the bottom of the page.

7. Click the **Sync Time** field and choose a suitable sync time.

8. Finally, click the **Sync Now** link to trigger the synchronization process immediately. This allows you to test that everything is working correctly and that the daily automatic synchronizations are likely to succeed.

9. Don't forget to click the **Save** button in the upper-right corner of the screen to save your changes.

After a few moments, you should receive a notification telling you that the CSV processing was successful, as shown in the following screenshot:

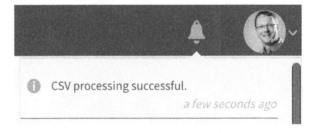

Figure 16.5 – The CSV processing successful notification

Let's check this out by returning to the **Internal Users** page of the admin role.

10. Click the **Back** button located at the top of the left sidebar to return to the Administrator home page.

11. Click the **Users** link located in the **Manage** section of the left sidebar.

12. Confirm that the information about the available users matches the data in the CSV file.

In this section, you have configured a workflow that automatically synchronizes the list of users in your ALM account. This allows you to automate not only the creation of new users but also the updating of existing users. All you need to do is configure your internal user directory to export the CSV file once a day to the ExaVault account, moments before Adobe Learning Manager imports the data.

This illustrates one approach to integrating Adobe Learning Manager with virtually any directory solution used in organizations around the world.

Automatic and manual CSV uploads are not compatible

Since you have configured a data source, manually importing CSV files using the process described in the *Importing users from a CSV file* section of *Chapter 5, Managing Users*, is no longer possible.

Out-of-the-box connectors cover the most popular enterprise applications and services used by organizations around the world. But in an ever-changing technology landscape, it is impossible to provide a dedicated connector for every possible external application. Chances are, the application used within your organization is not covered by any of these connectors. In such a case, you need to rely on the ALM API and some custom development to integrate your ALM account with the solution used in your organization. This is what will be discussed in the next section.

Developing applications with the API

API stands for **Application Programming Interface**. It is a type of interface commonly used by developers to have different application connect to each other and exchange data. Thanks to the Adobe Learning Manager API, any data contained in your account and any services provided by Adobe Learning Manager can be programmatically accessed and integrated into any type of custom application developed by your in-house development team.

Here are some of the most common use cases involving the Adobe Learning Manager API:

- Some organizations want to replace the default learner experience with a fully customized application or website. To do this, they develop their own website/application and use the Adobe Learning Manager API to access the necessary data and services (such as details about the logged-in user, the list of available courses, and completion statuses) and to report learner interactions to the ALM backend. This is referred to as using Adobe Learning Manager as a *headless* LMS.

- You can use the API to develop your own custom connectors when the built-in connectors are not enough.

- You can use the API to build a custom application that extends the native capabilities of Adobe Learning Manager.

These are just a few of the many instances in which the API is useful.

If this sounds a little technical, remember that the Adobe Learning Manager API is intended for developers. As an administrator or integration admin, you don't need to fully understand how developers implement the API in the applications they build.

The only thing you need to know is that the Adobe Learning Manager API uses a security framework called **OAuth 2.0** to authenticate and authorize external applications. This security framework requires that you generate security tokens for each external application that needs access to your ALM account via the API.

> **OAuth**
>
> **OAuth** stands for **Open Authorization**. If it is an open industry standard used to grant websites and other applications secure access to each other. More information on the OAuth standard can be found on the official OAuth website at `https://oauth.net/`. I strongly suggest you watch the video on their home page for a quick but thorough explanation of what OAuth is.

To experiment with this workflow, let's imagine you want to use Adobe Learning Manager as a headless LMS, so you need to develop a custom website/app that will serve as the learner experience for your users. This custom website/app will be hosted by you and will access the ALM backend through the API. Therefore, you need to register this application with your ALM account and generate the necessary security tokens by following these steps:

1. Log in to your account as an integration admin.

2. From the integration admin home page, click the **Applications** link located in the left sidebar.

3. Click the **Register** button located in the upper-right corner of the page to open the **Register a new application** page.

4. Type an application name in the **Application Name** field. This is nothing technical, so feel free to choose any name you deem appropriate. Note that this name cannot be changed afterward.

5. Provide the URL where your custom application will be hosted in the **URL** field.

   For the purpose of this exercise, just type the URL of your website or any other valid URL.

6. Type `https://*.<the_address-Of_your_website>` in the **Redirect Domains** field.

   These are the domains where it is safe to redirect users after they have authenticated with the OAuth server. Note that you can add multiple redirect domains in this field.

7. As a best practice, take the necessary time to provide a brief description of the application you are registering.

8. In the **Scopes** section, select the checkboxes required by your application.

   In this example, you are building a custom learner experience, but you will still be using the native ALM admin role to build courses and administer your LMS. So, you only need to select **Learner role read access** and **Learner role write access**.

   With this configuration, your custom application will be authorized to read and write anything related to the learner role, but you will not be able to use it to remotely administer your ALM account.

9. If you want this application to be visible to the other administrators of your ALM account, select the **No** radio button in the **For this account only?** field; otherwise, leave it as **Yes**.

10. When the **Register a new application** page looks as in the following screenshot, click the **Save** button in the upper-right corner of the page:

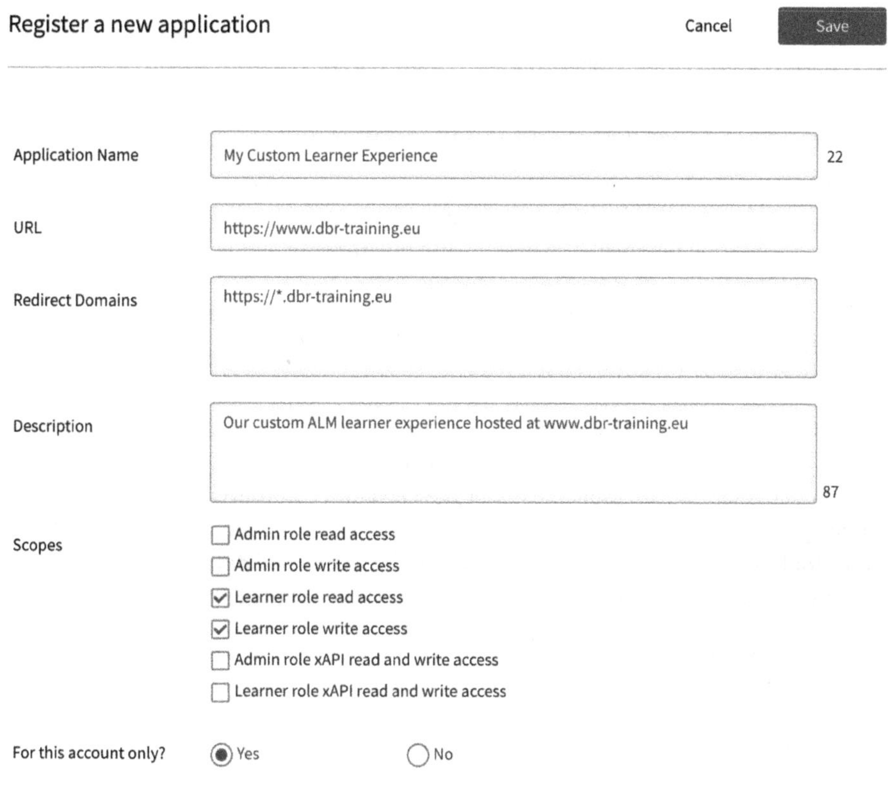

Figure 16.6 – The Register a new application page

11. As soon as you click the **Save** button, the page refreshes and displays the **Application ID** and the **Application Secret**. These are the security tokens that your developers need to include in every request they send to the Adobe Learning Manager API.

Application ID	4b705fd7-06bc-4fcb-afb4-8bd169ed1689
Application Secret	1ac0f4a4-6728-43b9-bf35-a964feb68f60
Application Name	My Custom Learner Experience

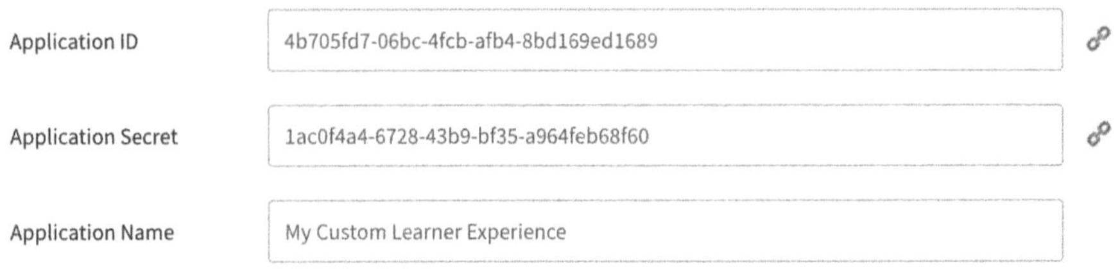

Figure 16.7 – The application ID and the application secret are generated when you click Save

12. Click the **Back to Applications** link located at the top of the left sidebar to return to the **Applications** page of the integration admin role.

When back on the **Applications** page, confirm that your newly registered application appears on the page. If needed, you can click this application to edit its details or delete it entirely.

> **Internal and external applications**
>
> The application you have registered in this section is considered an *internal* application. External applications are either provided by Adobe Learning Manager or developed by ALM partners. To register an application provided by a partner, use the **Approve** button located in the upper-right corner of the **Applications** page and enter the application ID that was provided by that partner. To use any of the applications provided by Adobe Learning Manager, use the **Featured Apps** tab of the **Applications** page.

When it comes to the API, your role as integration admin pretty much ends here. It is now up to your developers to take it further and make your custom application a reality. To help them out, all the necessary developer resources are available under the **Developer Resources** link located in the left sidebar. On that page, you find the Adobe Learning Manager **API Reference**, **Application Developer Manual**, and a tool to generate temporary access tokens for testing and development. If you are into development, these resources give you all the information you need to get started.

In this section, you learned how to register applications so developers can access your account programmatically using the Adobe Learning Manager API.

In the next section, you will briefly discuss the migration process, which facilitates the transition from your current enterprise LMS to Adobe Learning Manager.

Discovering the migration process

If your organization already has an LMS, the migration process helps you migrate the training data and content that exists in your current solution to Adobe Learning Manager.

To initiate a migration project, you must contact the ALM support team, who will activate the functionality in your account.

Basically, the migration process uses the following main steps:

- First, you need to export the data from your current LMS as .csv files.

- Next, you must match the information exported from your current LMS with the information expected by Adobe Learning Manager. The Adobe support team will help you by providing the necessary technical information on how to prepare the data so that it imports flawlessly into Adobe Learning Manager.

- Finally, you must use the migration wizard available in the integration admin role to import the data in ALM. This must be done in a certain order and data integrity checks must be performed throughout the entire process. Once again, the Adobe support team will help you get through this process and troubleshoot any issues that may arise.

To learn more about the migration process, please refer to the migration manual in the official ALM user guide at https://helpx.adobe.com/learning-manager/integration-admin/feature-summary/migration-manual.html.

Summary

In this chapter, you learned about the tools and features available in the Integration Admin role. These allow you to connect your ALM account to other enterprise tools and services used in your organization. All these tools and features are geared toward a single goal: enabling data exchange between ALM and the rest of your IT infrastructure.

To do so, Adobe Learning Manager includes a number of connectors that allow you to integrate your account with the most common enterprise applications used by organizations around the world. If there is no built-in connector for the solution your organization uses, or if your project requires additional custom development, you can use the Adobe Learning Manager API to programmatically access every aspect of your ALM account.

In this case, remember that Adobe Learning Manager uses the OAuth 2.0 security framework to authenticate and authorize external applications requesting access to your account via the API. Generating secure requests to the API is the responsibility of your developers. Your only responsibility as an integration admin is to register these applications in your ALM account and communicate the necessary security tokens to the development team.

Finally, you discovered the migration wizard of Adobe Learning Manager. This feature is designed to help organizations transition from their current LMS over to ALM. Keep in mind that the migration assistant is not enabled by default. You need to contact the Adobe support team to activate it so they can assist you with your migration project.

With the end of this final chapter, our journey together comes to an end. I hope you enjoyed the ride and found the necessary information for implementing ALM in your organization.

I thank you for reading this book and wish you a lot of success (and fun!) with Adobe Learning Manager.

Index

www.packtpub.com

Subscribe to our online digital library for full access to over 7,000 books and videos, as well as industry leading tools to help you plan your personal development and advance your career. For more information, please visit our website.

Why subscribe?

- Spend less time learning and more time coding with practical eBooks and Videos from over 4,000 industry professionals

- Improve your learning with Skill Plans built especially for you

- Get a free eBook or video every month

- Fully searchable for easy access to vital information

- Copy and paste, print, and bookmark content

Did you know that Packt offers eBook versions of every book published, with PDF and ePub files available? You can upgrade to the eBook version at packtpub.com and as a print book customer, you are entitled to a discount on the eBook copy. Get in touch with us at customercare@packtpub.com for more details.

At www.packtpub.com, you can also read a collection of free technical articles, sign up for a range of free newsletters, and receive exclusive discounts and offers on Packt books and eBooks.

Other Books You May Enjoy

If you enjoyed this book, you may be interested in these other books by Packt:

Next-Level Instructional Design

Susan Nelson Spencer

ISBN: 978-1-80181-951-0

- Explore the four key competencies in detail—teaching, writing, creating, and analyzing
- Understand the importance of building upon all four key competencies of an effective instructional designer
- Develop and grow each competency through helpful and practical tips, not just theory
- See what really happens in the "real world" of instructional design through myth busters
- Discover common pitfalls and mistakes made by almost every instructional designer
- Recognize practical teachable moments derived from real-world case studies

Moodle 4 Administration - Fourth Edition

Alex Büchner

ISBN: 978-1-80181-672-4

- Get expert techniques to handle courses, categories, and enrolments in Moodle
- Manage users, cohorts, roles, and authentication in a professional manner
- Configure and manage core and third-party plugins and integrations like a pro
- Explore different levels of technical and educational configuration
- Enhance Moodle's look and feel to create engaging user experiences and ensure compliance with your corporate branding
- Gain insights by creating powerful custom reports and learning analytics
- Ensure your Moodle or Moodle Workplace complies with the latest GDPR regulations
- Support different learning settings, including home-office based learning, mobile learning, and multi-tenancy

Packt is searching for authors like you

If you're interested in becoming an author for Packt, please visit authors.packtpub.com and apply today. We have worked with thousands of developers and tech professionals, just like you, to help them share their insight with the global tech community. You can make a general application, apply for a specific hot topic that we are recruiting an author for, or submit your own idea.

Share Your Thoughts

Now you've finished *Enterprise LMS with Adobe Learning Manager*, we'd love to hear your thoughts! Scan the QR code below to go straight to the Amazon review page for this book and share your feedback or leave a review on the site that you purchased it from.

https://packt.link/r/1-804-61887-X

Your review is important to us and the tech community and will help us make sure we're delivering excellent quality content.

Download a free PDF copy of this book

Thanks for purchasing this book!

Do you like to read on the go but are unable to carry your print books everywhere? Is your eBook purchase not compatible with the device of your choice?

Don't worry, now with every Packt book you get a DRM-free PDF version of that book at no cost.

Read anywhere, any place, on any device. Search, copy, and paste code from your favorite technical books directly into your application.

The perks don't stop there, you can get exclusive access to discounts, newsletters, and great free content in your inbox daily

Follow these simple steps to get the benefits:

1. Scan the QR code or visit the link below

https://packt.link/free-ebook/978-1-80461-887-5

2. Submit your proof of purchase
3. That's it! We'll send your free PDF and other benefits to your email directly

www.ingramcontent.com/pod-product-compliance
Lightning Source LLC
Chambersburg PA
CBHW081454050326
40690CB00015B/2794